SUPERMARKET
CONFIDENTIAL

SUPERMARKET CONFIDENTIAL

THE SECRETS OF ONE-STOP SHOPPING FOR DELICIOUS MEALS

By Joanna Pruess

The Lyons Press
Guilford, Connecticut
An imprint of The Globe Pequot Press

First Lyons Press edition, 2004

First published as *The Supermarket Epicure* in a different form by William Morrow and Company, Inc.

The Lyons Press is an imprint of The Globe Pequot Press.

10 9 8 7 6 5 4 3 2 1

Printed in the United States of America

Designed by LeAnna Weller Smith

ISBN 1-59228-562-7

Library of Congress Cataloging-in-Publication Data is available on file.

This book is dedicated to:

My wonderful children: Nicole, Ben, and Justin. You remain my constant source of joy, inspiration, and support.

My mother, Harriet Rubens, who nourished and nurtured an amazing brood. Your need to feed at least seven hungry people every day first brought me to the supermarket. The love you shared with our family for travel to far-off lands allowed me to discover the pleasures of different cuisines.

In loving memory of my father, Gerald Rubens, who taught me that if I asked enough questions, nothing was beyond my reach; and whose "crazy concoctions" inspired my own sense of invention.

Bob Lape, for new beginnings and the promise of a joyful future.

ACKNOWLEDGMENTS

In writing this book, I learned what almost every cookbook author before me has written: A book is the collective efforts of many people giving generously of their time, talents, and commitment to the cause. These thank-yous cannot begin to express my gratitude.

When this book was first written in 1987, it was shortly after I had spent five wonderful years as the director of the Cookingstudio at Kings Super Markets, in New Jersey, the cooking school I created inside the market. I went on become the director of communications for Fresh Fields, in the Washington, D.C. area, where I witnessed firsthand a new, cutting-edge variety of supermarkets. Fresh Fields later became part of Whole Foods, today this country's pre-eminent purveyor of healthful foods.

To Allen Bildner, and all his associates at Kings Super Markets, and Mark Ordan, and the entire creative staff at Fresh Fields, thank you for sharing your knowledge of the supermarket industry. And special thanks to all the Cookingstudio teachers, staff, and students.

To Sandy Talcott, who originally motivated me to write this book by asking for it again and again and again over the years. The original "team" of Barbara Soyster, Barbara Somers, Cheryl Kleinman, and Kathleen Kenny Sanderson—my four pillars of strength. Without your knowledge, humor, and loving support, as well as untold hours spend in reading and evaluating the recipes and text, this book would not have come into being.

To Karen Berk and Carole Walter, dear friends and enormously competent food professionals, by listening tirelessly to my ideas both old and new, you helped me to get through the rough spots and offered encouragement. Barbara Koplin and Moira Crabtree, thanks for telling me how much you've loved the food in this book over the years. And to Nicole, Ben and Justin, it fills my heart with joy knowing that each of you actually cooks some of these dishes.

To Judy Hausman and Bob Lape for reading this in the light of contemporary supermarkets and suggesting refinements to the text.

And finally to my superb team at Lyons Press/Globe Pequot Press: I am so grateful that you gave me the opportunity to make this book so much better and more useful. It has been my dream since it was first published. Thanks Jay Cassell for seeing the possibilities; Ann Treistman for your support, deft editing, and clear vision; Larry Dorfman for your incredible marketing skills; Jane Crosen for your astute copyediting, and finally, Leanna Weller Smith for breathing life into the book's design.

Joanna Pruess
September 2004

CONTENTS

INTRODUCTION

Supermarkets have been a part of my life for as long as I can remember. In my childhood, family outings were often coupled with a stop for weekly grocery specials. Five children—my brother, three sisters, and me—each checking out with two bottles of ketchup was not unusual. Through the years, I watched as modern convenience foods like TV dinners, cheese that made funny, squiggly designs when squirted from the can, and frozen vegetables made their debut. Canned spaghetti bore little resemblance to the Italian prototype or my Mom's slowly simmered version. But, it was easy and fast to prepare. Julia Child had yet to show us the joys of French cooking, and "good food" was simple, basic fare.

At twenty-one, I moved to France, where my ideas about what was good to eat were radically redefined. There I saw and tasted a broad range of foods I'd never known. Shopping at the local butcher, as well as at the cheese, fruit, and vegetable merchants, became an ever-changing ritual for almost eight years. Choices fluctuated daily, and each season brought new gastronomic reasons to celebrate. Even the smells and sounds varied. With time, my meals were inspired by what looked best in the market each day, and I became more demanding of products I chose.

A switch had flipped in my head, and I fell madly, passionately in love with food. Tender, thin green beans made me euphoric. A perfectly roasted chicken was a masterpiece. And ripe melons from Cavaillon were celestial gifts. Thanks to le Cordon Bleu and friends, I learned to touch, feel, and smell what I was buying. Big wasn't necessarily best and taste was more important than appearances. But appearances were part of the seduction, too.

Along the way, I also learned that shopkeepers had rigidly set hours. When I missed them (which was often), I found myself exploring the local supermarkets that stayed open when all other stores were closed. Although the food never seemed quite as fresh, my gnawing hunger pains and fascination with new products were more than nourished. The clerks were willing to let me sample or buy the tiniest portion of a pâté or salad. I watched as other shoppers carefully considered their choices. Under these conditions, I learned a valuable shopping lesson: No matter where you are, celebrate the best of what is available. By choosing carefully, asking questions, and experimenting, you can prepare great meals from ordinary sources.

When I returned to the United States, my first trips to the supermarket left me feeling like I was shopping in an impersonal, plastic-wrapped world. Apples were tightly sheathed in cellophane, meats were half concealed in cardboard, and salads were sealed in plastic tubs. There was no one to talk to about food, no one to ask questions of, no smells, and no tastes. I resolved to do all my shopping in the many specialty shops that were springing up not far from where I lived. A job and three infants soon made this a forgotten dream. Happily, times were changing in the supermarket world.

In the 1930s, the pioneers of the grocery industry had revolutionized shopping by creating one-stop food centers complete with everything from canned vegetables and fresh meat to laundry supplies. The idea was successful and it spread. But, by the fifties and sixties, modern technology had streamlined food handling to where it had all but replaced human hands. Meat was packaged on an automated line, and it was a rare market that had a butcher to ask for specialty cuts or how to cook something. Produce was wrapped, scaled, or weighed and protected from the view of knowing eyes. As big chains gobbled up small businesses, personal attention and individuality were sacrificed to the "bottom line." Eventually, customers felt alienated and began looking to smaller, more intimate food stores.

By the mid-seventies, supermarkets began taking a hard look at themselves, their lost customers, and how to win them back. What they found was their customers' needs had changed. Women with or without husbands were out the door and winning the bread. Fathers were raising children alone. Seniors and singles had their own demands. Interest in nutrition made mediocre, chemical-laden foods less desirable, while improved take-out and quick-heat items seized everyone's interest because of their ease of preparation. That was the point at which I approached Kings Super Markets in New Jersey.

In 1981, I had the great good fortune of being hired by the company to create and be the first director of the Cookingstudio, a cooking school within its Short Hills store. Among the thirty teachers who taught classes there were Jacques Pépin, Giuliano Bugialli, and almost every other luminary in the culinary field.

I also had the opportunity of expanding my own personal vision about cooking by giving classes designed specifically for those who were visually impaired, hearing impaired, and mentally challenged. Special cooking classes exclusively for men, classes on how to prepare wild game, and Friday and Saturday night sessions conceived as couples' dinner parties were only part of the curriculum. Five years later, the school had instructed close to 15,000 attendees, and there were three more Cookingstudios in other Kings locations.

After moving to Washington, D.C., I again had the chance to be on the cutting edge of the supermarket business when I became director of communications for Fresh Fields, a progressive market that ultimately became Whole Foods, still one of the industry's innovators.

Since working in this industry, I have seen the public become excited by high-quality foods. Today's shoppers are more willing to experiment and invest in newer, less-familiar foods. While the general trend may be away from cooking all the time, there is a strong renewed interest and pride in preparing at least part of the meal oneself. Couples cook and entertain together. Children, too, have taken to the kitchen—and not simply to make chocolate chip cookies.

Even the smallest stores now offer what was once considered exotic foods from around the world. Progressive supermarkets recognize that beyond high-quality ingredients, only personalized service and convenience can distance them from the competition. Catering managers, chefs, and cooking teachers are being added to their staffs, while the "super" part of their name is being expanded to include more nonfood products like fresh flowers, general merchandise, and party supplies. To keep customers informed, a wealth of printed and spoken information is available. Longer hours of operation, telephone ordering, and even entertainment are part of today's planning. The tide has definitely turned for many supermarkets.

With so much available in one place, some new problems have evolved: how to navigate these giant markets, deal with take-out and prepared foods, and buy, store, and present food to its best advantage? Having spoken with thousands of shoppers, I know that to be a smart shopper, a strategy is necessary. To assist you, the chapters of this book are divided like the sections of your supermarket: Vegetables, Fruits, Poultry, Meat, Fish, Dairy, Baking Goods, Staples, Frozen Foods, even Prepared Foods and Take-Out. There is general information in the introduction to each chapter and specific information about buying the main ingredients in the recipe headnotes. At the end of many recipes, there are "Did you know?" and other sidebars. They offer tips on smart buying, storing, and preparing your food, as well as recipe variations.

Finally, between chapters there are strategy pages dealing with larger supermarket issues, such as: "Label Literacy," "Buying by the Seasons," and "Let Your Supermarket Work for You."

With some practice and thought, these skills will help you to translate your purchases into meals worthy of some star chefs. Your table may or may not be graced with the latest exotica from far-off lands, but you will dine very, very well.

In the end, food is an intensely personal experience. Discover what pleases you and carefully choose what is really best that day in the market. That's the beginning. Most recipes are only meant to be a guideline. (Baking is the exception.) If basil is called for and oregano is more to your liking, make the substitution. If the broccoli looks great and the asparagus spears are old, the choice should be obvious, even if the recipe suggests asparagus. Great cooks in Paris and Chicago don't dwell on what isn't; they celebrate the positive.

Finally, it takes more than correctly prepared recipes to make a great meal. Success comes from proper selection and storage. Presentation and even table décor play an important role in creating the total experience. A meal should be a temptation for all the senses. Eyes see and noses smell before a morsel of food reaches the mouth. Many of the tools for creative entertaining and wonderful everyday eating are found in today's markets. Throughout this book I've added suggestions and tips on how best to master today's supermarket in the hopes that you, too, will feel as I do: that you can create wonderful dining experiences from your local supermarket.

SUPERMARKET

CONFIDENTIAL

129
199
89
79
99

LET YOUR SUPERMARKET WORK FOR YOU

Supermarkets have made monumental strides in updating their images from one-stop utilitarian food markets to one-stop "super" stores, offering an abundance of food—both fresh and prepared—and nonfood products and services formerly available only in food boutiques or specialty stores.

In order to survive today's dramatically larger (45,000 to 50,000 square feet is not unusual) and more complicated markets, customers should choose the supermarkets that best meet their needs. Confronted with this task, I have developed certain criteria to help me make the decision after visiting the quality markets in an area.

For me, the two most important considerations are *Cleanliness* and *Consistency*.

Cleanliness is vital to how good I feel about a market; it tells me a lot about the food sold there and how to avoid the constant threat of food-borne illness. First impressions lead me to certain conclusions about quality and the degree of management's concern for food safety.

Even before entering the store, I make judgments: If garbage is strewn carelessly around, I think the same might be true in the meat-packing room or elsewhere. If the containers in the Take-Out or Deli sections are dirty, the food looks old, or clerks are sampling while serving customers, I fear that bacteria are lurking nearby and I may end up sick. If spills are not quickly wiped up, leaving treacherous puddles, or there are unpleasant odors, I know that this is not where I want to do my shopping on a regular basis.

Consistency is more important to me than finding the newest variety of herb or most exotic fish. Why? Because initially I always spend a lot of mental energy sizing up where I shop and getting used to cooking with certain kinds of ingredients.

There is comfort in a more or less predictable quality. Sure, foods vary from day to day. But if, on a regular basis, you can do your general shopping or dash in at the last moment and still find respectable ingredients, it is a great time-saver. I also look for consistent store policies and clerks or department managers who are usually willing to be helpful. It is a luxury to know that specially ordered products will be delivered as promised.

Along with consistency, I look for markets that are neat and well-organized, bright, and easily navigated. Especially in smaller markets with narrower aisles, if the store is well lit and well signed, shopping is easier and less claustrophobic.

Service and Cooperation make shopping easier, too. They are part of the market's desire to meet customer needs. More than any other product, today's stores offer a variety of services to distinguish them from their competition. How successful they are seems to be as much a result of their attitude as the actual assistance they give. I think about how helpful the staff is and whether I feel that they sincerely care about my requests. On more critical issues, such as food recalls, complaints, or even simple returns, the staff's reaction affirms or denies a commitment to the store's customers.

Finally, **Flexibility** and **Change** show me that a supermarket is trying to keep abreast of current food trends and improved technology.

To make shopping easier and more efficient, I suggest preparing a market list in the order of the store's layout. Use it as a guide, but don't overlook the choicest item or best buy in the store because you are so intent on finding the next item on your list. Shopping once or twice a week and planning ahead helps avoid wasteful impulse buying. However, only buy the amount of fresh food you can use to best advantage.

Whether you choose your produce, meat, fish, or poultry first is not significant. Rather, keep in mind that if the food you want is too highly priced, not of top quality, or unavailable, you should make a substitution on the spot. Often these spontaneous changes have become some of my greatest successes.

Investigate the newer special services now available in many markets before you actually need them. For catering I ask for references from past catering jobs. I also taste this department's food and watch how platters and take-out foods are prepared.

And take it from one who knows: If possible, don't go to the market when you are hungry!

CHAPTER ONE: **VEGETABLES**

INTRODUCTION

The vegetable section of the produce department is one of the largest and most changeable areas of a supermarket, often fluctuating daily because of seasonality and availability. An appreciation for ethnic cuisines and an awareness of the important role vegetables play in good health have prompted merchandisers to offer us less-familiar produce and herbs along with staples like carrots, onions, and celery. Although many markets are selling vegetables unwrapped, careful selection and storage is vital if you want the best quality. Be sure to glance at the tips included with each recipe.

Your choices change hourly in a supermarket. With a little flexibility on your part—choosing what is best rather than what you had written on a list—the possibilities are tremendous. In this era of health consciousness, vegetables deserve resounding kudos. They are filling, fibrous, and often nonfattening. For me, they are also my favorite foods.

General Buying Suggestions

✓ Look carefully at every vegetable you buy. Turn it over, look at the roots or leaves, check for bruises and drying.

✓ Bulk-packed vegetables save you money—but only when used within a reasonable period of time. Be sure to evaluate the overall quality. Money spent on discarded foods is also thrown away.

✓ Where uniform size is important to even cooking or appearance, take the time to *hand-pick* vegetables, if possible. If they are plastic wrapped, examine the packages carefully for broken or damaged product. Some produce clerks will actually open containers for you if asked.

✓ Some vegetables, like celery and carrots, are frequently sold cello-packed. Look to see that the bright orange color is on the carrots, not a grid pattern on the bag. Sometimes, larger vegetables like cabbage and squash are cut in half and also sold plastic wrapped. With sealed bags, like packages of spinach, check for broken, wet leaves. They decay quickly.

✓ Make a point of becoming friendly with the produce manager. He or a clerk can sometimes find fresher produce from the storage room if asked, or he can order an item specially. When in doubt on how much to buy or how to cook a new vegetable, look for printed materials or ask for advice.

- ✓ Newer produce items, such as miniature vegetables, nopales (cactus leaves), and exotic mushrooms, often come with recipe folders to give you additional storage and cooking tips. Unless your market has a good turnover on these items, examine them carefully. In some markets they tend to get old before they are bought. When faced with unfamiliar vegetables, I read about them, then cook them for myself to become familiar with their taste and texture, before I use them for entertaining.

Salad Greens

Not long ago, iceberg, romaine, and Boston lettuce were usually the entire "salad greens" department of a market. Today, that trio has exploded into a seemingly endless array of leaf and head lettuces, sprouts, and even edible flowers. No matter how many choices there are, each item should be carefully stacked in a cool bin and frequently misted to remain fresh looking. With attention to the selection, storage, and preparation of your ingredients, an unlimited variety can be yours.

Just about everyone loves a good salad, from crisp mixed greens to those composed of more exotic ingredients. Nothing has revolutionized the vegetable department more than those bags of pre-washed lettuces and shredded broccoli slaw. There are also "breathable" packages of vegetables that you can put right in the microwave. They are convenient and I wholeheartedly endorse them because they make preparing and eating salads and vegetables so easy. However, two cautionary points: (1) It's probably a good idea to wash these "pre-washed" packed veggies another time, and (2) be sure to check the dates on the bag and always look at the contents before throwing the bags into your shopping basket.

Knowing that greens are delicate, choose them carefully. Slip each choice into a plastic bag and put them in the shopping cart where they will not be damaged. At the checkout register, unpack them last from your cart so they don't get squashed at the end of the belt, then ask that they be packed separately from the rest of the order—with potatoes, onions, and other heavy items at the bottom of the bag, more crushable items on top.

Selection

- ✓ Look over each head of lettuce carefully for damaged outer leaves and brown spots. Colors should be bright. Some stores trim lettuce for better value and to make it more saleable.

- ✓ Whether soft-leafed (Boston) or crisp-leafed (romaine), lettuce should not be limp. If it is, it may have been soaked in water or otherwise mistreated. Don't buy it. Lettuces should be misted periodically and kept cool.
- ✓ Choose heads that feel firm and heavy.

Storage

Whole Heads

- ✓ Keep lettuces whole until needed. They will last longer—two to four days at most.
- ✓ Don't wash them (it causes rust), but remove excess dirt and damaged leaves that may hasten decay. Put each head in a plastic bag, squeeze out excess air, fasten, and refrigerate in the vegetable bin.

Washed Leaves

- ✓ Put washed leaves on paper towels in layers and put them into sealed plastic bags. Punch a few holes in the bags to allow air to circulate. Leaves will stay fresh up to two days.
- ✓ Do not store lettuces near any fruit, such as cantaloupes or apples, which gives off ethylene gas. It will cause rust spots.

Preparation of Lettuce for Salads

- ✓ Lettuce is a delicate green, so it needs to be treated carefully. It bruises when forced into a small space, and it wilts when not chilled.
- ✓ Fill the sink with lukewarm to cool water. Break off the leaves and discard the core. Swirl the lettuce gently in the water. Then rinse each leaf separately (except iceberg), and remove any rust spots and thickened ribs.
- ✓ Spin-dry in a salad spinner or swing in a lettuce basket. Pat the leaves dry with paper towels, if necessary.
- ✓ Store whole leaves, wrapped in paper or cloth towels, in the refrigerator to chill and crisp before being dressed. Or, tear the leaves, put them in a salad bowl, cover with a slightly dampened towel, and refrigerate, for up to two hours.

Combining Ingredients

Combine crisp, sharper-flavored lettuces like chicory, watercress, or radicchio with subtler leaves like Boston or green and red leaf. Vary textures and colors, but be selective. Three or four different lettuces are plenty.

Dressing a Salad

✓ Don't overdress a salad. Eight cups of lightly packed leaves need only 1/4 to 1/3 cup of dressing.

✓ Vary the oils, vinegars, and herbs. Walnut oil goes well with delicate greens such as Bibb lettuce or arugula. Crunchy romaine likes a fruity olive oil. This is where your own taste and creativity are important.

✓ Dress salads just before serving. Otherwise the acid of vinegar or lemon juice will cause lettuce leaves to go limp.

Some of My Favorite Salads

- Blanched green beans, minced shallots, boiled and sliced new potatoes, and cubed beets, tossed with Mustard Vinaigrette (page 271) and served on red lettuce leaves.
- Arugula, radicchio, crumbled goat cheese, walnuts, and torn Boston lettuce leaves, tossed with Mustard Vinaigrette (page 271), substituting raspberry vinegar and walnut oil for lemon juice and olive oil.
- Torn romaine lettuce, julienned turkey breast, red onion rings, broken walnut pieces, and pear slices arranged on plates with Roquefort Vinaigrette (page 272) spooned on top.
- Blanched snow peas or sugar snaps, yellow pepper slices, cherry tomato halves, shredded carrots, and blanched cauliflower florets tossed with Sweet and Tangy Asian Vinaigrette (page 274) and served on Bibb lettuce leaves.
- Avocado and papaya slices arranged with chopped eggs and watercress sprigs on a bed of Boston lettuce leaves with Curried Mayonnaise (page 277).
- Boiled shrimp, blanched snow peas, cubed jicama, and diced red pepper tossed with Spicy Old Bay Tomato Dressing (page 273) and served in a steamed artichoke with the choke removed. Or serve on toasted sourdough bread.
- Sliced zucchini, red or yellow pepper slices, quartered small mushrooms, toasted pine nuts, sprouts, and thinly sliced scallions tossed with Puréed Chickpea Vinaigrette (page 272) served on a bed of chicory and field greens.

- Cucumber slices, cubed beets, sliced boiled potatoes, and tomato slices, tossed with Tuna Niçoise Vinaigrette (page 284) served on a bed of romaine and endive leaves with garlic croutons.

Herbs

The explosion of greens in supermarkets includes fresh herbs as well. Contemporary lighter cooking stresses that herbs are an excellent way to add lots of flavor but no calories to our foods. Here, freshness counts a lot. And since we often use a small amount of most herbs, markets and growers have taken a cue from their customers' needs in their merchandising, selling herbs in a variety of ways.

Selection

With all herbs, look for brightly colored, fresh-looking leaves, free of bruised spots, excess moisture, or wilting.

✓ Herbs growing in small plastic pots afford the potential advantage of continual growth on your window sill or of being transplanted. Since they need to be watered, if the soil seems very dry and the leaves are wilted in the market, pass them up. Remember to attend to this at home, too. I've had the greatest success with chives, which seem to thrive in the steamy atmosphere near the kitchen sink. If the plant flowers, great! Add the blossoms along with other edible flowers, such as nasturtiums, to your salad. Freeze-dried chives, by the way, are usually limp and tasteless. Substitute fresh scallions.

✓ Hydroponically grown herbs sealed in plastic bags are available for immediate use, since they are quite clean. However, the flavor is usually milder. Be sure to check the bag for condensation and moisture-wilt.

✓ Larger bunches of familiar herbs like flat-leaf and curly parsley, dill, and basil are usually available to use immediately or to store in your refrigerator. As you choose each bunch, put it into a plastic bag to keep it moist. The smaller tied bunches of thyme, rosemary, oregano, marjoram, and the like are appearing year-round from local growers. Look at their condition carefully. If they are withered and limp, you may be better off with a new bottle of the dried version of the herb.

✓ Even tiny plastic see-through boxes with a tablespoon or two of chopped herbs are found in many markets today. Here, all the work has been done for you. There is often information concerning the use of an herb on printed cards alongside, and the boxes should be dated. But, be aware that the leaves can be moldy or wilted and thus unusable, making the already high price exorbitant.

Care of Fresh Herbs

- Once home, use herbs quickly or prepare them for storage. Do *not* wash herbs before refrigerating. Properly wrapped and sealed in a plastic bag, most herbs make their own mini-environment and will stay fresh in the refrigerator for up to a week.
- If there are no roots, wrap a damp paper towel around the stem ends, pull off any wilted leaves, and put the herb in an airtight plastic bag. If the leaves are very moist, a dry paper towel in the bag will help absorb excess moisture.
- Herbs with roots should be put in a glass with a couple of inches of water. Use a plastic bag to tent the top.
- When herbs begin to wilt, they may be washed, dried, and then frozen for four to six months in small, airtight bags with the air pushed out before sealing. Or, they may be puréed first, frozen in a small amount of water in an ice-cube tray, and then stored in bags. Although they will not retain their appearance, their flavor will remain quite fresh-tasting, and they can be used in cooking or in herb butters and vinegars.
- Another solution is to dry herbs. While some dried herbs have more flavor than commercially jarred products, they are, after all, still dried. Generally, when substituting dried herbs for fresh in a recipe, use one-third the amount: 1 teaspoon dried thyme leaves in place of 1 tablespoon fresh.

Using Herbs

- Because herbs are so delicate, they need to be handled with care when washed and chopped.
- Rinse herbs under cool water and gently pat them dry with paper towels, or dry them in a salad spinner.
- Where appearances are important, a sharp knife bruises delicate

leaves less than a food processor. If using a food processor, it is important to *pulse* the ingredients a minimum of times.

- Add fresh herbs toward the end of cooking, but crumble dried herbs and add them early to release their flavor.

JUST A HINT: An easy way to remove the tiny leaves of herbs with inedible coarse stems is to grasp a stem between your thumbnail and index fingernail, and with light pressure, strip the leaves opposite from their growing direction, i.e., from tip to root end.

A sprig of fresh rosemary is wonderful in a soup or stew, but also see how herbs are used in my Herbed Cream Cheese Dip (page 200) or in Mustard Vinaigrette (page 271). Herb butters are a combination of finely minced herbs and softened butter (about 1 tablespoon herb to a stick of butter, depending on how pungent the herb is and personal taste). Use unsalted butter. Salt may be added afterward. Pipe the herbed butter into rosettes; or form it into a cylinder, chill, and slice as a garnish for grilled fish, meats, poultry, or soups and stews. Frozen, these butters last for up to three months.

Basic Kitchen Herbs from the Supermarket

BASIL is very fragrant with a mildly spicy flavor. It is a staple of Italian cooking since it goes so well with tomatoes, vegetables, and pasta. Try it, too, in salads, soups, and stews. It does not withstand long cooking, so add it at the end. When using as a garnish, cut it at the last minute since it quickly turns black. The taste of opal basil is the same as that of green leaf. Lemon basil has a subtle hint of citrus.

BAY LEAF is a pungent leaf of the laurel tree. Use it sparingly in soups and stews; it should be removed before serving, since the leaf does not soften during cooking.

CHERVIL has recently become easier to find fresh. It is a delicate cousin of parsley and complements vegetable and egg dishes. It is used in *fines herbes.*

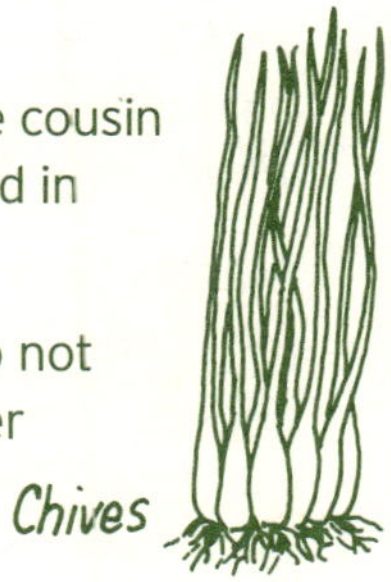

CHIVES are a mild-flavored relative of the onion family. They do not withstand cooking, so they are often stirred into soups or other dishes at the end of cooking, chopped and sprinkled on salads, or used whole as a garnish.

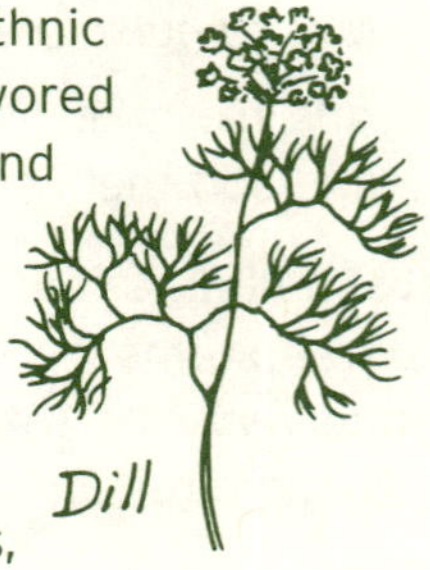

CILANTRO is also known as coriander or Mexican or Chinese parsley. The leaves add a distinctive taste to many ethnic dishes, such as Salsa (see page 42). The sweet-flavored seeds are ground for curries and baked into breads and cookies. Add some whole leaves to your favorite mixed green salad, too.

DILL leaves have a subtle licorice taste and are used in soups and vinaigrettes, and with potatoes, cucumbers, and fish. The seeds are used for breads, pickles, and soups.

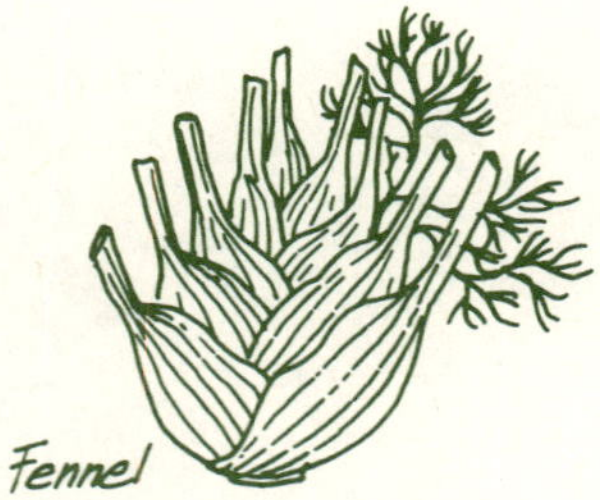

FENNEL has a strong licorice flavor in its feathery leaves or edible bulb, which is made milder by cooking. The seeds are commonly used to season sausages and richly flavored meat dishes. Eat the raw or braised bulb as you would celery.

LEMONGRASS grows in thin stalks and has a lovely citrus flavor used often in Thai and other Asian cuisines. It looks a bit like a tough scallion. Remove the tough two or three outer layers, then mince the inside bulb.

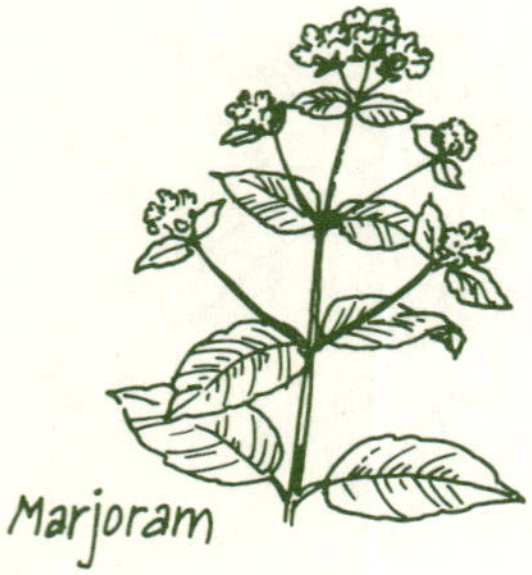

MARJORAM is a mild cousin of oregano, frequently used in Italian cooking or with creamed vegetable soups, poultry, and stuffings.

MINT has a cool, refreshing flavor. Spearmint and peppermint are the most common varieties found in markets. It is used in Middle Eastern foods, jellies, sauces, and desserts, as well as with peas and new potatoes.

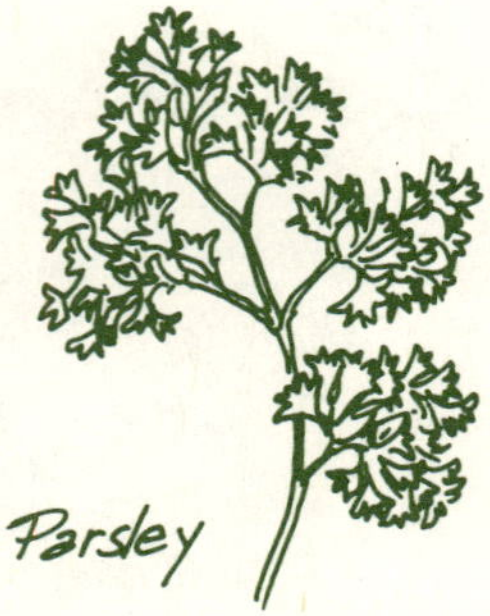

OREGANO is similar to its relative marjoram but has a more pronounced flavor. It is used for foods like pizza, stews, and other full-flavored dishes where its robust flavor will not overpower.

PARSLEY is the most widely used of the culinary herbs. Curly parsley is mild and most often used as a garnish. Flat-leaf parsley, also called Italian parsley, has a more distinct flavor and is used to enhance the flavor of other herbs and many foods. When chopping parsley, note that the stems have the most flavor.

ROSEMARY has a pine-like scent that can be overpowering if the herb is used to excess. Use it in small amounts to season lamb, beef, veal, and game, as well as some sauces. It is especially nice with garlic.

SAGE has a strong flavor that can easily dominate others. It is best used with game, poultry, and cheese and is found in many sausages. Fresh sage leaves don't taste as musty as the dried or powdered herb.

TARRAGON is a sweet herb with an anise-like taste, often used in French cooking to enhance delicately flavored chicken, fish, veal, and egg dishes, as well as sauces such as Béarnaise (see page 207) and beurre blanc.

THYME has a pungent, distinctive scent. It is a popular herb used in strongly flavored stuffings, pâtés, and soups, as well as poultry and fish dishes.

With herbs more readily available, it is becoming easier for supermarket cooks to experiment with these culinary treasures.

Salad Bars: Convenient or Passé?

When salad bars were the "new kid on the block," everyone was piling fixings into containers along with salad dressings and toppings. With expanded Deli Sections, Olive Bars, and convenience foods—including more hygienic, pre-packed "grab and go" salads—much of the allure has been supplanted.

If you use the Salad Bar in your market, look at it carefully.

- First impressions count. What you see often indicates the quality of the Salad Bar. Look for one that is appetizing.
- It should be well tended, with appropriate utensils in place for each item.
- There should be no spillage.
- Food trays should be set in ice, and a protective "sneeze" guard should extend upward or down from above to prevent shoppers from leaning over the food.
- Containers, lids, and a selection of dressings should be neat and easily accessible.
- Empty trays should be refilled promptly. A high turnover is a good indication of freshness.

- Consider the cost. If all you are buying is lettuce, radishes, and shredded carrots, then $4.99 or more a pound is extravagant.
- If you want olives, marinated artichoke hearts, a few nuts, or berries for garnish, then what you are paying for is the convenience of preparation and the savings realized from the availability of small portions.
- Be sure to ask if they use chemical preservatives.

FETTUCCINE WITH ASPARAGUS AND LEMON CREAM

Serves 4 to 6 as a main course or 8 as a first course

This colorful pasta dish with lemon-scented cream, red peppers, and asparagus is perfect for spring—just when asparagus comes into season. It's worth waiting for these graceful stalks since the out-of-season ones can be expensive and less flavorful.

Asparagus only lasts a couple of days, even when stored well, so I buy them as close to eating time as possible. Try to select spears that are of uniform size (I prefer narrow ones, about 1/2 inch in diameter), with closed buds and stiff stalks. That's the surest way to guarantee even cooking. If the only choice you have is rubber-banded bunches, select carefully for size and quality. Once the bright green begins to get slightly mottled or the stalks droop, the magic is gone.

- 1 pound dried fettuccine pasta or Quick Homemade Fettuccine (page 289)
- Kosher or coarse salt
- 4 tablespoons (1/2 stick) unsalted butter
- 1 1/2 cups heavy cream
- Grated zest of 1 large lemon
- Salt and white pepper to taste
- Pinch of freshly grated nutmeg
- 1 1/2 pound tender, young asparagus, cleaned, trimmed, and cut into 1 1/2-inch pieces (see "Did you know?")
- 1 small red bell pepper, peeled, seeds and membranes removed, cut into fine dice
- 1 cup freshly grated imported Parmesan cheese
- 1/4 cup coarsely torn flat-leaf parsley leaves, for garnish

1. Bring a large pot of salted water to a boil. Add the dried pasta, stirring to separate the strands. Cook according to package directions until al dente, 10 to 15 minutes. If using fresh pasta, cook for 1 to 2 minutes after the sauce is ready.
2. Meanwhile, melt the butter in a large, heavy skillet over low heat. Stir in the cream, lemon zest, salt, pepper, nutmeg, and asparagus. Simmer until the asparagus are crisp-tender, about 7 to 8 minutes, shaking the pan occasionally. Stir in the red pepper and continue cooking for another 2 to 3 minutes. Taste to adjust the seasonings, if necessary.
3. Once the pasta is cooked, drain it, and stir into the sauce. Sprinkle half of the Parmesan cheese over the pasta and toss to blend well. Transfer to a heated serving platter, garnish with parsley leaves, and serve immediately. Pass the remaining cheese at the table.

Did you know? Wait to clean asparagus until you are ready to use them. Otherwise, they dry out. Break off the fibrous bottoms, then peel off the thin outer layer almost up to the bud. The spears cook faster and are more uniformly tender this way. If you must keep asparagus for a day or two, stand the spears upright in a container with about an inch of water or wrap the bottoms with wet paper towels. Cover with plastic to maintain the moisture.

Asparagus may be frozen, too. Clean and blanch the spears for 2 to 4 minutes, depending on the size, then shock under cold water and pat very dry on paper towels. Put them in resealable plastic bags, press out the air, and freeze. Cook the frozen asparagus in simmering water until tender, 12 to 16 minutes.

CHILLY BEET SOUP

Serves 8 as a first course

When days are hot, this chilly dark pink soup with wispy chives is a perfect pick-me-up. The surprising combination of beets, green apples, cucumbers, leeks, and yogurt is creamy and slightly sweet, with a little tangy bite. For a light summer meal, serve a larger bowl of the soup accompanied by a sandwich. For soups and purées, canned beets are fine.

Fresh beets have a truly wonderful taste and texture. Select bunches of a uniform size with fresh, unwilted greens. I like them roasted, cooled, and sliced in a salad with goat cheese and arugula, drizzled with extra-virgin olive oil and balsamic vinegar. You may even find candy-cane-striped and yellow beets. Their taste is similar to red beets.

3 medium leeks, white parts only, washed and thinly sliced

1½ cups chicken or vegetable stock

3 8½-ounce cans sliced beets, undrained

2 large Granny Smith or other tart green apples, washed and seeded but unpeeled

1 medium cucumber, peeled, quartered, and seeds removed

2 cups plain low-fat yogurt

Chives or ¼ cup thinly sliced scallion tops for garnish

1. In a small saucepan, combine the leeks and ½ cup of stock. Bring to a simmer and cook for 1 to 2 minutes, or until the leeks soften. Transfer to a small bowl and set aside to cool.
2. In the bowl of a food processor or in an electric blender, purée the beets until almost smooth. Add the apples and cucumber and process until slightly chunky, scraping down the sides of the bowl as needed.
3. Blend the remaining cup of stock with the yogurt in a small bowl. Scrape into the beet purée and process just until well blended. Pour into a large bowl, stir in the leeks, cover, and chill until cold. To serve, ladle the soup into bowls, and add 2 or 3 chives or some scallions in the center of each bowl.

Did you know? To cook evenly, select bunches of even-sized beets. Cut off the greens and reserve. Wrap the beets in foil and bake in a 375°F oven until tender, at least 1 hour. When cool enough to handle, peel (wearing rubber gloves will help with this messy chore). Sautéed beet greens with melted butter, orange juice, salt, pepper, and chopped parsley are delicious.

ASIAN BROCCOLI SALAD

Serves 8 for lunch

- 1 large bunch (1 ¾ pounds) broccoli, rinsed, leaves removed, stalks separated and cut into thirds, or 10 cups broccoli florets
- 1 large onion, peeled and thinly sliced
- 2 large red bell peppers, peeled, seeded, and sliced
- 8 ounces firm tofu, cut into small cubes
- 1 recipe Sweet and Tangy Asian Vinaigrette (page 274)
- 3 tablespoons sesame seeds, toasted until light brown

In this flavorful salad, bright green broccoli and sweet red bell peppers are combined with firm-style tofu found in your Dairy case. Tofu's creamy color, slightly soft texture, and delicate taste are a satisfying foil for the broccoli and tangy ginger-soy dressing (Sweet and Tangy Asian Vinaigrette, see page 274). However, if you prefer, substitute diced cooked chicken breasts or shrimp.

Broccoli is one of the most consistently good buys in supermarkets, providing it has been kept cool. And it's so versatile. Select a bunch that is dark green with tightly closed florets. The stalks should be firm, without leggy branches. As broccoli ages, the color lightens and the stalks become fibrous and hollow. Turn the bunch over and look. Also, the stronger broccoli smells, the older it is.

Another broccoli-type vegetable is broccolini. With slim stems and broccoli-like buds, it's a cross between broccoli and kale. Rapini, also known as broccoli rabe or rape, has a slightly bitter taste and is usually steamed, then sautéed in olive oil and garlic. Although its flowers look like broccoli florets, it is not broccoli; however, both are members of the brassica family of vegetables known for their healthful properties.

1. With a sharp paring knife, remove the tough outer layer of the broccoli stalks, then steam them in a large pot until just tender, about 4 to 5 minutes once the water boils under the steamer. Drain in a colander, rinse under cold water to stop the cooking, and blot dry, and then cut it into bite-sized pieces.
2. Put the onion in a bowl, pour boiling water over it, and let it wilt for about 1 minute. Drain and blot dry.
3. In a large bowl, combine the broccoli, onion, red pepper, and tofu, and toss with approximately half of the vinaigrette. Chill for about 2 hours.
4. Add the sesame seeds and approximately half of the remaining dressing (see note below). Toss and serve.

NOTE: Salads made with steamed vegetables and other porous ingredients like pasta tend to absorb the dressing and, after a while, lose their taste. Therefore, if chilling the salad before serving, add about half of the vinaigrette to the salad before refrigerating to moisten and allow the flavors to blend. Then, add some more dressing just before serving to refresh the flavor.

Did you know? Although many supermarkets sell broccoli florets, if you buy a whole bunch, after cutting off the florets, you can julienne the stalks and make a crunchy slaw with them (see Mexican Coleslaw on page 21). Or blanch the stalks for a couple of minutes, drain and blot dry, then freeze in resealable plastic bags if you won't use them within a couple of days.

BROCCOLI AND CHEESE IN GOLDEN PHYLLO DOME

Serves 8 as a first course or vegetable side dish

Two broccoli florets visually identify the main ingredient in this green-centered golden dome. After the first bite, you'll detect cheese and dill as well. Serve as an accompaniment to roast chicken or grilled fish, or as an attractive first course.

When stored with wet paper towels around the stalks, broccoli will remain in good condition in a cold refrigerator for up to a week. I usually don't buy frozen broccoli because the texture seems soft and mushy. However, since the vegetable is puréed in this recipe, frozen stalks or pieces would be a satisfactory choice. Cook broccoli uncovered in a non-reactive pan to retain its bright green color.

Vegetable or olive oil

1 large bunch (1 3/4 pounds) broccoli, rinsed, leaves removed, and stalks peeled and cut into thirds

5 tablespoons unsalted butter

1 medium onion, peeled and finely chopped

1 cup shredded Gruyère or Swiss cheese

2 eggs, beaten

2 tablespoons finely chopped fresh dill or 2 teaspoons dried

1/4 teaspoon freshly grated nutmeg

1/4 teaspoon dry mustard

Pinch of ground red pepper

Salt and freshly ground black pepper to taste

8 phyllo leaves (see page 22)

1. Oil a 7-cup oven-safe bowl and preheat your oven to 375ºF.
2. Steam the broccoli just until tender, about 5 to 6 minutes after the water under the steamer boils. Reserve 2 florets for the garnish and transfer the remaining broccoli to the bowl of a food processor.
3. Melt 1 tablespoon of the butter in a small skillet. Add the onion and sauté over medium-high heat until wilted and lightly colored, about 5 to 6 minutes. Add to broccoli and pulse until fairly smooth, scraping down the sides of the bowl as needed. Add the cheese, eggs, dill, nutmeg, dry mustard, red pepper, salt, and black pepper. Process until blended.
4. Melt the remaining 4 tablespoons of butter. Lay 1 phyllo leaf, long end near you, on a clean surface and brush lightly with butter. Cover the remaining phyllo with a towel so it doesn't dry out. Fold the phyllo in half lengthwise, then in half lengthwise again, forming a long strip of 4 layers. Drape in the oiled bowl, crossing in the center and leaving the ends extended over the edge. Repeat with a second leaf, placing it at right angles to the first. Use the remaining 6 leaves in the same fashion, covering the entire inside of the bowl.
5. Scrape the broccoli mixture into the bowl and smooth with the back of a spoon or a spatula. Turn the ends of the phyllo strips over the filling, starting with the last strip and ending with the first. Brush with the remaining butter. Bake in the middle of the oven until the top is golden brown, about 40 minutes.
6. Remove from the oven and invert onto an oven-safe platter. Remove the bowl and return the phyllo dome to the oven until the top is golden brown, about 8 minutes. Remove and let it stand for 10 minutes. Add the 2 reserved florets in the center of the timbale. Slice into wedges with a serrated knife and serve.

Did you know? Paring the tough, fibrous outer layer of broccoli helps it cook faster, makes it easier to digest, and it is more attractive when served as a crudité. Even on a raw vegetable platter, I prefer to blanch the florets for a couple of minutes to brighten the color and remove the slightly dusty look of the raw buds. Serve broccoli with Tapenade (page 277) or Curried Mayonnaise (page 277) as an hors d'oeuvre.

MEXICAN COLESLAW

Serves 6 to 8

This coleslaw is hardly mild-mannered. Tossed with a sunny Mexican mole-flavored sauce, the vibrant colors and crunchy textures of sliced radishes and finely chopped green peppers add a festive touch. You could also use daikon radish, a cylindrical white Asian variety that is slightly hotter than red radishes.

When buying radishes, the freshest ones are those in a bunch with the leaves still attached. The greens should be crisp and the radishes should look firm and smooth. Smaller, round radishes are usually milder than larger ones and have a crisper texture. At home, remove the greens before storing the radishes to prevent moisture loss. They only last a few days. The greens may also be eaten as a vegetable.

1 tablespoon apple cider or red wine vinegar

2 tablespoons prepared dark mole sauce

3 tablespoons vegetable oil

1 8-ounce can crushed pineapple packed in juice, drained, juice reserved

1 teaspoon tomato paste

1/8 teaspoon celery seeds

1/2 cup commercial sour cream

1 1/2 pounds white or green cabbage, cored and finely shredded, or shredded broccoli stalks

1 large green pepper, seeds and membranes removed, minced

1 cup thinly sliced radishes

Salt and freshly ground black pepper to taste

1. In a small bowl, combine the vinegar and mole sauce, stirring to blend well. Whisk in the vegetable oil, reserved pineapple juice (approximately 2 tablespoons), tomato paste, celery seeds, and sour cream, cover, and set aside.
2. Combine the cabbage, pepper, radishes, and pineapple in a large bowl. Spoon the sauce on top, season with salt and pepper, and toss to blend. Serve at once. This salad tends to get watery when it sits around.

Another idea . . . For a quick and colorful vegetable dish, sauté small radishes in a little butter for 3 to 4 minutes over medium–high heat. Stir in a little sugar, cook until it melts, then serve.

CARAMELIZED CABBAGE IN STRUDEL

Serves 6 to 8

- 8 tablespoons (1 stick) unsalted butter
- 2 large onions, peeled and chopped
- 1 large green or white cabbage, approximately 2 pounds, cored and shredded
- Salt and plenty of freshly ground black pepper to taste
- 7 phyllo leaves
- 3 tablespoons toasted fresh bread crumbs

When I first tasted the caramelized sweetness of slowly browned onions and cabbage wrapped in flaky pastry, I understood why my Hungarian great-grandmother loved this dish. It quickly became a favorite of mine and I often made it for my own grandmother. With the convenience of purchased strudel leaves (phyllo) available fresh in the Dairy department or in the Frozen Foods aisle, you can easily prepare this satisfying side dish for roasts and game. To embellish it, you could add a handful of dried wild mushrooms that have been soaked in warm water and squeezed dry. Like cabbage, this strudel seems to go with cold-weather foods.

When buying cabbage in the market, look for the familiar white, green, and purple heads to feel solid with no signs of damage to the outer leaves. These cabbages last in a vegetable crisper for at least 10 to 12 days. Elegant curly-leafed savoy, napa, and Chinese cabbage used mainly in stir-frying last only a week before the leaves look limp. Cabbage is reasonably priced, low in calories, and quite healthful.

1. Heat 4 tablespoons of butter in a heavy pot large enough to hold all of the cabbage. Add the onions and sauté over medium-high heat until lightly colored, about 7 to 8 minutes. Stir in the cabbage and cook until softened and golden brown, 40 to 45 minutes. If the cabbage begins to brown before completely softened, stir it well, adjust the heat down to low, and cover the pot for a few minutes until moisture forms on the lid. Then remove the lid, stir, turn the heat back to medium, and continue. Or, add ½ cup water, stir up the browned cabbage, and continue cooking. The water should evaporate. (You may have to do this a couple of times, stirring each time so that the cabbage at the bottom of the pot does not burn.) Stir in the salt and plenty of pepper. Set aside uncovered.
2. Preheat your oven to 375ºF; butter a cookie sheet or jelly-roll pan.
3. Melt the remaining butter. Spread a clean towel on a flat surface. Lay 1 leaf of phyllo with the long side close to you on the towel and brush lightly with butter. Keep remaining phyllo covered with a towel. Sprinkle about 1 tablespoon of bread crumbs over the phyllo. Add a second leaf of phyllo, brush with butter, but *do not* add bread crumbs. Continue with the remaining leaves of phyllo, using bread crumbs only on the fourth and sixth leaves. *Do not* brush the last (seventh) leaf of phyllo with butter.

4. Spoon the cabbage mixture into a strip along the long edge of the phyllo, forming it into a compact cylinder, leaving about a 1 1/2-inch border at each short end. Using both hands, flip the sides of the towel toward the back, causing the front edge of the strudel to roll back over the cabbage. Turn the sides of the phyllo in and continue rolling in the same manner. With the last roll, flip the strudel onto the jelly-roll pan with the seam on the bottom. Brush the top and sides of the strudel with the remaining butter. With a sharp, pointed instrument (like a trussing needle or awl) make 6 to 8 small holes through the strudel dough to the filling to allow excess moisture to escape.
5. Transfer the pan to the middle of the oven and bake until the top is crisp and golden brown, about 25 to 30 minutes. The strudel may be kept in a 250°F oven for at least 1 hour. To serve, cut crosswise with a serrated knife into 1 1/2-inch slices.

NOTE: Cabbage strudels may be made 1 or even 2 days ahead of time, covered with a buttered piece of aluminum foil, and refrigerated until ready for baking. If the foil is stuck to the phyllo, begin baking the strudel with the foil. Once the butter melts, it will lift off easily.

Another idea . . . Have you tried Bubble and Squeak? I first tasted this well-known English boarding-school dish at a very upper-class eating club in London. It's made with leftover browned cabbage, onions, and mashed potatoes, smoothed into a heavy skillet with some melted butter and salt and pepper, and cooked until crisp on the underside, then inverted onto a plate. Sometimes it has sausages in it, as well. The name supposedly comes from the sound your stomach makes when you eat this delectable concoction!

HOLIDAY CRANBERRY CARROTS

Serves 8

- 2 pounds baby carrots
- 4 tablespoons (½ stick) unsalted butter
- 1½ tablespoons grated orange zest
- 8 cardamom pods, hulled and seeds pounded in a mortar or ¼ teaspoon ground cardamom
- ¼ cup dry Marsala wine
- ¾ cup fresh cranberries
- Salt to taste

I love carrots for their versatility and sweet flavor as well as for the color contrast they add to any plate. In this festive recipe, bags of baby carrots offer great convenience. Their orange tone is intensified by the cranberries that pop during cooking and blend with the Marsala wine to form an attractive glaze. Orange zest and cardamom add a subtle warmth and richness to the taste.

Select the thinnest, brightest carrots you can find. Since they are available all year, this should not be a problem. Older carrots are often large, cracked, and pale colored. They may even be sprouting roots. You can be pretty sure they will be tasteless and tough. I prefer to buy mine with the tops still on as a guarantee of freshness. This way, carrots keep for a couple of weeks in a refrigerator. With few exceptions (such as purées), I don't use frozen carrots because their texture is inferior.

1. Steam the carrots until tender, about 5 to 6 minutes. *Do not overcook.*
2. Melt the butter in a large, heavy skillet over medium-high heat. Add the carrots, orange zest, and cardamom. Cook, stirring occasionally, for 2 to 3 minutes. Add the Marsala and cranberries, turn the heat to high, and cook until the liquid has evaporated, about 3 to 5 minutes, stirring frequently. The cranberries will pop during this time. Season to taste with salt.

NOTE: This dish may be prepared several hours or even a day ahead of time and reheated over low heat.

Did you know? Another method of peeling carrots, parsnips, or salsify for cooking is to boil or steam them whole for a few minutes, then run them under cold water. Their skins will slide off. Then slice, julienne, or cook them longer, as needed. This works well when there are lots of carrots to be cleaned.

CAULIFLOWER AND POTATO PURÉE WITH PARMESAN

Serves 8

When combined with potatoes and Parmesan cheese, cauliflower is subtle-tasting and a nice balance to more highly seasoned meats or vegetables. For a low-carb version, omit the potato. Pipe this purée through a pastry bag to add visual appeal and texture to a plate. It's a fine compliment to Noisettes of Lamb Florentine (page 143).

Cauliflower is another winter vegetable whose aroma gets stronger as it gets older. And if the smell is pungent, the taste will be less than sweet. Use cauliflower within a couple of days of buying it. Look for heads that are firmly bunched and uniformly pale-colored without any brown spots.

1 head of cauliflower, approximately 1 1/4 pounds, broken into florets
1 large red potato, peeled and cubed
3 tablespoons light cream or milk
2 tablespoons unsalted butter
1/4 teaspoon freshly grated nutmeg
Salt and white pepper to taste
1/2 cup freshly grated Parmesan cheese

1. Steam the cauliflower over boiling water until tender, drain well, and transfer to the bowl of a food processor. In a separate pot, boil the potato until tender, drain, and keep covered until needed.
2. Add the cream or milk and butter to the cauliflower and process until smooth. Add the potato, nutmeg, salt, and pepper; pulse until smooth. Overprocessing will make the potato gummy.
3. Add the Parmesan and pulse a few times to combine. Taste and adjust seasonings, if necessary.
4. Pipe the purée through a pastry bag fitted with a large star tip into a circular mound on each plate, or serve more simply.

Did you know? Vegetable purées add variety to a meal. They are a cinch to make in the processor. Make sure the non-starchy vegetable is very smooth before adding the cooked potato, since overprocessing potatoes releases starch and produces a gummy texture. Using a food mill is a way of making a more textured purée.

ROASTED EGGPLANT WITH TAHINI ON ENDIVE LEAVES

Serves 6 as a first course

- 1 tablespoon + 1/3 cup extra-virgin olive oil
- 2 medium eggplants, wiped
- 3 large cloves garlic, peeled and cut into slivers
- 2 plum tomatoes, peeled
- 1/2 cup tahini
- Salt and freshly ground black pepper to taste
- 2 tablespoons minced flat-leaf parsley
- 7–8 tablespoons fresh lemon juice
- 1/3 cup pine nuts, toasted until light brown
- 30 Belgian endive leaves, approximately the same size
- 6 cherry tomatoes, for garnish

This do-ahead dish easily doubles as an hors d'oeuvre or vegetable accompaniment for roasted lamb or grilled chicken. The tangy, sweet Middle Eastern flavors of roasted eggplant and tahini seem to improve with time. (Check in the Ethnic or International Foods section for the ground sesame seed purée.)

We are fortunate to have excellent eggplants available almost all year. Besides large purple ones, there are small Japanese ones (look at the end of this recipe for an idea on how to use them), as well as long Chinese, round white, and purple-and-white-striped varieties. They all taste alike.

Your fingers are the best guide to good selection. Eggplants should have shiny, tight skin without any brown spots, and the crown should be green. But don't judge by appearances alone. Gently push with your thumb or forefinger. If the flesh gives slightly, then bounces back, it is ripe. If the indentation remains, it is overripe and the insides will be mushy. If there is no give, the eggplant was picked too early. Use them within a few days. If refrigerating, do so without wrappings. Since they don't like extreme cold, keep them in the top part of the refrigerator; a cool pantry is even better. Eggplant yield: 1 pound equals 3 to 4 cups chopped.

1. Preheat your oven to 375°F. Brush a cookie sheet with 1 tablespoon of oil.
2. Cut the eggplants in half lengthwise and make several deep gashes in the flesh but do not pierce the skin. Insert the garlic slivers into the eggplants and put cut side down on the cookie sheet. Bake for about 40 minutes, or until the flesh is very soft.
3. Remove from the oven and cool slightly. Scoop out the pulp and put it into a food processor or mash with a fork. Be sure to include the garlic. Add the tomatoes, tahini, salt, pepper, parsley, olive oil, and most of the lemon juice and process until smooth. If doing by hand, mash the tomatoes, then mix all the ingredients together. Scrape into a bowl, cover, and cool to room temperature or refrigerate for several hours or overnight.
4. Before serving, stir in the pine nuts and taste to adjust seasonings, adding additional lemon juice, if necessary. To serve as an appetizer: Put 5 endive leaves in a petal design on each plate, the tapered end pointing out. Spoon a large tablespoon of the eggplant mixture onto each leaf and put a cherry tomato in the center. Little slices of toasted French bread, brushed with olive oil and lightly dusted with crumbled tarragon leaves, would be a nice addition.

Did you know? Tahini is made from ground raw, hulled sesame seeds. You may find it with baking supplies or with health foods in the market. It is frequently used in Middle Eastern cooking. Once opened, this fragile condiment should be refrigerated, as it goes rancid easily. Use it within 1 to 2 months.

Another idea . . . To make grilled Japanese eggplant, buy 1 eggplant per person, using the same selection guide as above. Split the eggplants in half lengthwise, brush all over with a little sesame oil, and put on a hot grill or barbecue, cut-side down. Turn once after 2 to 3 minutes, brush lightly with some hoisin sauce (from the Asian section), and cook for another 2 minutes or until the eggplants are tender when pierced with a fork. Sprinkle on a few sliced scallions and serve.

IBERIAN EGGPLANT CASSEROLE WITH SAUSAGES AND SHRIMP

Serves 4 to 6

You'll discover lovely layers of flavor in this exciting partnership of eggplant, lamb sausages, shrimp, and Pimentón de la Vera, the fragrant, smoky, dried red pepper powder from the southwest of Spain. The dish is sprinkled with crumbled Spanish goat cheese before cooking. Increasingly, the exciting provisions from countries around the world are turning up in supermarkets as they respond to global influences. Spain is one of the culinary world's newest darlings.

3 tablespoons olive oil + additional oil to drizzle on top

4 ounces lamb sausage, casings removed and coarsely chopped

1 pound eggplant, peeled and cut into ¾-inch cubes

1 large onion, coarsely chopped

1 large green bell pepper, diced

½ medium red bell pepper, diced

1 rib celery, chopped

1 large clove garlic, chopped

½ pound medium shrimp, peeled and deveined

1 cup cooked rice

¼ cup chopped flat-leaf parsley

2 tablespoons fresh thyme leaves

1 teaspoon hot Pimentón de la Vera or smoked paprika

Salt to taste

3 ounces crumbled goat cheese

1. Preheat your oven to 350°F. Lightly oil a large casserole or individual ramekins.
2. Heat the olive oil in a large casserole over medium-high heat. Add the sausage and cook until the pieces are no longer pink in the middle, about 6 to 8 minutes, chopping them into small pieces with a spatula. Stir in the eggplant, onion, bell pepper, celery, and garlic, and cook until softened, about 15 minutes, stirring occasionally.
3. Add the shrimp, rice, parsley, thyme, Pimentón de la Vera, and salt, and cook until the shrimp turn pink. Transfer mixture to a deep baking dish, sprinkle with goat cheese, and drizzle with a little olive oil. Bake until cheese is melted and mixture is heated through. Serve either hot or at room temperature.

Did you know? Many recipes routinely call for salting sliced eggplant, letting it stand for at least 30 minutes, then rinsing, draining, and drying. This is done to remove any bitterness as well as some of the moisture. Modern eggplants are less bitter, so this salting is less essential for that function. However, when sautéing slices of the vegetable, those that are pre-salted and drained absorb far less oil.

FENNEL, ORANGE, AND SAGE SALAD

Serves 6

- 2 heads of fennel, cored and thinly sliced
- 1 red onion, julienned
- 3 navel oranges
- 1 bunch (1 ounce) fresh sage + fresh sage leaves, to garnish
- ½ cup extra-virgin olive oil
- ¼ cup balsamic vinegar
- Salt and freshly ground black pepper to taste
- Arugula leaves, to garnish

This lovely salad is a fixture at my house in the fall. It vies with a combination of thinly shaved fennel and green apples with Parmesan cheese and imported black olives tossed with the same oil-and-vinegar combination.

Fennel is at its very best from late September through November, although it is available for most of the year. Look for firm, roundish, and creamy white heads. If it is all green, it is a sign that it was harvested when immature and will be tough. The fresh green foliage should be attached and shouldn't appear dry in any way.

Arugula, an aromatic salad green also known as rocket or rucola, is a staple of Italian salads. Buy bunches with crisp leaves. Separate the leaves, discarding the thick stems. Rinse under cool water and blot dry on paper towels, then wrap leaves tightly in plastic or a resealable plastic bag. It is best if used within 2 days.

1. Combine fennel and onion in a bowl. Peel the oranges, cut them in half lengthwise, and then slice into semicircles. Cut the bunch of sage into chiffonade, by slicing the leaves crosswise into thin strips.
2. Toss all ingredients gently with the oil and vinegar, and season to taste with salt and pepper. Let stand at least 1 hour before serving. Garnish with additional sage and serve on arugula leaves.

Have you tried? In Italy, fennel is sometimes served as an appetizer called Finocchio in Pinzimonio: Trim the fennel stalks at the point where they meet the bulb, and shave a narrow slice off the base. Rinse under cold water, then cut the bulbs into quarters or eighths. Arrange on a small serving dish that also holds small bowls of extra-virgin olive oil and coarse salt. Pick up a piece of fennel *(finocchio)* with your fingers *(in pinzimonio)* and dip it first into the oil and then the salt. This also makes an interesting variation for your favorite crudité.

GREEN BEAN AND NEW POTATO SALAD FROM VERNON

Serves 8

Many French towns are renowned for producing the finest quality of a certain product: Cavaillon for small, perfumed melons; Bresse for its prized white chickens. Vernon, northwest of Paris on the way to Rouen, justly prides itself on its tender green beans. Friends from that region first introduced me to this simple salad with its garlicky vinaigrette, an addicting combination for bean and potato lovers like me. In an effort to duplicate their dish, I have been known to pick out each thin, crisp, deep green bean individually from the produce bin. Uniformity shows in the appearance and taste. Some markets also sell haricots verts, the pencil-thin variety of green beans. Their sky-high price would be an unnecessary expenditure here.

At home, refrigerate beans in a partially opened plastic or brown paper bag, or punch a couple of holes in a sealed bag. Moisture causes beans to become moldy. If you won't use them within 2 days, boil or steam the beans until bright green but still crisp, then rinse them under cold water to stop the cooking, blot dry, wrap, and refrigerate. They will stay in top condition for 3 or 4 days this way. Or you can freeze them, partially cooked and well dried, in an airtight wrapping for up to 6 months.

- 1 1/4 pounds tender young beans, rinsed, tips removed
- 1 pound of red potatoes, of equal size, scrubbed
- 1 recipe Mustard Vinaigrette (page 271)
- 2 large cloves garlic, peeled and crushed
- 2 tablespoons finely chopped flat-leaf parsley
- Freshly ground black pepper to taste

1. Bring a large pot of salted water to a boil. Cook the beans until just tender, about 3 to 4 minutes once the water returns to a boil. Drain in a colander or strainer, rinse with cold water, and then blot dry on paper towels. (The beans may also be steamed.)
2. Add more cold water to the pot along with the potatoes, and boil until just tender, about 12 to 14 minutes. They should be easily pierced with a knife, but not crumbly. Drain and cool until slightly warm. Do not rinse them. With a sharp knife, cut them into 1/4-inch slices without peeling.
3. Mound the beans in the center of a large bowl and lay the potato slices overlapping one another around the outside edge. If you are not serving this right away, drizzle a little olive oil over the potatoes to keep them from drying out. Before serving, prepare the Mustard Vinaigrette with the extra garlic and parsley, and pour over the beans and potatoes. Add plenty of black pepper. Toss carefully and serve.

NOTE: Occasionally I add diced leftover roasted chicken or turkey breast to this salad for a more substantial picnic dish or as a light main course.

GNOCCHI WITH PEAS AND TOMATO SAUCE

Serves 8 to 10 as a first course

A Tuscan farmer woman first taught me to make these heavenly potato dumplings (or gnocchi). Her sauce included the giblets from the fresh chicken cooked to crunchy perfection that she served at the next course (see Crunchy Oven-Roasted Chicken, page 100). This recipe is rustic and very satisfying. There are some fine ready-to-cook fresh or frozen gnocchi that would make this very quick and easy to serve. Be sure to test purchased convenience foods once before serving them to guests.

FOR THE SAUCE:

2 tablespoons olive oil

1 small clove garlic, peeled and minced

1 small onion, peeled and finely chopped

1 small carrot (or 1/2 medium), peeled and finely chopped

1 small rib celery, finely chopped

4 ounces thickly sliced prosciutto or similar-type cured ham (not smoked), chopped

Giblets from 1 chicken (neck, liver, heart, and gizzard), cleaned and chopped, optional

1/4 cup freshly chopped flat-leaf parsley

1 tablespoon chopped fresh basil or 1 teaspoon dried

1 28-ounce can Italian tomatoes, drained and puréed

Salt and freshly ground black pepper to taste

1/2 cup shelled peas or small frozen peas, defrosted

4 ounces freshly grated Parmesan cheese

FOR THE GNOCCHI:

1 1/2 pounds boiling potatoes, quartered

2–3 cups all-purpose flour

1/2 tablespoon salt

1. Prepare the sauce: Pour the oil into a large, heavy pot and heat over medium-high heat until fragrant. Add the garlic, onion, carrot, and celery, and sauté until wilted, 7 or 8 minutes. Add the prosciutto, giblets, if using, parsley, and basil, and cook until the giblets are browned and separated. Stir in the tomatoes, salt, and pepper, and simmer for 20 minutes or longer while preparing the gnocchi. Toward the end of the cooking time, add the peas and cook until tender, about 5 to 7 minutes, if using fresh peas.
2. Prepare the gnocchi: Boil the potatoes in a large pot of salted water until tender when pierced with a knife, about 12 to 14 minutes, then drain, and peel while still warm. Set aside until just cool enough to work with.
3. Sprinkle a large work space lightly with flour. Press the potatoes through a potato ricer or food mill *(not a processor)* and spread them out to cool. Begin incorporating flour by 1/2 cupfuls into the potatoes, dusting your hands, the board, and the potatoes with flour repeatedly as you work until the dough is smooth, uniform, and slightly sticky. (Some potatoes take more flour than others do, so amounts may vary by up to 1 cup.) Knead gently for 3 to 4 minutes more, then form the dough into a large cylinder about 4 to 5 inches in diameter.
4. Cut off slices about 1 inch thick, then cut these slices into 1-inch strips (see illustration). Roll each strip into a cylinder about the thickness of your thumb. Cut it into 1-inch lengths. Put the gnocchi on a floured board and do not handle them.

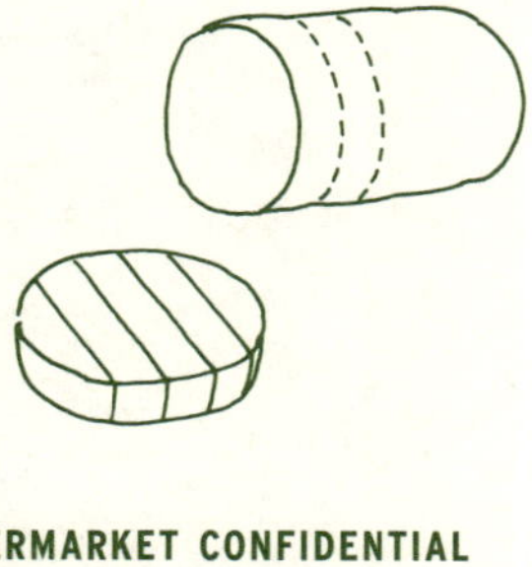

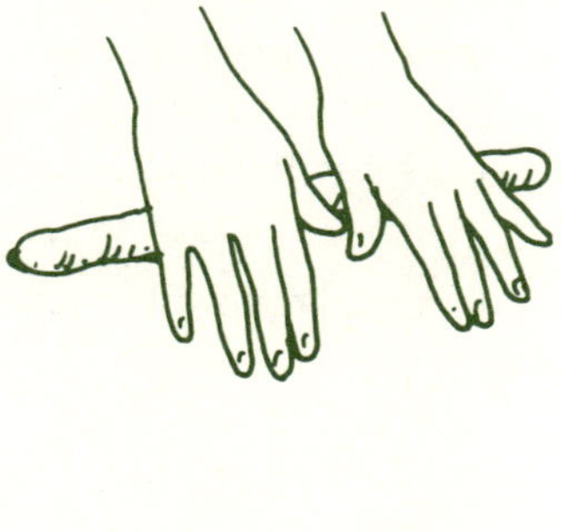

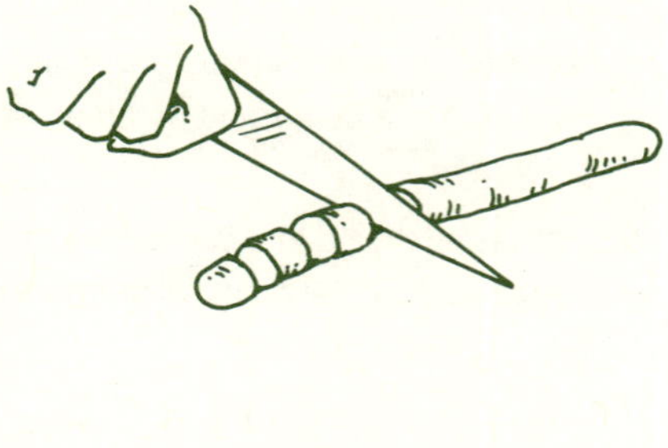

5. Bring a large pot of salted water to a boil. Add about 2 dozen gnocchi at a time. After the water returns to a boil and the gnocchi rise to the surface, cook for another 30 to 40 seconds. Remove with a skimmer or wide-slotted spoon to a large, warmed serving bowl. Repeat with the remaining gnocchi. You will have about 4 or 5 batches of gnocchi.

TO SERVE: Alternate layers of the gnocchi with large spoonfuls of the sauce. (You will need only about half the amount of sauce prepared above. Pass extra sauce at the table and/or freeze the leftovers.) Sprinkle with Parmesan, toss gently, and serve about 8 to 10 gnocchi per person.

Did you know? I think the best mashed potatoes are made the old-fashioned way—with a potato ricer or masher rather than a processor, which can make them gummy if you let the machine run. (I use the processor when I make vegetable purées and add the potato at the last minute.) Or use a handheld mixer for rustic "smashed" potatoes.

Peel and quarter the potatoes, then boil them in salted water until tender. Drain and let them dry out slightly, either in the pan over low heat for a minute, or in a bowl partially covered with a clean towel. Then mash them by hand. Beat in some milk or a little of the boiling liquid, some butter, a pinch of nutmeg (if you like), and salt and pepper to taste. Don't keep stirring! Thin-skinned, boiling potatoes make creamier mashed potatoes than the baking variety (russets). Be sure to cut off any green spots on the potatoes before cooking them.

SAUTÉED JULIENNE OF LEEKS AND CUCUMBERS

Serves 4 to 6

- 4 young leeks, about 1 1⁄4 inch in diameter, outside leaves removed
- 2 tablespoons unsalted butter
- 2 medium-sized cucumbers, peeled
- Salt and freshly ground black pepper to taste
- 1 tablespoon light cream (optional)
- 2 teaspoons fresh lemon juice
- 1 generous teaspoon minced flat-leaf parsley

This pale green vegetable dish is delicate yet flavorful. The cucumbers, cut into crescent shapes, are blanched and then sautéed with matchstick-thin strips of leeks. The result is a refreshing accompaniment for fish, poultry, or pork. Texture is important here, so choose the vegetables with care. Long, English hothouse cucumbers and small Kirby cukes, while both more costly, can often be better than the mushy "garden" variety.

Unfortunately, cucumbers in supermarkets are often shipped with a waxy coating I abhor, even though it's meant to retard moisture loss. I generally leave them in a plastic bag from the Produce department and peel them just before using. Feel each cuke to be sure it is solid and without any soft spots. I prefer medium-sized cucumbers because large ones often have big seeds, as well.

Size is also important with leeks. Once the root end is enlarged, a leek is likely to be tough and not as sweet tasting. Leeks are best when firm and young with bright green leaves. They should measure under 1 1⁄2 inches in diameter at the base. Wrapped in plastic bags in a refrigerator, they will keep for at least 10 days before turning brown.

1. Trim off the root end of the leeks and the green leaves about 1 inch above the white part. Insert the tip of a sharp paring knife about 1⁄4 inch from the trimmed root and make a deep incision up the length of the leek. Spread the leaves apart with your fingers and rinse under cold running water to remove any sand. Cut them in half lengthwise, then in thirds crosswise, and finally into thin lengthwise strips.
2. Melt the butter in a large, heavy skillet over medium heat. Add the leeks and slowly sauté them until softened, but not browned. Set aside.
3. Cut the cucumbers into half lengthwise, and scoop out the seeds with a pointed spoon or melon baller. Cut crosswise into thin crescent shapes. Bring some water to a boil in a medium-sized saucepan. Add about a teaspoon of salt, then drop in the cucumbers and cook for about 30 seconds until they are just transparent. Remove with a skimmer or slotted spoon and blot dry on paper towels. Add to the skillet with the leeks, toss to combine, and raise the heat to medium.
4. Add the salt, pepper, and cream, shaking the pan until the cream evaporates. Add the lemon juice and parsley, toss again, and taste to adjust the seasonings, if necessary.

PESTO MUSHROOMS

Makes 16

Fresh basil is a sure sign of summer and a passion of many cooks. In season, a walk in the Produce department reveals bunches of this tender aromatic herb—hopefully misted and not left to become limp or bruised. There may even be purple (opal) or other varieties to experiment with (their taste is similar).

But, what about the bags of hydroponic basil that we typically find in winter? They certainly are clean and easy to use. Pick off a leaf and rub it between your fingers. Sometimes all this clean living diminishes the intensity of flavor.

For years, pasta with pesto has been a staple in my house. When I have leftover pesto, I sometimes add a little cream cheese to soften the flavors and stuff mushrooms with it. The barely warmed crunchy caps and soft filling are a decadent hors d'oeuvre. Or, serve one large pesto mushroom with other vegetables to accompany a main course. As for prepared pestos in the Produce and other departments, too often they taste of chemicals and other odd additions.

2 cups loosely packed fresh basil leaves, rinsed and gently blotted dry

1/4 cup olive oil

2 tablespoons pine nuts

2 tablespoons walnuts or all walnuts, if desired

2 large cloves garlic, peeled and split

1 teaspoon salt

Freshly ground black pepper to taste

2 ounces cream cheese

1/3 cup grated imported Parmesan cheese

1/3 cup grated Romano cheese or use all Parmesan cheese

16 medium-large mushrooms

2 tablespoons unsalted butter

1 large clove garlic, peeled and minced

Salt and freshly ground black pepper

1. Combine the basil, olive oil, pine nuts, walnuts, garlic cloves, salt, and pepper in the bowl of a food processor and process until smooth. Scrape down the sides of the bowl, add the cream cheese, and process until smooth.
2. Scrape the basil mixture into a bowl and stir in the cheeses. Adjust the seasonings, if necessary.
3. Remove the stems from the mushrooms and wipe the caps. (Reserve stems for stock or soup, or discard.) In a small skillet, melt the butter and stir in the minced garlic; cook over low heat for 30 seconds, then turn off the heat. Brush caps inside and outside with oil and season with salt and pepper.
4. Put in a shallow baking dish. Fill each cap with pesto, mounding it slightly in the center. Cover loosely with plastic wrap and refrigerate for 1 to 2 hours. (This recipe may be prepared up to this point at least a day ahead of time.)
5. Preheat your oven to 400°F. Bake mushrooms uncovered for 5 to 6 minutes or until the filling is softened and the mushrooms are warm but still firm. Serve at once. As an hors d'oeuvre, I generally put each cap in a small decorative fluted paper cup, like the mini-muffin liners often found in the Baking section of the market.

Did you know? When buying cultivated white mushrooms, buy the freshest, whitest ones you can find. If they are loose, turn them over to inspect the undersides. As mushrooms lose moisture, the ridged part of the cap separates from the stems. When appearances are less important, pre-packed baskets are generally a better buy.

When storing mushrooms in the refrigerator, keep them in a brown bag or plastic bag with holes cut into it to let them breathe. Cultivated mushrooms are usually so clean that a wipe with a damp towel is all they need.

Portobello, crimini, and shiitakes are just some of the wonderful varieties of mushrooms available in supermarkets. They are all fragile and should be used within a day.

INCREDIBLY LIGHT ONION RINGS

Serves 4

Onions in every shape and size are a personal passion of mine. The wire basket that hangs in my kitchen overflows with white, red, and yellow onions, as well as garlic, all year long. Wherever you store them, it's important to avoid direct sunlight. I adore onions thinly sliced and raw on sandwiches, but also baked, braised, or fried to a crisp. These crunchy, ungreasy onion rings are the easiest and best version I've tried. What's more, they can be made at least an hour ahead of time and left in a warm oven. Be warned, they disappear quickly!

Choose onions individually, feeling them to be sure they are solid, without any soft spots, and that the skins are dry and papery. Smell them, too; they should be sweet. Only a deteriorating onion will smell pungent before it is cut. Mild shallots, too, go in my basket. Scallions and tiny pearl onions, however, I leave in an opened plastic bag in the vegetable drawer of my refrigerator.

FOR THE BATTER:

1 cup cold water

1 cup unbleached all-purpose flour

2 tablespoons white wine or beer (optional)

1/2 teaspoon salt

FOR THE ONIONS:

2 very large yellow onions, peeled, thinly sliced, and separated into rings

Olive oil or a combination of olive and vegetable oils for deep-frying

Salt to taste

1. Prepare the batter: Pour the water into a large bowl. Using a strainer, slowly sift in the flour, stirring with a wooden spoon or whisk to incorporate evenly. Add the wine or beer, if using, and salt. The batter should be smooth and the consistency of light cream. Set aside for 10 minutes.
2. Add the onions to the batter, turning to cover.
3. Turn your oven on to 275°F. Line a cookie sheet with paper towels.
4. Pour the oil into a large, heavy skillet to a depth of 1/2 inch and heat until very hot but not smoking, 300°F on a deep-fat thermometer. (If the oil becomes too hot during cooking, remove the skillet from the heat for 1 or 2 minutes to cool slightly.)
5. Remove some of the onion rings from the batter with a fork or slotted spoon, allowing excess batter to drip back into the bowl. Fry only as many rings as will fit comfortably in the pan at a time, keeping the oil very hot. Do not crowd the pan. Fry until both sides are golden brown, turning once, about 3 to 4 minutes. When golden brown, remove with tongs or a fork to the cookie sheet to drain. Transfer to the warm oven and continue with the remaining onion rings. Sprinkle with salt to taste before serving.

Have You Tried? This flour-and-water batter is excellent for deep-frying sage leaves, too. Hold each leaf by the stem and dip it completely into the batter. Lift out and let any excess batter drip back into the bowl. Carefully put each leaf into hot oil and fry it until golden brown on the first side, then turn and continue cooking until the second side is well colored. Only fry as many leaves as will fit comfortably in the skillet at a time.

Drain on paper towels and sprinkle with salt. I usually squeeze on a few drops of lemon juice for flavor. Serve at once. This is an hors d'oeuvre to make for your friends in the kitchen. Or leave the fried leaves in a warm oven and serve them within an hour.

MARINATED THREE-ONION SALAD

Serves 6 to 8

This simple creamy dill-flavored salad is a colorful side dish for an informal dinner or buffet. Don't worry about the onions' pungent bite. Blanching subdues them. Serve with Smoky Turkey Meatloaf (page 104), pâtés, and roast chicken. This low-fat yogurt sauce is also a great dipping sauce for raw vegetables or as a sauce for sliced mushroom, endive, and beet salad.

Both large Spanish and red Bermuda onions seem milder to me when bought in the late spring. They are my first choice for eating raw if I cannot find some of the newer sweet onions sold seasonally like the Vidalia (from Georgia), Walla Walla (from Washington), or Maui (from Hawaii). All three make wonderful eating, but watch the price ticket—these "gourmet" varieties are apt to be a couple of dollars more a pound than yellow onions. If you are putting them into a stew, the special flavor of these gourmet onions will be lost.

2 large yellow or Spanish onions, peeled, thinly sliced, and separated into rings

2 large red Bermuda onions, peeled, thinly sliced, and separated into rings

1 large bunch scallions, trimmed and thinly sliced (including most of the green parts)

2 tablespoons salt

2 teaspoons Dijon mustard

3 tablespoons fresh lemon juice

2 tablespoons olive oil

1 cup plain low-fat yogurt

1 tablespoon sugar

1/3 cup finely chopped fresh dill leaves

Freshly ground black pepper to taste

1. Put the onions in a large bowl. Cover with boiling water, add the salt, and let stand for about 10 minutes, or until wilted. Drain and blot well on paper towels.
2. Rinse and dry the bowl. In the same bowl, combine the mustard and lemon juice, then whisk in the olive oil and yogurt. Add the sugar, dill, and pepper. Stir in the onions and scallions. Mix well and refrigerate for at least an hour. The flavor improves as the salad sits.

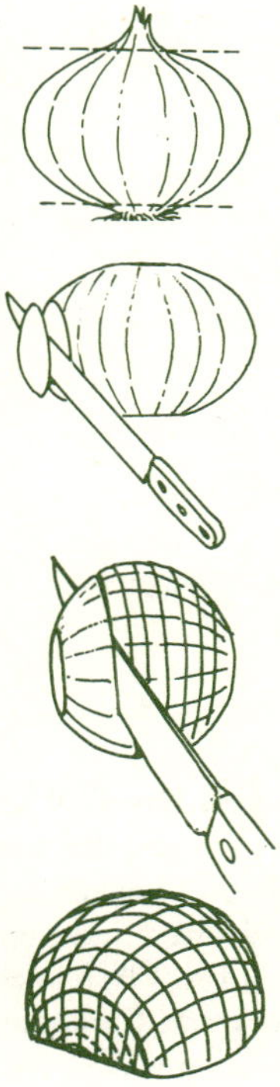

Did you know? When asked what is the best way to slice or chop an onion, I always answer, "Quickly!" The easiest way I know is to cut a narrow slice off the top and bottom, and make a small incision along the side, through the skin and one layer of the onion, and remove. Then, cut a thin slice off one side, creating a flat base so that the onion will not slip or rock as it is being cut.

Place the flat, cut part on the board and make even slices almost through the onion, working from the right (or left) to the center. Once at the center, turn the onion 180 degrees and then slice the other half, holding the first slices together against the middle so that all the slices are equally thick or thin.

To chop, trim off the top and only the smallest amount from the root end of the onion. It should stand steady. You do not need to slice off anything from the side (as above). Cutting from the top down, make narrow or wide slices almost to the root. Turn the onion 45 degrees and slice the onion, again almost to the root. Then, cut the onion in half through the root in the center, and with the flat part on the work space, slice the onion into pieces working from the top to the root end.

PARSNIPS AND POMEGRANATES

Serves 8

8 medium parsnips, tops and tips trimmed, cut into 2-inch lengths, wider top split in half lengthwise

2 tablespoons unsalted butter

1 1/2 cups orange juice

1/2 teaspoon salt, or to taste

3/4 cup fresh pomegranate seeds, white membranes removed, about 1 large pomegranate

2 tablespoons finely chopped chives

Although parsnips and pomegranates have been used in cooking for centuries, I've never seen them combined before. But cooking is creative, and there are very few rules in the kitchen. Parsnips have a lot of natural sugar that caramelizes during sautéing or frying. With a hint of orange and the jewel-like pomegranate seeds, this vegetable dish is a regal addition to any fall meal—just the season to find these items in your market.

Try to buy parsnips loose; they'll keep better (at least a couple of weeks) when not wrapped airtight. Even though their size varies dramatically, unless a parsnip is wrinkled and dehydrated-looking, it should still be delicious. When cooking them, if some are very thin and others thick, cut the parsnips into equal-sized pieces, and split the wide end in half.

1. Bring a large pot of salted water to a boil. Add the parsnips, cover, and return the water to a boil. Remove the lid and cook until the parsnips are just tender when pierced with a knife. Drain and rinse under cold running water. The skins should slip off. Thicker ends will take longer. Do not let the parsnips get too soft. Cut the pieces into approximately 1/2-inch cubes and blot dry on paper towels.
2. In a large, heavy skillet, melt the butter over medium-high heat. Add the parsnips, shaking to coat them evenly and cook, turning occasionally, until they start to color, about 7 to 8 minutes.
3. Pour in the orange juice, turn up the heat, and boil until the orange juice evaporates, about 3 to 4 minutes. Stir in the salt. Add the pomegranate seeds and chives and gently turn to mix and warm the seeds. To serve, spoon the parsnips onto a dish in a ring shape with another green vegetable, such as baby peas, in the center.

Have you tried? There are lots of things you can do with parsnips other than boiling and puréeing them. They are wonderful sliced and sautéed with tangy apple slices. Or, blanched and shredded, they add texture and taste to salads of mixed greens or chicken.

SAUTÉED SUGAR SNAPS, RADISHES, AND CHERRY TOMATOES

Serves 3 to 4

This colorful medley of vegetables literally takes only a minute to cook. Blanched sugar snap peas are tossed with split cherry tomatoes and icicle or regular radishes, splashed with a little balsamic vinegar, and the magic is done. Plenty of crunch and a subtle touch of sweetness make this a terrific side dish for roasted chicken or Indian Game Hens Marinated in Yogurt and Spices (page 112).

Unlike fresh green peas in the shell, sugar snaps and snow peas are found almost all the time. I prefer small ones of a similar size that are bright green and very crisp. Buying trays of them can be risky because there are sometimes many broken or oversized ones. In that case, buy a bit more than you need. As soon as you return home, punch holes in the wrapping and refrigerate. Use them within a couple of days.

Although bagged radishes may seem convenient, in most cases they are often old and of inferior quality.

- 6 ounces snow peas or sugar snaps, tips and strings removed
- 2 tablespoons unsalted butter
- 1 1/2 cups sliced radishes
- 1 1/4 cups split cherry tomatoes
- 1 tablespoon sugar
- 1 tablespoon balsamic vinegar
- Salt and freshly ground black pepper to taste

1. In a medium-sized saucepan of boiling salted water, blanch the snow peas for 25 to 30 seconds to set the color. Drain and rinse with cold water. Blot them dry on paper towels.
2. In the same saucepan, melt the butter over medium-high heat. Add the radishes, cherry tomatoes, sugar, and balsamic vinegar and shake the pan to coat the vegetables, cooking for about 30 seconds. Add the snow peas, season with salt and pepper, and toss. Serve at once.

Did you know? The French call Chinese snow peas mange-tout, which means "eat it all."

RED PEPPER BUTTER

Makes 1 cup; about 16 to 18 rosettes

- 2 large red bell peppers, peeled, seeds and membranes removed, or 2 red peppers from a jar, packed in water (not oil and vinegar) and blotted very dry
- 1 large clove garlic, peeled
- 12 tablespoons (1 1/2 sticks) unsalted butter, at room temperature
- 1/2 teaspoon Worcestershire sauce
- 3/4 teaspoon salt
- 1 tablespoon freshly snipped chives or finely chopped scallions

This colorful composed butter is easily made ahead of time, piped into decorative swirls, and refrigerated until serving time. It is a festive addition to grilled swordfish, venison, or tuna steaks. Try it on broiled chicken breasts, grilled venison steaks (page 150), or steamed broccoli and asparagus.

Bright, firm, sweet red bell peppers always capture my eye in the market. I buy only those that have no bruises and feel the heaviest. As these peppers (which are ripe green bell peppers) get older, they become dehydrated and their skin wrinkles. Store them unwrapped in a vegetable crisper. Unlike their green cousins, these beauties are already ripe, and their good looks fade after only a couple of days.

1. To peel the peppers, char them over a gas flame or under a broiler, turning to blacken all sides of the flesh. Transfer to a small brown paper bag, close tightly, and allow them to steam and to cool enough to handle. The charred skin will peel easily with the help of a small paring knife. If needed, run them under cold water to remove any blackened bits. Blot dry, and remove the seeds and membranes before using.
2. Combine the peppers and garlic in the bowl of a food processor and process until smooth, scraping down the bowl as needed. Add the softened butter, Worcestershire sauce, and salt; process, starting with an on-off motion, into a smooth mixture.
3. If desired, fill a pastry bag fitted with a star tip with the butter. Pipe swirls of butter about the size of a half-dollar onto waxed paper. Or roll the butter into a cylinder about 1 1/4 inches in diameter, wrap in plastic wrap, chill, and then cut into 1/2-inch slices. Sprinkle chives on each swirl or slice. Refrigerate until needed. If the butter won't be used for several hours, place swirls on waxed paper in a flat dish and cover with foil or plastic wrap. Add the chives shortly before serving.

Another idea . . . Here's a Quick Fresh Red Pepper Sauce to serve with grilled scallops or roasted chicken breast that has been sliced and fanned:

Combine 2 large peppers (peeled and seeded), 2 tablespoons of olive oil, salt, and pepper together in a food processor. Purée them until smooth. Transfer to a bowl and stir in 1/4 cup finely chopped flat-leaf parsley. Makes 1 cup. I like the combination of grilled foods with a room-temperature sauce.

Did you know? Some Deli sections sell roasted red bell peppers. Some are marinated in vinegar and oil, others are simply roasted, peeled, and packed in a little olive oil. Be sure to taste both for seasonings and freshness. Jarred red peppers also vary greatly in quality and taste. If using in place of freshly roasted and peeled peppers, look for those packed in water with a minimum of preservatives for this recipe.

PUMPKIN AND PORCINI

Serves 6

Porcini are Italian wild mushrooms, called cèpes in French, with a woody, pungent flavor. They are sold dried and packed in small cellophane bags in many markets, often in the Produce department. Or check in the aisle with canned mushrooms; they are sometimes found there hanging on J-hooks. Porcini are quite expensive, so select the package with the largest number of whole pieces. Dried porcini keep for months in a cool pantry. Combined with the sweetness of fresh pumpkin and the other aromatic ingredients, they make a colorful and unusual side dish for autumn game dinners.

Pumpkins will remain in perfect condition for at least a month if stored in a cool, dry spot. Once bruised or cut, they need to be covered, refrigerated, and used within a week.

1 ½ ounces dried porcini mushrooms
Flour and salt for dredging
4 cups pumpkin, peeled, seeded, cut into 1-by-1-by-½-inch pieces (see note)
6 tablespoons olive or vegetable oil
3 ounces thick-sliced bacon, cut into ½-inch pieces
1 cup finely chopped onion
½ cup dry Marsala
5 juniper berries, crushed
1 teaspoon salt, or to taste
Freshly ground black pepper to taste
2 tablespoons balsamic vinegar

1. In a small bowl, cover the mushrooms with warm water and soak for about 25 to 30 minutes until soft. Transfer to a clean bowl and remove all grit and fibrous pieces. Pour the liquid through several layers of cheesecloth and reserve for use at another time. It's wonderful in Sautéed Veal Cutlets with Mustard, Capers, and Peppers (page 138). Rinse the mushrooms again and squeeze gently to remove excess water.
2. Combine the flour and salt in a flat dish. Dredge enough pumpkin cubes to cover the bottom of a large, heavy skillet without crowding and shake off excess flour. Heat 4 tablespoons of oil over medium-high heat until hot and almost smoking. Sauté the cubes until lightly colored, turning to color all sides. With a slotted spoon, remove to a bowl and continue dredging and sautéing until all the pumpkin is cooked.
3. Wipe out the skillet. Pour in the remaining 2 tablespoons of oil, heat until hot and fragrant, add the bacon, adjust the heat to medium, and sauté until the pieces are separated and translucent, about 2 to 3 minutes. Add the onion and continue to cook slowly another 10 minutes, stirring occasionally, until the onion is light brown.
4. Stir in the Marsala, add the juniper berries, mushrooms, salt, and pepper. Raise the heat and bring the mixture to a boil, cooking until the liquid is reduced by half. Add the vinegar and pumpkin and cook for a few minutes longer to warm the pumpkin through. Adjust seasonings, if necessary.

NOTE: Other squashes or sweet potatoes may be substituted for pumpkin, if desired.

Did you know? If you have saved the soaking liquid from dried porcini mushrooms, strain it through several layers of cheesecloth or paper towels and use part of it in place of stock (about 1 to 1½ cups) to add an earthy flavor to soups and stews.

THOSE POTATOES!

Serves 6 to 8

This potato dish is so popular that I usually double the recipe when friends come over. The serpentined pepper strips make a beautiful design. And the aroma from the garlicky potatoes will fill your room. Gratins will be crunchier if baked in a porous dish so moisture can escape. The terra-cotta ovals or rectangles made in France and Italy are perfect.

If you eat a lot of potatoes, buying in bulk is fine. However, large quantities of foods left to go bad often end up costing more money because of what is thrown away. Try to select each potato separately so they are the same size and check for cracks and blemishes. At home, I leave potatoes loose in a drawer or cool pantry.

1 tablespoon unsalted butter

2 pounds medium-sized red or other waxy potatoes, peeled and cut into 1/8-inch slices

2 large red bell peppers, peeled, seeds and membranes removed, cut into thin strips

1/2 cup milk

1/4 cup + 2 tablespoons cream or all milk

2–3 large cloves garlic, peeled and minced

1 teaspoon salt, or to taste

1/8 teaspoon white pepper

2 tablespoons chopped flat-leaf parsley, for garnish

1. Preheat your oven to 350°F. Butter a large (10-by-14-inch) earthenware or porcelain baking dish.
2. Lay potato slices in an overlapping pattern in the dish, reversing directions from one row to the next. Drape strips of peppers around the edges of the potato slices, forming an undulating design. Use any extra pieces of pepper around the edge of the dish.

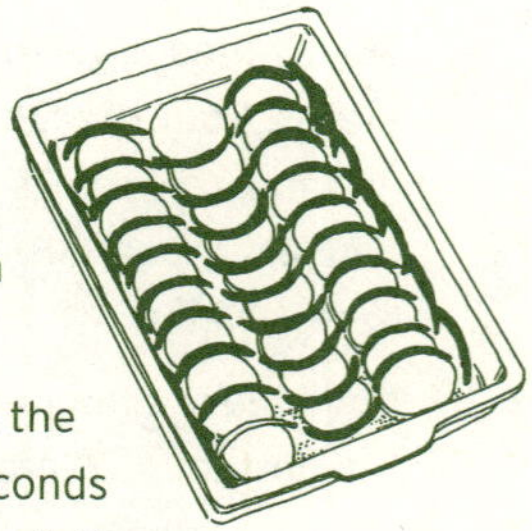

3. In a small saucepan, bring the milk and 1/4 cup of cream, the garlic, salt, and pepper to a simmer and cook for 30 seconds over low heat, then pour over the potatoes, including all the garlic, and transfer to the lower third of the oven. After 1 hour, spoon the remaining 2 tablespoons of cream over the potatoes. Bake until the top is crusty and well colored, about 1 hour and 20 minutes. If the potatoes become too dry during cooking, drizzle on a couple more tablespoons of cream.
4. Remove from the oven, sprinkle on parsley, cut into portions along the edges of the potato slices, and serve.

NOTE: This dish may be cooked ahead of time and reheated for 10 to 15 minutes in a 350°F oven. Add a little more cream, if needed, to make the top shiny.

As a variation . . . Sauté 2 to 3 thinly sliced large onions in some butter or olive oil until lightly browned. Spread them evenly in the gratin dish and layer the potatoes over them. Continue as above, omitting the red pepper and stirring a teaspoon of Dijon mustard into the cream. Ten minutes before removing the potatoes from the oven, sprinkle 1/2 cup of Parmesan cheese on top and return the dish to the oven until the top is brown.

TOMATO COULIS

Makes 1 1/2 cups

This simple uncooked tomato sauce is a celebration of how wonderful real tomatoes can be. Use it on Zucchini Gratin (page 49).

For the most part, those perfectly shaped, uniform-sized light red rocks—found during most of the year and marketed under the misnomer t-o-m-a-t-o-e-s—taste like cellulose to me. With few exceptions I don't buy fresh tomatoes in the supermarket except in late summer. Some imported tomatoes have reasonably good flavor, as do some locally grown vine-ripened varieties. Even at other times of the year, fresh plum tomatoes are often a quite good choice for cooking.

The secret is to smell them. Do they smell tomatoey? If they feel very hard, leave them. Finally, please don't put tomatoes in a refrigerator unless they are cut. They taste much better at room temperature. For sauce, barring any decent alternatives, I prefer canned imported Italian tomatoes from the San Marzano region of Italy or Muir Glen California tomatoes. I use them in Chunky Homemade Tomato Sauce (page 282).

3 firm, ripe tomatoes, peeled and seeded
1/2 teaspoon salt, or to taste
Freshly ground black pepper to taste
1/2 teaspoon sugar
1 tablespoon freshly chopped mint or basil

1. To peel and seed the tomatoes, drop them in a saucepan of boiling water for about 20 to 30 seconds. Remove with a slotted spoon and use a sharp paring knife to peel away the skin. Then, cut the peeled tomatoes in half horizontally. With the rounded side in the palm of your hand, squeeze gently to extract the seeds.
2. Process the tomatoes in a processor. The purée can be very smooth or chunky, depending on the texture you want. Add the salt, pepper, sugar, and mint or basil and taste to adjust seasonings, if necessary.

Did you know? The word coulis originally referred to all sauces that were derived naturally from cooking meat. Later it came to mean a thick purée of meat, poultry, fish, game, or vegetables that was also used for sauces and soups. Today we usually use the word to refer to a cold, puréed sauce made from uncooked or only slightly cooked ingredients, such as this tomato coulis. The raspberry sauce for the Fresh Pear Tart with Ginger Cream (page 75) is another coulis.

SALSA

Makes 2 ½ cups

- 1 cup minced onion
- 1 ½ cups finely chopped firm, ripe tomatoes
- 1–2 large jalapeño peppers (about 2 inches long), membranes and seeds removed, minced (see note)
- 2 cups washed and loosely packed cilantro leaves, chopped
- 2 tablespoons red wine vinegar
- Freshly ground black pepper to taste

Salsa is that addicting uncooked chunky tomato sauce that almost every Tex-Mex restaurant serves with baskets of tortilla chips. It can vary from mild to three-alarm blazing hot. I've developed a real passion for salsa, since it's low in calories and very flavorful. Use it, mixed with yogurt, for dipping raw vegetables, or stir it into sour cream to make a piquant dressing. Ladled over an omelet, it's colorful and zesty. You need flavorful tomatoes for this sauce.

Cilantro, also called fresh coriander or Chinese parsley, looks like flat-leaf parsley. It is a staple of Asian and Mexican cooking. The best way to maintain it is with a damp paper towel wrapped around the roots and stems and stored in a resealable plastic bag. It should last 4 or 5 days. If it's very wet, blot first with dry paper towels. This also works well for parsley and mint.

1. Combine all of the ingredients in a small bowl. Refrigerated in a glass jar with a tight lid, salsa will last for up to a couple of weeks.

NOTE: Working with hot chile peppers can be risky. The oil in the peppers can get on your hands, under your nails, or just about anywhere. *Do not touch your eyes* after you have been working with peppers, even if you have washed your hands. The hottest parts of the peppers are the seeds and membranes. Remove as much of these as your taste allows. Peppers vary widely in heat. One jalapeño might be enough today. But, a second may be needed another time.

Did you know? The smaller the top of a chile pepper, the hotter it is likely to be!

As a variation . . . There are several variations of salsa without tomatoes. One of my favorites is to combine 2 peeled and diced ripe mangoes, 1 seeded and finely chopped red bell pepper, ½ cup finely chopped red onion, 2 finely chopped jalapeños with the seeds and membranes removed, 1–2 tablespoons chopped cilantro, 2 tablespoons olive oil, the juice of 1–2 limes, and fine sea salt to taste. Serve on grilled duck or chicken breasts.

SUMMER TOMATO SOUP WITH BASIL CREAM

Serves 6

This delicate tomato soup is a perfect celebration for August and September, when tomatoes are at their best and now featured in markets. Served lukewarm or cool, it is a refreshing and colorful beginning to a meal or a marvelous partner for sandwiches at a light meal. Served with lightly salted basil-scented whipped cream, it is elegant.

Chopping basil is best done by hand with a sharp knife. A food processor bruises the leaves.

2 tablespoons unsalted butter

4 large shallots or 1 medium onion, peeled and thinly sliced

2 1/2 teaspoons salt, or to taste

3 pounds juicy, ripe tomatoes, peeled, seeded, and coarsely chopped

1 pint rich chicken stock (see note)

1 pint milk

White pepper to taste

1/2 cup heavy cream, chilled (optional)

1/2 cup loosely packed fresh basil leaves, finely chopped

Small basil leaves for garnish (optional)

1. In a heavy, medium-sized saucepan, melt the butter over medium heat. Add the shallots or onion, and sauté until wilted and very lightly colored, about 7 to 8 minutes. Stir in 2 teaspoons of salt and the tomatoes, cover tightly, and simmer until the tomatoes are soft, about 12 minutes.
2. Transfer to the bowl of a food processor or electric blender and purée until smooth. Or, for more texture, pass through a food mill. Return the purée to the saucepan, stir in the chicken stock and milk, season with white pepper, and heat gently for a few minutes. Set aside to cool.
3. If desired, beat the heavy cream in a chilled bowl just until it forms soft peaks. Stir in 1/2 teaspoon salt and the basil. Otherwise, stir the chopped basil into the soup. Ladle the soup into bowls, add a good-sized dollop of the basil cream in the middle of each bowl, if using, and add a couple of basil leaves in the center.

NOTE: To enrich a canned or weak chicken stock, add 1 medium celery stalk, chopped; 1/2 small onion, chopped; 1 small carrot, peeled and chopped; a couple of sprigs of parsley; and a couple of black peppercorns to 3 1/2 cups (2 cans) of stock. Bring the liquid to a boil, then lower the heat and boil gently until the liquid has reduced to 2 cups approximately 15 to 20 minutes. Strain.

Did you know? Tomatoes cooked in an aluminum pan lose their natural red color and turn slightly brownish during simmering. They develop a metallic, bitter taste as well.

FRIED TURNIP CRISPS

Serves 8

- Vegetable oil for deep frying
- 6–8 medium-sized turnips, peeled and cut into ⅛-inch slices
- Salt
- Fresh lemon juice (optional)

I always laugh when I serve these crunchy, almost sweet chips to my friends. They never suspect these delicious morsels are turnips. Turnips, parsnips, celery root (celeriac), and sweet potatoes, when thinly sliced, become crisp like potato chips. They are a delightful pre-dinner snack or can be served in place of a starch. If you have a food processor, use the slicing blade to do the cutting for these crisps. Although wonderful varieties of fried vegetables are sold in market Snack sections, these are far less expensive and fresher.

Turnips are the best in spring, when tender, smaller ones are in the market. Alas, so many people turn up their nose at this vegetable and its bigger cousin, the rutabaga, that they have no idea how wonderfully sweet they can be. Store turnips without their greens in the refrigerator for up to a week. And, try Roasted Squabs Stuffed with Turnips, Olives, and Figs (page 120) for a special meal.

1. Pour the oil into a deep skillet to a depth of about 1 inch and heat until hot but not smoking.
2. Pat the turnip slices dry on paper towels. Add them in small bunches so the oil remains hot. Continue cooking until they are golden brown, stirring frequently so that all the crisps cook evenly, about 7 to 8 minutes. Remove to paper towels and serve while still hot, or keep warm in oven. Continue with the remaining turnips. Sprinkle lightly with salt and, if desired, drizzle a little fresh lemon juice over them.

Did you know? Turnips and other root vegetables, as well as squashes, eggplants, and even green beans, may be tossed with a little oil or prepared salad dressing and roasted until crisp.

Another idea . . . For Herbed Oven Roasted Vegetables, combine 6 seeded and quartered plum tomatoes, 3 peeled and diced medium turnips, 2 medium zucchini and 2 yellow squashes cut into ¼-inch diagonal slices, and 2 each red, yellow, and green peppers, julienned. Toss with 1 cup olive oil and ½ cup balsamic vinegar or 1½ cups high-quality purchased Caesar dressing, 4 tablespoons chopped fresh rosemary leaves, 4 tablespoons fresh thyme leaves, 3 cloves minced garlic, and salt and freshly ground black pepper. Bake in a flat dish for 20 minutes in a 350°F oven. Turn, sprinkle on Parmesan cheese, and bake for 20 minutes more. Drain any liquid and serve either hot or at room temperature. Serves 8.

WINTER VEGETABLE STEW DIJON STYLE

Serves 6 to 8

Dijon, France, is renowned for its spicy mustard; many varieties are now available from whole grain to herb-seasoned. In this hearty vegetarian dish, any of those mustards will add a rich flavor to the sauce and practically no calories—a boon to dieters. Notice that the only cream is half-and-half; the sauce is thickened with a little cornstarch. I don't think you'll feel cheated. When served over brown rice or barley, the varied texture and colors of this medley are especially satisfying. While vegetables at the peak of freshness are my preference, this is a good spot to use up those that may have been slightly neglected.

4 tablespoons (1/2 stick) unsalted butter

1 tablespoon vegetable oil

3/4 pound tender carrots, peeled and sliced about 1/4 inch thick (approximately 3 cups)

1 head cauliflower, broken into small florets

3/4 pound yellow onions, peeled and sliced 1/4 inch thick (approximately 3 1/2 cups)

1/3 cup white wine

2 cups vegetable or chicken stock

2 teaspoons salt, or to taste

Freshly ground black pepper to taste

2 tablespoons freshly chopped dill or 1 tablespoon dried

1/2 cup half-and-half

4 tablespoons Dijon mustard

1 1/2 teaspoons cornstarch

1 10-ounce package frozen petite peas, defrosted

Chopped toasted pecans for garnish, optional

1. Melt the butter and oil in a large, heavy casserole over medium heat. Add the carrots and sauté for 2 to 3 minutes; add the remaining vegetables except the peas and continue cooking until they start to wilt, 5 to 6 minutes longer. Pour in the wine and bring to a boil. After 1 minute, add the stock, cover, adjust the heat down, and simmer until the vegetables are almost tender, 8 to 10 minutes.
2. Add the salt, pepper, dill, and half-and-half into which you have stirred the mustard. Stir to blend and continue cooking slowly over medium-low heat for another 8 to 10 minutes.
3. Remove about 1/2 cup liquid and stir in the cornstarch. Return the liquid to the casserole and blend well, cooking gently for a few minutes more until the liquid thickens. Adjust the seasonings, adding more mustard if needed. Stir in the peas. Serve over noodles, cooked barley or brown rice, or other grains. Top with chopped nuts, if desired.

As a variation . . . Stews are ideal for adding or changing ingredients to suit your own taste. For non-vegetarians, this stew would be delicious with cubes of leftover chicken or turkey added at the end to warm them through. Or fresh shrimp, again added at the end and allowed to turn pink, would be a flavorful and colorful addition. Or, how about broccoli florets or roasted red peppers? I have used all of them at various times.

COOL AND TANGY WATERCRESS SAUCE

Makes 3 cups

2 large bunches watercress, washed
1/2 cup mayonnaise
1/2 cup plain low-fat yogurt
1/2 cup heavy cream, whipped to soft peaks
Salt and freshly ground black pepper to taste

This is a refreshing and light sauce for fish in pastry or grilled trout. Crisp dark green bunches of watercress—essential here for color and taste—need to be wrapped in damp towels and refrigerated with a light protective wrapping if they are to last more than a day. Once again, don't make the mistake of wrapping airtight. Vegetables need air circulation.

1. Remove any yellow leaves and trim the coarse stems from the watercress. Put it in the food processor and purée. Add the mayonnaise and yogurt and pulse just until blended. Transfer the sauce to a bowl and fold in the cream, salt, and pepper.

CRISPY YUCCA WEDGES

Serves 4 to 6

With interest in Latino and other ethnic cuisines, tubers like yucca are found near familiar potatoes. The delicate sweet flavor of yucca "fries" is a perfect complement to spicy dishes. Yucca's almost neutral flavor takes well to a light dusting of green tea ground with coarse salt.

Also known as manioc, tapioca, and cassava, this starchy root is a native to Brazil and is used from appetizers to desserts. Hispanic dishes frequently use yucca to thicken dishes, while in the Caribbean it's often fried.

2 pounds yucca, peeled and cut into 4-inch lengths

Peanut or other vegetable oil, for frying

1 tablespoon green tea leaves

1 tablespoon coarse salt

1. Bring a large pot of salted water to a boil. Add the yucca and cook until a fork easily penetrates the flesh, at least 18 to 20 minutes. Test each piece separately and watch that you don't overcook them. Drain the yucca and blot dry, then cut into thick, irregular wedges, like steak fries.
2. Pour enough oil in a deep skillet to measure ½ to ¾ inch and heat until hot. Add the wedges, a few at a time, and cook over medium-high heat until golden brown, about 15 to 20 minutes, turning to color on all sides. Blot on paper towels.
3. Combine the tea and salt in a spice grinder or clean coffee grinder and pulse until finely ground. Sprinkle on yucca and serve.

HOT AND SPICY STIR-FRIED ZUCCHINI

Serves 6

These spicy gingery zucchini slices take just minutes to stir-fry in a wok, and they'll remain quite fresh for a hour. To make last-minute work easier, do all the cutting and measuring in advance. Refrigerate cut-up vegetables in resealable plastic bags. Salting the zucchini before cooking prevents them from absorbing a lot of oil.

- 1½ pounds medium zucchini, washed, trimmed, and cut into ¼-inch slices
- 1 tablespoon kosher or coarse salt
- 1 tablespoon cornstarch
- 3 tablespoons rice wine vinegar
- 1–2 tablespoons vegetable oil
- 1–2 tablespoons toasted sesame oil
- 2 tablespoons finely minced fresh gingerroot
- 2 tablespoons minced scallions, including most of the green parts
- ½ tablespoon red pepper flakes, or to taste
- 1 tablespoon soy sauce
- 1½ tablespoons sugar

1. Put the zucchini in a large colander, toss with the salt, and set in the sink to drain for 15 minutes, turning a couple of times. Remove slices and blot dry on paper towels. Stir the cornstarch into the vinegar and set aside.
2. Heat the smaller amounts of both oils in a wok until very hot. Add the zucchini, turning with a wide spatula, until it is lightly colored and begins to soften, about 3 minutes. Add the extra oil, if needed. Add the ginger, scallions, and pepper flakes and cook briefly. The flakes will darken but do not let them burn.
3. Stir in the cornstarch and vinegar mixture, soy sauce, and sugar and cook until the sauce thickens and coats the zucchini, 1 to 2 minutes. The slices should still be quite crisp. Serve at once or leave in the wok for up to an hour.

Did you know? Rice wine vinegar, found with other Asian ingredients or vinegars, has an acidity level of about 4 percent, making it lower than red wine and many other vinegars, which average between 5 and 6.5 percent. If substituting another vinegar, dilute it with some water to cut back on the sharpness.

Did you know? Sesame oil used in Asian cooking is generally made from toasted seeds. The untoasted variety has far less flavor.

ZUCCHINI GRATIN

Serves 8

This versatile late-summer dish can be served warm or at room temperature. I first tasted it near Grasse, in the south of France, where the vegetables had come fresh from the garden. If you do not grow zucchini, summer squash is one of the easiest vegetables to find in a supermarket. Serve it with a fresh Tomato Coulis (page 41).

I prefer small zucchini—no longer than 6 inches—that are solid and with no signs of dehydration. Since zucchini have such a high percentage of water, they will last only a few days in the refrigerator. Make sure to remove them from the plastic bag.

3 tablespoons unsalted butter

1 tablespoon vegetable oil

3 medium zucchini, washed and cut into 1/4-inch slices

2 large shallots, peeled and finely chopped

2 eggs

1/2 cup milk

1/2 cup freshly grated imported Parmesan cheese

1/3 cup cooked white rice

1/4 teaspoon freshly grated nutmeg

Salt and freshly ground black pepper to taste

1 recipe Tomato Coulis (page 41)

1. Preheat your oven to 350°F. Butter an 8-inch-square baking dish with 1 tablespoon of butter. Set aside.
2. In a large, heavy skillet, melt the remaining 2 tablespoons of butter and the oil over medium-high heat. Add the zucchini and sauté until wilted and lightly colored, about 5 minutes, shaking the pan often. Reduce heat to medium, stir in the shallots, and cook for 2 minutes longer, until the shallots are wilted.
3. In a bowl, beat the eggs and milk together. Add the zucchini mixture, half the grated cheese, the rice, nutmeg, salt, and pepper. Stir and adjust the seasonings, if necessary. Pour the mixture into the prepared baking dish, smooth the top, and sprinkle on the remaining cheese.
4. Bake in the center of the oven until a knife inserted in the center comes out clean, about 20 minutes. Meanwhile, prepare the Tomato Coulis. Remove the gratin from the oven and cool on a wire rack for at least 10 minutes. Cut into squares and serve with Tomato Coulis.

BUYING BY THE SEASONS

So many foods are flown in from growers around the world that we can be fooled into thinking we no longer need to wait for peaches in the summer, pears in the fall, or tomatoes in August. While it's true that sophisticated farming and shipping technology affords us many more varieties of fruits, vegetables, fish, and meat throughout the year, an intelligent shopper must still consider seasonality as an important issue when buying in a supermarket for several reasons.

The more delicate a food, the more important the question of seasonality becomes. To enjoy food in optimum condition, with the longest shelf life, and at the best price, supermarket shoppers are best served by selecting foods in their prime growing and shipping times. This doesn't mean there are no exceptions. I have bought plums and nectarines in February that were sensational. But I've gambled and lost, as well. If the market offers samples, then your decision is made easier. Otherwise, the facts are overwhelmingly in favor of seasonal buying.

Produce

Many fruits and vegetables stop ripening once they are picked. Since tree- or vine-ripened fruits, such as peaches or tomatoes, are extremely perishable, they are often picked under-ripe for easy transport. This is especially true for long-distance shipping where a longer shelf life translates into less spoilage and higher revenues for grocers. While the color may brighten and the fruit may soften, no more sugar is being produced, so the produce cannot develop optimum flavor and texture, even when left to ripen at room temperature.

When fruit is picked ripe—as with berries shipped from South America—by the time it arrives in the supermarket, it is usually at the tail end of its shelf life. If not used that day, it is wasted. Where possible, ask for fruit from the closest grower.

Price is another consideration. Out-of-season items can cost at least twice as much as seasonal ones. For my money, the risk of having to discard spoiled or tasteless produce isn't worth it. In season, even the least expensive supermarket should have a good selection of produce to choose from. Just pick carefully and read the selection tips with each recipe.

Respecting seasonality also means recognizing that some foods, while available all year, go through different stages. Garlic, for example, is usually milder in spring and summer. Split a clove during the winter months, and you are likely to find a green shoot growing inside; this can be bitter and should be discarded before use.

Other foods in the Produce department can be a better buy in another form—such as flash frozen—during most of the year: The wonderfully sweet fresh green peas of summer come and go quickly, leaving behind only large, waxy green marbles. On the other hand, boxes of frozen petite peas are delicious. When fresh unblemished spinach is hard to find, boxes of frozen are more than acceptable.

Tomatoes for sauces and soups are another disappointment. Experience has taught me that showy hothouse and imported varieties are usually inferior to the canned imported Italian (San Marzano region) ones.

Modern technology allows growers to individually flash freeze berries in the fields at the height of their growing season. During winter, these packages are a more reliable choice than imported fresh berries when appearance is less important. While fresh-squeezed orange or grapefruit juice is wonderful, it is no more nutritious than frozen juice, which is usually substantially less expensive.

Meat, Poultry, and Fish

Although supermarkets sell meat, poultry, and fish all year, they do gear up for holiday and seasonal merchandising. You might consider buying during peak availability, when prices are lower, especially if you have a freezer in which to store multiple purchases.

Lamb is often featured for Easter but is available 12 months of the year. Traditionally the price is lower in the spring when young animals come to market.

A more diversified selection of fish is featured during the Lenten season when markets run plenty of specials. This is a good time to sample unfamiliar fish or to discuss a new recipe with the manager or savvy salesperson in the Seafood department. He should also be informed and able to address questions and concerns about mercury and PCBs in swordfish and/or tuna.

Turkeys are a traditional Thanksgiving mainstay. But with more cuts and sizes available, this bird's popularity is spreading, particularly as a substitute for pricier veal.

More adventurous markets sell game birds, usually in the fall and winter months, when heartier fare is more appealing. Ask, and they will usually order them for you.

Certain cuts of meat are seasonal favorites. Steaks are a barbecue special; as a result the price is often lower in winter when there is less demand, and pork chops are less costly in summer. Buy at the lower price and freeze them.

Dairy

Seasonal differences here are not as noticeable.

But, as June is National Dairy Month, look for butter to be cheaper. It freezes well for a long time, so it's a good buy. Wrap it tightly and freeze.

The variety of cheeses is highest during the cool months and during Lent.

For holiday baking, heavy cream is sold in quart cartons. The rest of the year, pints and half-pints are the norm. If your market sells "pasteurized" cream in addition to "ultra-pasteurized," it is more often available during winter months when it is less likely to spoil.

Staples

The center shelves of the market appear about the same all year, but there are subtle changes you might notice. It is difficult to convince supermarkets to change their familiar ordering patterns. But with enough requests, they often listen.

Specialty flours, candied fruits, chocolates, and some nuts are associated with autumn and holiday baking. During the rest of the year, they may be missing or in short supply, since shelf space is always at a premium. If you use these items regularly, be sure to check with the department manager about special orders or, if your space at home permits, buy extra.

Other baking supplies, such as parchment paper and decorative foil cups, are also easier to find in the fall.

Chestnuts, currants, and dried fruits are more often used in winter cooking.

During the warmer months, barbecue sauces, seasonal decorative paper plates and napkins, charcoal, and other paraphernalia for outdoor cooking are more in demand, and there will be more variety.

CHAPTER TWO: **FRUIT**

INTRODUCTION

Recently, supermarket produce buyers have gone back to school and to the fields to familiarize themselves with many varieties of fruit that were formerly unavailable. With technological advances and global marketing, an ever-widening supply and variety of products are in the market. The spread of smaller ethnic markets has afforded interested cooks the chance to sample less familiar fruits like pluots and fresh lichees. These customers, in turn, then look for these products in their supermarkets. A bit of healthy competition has certainly helped the consumer.

Such plenitude has made fruit even more popular in every dimension of cooking from breakfast through dessert; from juicy berries on cereal to Individual Apple Strudels (page 57). Fruit in combination with other foods adds a sweet acidity to balance flavors. Pineapple Boats with Pork, Black Beans, and Mole Sauce (page 78) or Sautéed Turbot Fillets with Sliced Starfruit (page 81) are but two examples. And, the fruit can be beautiful enough to make the most exquisite centerpieces.

To meet high expectations, customers need to spend a minute analyzing how good the fruit they reach for actually is. Fortunately, fruit is wrapped far less than it used to be, as looks can be very deceiving. Aside from a visual examination for bruises and texture, the aroma and feel of the fruit can give you some important clues to the taste and texture. A peach, for example, may look beautiful. If it is hard as a rock and there is no fragrance, however, chances are poor that it will get any better even sitting out on your kitchen counter. Tempting though it may be, you will be better off passing it by.

Soft fruit can also be misleading. Remember that each time someone gently pushes the bottom of a melon, it is bruised a little more. Eventually, it may become soft, but it is a long way from ripe. In a bag of apples or oranges, the adage about one bad piece of fruit spoiling the barrel is true. Make sure to inspect these bags carefully. Once home, you should discard rotten fruit immediately.

Another source of concern in the fruit section is preservatives and dyes. Markets and growers need to make a profit, and this may lead to undesirable practices, such as applying a waxy protective coating to make apples look shiny and cushion them against bruises. If you have concerns, be sure to ask. Here, as elsewhere throughout the market, it pays to ask a friendly manager. Not only should he answer questions, he can help with special orders and assist you in selecting the best of what is available that day.

Seasonal buying, for me, is still the safest and most economical way to buy fruit. Look at the Strategy Pages on seasonality just preceding this chapter and stay abreast of health concerns with produce from foreign sources. Another good way to verify quality is to sample fruit from the same crop. Markets know that this often boosts sales and frequently have cut-up fruit ready and waiting. It's also an appealing way to discover unfamiliar items, provided that the display is clean.

We are fortunate to have a variety of fruits available in supermarkets today. We no longer suffer with ugly cold-storage apples in the spring. Strawberries have become almost seasonless. With a little care in selection, each piece of fruit you eat, if consumed in a timely manner, will be delicious.

INDIVIDUAL APPLE STRUDELS

Makes 8

Apple strudel is one of my favorite desserts. Even thinking about crisp, flaky pastry wrapped around tangy apples laced with walnuts and raisins, cinnamon, and a dash of rum makes my mouth water. Thanks to phyllo, these miniature strudels are easy to make and serve in individual portions. No more flakes and broken slices, and everyone gets plenty of crunchy "ends."

It should come as no surprise that Americans eat more apples than any other fruit. However, of the several hundred varieties grown, most are eaten locally and aren't seen in the market. Until a few years ago, even in fall—peak apple season—grocers stocked only a few choices like Rome Beauty, red and yellow Delicious, McIntosh, and Greening. Recently, I have found other varieties—Macouns, Empires, Granny Smiths, and Cortlands, along with Jonathans and Winesaps—in markets around the country. If you look for locally grown varieties, you surely will be rewarded. Most recently, I have enjoyed crisp Fuji apples.

When choosing apples, buy firm, brightly colored (appropriate to the variety) fruits. If the skin looks shriveled or there are bruises, leave them. Most apples last at least 2 weeks in the refrigerator. They keep nicely in a dark cellar, as well.

- 1/2 cup golden raisins
- 1/3 cup amber or dark rum
- 8 tablespoons unsalted butter
- 5 large Granny Smith or other tart apples, peeled, cored, and coarsely chopped (approximately 6 1/2 to 7 cups)
- 6 tablespoons sugar
- 2 tablespoons lemon juice
- 1 teaspoon cinnamon
- Zest of 1 large lemon, minced
- Pinch of salt
- 3/4 cup finely chopped walnuts
- 1/4 cup toasted bread crumbs
- 12 sheets phyllo
- Confectioners' sugar for dusting (optional)
- 1/2 pint lightly whipped heavy cream, sweetened with sugar (optional)

1. Combine the raisins with the rum in a small bowl and set aside.
2. In a large, heavy skillet, melt 3 tablespoons of butter over medium heat. Add the apples and cook for about 5 minutes until slightly softened, turning to coat with butter. Add the raisins and rum, sugar, lemon juice, cinnamon, lemon zest, and salt. Adjust the heat to medium-high and allow the mixture to boil until almost all the liquid has evaporated, about 3 to 4 minutes. Stir in 1/2 cup of the walnuts and set aside.
3. Butter a cookie sheet or jelly-roll pan and preheat your oven to 425°F.
4. Combine the bread crumbs with the remaining 1/4 cup walnuts in a small bowl.
5. Melt the remaining 5 tablespoons of butter in a small pan.
6. On a clean work space, lay 1 sheet of phyllo horizontally on a towel and brush lightly with butter; cover the remaining phyllo with a towel. Sprinkle a scant tablespoon of the bread crumb mixture over the phyllo. Lay a second sheet on top of the first, and again brush lightly with butter, and sprinkle on another scant tablespoon of crumbs. Put on a third sheet and cut the stack in half vertically. Spoon about 1/8 of the filling along the lower edge of each stack of phyllo, leaving about a 1 1/4-inch border on each side.

7. Holding the lower edges of the towel, flip the towel, causing the phyllo to roll over on itself. Fold in the sides of the phyllo and continue to roll. Carefully transfer each strudel to the cookie sheet with the seam side down. Brush the tops with butter. Continue with the remaining phyllo and filling until all 8 strudels are rolled.
8. Bake in the middle of the preheated oven for 12 minutes or until the strudels are crisp and golden brown. Remove and let them stand for at least 10 minutes before serving. Strudels will keep well in a turned-off oven for at least 1 to 2 hours. Sprinkle with confectioners' sugar. Serve with lightly whipped cream, if desired.

LEMON-GLAZED APRICOTS

Serves 4

6 ripe apricots, washed and split
1/4 cup Lemon Curd (page 69)
1/2 teaspoon ground ginger
2-3 tablespoons sugar
Vanilla ice cream (optional)

This is a simple, refreshing dessert to make for summer meals. Tangy Lemon Curd (page 69) with a dash of ginger is spread on fresh apricot halves and baked for a couple of minutes. If you are on the lookout for apricots, buy large, round, golden-yellow ones in season. They should still be firm (not hard). Let them ripen in a bag on your kitchen counter for a couple of days. Don't waste your money on small apricots; they will be mostly pits.

Apricots are an almost forgotten luxury in most supermarkets and specialty stores. Modern technology has concentrated on shipping fruit that will not bruise, so the ripe fruit's exotically sweet flavor often never develops fully, especially with mid-winter imported varieties. Yes, they get soft, but they are also mushy and of little interest. Cooking brings out their flavor.

1. Preheat your oven to 375ºF. Adjust the broiler pan to 2 to 3 inches from the heat.
2. Put the apricot halves in a flat, oven-safe dish. Combine the lemon curd and ginger in a small bowl and spoon it over the apricots. Sprinkle on the sugar and bake apricots for about 2 minutes, or until just warm.
3. Transfer to the broiler until the tops are glazed. Watch carefully to prevent burning. Remove and serve 3 apricot halves per person. If desired, add a scoop of vanilla ice cream.

NOTE: If you have a *baked* Tart Shell (page 229), double this recipe, spread another 3/4 cup of Lemon Curd over the tart shell, and arrange the baked apricots on top.

Another idea . . . Try this glaze on ripe nectarines, freestone or white peaches, or those amusing donut-shaped peaches.

BANANA-FILLED CRÊPES FLAMBÉES

Serves 6

Bananas in caramelized rum syrup, wrapped in crêpes and set aflame, are a favorite old-fashioned temptation of mine. To gild the lily, I add softly whipped cream or vanilla ice cream. This is an easy and impressive dessert to make when time is limited. Since the crêpes are made ahead of time, with a short interlude you can ignite the bananas and make a grand entrance. Some markets also sell ready-made crêpes.

Bananas are one of the easiest and best fruits to buy anywhere. They are available all year. Rather than looking for perfectly ripe fruit, I buy slightly green ones without bruises and marks and let them ripen on my counter. In my house, some of us like bananas with tiny brown sugar spots while others like them pure yellow. Only after they are as ripe as I want them do I think of refrigerating them. Even though refrigeration turns the skin brown, the bananas are fine.

FOR THE CRÊPES: (SEE NOTE)

1 scant cup unbleached all-purpose flour

1 1/4 cups low-fat milk or 1 cup milk + 1/4 cup water

1 tablespoon + 1/4 cup sugar

1 teaspoon salt

1 teaspoon vanilla extract

2 eggs

3 tablespoons + 1/2 teaspoon unsalted butter, melted

FOR THE BANANAS:

6 firm, ripe, medium-sized bananas without blemishes

Flour for dusting on bananas

5 tablespoons unsalted butter

1/2 cup sugar

2 tablespoons + 1/4 cup water

1/3 cup dark or light rum

1 cup heavy cream, softly whipped with the grated zest of 1 lemon and a little sugar (optional) or vanilla ice cream (optional)

1. Prepare the crêpes: In a large bowl, whisk together the flour, milk, sugar, salt, vanilla, and eggs until smooth. Add the 3 tablespoons of melted butter and mix again quickly. The batter should be the consistency of light cream. Cover and refrigerate for at least 1/2 hour.
2. Heat the remaining 1/2 teaspoon of butter in an 8-inch skillet over medium-high heat until hot, rotating the pan to cover the bottom completely. Stir the batter, then ladle about 2 tablespoons into the pan toward one side. Lift the pan and rotate it quickly to cover the bottom evenly. Replace the pan on the heat and cook until the crêpe's edges are light brown, about 1 minute. Adjust heat to medium if the crêpes seem to be burning before they are cooked through.
3. Slip the edge of a spatula or rounded knife under the edge of the crêpe, grab it with your fingertips, and flip it to the other side. Cook the second side for 20 seconds, or until lightly browned in spots. Flip the crêpe onto a plate and continue with the remaining batter. Cover the plate with a second plate inverted on top of the crêpes. If not using the crêpes immediately, let them cool slightly, then cover. Or separate them into piles of 4 with waxed paper between each group. Put them in a resealable plastic bag, push out the air, and freeze for up to 3 months. Defrost completely before trying to separate them.
4. Cook the bananas: Peel the bananas and remove the strings from the sides. Dust lightly with flour.

5. In a large, heavy skillet, melt the butter over medium-high heat. Add the bananas and brown lightly on all sides, turning with a wooden spatula. Sprinkle with 1/4 cup of the sugar, add 2 tablespoons of water, and continue cooking over medium-low heat for another 5 to 6 minutes, or until the bananas are warmed through.

6. Have 6 crêpes ready. Using 2 spatulas, carefully lay a banana on one side of each crêpe. Roll up and put on a plate while finishing the sauce.

7. Stir the remaining 1/4 cup of sugar and 1/4 cup of water in the skillet. Bring to a boil over high heat and cook until the syrup turns light brown. Immediately add the rolled crêpes, spooning the syrup over them. Heat the rum in a small saucepan, and pour it over the crêpes. Carefully ignite, shaking to loosen any caramelized sugar on the bottom of the pan. Serve 1 crêpe to each person, spooning some syrup over it. Add a dollop of whipped cream or vanilla ice cream that has been allowed to soften slightly.

NOTE: This recipe makes 12 to 14 crêpes. Either make all the crêpes and freeze the extras, or refrigerate the extra batter in a covered container for up to a week.

Did you know? Three categories of rum are usually sold in U.S. liquor stores. Light-colored, light-bodied rum is from Spanish-speaking areas of the Caribbean. The best is from Puerto Rico. Amber rum, made from sugar-cane juice, has medium body and comes from Haiti and Martinique. Rich and pungent dark rum is made from fermented molasses and other by-products of sugar production. It comes from English-speaking countries. Jamaican is the best. Which one to use in a recipe is often determined by personal taste.

BLACKBERRY TART

Serves 8

Finding beautiful half-pint containers of blackberries neatly lined up in the market of a late-June morning, I celebrated by making a luscious almond-flavored crust with the berries just peeking out from a sweet glaze. While the best berries may be those picked from the bush, I've often found dark, succulent blackberries in season (late May through September) that are superbly flavorful.

Be alert when berry buying. Containers should be covered without any signs of leakage. Each long, plump berry should be dark in color because even a little redness means the fruit is sour. Ask the clerk if there are fresh containers in back if those on display look picked over. Once home, sort the berries as soon as possible. Bruised and moldy berries can ruin the rest within hours. Store berries covered and refrigerated for up to 2 or 3 days. Then rinse or mist them with cool water just before serving.

- 1 Walnut Pastry Crust (page 230), substituting almonds for walnuts, baked
- 1 1/2 pints blackberries
- 1 tablespoon cornstarch
- 2 tablespoons kirsch
- 1/2 cup red currant jelly
- 3 tablespoons sugar
- Grated zest of 1 lemon
- 4–5 slivered almonds, for garnish
- 1 cup heavy cream, whipped and flavored with a little crème de cassis, or vanilla ice cream (optional)

1. Fill the baked tart shell with blackberries.
2. Dissolve the cornstarch in the kirsch in a small bowl. In a small saucepan, combine the jelly, sugar, lemon zest, and kirsch-cornstarch mixture and bring to a boil. Boil until the sugar is dissolved, the jelly is melted, and the mixture coats the back of a spoon, about 3 minutes. Remove the pan from the heat, stirring to cool the glaze slightly, then pour evenly over the berries. It should just about cover them. Let the glaze set, then add the almonds in the center. Serve with whipped cream or ice cream, if desired.

Did you know? Like blueberries, blackberries can be frozen by placing them directly on a cookie sheet in the freezer (see page 233). They will last for up to 9 months or a year if correctly stored. While they won't be as firm as fresh fruit, the taste will be perfect. Use them for a shortcake (see page 65), or Mosaic of Peaches and Berries in Wine (page 74). They look better if you do not defrost them before using.

OLD-FASHIONED BLUEBERRY PIE WITH LEMON CRUST

Serves 8

Lemon and blueberries seem made for each other, especially in this delectably homey pie, first served to me by my friend Anne Semmes. The lemony lattice crust holds juicy, fat blueberries laced with lemon and a touch of crème de cassis. Since blueberries give off so much liquid, I partially cook some of the berries and combine them with uncooked berries. The results are a spectacular pie!

Luckily for blueberry lovers, these versatile berries are simple to buy from late May through September, and quite resilient in the refrigerator. They last for at least 10 days in the refrigerator. Look for plump, dark fruit, with a minimum of tiny green berries. If the skins look wrinkled or soft, pass on that basket. Be sure to check the berries for mold or bruises and wash just before eating. Frozen berries also work well for this pie. If you don't defrost the 2 cups of the berries before adding them to the cooked mixture, they will keep their shape better.

FOR THE LEMON PASTRY:

2 cups unbleached all-purpose flour

3/4 teaspoons salt

2 teaspoons sugar

1 teaspoon grated lemon peel

8 tablespoons (1 stick) unsalted butter, chilled and cut into small pieces

1/4 cup solid vegetable shortening

1 tablespoon fresh lemon juice

2–4 tablespoons ice water

1 egg white, beaten

FOR THE FILLING:

5 cups fresh blueberries

2 tablespoons water

3 tablespoons cornstarch

2 tablespoons crème de cassis

3/4 cup sugar

2 teaspoons fresh lemon juice

1. Prepare the pastry: In the bowl of a food processor, combine the flour, salt, sugar, and lemon peel, and process for about 15 seconds. Add the butter and shortening and pulse until the mixture resembles coarse meal.
2. Combine the lemon juice with 2 tablespoons of water. With the machine running, add the lemon water through the feed tube, and process just until the pastry begins to pull into a ball, adding extra water by the teaspoon, if necessary. Remove the dough, divide into 2 uneven balls, one slightly larger than the other, and pat into flat discs, lightly dust with flour, wrap with plastic wrap, and refrigerate for at least 2 hours.
3. Preheat your oven to 425°F.
4. Lightly dust a work space with flour. Roll out the larger disc into a circle measuring about 12 inches across and 1/8 inch thick. Line a 9-inch pie plate with the pastry, leaving the overhanging edge untrimmed. Brush with egg white.
5. Combine 3 cups of the blueberries in a medium-sized saucepan with the water, cover, and bring to a boil. Adjust the heat to medium and cook uncovered for 4 or 5 minutes, or until the berries have begun to pop. Stir the cornstarch into the crème de cassis. Drain off approximately 1/2 cup of the liquid, then add the sugar, lemon juice, and crème de cassis along with the remaining blueberries. Cook for 2 minutes longer over high heat. The fruit mixture should be quite thick. Let cool for 15 minutes, then scrape into the pie shell.

6. Roll the smaller disc of dough into a 9-inch circle and cut it into ½-inch strips. Arrange over the pie in a lattice pattern and trim. Bring the edge of the bottom crust over the rim and crimp the edge. If desired, decorate the lattice with leaves and berries cut from the extra pastry scraps.

7. Put the pie on a cookie sheet and bake in the middle of the oven for 8 minutes, or until the crust is light brown. Turn heat to 350°F. and continue baking for 25 to 30 minutes, or until the crust is golden brown and the juices begin to bubble. If the crust becomes too brown before the end of the cooking time, cover with strips of aluminum foil. Remove the pie from the oven and cool for at least 30 minutes before serving.

Did you know? Because blueberries give off so much juice, many people make their pies from canned berries. It is easy to drain off the liquid from them, but it's almost as easy to cook your own. If using a canned product, note that canned berries are superior to canned "pie filling," which has a lot more sugar and starch in relation to the fruit.

Another idea . . . Bake and cool an 11-inch Pâte Brisée or Walnut Pastry Crust (page 229 or 230), spread 1 cup of Lemon Curd (page 69) over the bottom, and fill it with 1½ pints (3 cups) blueberries dusted with confectioners' sugar. Extra dough may be cut in lemon shapes, baked with the tart shell, and glazed with Lemon Curd. Add some bright green, non-poisonous leaves next to each lemon cutout on top of the berries as garnish, if desired.

NUTMEG-SCENTED CANTALOUPE SHERBET

Makes 1 1/2 quarts

1 large ripe cantaloupe, peeled and seeded
2 tablespoons strained fresh lemon juice
1/2 cup superfine sugar
1/2 teaspoon salt
1 teaspoon freshly grated nutmeg
3 cups cold milk
Freshly grated nutmeg, for garnish

The celebrated American food writer M. F. K. Fisher once told me that her father used ground nutmeg on his melon. That combination of creamy sweet melon, with a delicate hint of warm spiciness, proves ethereal in the following sherbet. Serve with gingersnaps or Molasses Spice Cookies (page 242).

When buying cantaloupes, don't waste money on those small melons in April and early May. While some are tasty, they are usually disappointing. Instead, wait until late May through early September for firm (not rock hard) round or oval melons with no green under the webbed skin. They are best when blushed with yellow. Check the stem end. It should be smooth and slightly indented. While it may give slightly to pressure, a better test of ripeness is a fragrant aroma at the stem end. Any cantaloupe with bruises and sagging-looking skin has seen better days. If the melon is quite firm, it will taste better if left at room temperature for a couple of days to soften.

1. Purée the cantaloupe in the bowl of a food processor. There should be about 2 1/2 to 3 cups purée. Add the lemon juice, sugar, salt, and nutmeg and process to blend until smooth, about 30 seconds.
2. Scrape into a large bowl and stir in the milk. Transfer to an ice-cream maker and follow the manufacturer's directions. Once processed, serve within 2 hours. Otherwise, scrape the mixture into a metal container, such as a cake pan, cover, and freeze until solid, at least 3 hours.
3. About an hour before serving, cut the frozen sherbet into cubes, and put them in a food processor. Begin by pulsing and then process until the sherbet is very smooth and light in color. Serve at once for a softer consistency or return to the freezer for about 1 hour. The sherbet may be reprocessed if serving it on a second or third occasion. Serve in small scoops with a light dusting of freshly grated nutmeg on top.

NOTE: If you do not have an ice-cream maker, the following method may be used. While the texture will not be as smooth, the taste will still be delicious:

1. Combine the cantaloupe purée, lemon juice, and sugar in a bowl and let stand for at least 1/2 hour. Stir in the salt, nutmeg, and milk, then scrape the mixture into a flat metal container, such as an 8-by-8-inch square brownie pan, and cover and freeze until almost solid, at least 4 to 6 hours.
2. Cut the mixture into cubes, transfer to the bowl of a food processor, and pulse until smooth. Scrape back into the metal pan, cover, and freeze until firm.

Did you know? The melon we call cantaloupe in the United States is actually a musk-melon, as is its large cousin, the Persian melon. True cantaloupes, like the famous Cavaillon melons of France that are sometimes available in the United States, have smooth skins and are not grown in the United States.

CHERRY-ALMOND SHORTCAKE

Serves 8

This old-fashioned shortcake is an ideal base for any seasonal fruits. It also shows how special homemade biscuits can be. If you love sweet dark cherries, this is a dessert to make for your Fourth of July celebration or any other summer meal when cherries are abundant. Although it takes about 5 or 10 minutes to remove the pits, you won't remember it by the time you bring out this down-home treasure, topped with whipped cream, vanilla yogurt, or sour cream. Add toasted almonds and cherries, as well.

Giant bins of fruit mounded high with dark-red cherries are so tempting. They are perfect eaten out of hand. But take a moment to gently feel the fruit (even if that means through cellophane packaging). Are the cherries firm and shiny? A few sun-cracked cherries are okay, but if the lot looks that way, wait for the next shipment. I reach toward the back of the display for less-picked-over fruit. Wash cherries when you are ready to eat them. Store them either loosely wrapped or open in a bowl. Eat within a couple of days.

FOR THE FRUIT TOPPING:

1 1/4 pounds sweet dark cherries, pitted

2 tablespoons kirsch

2 tablespoons sugar

1/4 cup fresh orange juice

FOR THE SHORTCAKE:

1 3/4 cups sifted unbleached all-purpose flour

1/4 cup + 2 tablespoons sugar

4 teaspoons baking powder

1 teaspoon salt

8 tablespoons (1 stick) unsalted butter, chilled and cut into small pieces + 1 tablespoon melted butter

1/2 cup milk

1 cup heavy cream

1/4 teaspoon almond extract

1/2 cup slivered almonds, lightly toasted, to garnish

1. Make the topping: Combine the cherries, kirsch, sugar, and orange juice in a medium-sized saucepan. Bring to a boil, then reduce the heat and simmer for 4 to 5 minutes. Set aside to cool.
2. For the shortcake: Preheat your oven to 425°F.
3. In a large bowl, sift together the flour, 1/4 cup of sugar, baking powder, and salt. Add the chilled butter and, with your fingers or two knives, cut it into the dry ingredients until it is the size of small peas. Pour in the milk and quickly mix just until blended.
4. Turn the dough onto a lightly floured board and knead for about 30 seconds until smooth. Transfer to a 9-inch round unbuttered cake pan, patting to smooth with your fingertips. Brush the top with the tablespoon of melted butter and bake in the preheated oven for 25 minutes, until it has risen and the top is golden brown. Remove from the oven and cool for about 30 minutes in the pan.
5. While the cake is baking, whip the cream with the remaining 2 tablespoons of sugar and the almond extract into soft peaks.
6. Assembly: Transfer the shortcake to a cake plate. Ladle the cherries and juice over it. Sprinkle on the slivered almonds. Once the cake is cut, ladle a generous spoonful of whipped cream over each slice.

Have you tried . . . There are commercial cherry pitters available in the Kitchen Tools section of the market. Otherwise, split each cherry and use your fingers, a tiny spoon, or even a paper clip to pop out the pit.

CRANBERRY, PEPPER, AND ONION CONSERVE

Makes about 3 cups

- 2 tablespoons unsalted butter
- 1 tablespoon vegetable oil
- 3 large onions peeled and sliced very thin
- 6 tablespoons apple cider vinegar
- 1/2 cup sugar
- 3 cups fresh cranberries, washed and picked over
- 2 large red bell peppers, peeled, seeds and membranes removed, cut into 1/4-inch slices (see page 38)
- 1/4 teaspoon ground cardamom
- 2 tablespoons tiny capers

While we often think of cranberries in sweets, this tangy relish is a terrific condiment for pâtés, game meats, and that holiday favorite, turkey. The vibrant rosy tones and spicy flavors last for months. It's an easy holiday gift to make.

Cranberries are usually plentiful from early autumn right through midwinter. For the remaining months, cranberry fanciers can keep them in their plastic bags for at least a month in the refrigerator or freeze them for almost a year. The Cranberry Holiday Braid (page 238) would be lovely on a chilly morning. Be sure the berries are bright and firm.

1. In a large, heavy skillet, melt the butter and oil. Add the onions and sauté over medium-high heat for about 12 to 14 minutes, or until lightly colored. Shake the pan occasionally to cook evenly. Stir in the vinegar and sugar and cook until the sugar dissolves, about 2 to 3 minutes. Stir in the cranberries and peppers, cover, and cook gently for about 12 to 15 minutes.
2. Remove the lid and crush most of the berries with the back of a wooden spoon. Stir in the cardamom and capers, then remove from heat and let cool. Transfer conserve to clean jars, cover, and refrigerate for at least 2 days for the flavor to develop. This conserve lasts for many months in the refrigerator.

MINTED PINK GRAPEFRUIT SORBET

Serves 8

Tangy, citrus-flavored grapefruit and cool crème de menthe are a wonderfully refreshing combination. This delicate sorbet is like an icy breath of fresh air between courses or at the end of a meal. Fresh mint leaves and a segment of the fruit make an elegant presentation. Although grapefruits are found all year round in the market, the very best ones appear in the late-winter to early-spring months. If you find the beautiful "Ruby Reds" from Texas, your sorbet will be vivid pink. But the flavor will be quite similar with pink or white grapefruit. The skin should look smooth without any soft, brown, or spongy spots. Don't worry about tiny lines or defects; they won't affect the taste. As you pick up each grapefruit, it should feel heavy and firm. Grapefruits will keep in your refrigerator for at least 7 days.

2–3 very large red or pink grapefruit

2/3 cup sugar

5 tablespoons white crème de menthe (see note)

1/4 cup water

Mint leaves, for garnish

1. Peel the skin and white pith from grapefruit. Break in sections, reserving 8 whole segments for garnish. Remove as much of the membranes as possible from the sections. Combine the grapefruit, sugar, crème de menthe, and water in the bowl of a food processor and purée until smooth. You should have about 3 cups. Let mixture stand for 30 minutes, then pour into a shallow glass dish and freeze for 12 to 24 hours until frozen solid.
2. Transfer the mixture to the bowl of a processor and pulse until smooth. Return to the shallow dish and refreeze for 1 to 1 1/2 hours. Remove the dish from the freezer and let stand at room temperature for about 10 minutes before serving to soften slightly. Scoop into small balls. Serve in bowls with a grapefruit segment and a couple of mint leaves to garnish.

NOTE: If pink or red grapefruit are unavailable, white grapefruit are fine. In that case, you can use 2 tablespoons of *green* crème de menthe, if you desire.

MARGARITA'S FRUIT SALAD IN A HONEYDEW MELON

Makes 7 to 8 cups

- 1 large ripe honeydew
- 2 tablespoons fresh lime juice
- 3 large bananas, peeled and cut into slices
- 1 large mango (about 1 1/4 pound), peeled and cut into 3/4-inch cubes
- 1 cup dark sweet cherries, split and pitted
- 2 tablespoons tequila (see note)
- 3 tablespoons triple sec or Curaçao
- 1 cup shredded sweetened coconut, lightly toasted

Here is another south-of-the-border inspiration to enliven a buffet table or to present as a colorful summer dessert. Carve a handsome honeydew melon into a bowl and fill it with fruit and coconut laced with the margarita-like flavors of tequila, triple sec, and lime juice to make this a memorable salad.

Choosing a good honeydew melon in the market can be a bit problematical. First, unlike melons such as cantaloupes, honeydews frequently do not give off a sweet smell to let you know when they are ripe. Second, although the flat stem end may give to slight pressure, this area may have been pushed by several shoppers ahead of you. Select a solid, heavy honeydew with a creamy, almost white rind without any traces of green. Soft spots indicate deterioration. At home, leave a honeydew on the counter to soften for a couple of days, unless you are certain it is ripe. Then refrigerate for up to 3 days longer. Best time to find a great melon in a supermarket: late May to the end of September.

1. If the melon is not steady, cut a tiny slice off the smooth end. Using a wide zigzag pattern, remove the top quarter near the melon's stem and set aside. Scrape out and discard the seeds. With a sharp paring knife, trace an incision around the melon about 3/4 inch in from the outer edge. At the point where the zigzag pattern makes a V, cut down the flesh on the inside toward the center, and scoop out the flesh with a long serving spoon, leaving about a 3/4-inch wall of melon. Cut the melon into bite-sized cubes (there should be about 4 cups) and return them to the melon or a large mixing bowl.
2. Add the lime juice, bananas, mango, cherries, tequila, and triple sec and toss gently. Before serving, add the coconut and toss again.

NOTE: Unless you make margaritas, you may not find many uses for tequila, the liquor distilled in Mexico. I'd buy a miniature bottle so you don't clutter your shelf.

Did you know? Like honeydew melons, mangoes can also be difficult to buy. You need to find fruit that is firm but gives to slight pressure. When ripe, the skin will be shot with yellow and deep-orange streaks through the green, and the smell will be slightly floral. Let mangoes ripen outside the refrigerator, then use them within a day. Although mangoes are shipped from South and Central America during the winter months, they are a better buy during the summer.

LEMON CURD

Makes 2 ½ cups

Lemon curd is one of those magical ingredients that can suddenly turn simple ingredients into stars. Keep some on hand in the refrigerator and use it as a glaze for Lemon-Glazed Apricots (page 58), or spread on simple cookies, like Pogachel (page 243).

Lemons are available the year round to spark up the flavor of all kinds of foods from savories to sweets. Look for thin-skinned lemons that feel heavy. Avoid any with brown or moldy spots. Sometimes, smaller lemons sold in plastic bags are actually a better buy than larger lemons. The reason: Some giant lemons have a thick skin that is virtually impossible to squeeze the juice from. In other cases, bagged lemons are old and mushy. Separate bagged lemons at home. They will last for at least 10 days to 2 weeks in the refrigerator.

3 eggs

1 cup sugar

8 tablespoons (1 stick) unsalted butter, melted

¾ cup fresh lemon juice (3 to 4 lemons)

Zest of 3 lemons, minced or finely julienned

1. In a heavy saucepan, stir the eggs and sugar with a wooden spoon until smooth and light in color. Add the melted butter and lemon juice, stir to mix well, and set the pan over medium-low heat. Stir the mixture continuously until it is thick and coats the back of the spoon, about 6 to 8 minutes. It is important not to cook this mixture too quickly, or the eggs will scramble. Stir in the lemon zest, and scrape the mixture into a clean glass jar. It will keep for at least 1 month in the refrigerator. (If you prefer, you may strain the lemon curd to remove the zest.)

Did you know? It is easier to extract the juice of lemons and limes if you first roll them a couple of times on a counter, using relatively firm pressure. Or microwave them for 10 to 15 seconds.

LIME SORBET IN LIME CUPS

Makes 8 small servings or 4 dessert servings

- 2/3 cup sugar
- 2/3 cup water
- 5–6 medium-large limes
- 1 egg white
- 2 tablespoons gin (optional)
- Zest of 1 lime, finely shredded, for garnish (optional)

When it's very hot and a small chilly dessert is in order, or a meal is heavy and a palate refresher is called for, these delightful lime cups fill the bill. Make them ahead of time.

Limes are readily available most of the year but are more abundant in the summer, when they add a crisp tangy touch to cooled drinks and fresh fruit. Select limes that feel heavy and have firm skins.

1. In a small saucepan, cook the sugar and water over medium-high heat until the sugar dissolves. Remove just before the mixture comes to a boil, pour into a covered jar, and refrigerate until cold.
2. Carefully divide 4 limes in half using a zigzag pattern if you wish to serve the sorbet in lime cups. Remove the zest from another lime, if using it for garnish, and squeeze the juice from the limes. You should have 1 cup of juice.
3. Combine the lime juice and sugar syrup, pour into a flat metal container, cover, and freeze for several hours. When solid, cut into cubes, put in the bowl of a food processor, and process until smooth and frothy. Add the egg white and gin, if using, and blend. Return the mixture to the metal pan, cover, and refreeze for at least 3 hours.
4. To serve between courses of a meal, scrape out the membranes from the 8 lime halves with a grapefruit spoon or other sharp implement. Cut a thin slice off the bottom so that the cups are steady. Using a small (1 1/2-inch) ice-cream scoop, fill each cup with a ball of sorbet and add a few strands of zest on top. Or, serve the sorbet in large scoops with a plate of cookies for dessert.

Did you know? Look in the Kitchen Tools section of your market. There is a tool that cuts a zigzag pattern in fruits and vegetables sold in many places. Some make a wide V, others are narrower. They are useful for cutting melons, lemons, and tomatoes, as well.

ORANGE, JICAMA, WATERCRESS, AND OLIVE SALAD

Serves 6

Get set for an explosion of flavors with this colorful salad. Tangy, sweet orange slices are combined with salty Greek olives, peppery watercress, and delicate jicama—also known as Mexican potato—and tossed with fruity extra-virgin olive oil. It's a fresh delicious first course for any time of the year.

While some varieties of oranges are found all year, the best ones arrive just when we need them most: in the winter, when most fruits are a fond summer memory. I like navel oranges for salads because they have no seeds. Jicama, on the other hand, is available all year round. Look for this large tuber with dark-brown skin. Inside, the creamy white flesh is crunchy and has a slightly sweet taste. It is almost non-caloric and lasts for at least a week in the refrigerator. Once cut, it should be covered with plastic wrap.

- 2 navel oranges, peeled with all pith removed
- 8 ounces jicama, peeled and cut into fine julienne strips (about 2 cups)
- 1/3 cup Greek olives, pitted and coarsely chopped
- 2 large bunches watercress, thick stems removed
- 1/2 cup extra-virgin olive oil
- Salt and freshly ground black pepper to taste
- 1-2 heads of Bibb lettuce, washed and dried well

1. Cut oranges crosswise into 1/4-inch slices. Add the jicama, olives, and watercress. Pour on the olive oil, season with salt and pepper, and toss gently. Line 6 salad plates with lettuce leaves. Divide the salad among the plates and serve.

Have you tried . . . To peel jicama, use a sharp paring knife to pull off the fibrous skin in sheets. It is easier than using a vegetable scraper.

Did you know? Greek olives are found either on the shelves with other olives or in the Deli section. They are also sold already pitted.

ORANGES IN ORANGE SAUCE WITH ORANGE SHERBET

Serves 4

- 3 navel oranges
- Zest of 2 oranges, finely julienned
- 1/4 cup boiling water
- 1 1/2 tablespoons sugar
- 1/4 cup Grand Marnier, triple sec, or other orange liqueur
- Easy Orange Sherbet (page 314)

This refreshing triple-orange combination is reminiscent of desserts enjoyed in refined Italian restaurants. With minimal practice, you can cut the orange sections so that only the juicy fruit remains. The thin strips of zest are candied and combined with orange liqueur for the sauce. A chilly dollop of homemade or purchased sherbet goes on top.

While navel oranges are usually available during the winter months, we have Valencia and other varieties to give us sweet tangy juice and vitamin C all year. Choose oranges that are firm, without soft, mushy spots. While some varieties have thinner skins, try to avoid oranges that feel light in comparison to their size.

1. Wash oranges to remove any wax or dirt. Remove the zest from 2 of the oranges with a zester or sharp paring knife, avoiding the white pith. If using a knife, cut the zest into thin strips.
2. In a small saucepan, pour the boiling water over the zest. Add the sugar and boil, stirring occasionally, over high heat until the liquid has almost evaporated, 5 to 6 minutes. Do not let it brown. Stir in the Grand Marnier, then pour into a bowl to cool.
3. Remove the pith from the oranges with a sharp knife. Remove the sections by cutting off a narrow slice at the top and bottom of each orange. Make an incision next to the membrane of 1 section and another cut on the other side of the section. Continue working around the orange, putting the sections into a bowl as they are released. Once all sections are removed, squeeze all juice from the remaining core and membranes of the oranges over the zest. Mix and pour this sauce over the oranges. Chill for at least 1 hour.
4. To serve, divide the orange segments among 4 plates, spooning the zest and sauce over them. Put a small ball of orange sherbet in the center with a few strands of zest on top. Serve at once.

Did you know? While orange-based liqueurs may generally be used interchangeably in cooking, there are differences to recognize. Both Curaçao and triple sec are generic names referring to a liqueur distilled from orange peels, originally produced on the Dutch island of Curaçao, off Venezuela. Of the two, Curaçao tends to be sweeter. Triple sec was the name that Cointreau originally used for its own style of the liqueur made from Valencia oranges. When so many companies took this name, they simply switched to Cointreau. Grand Marnier also uses orange peels added to a cognac base. And, Drambuie is a Scotch-based, somewhat spicier orange liqueur sweetened with honey.

PAPAYA, AVOCADO, AND CHICKEN SALAD

Serves 4

What beautiful colors nature affords us. In this cool salad, slices of pale orange papaya, yellow-green avocado, and white chicken breast are ribboned with a tangy deep pink dressing. Simple to make; sensational taste.

Of the two types of papayas, the Hawaiian varieties are typically sold in supermarkets. When ripe, the pear-shaped fruit has yellow skin, pink or bright orange flesh, and small black seeds clustered in the center. Mexican papayas are much larger, up to several pounds, and the flavor is less intense than that of the Hawaiian papaya.

Papayas are available all year long in some markets. Unfortunately, they are often shipped quite green, which means that they must be allowed to ripen before you can experience their ambrosial taste. They are ready to eat when the skin is almost totally yellow and gives to slight pressure. Leave papayas outside of your refrigerator until they are ripe. Then refrigerate them for up to a week.

Romaine lettuce leaves, coarse stems removed, washed and dried

1 pound boneless, skinless chicken breasts, cooked and cut into thin slices lengthwise

2 ripe medium-sized papayas (about 14 ounces each), peeled, seeded, and cut into thin slices lengthwise

1 large avocado, peeled, pit removed, cut into thin slices lengthwise (see note)

1 cup Spicy Old Bay Tomato Dressing (page 273)

4 cherry tomatoes, for garnish

1. Put the lettuce leaves on each plate with the stem ends all together. Divide the chicken, papaya, and avocado slices among the plates in an alternating fanlike design, with the narrow ends toward the stems of the lettuce (see illustration).
2. Spoon a couple of tablespoons of the dressing in a ribbon across each plate and garnish with a cherry tomato. Pass extra dressing at the table.

NOTE: To loosen the flesh of avocados for easy peeling, run the back of a knife over the skin. To keep the slices from turning brown, put them in ice water.

Did you know? While some people like the spicy-peppery taste of papaya seeds, others have a quite strong toxic reaction to them. I'd avoid using them.

Did you know? Papain, a natural enzyme found in papayas, rapidly breaks down meat fiber and tenderizes it. Combine a puréed papaya with some lime juice, and a clove of crushed garlic. Marinate a flank steak or chicken breasts for 45 minutes to an hour, and then grill it. It will not only be tender, but full of flavor.

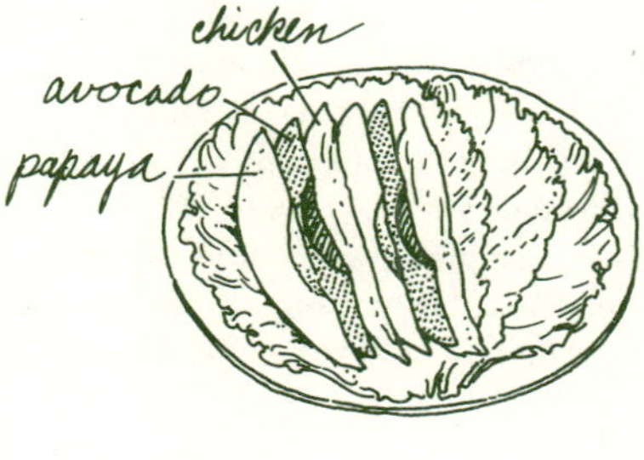

MOSAIC OF PEACHES AND BERRIES IN WINE

Serves 10 to 12

- 1 liter red or rosé wine (cabernet sauvignon, white Zinfandel, etc.)
- 1 stick cinnamon
- 6 whole cloves
- 1/2 cup sugar
- 1 2-inch strip orange zest
- 3 envelopes unflavored gelatin
- 3/4 cup cold water
- 4 large ripe peaches, peeled and cut into thin slices, about 3 cups (see note)
- 1/2 pint blackberries
- 1/2 pint blueberries
- Zabaglione Sauce (page 79) (optional)

The beautiful patterns of summer fruits, chilled in spiced gelled wine, remind me of the tile mosaics one sees in Italy. Each slice is different, and you can choose the variety of wine and fruit to suit your own taste. This hot-weather dessert is low in calories and splendidly refreshing. For a richer variation, add Zabaglione Sauce (page 79).

I haven't had extraordinary luck with supermarket peaches except in summer, when locally grown fruit is your best choice. South American imports at other times of the year are never very satisfying because peaches must ripen on the tree in order to be sweet and juicy. Ripe peaches are extremely perishable.

Select peaches where the ground color—not the blush—is either entirely cream or golden orange with no green showing at all. They should feel firm, not stone hard, and smell peachy. At home, leave them on the counter in a brown bag with a couple of holes punched in it for a couple of days, and then eat them. They last a day or two in the refrigerator.

1. Lightly oil a 9-by-5-by-3-inch glass or porcelain loaf pan.
2. Combine the wine, cinnamon, cloves, sugar, and orange zest in a saucepan and bring to a boil over medium-high heat. Reduce heat to medium, partially cover, and simmer for 20 minutes. Meanwhile, sprinkle the gelatin over the water to soften.
3. Remove the cinnamon, cloves, and orange zest with a slotted spoon and stir in the gelatin. Pour into a large bowl, cool for 1 or 2 minutes, then gently stir in the fruit. Carefully ladle the fruit-wine mixture into the pan. If any liquid remains, reserve until after the mold begins to solidify, about 1 to 2 hours, then pour it into the mold. Cover and refrigerate until solid, at least 8 hours or overnight.
4. To unmold, run a sharp knife around the edges and shake gently. Cover pan with a serving platter and invert. The mold should slide free after a few seconds. Cut into 3/4-inch slices with a sharp serrated knife, using a sawing motion, so as not to dislodge the berries and peaches. A wide spatula will help you to transfer the slices to individual plates. Serve with a wide ribbon of Zabaglione Sauce, if desired.

NOTE: If the peaches are not ripe, they may be poached with the wine and spices until tender.

As a variation . . . In cold weather when fresh peaches and berries are not in season, use pears, apples, and bananas. Small pieces of fresh pineapple may be used, too, but simmer it first for about 1 minute; otherwise, the fresh juice will prevent the gelatin from gelling.

Did you know? To soften gelatin so that it is evenly distributed, first sprinkle the granules in a small amount of cold liquid and wait until it is absorbed. Then combine this mixture with a hot liquid to melt it.

To determine how much gelatin you will need to solidify a liquid, you should estimate that 1 envelope of gelatin will gel 2 cups of liquid.

FRESH PEAR TART WITH GINGER CREAM

Serves 8

In the dead of winter, when sweet juicy pears rescue us from cold-weather doldrums, this gloriously rich tart with ginger cream will surely warm your spirits. The tangy raspberry sauce (made from frozen berries) balances the tastes and adds a pretty splash of color.

Good pears are easy to find in all markets from early autumn through the winter. Bartlett and Anjou are the most popular, although beautiful red ones are now available. Although it is difficult to find perfectly ripe pears—when the flesh is delicate and the pears bruise easily—well-chosen ones ripen within a few days. Even though they are frequently chilled, most ripening pears will give off a lovely fragrance. The flesh should feel firm, with a slight give, but never hard. Avoid those with bruises and irregular shapes.

1 11-inch Pâte Brisée tart shell (page 229), baked

FOR THE GLAZE:

1/2 cup red currant jelly

3 tablespoons sugar

FOR THE FILLING:

5 large Anjou, Bartlett, or Bosc pears, firm but almost ripe

2 tablespoons unsalted butter

1/3 cup + 2 tablespoons sugar

Grated zest of 1 lemon

2 tablespoons freshly grated gingerroot

1/4 cup Calvados or applejack

2 cups (1 pint) heavy cream

FOR THE RASPBERRY COULIS

1 12-ounce package unsweetened frozen raspberries, defrosted

1/2 cup confectioners' sugar, sifted

1/4 cup fresh lemon juice

1. For the tart shell: Bake the tart according to the directions on page 229. Roll out excess dough and cut out the shapes of a pear and 2 leaves. Bake the cutouts on a lightly buttered cookie sheet along with the tart, pricking them when they puff up.
2. Prepare the glaze: While the tart shell is cooking, combine the jelly and sugar in a small saucepan and boil over high heat until the sugar is dissolved and the glaze coats the back of a metal spoon, about 3 minutes. Brush the inside of the tart and the cutouts with the glaze.
3. For the pear filling: Peel, core, and cut each pear into 16 slices. In a large, heavy skillet, melt the butter over medium heat. Add the pears and, depending on their ripeness, cook until they start to soften, shaking and gently turning with a wooden spatula about 3 to 5 minutes.
4. Sprinkle on 1/3 cup of sugar and continue cooking until the sugar melts into a syrup, about 7 to 10 minutes. The pears should be tender without any hard spots. Remove to a bowl with a slotted spoon.
5. Stir the lemon zest, ginger, Calvados, and cream into the poaching syrup, raise the heat to medium-high, and boil until the mixture thickens and is reduced by half, about 15 minutes, stirring continuously with a wooden spoon. As the cream thickens, adjust the heat down so it gently bubbles.
6. Drain any liquid from the pears into the cream mixture and boil for 1 minute longer. Arrange the pears in an overlapping decorative pattern in the shell. Pour the cream over the pears, spreading it with the spoon. Sprinkle on the remaining 2 tablespoons of sugar.

7. Run the tart under the broiler for a few minutes just to brown the top or use a salamander. (A salamander is a long-handled metal tool used to caramelize sugar. It is heated directly on the stovetop until red hot, then held close to the surface of foods to turn them brown.) To avoid burning the crust, cover with aluminum foil. Remove the tart from the broiler, put the cutouts of pear and leaves in the center, and cool to lukewarm or room temperature.
8. Prepare the raspberry coulis: While the tart cools, or ahead of time, combine the raspberries, sugar, and lemon juice in the bowl of a food processor and purée until smooth. Pass through a strainer into a serving bowl. Spoon a generous ribbon of coulis around each slice of the tart.

Did you know? Of all the varieties of pears, the comice is usually the most expensive and the finest for eating out of hand. The skin should be smooth, firm, and either green-yellow or yellow with a red blush. Unlike other pears, Bosc pears have a rusty brown skin without any gloss to it. The neck is longer than that of other pears. Boscs are very juicy and sweet when ripe. Small Seckel pears, ranging from green to almost ochre, are slightly spicy and sweet and are often used in preserves. Newest in American markets is the Asian pear. It is far larger than other pears, has a mottled skin, and crunchy flesh almost like an apple.

PEARS POACHED IN PORT WITH STILTON CREAM

Serves 4

The English frequently serve pears and Stilton or other blue-veined cheeses along with a glass of port for dessert. Here I combine them into an elegant winter dessert that can be made ahead and await you for a smashing final course. A plate of crisp cookies would be most welcome, too. If you do not find Stilton in your Dairy department, Gorgonzola or a good-quality Roquefort are fine substitutions.

Buying pears for cooking is tricky. It is important that they not be completely ripe, lest they fall apart. On the other hand, if they are rock solid, they will have no taste. Try to buy large, firm, regular-shaped fruit and leave it in a brown bag for at least a day or two. Once the pears are almost ripe, with green skin just turning golden (or red with some varieties of Bartlett), they are ready to poach. If pears start to ripen too quickly, refrigerate them. Chilled pears will keep for up to 5 days.

FOR THE PEARS:

2 large Anjou or Bartlett pears, firm but almost ripe
1 1/2 cups port
1/2 cup water
Zest of 1 lemon, minced
1 stick cinnamon
1/4 cup sugar

FOR THE CHEESE TOPPING:

2 ounces Stilton or other blue-veined cheese, such as Gorgonzola, softened
1/4 cup heavy cream, chilled
4 pecan halves, toasted, for garnish

1. Poach the pears: With a sharp paring knife, peel the pears, cut them in half lengthwise, and carefully remove the core. A melon baller works well to remove the center part. Cut off a small slice from the back of each pear half so they do not rock.
2. In a large, heavy skillet, combine the port, water, lemon, cinnamon stick, and sugar. Lay the pears flat-side down in the pan and slowly bring the liquid to a boil over medium-high heat. Reduce the heat so the liquid is barely simmering, cover the pan, and poach for about 15 minutes, or until just tender, turning with a wooden spoon after about 8 minutes. Once tender, turn off the heat and cool the pears in the liquid for 5 to 10 minutes, then remove to a wide bowl with a slotted spoon and set aside.
3. Bring the poaching liquid to a slow boil and reduce for 10 to 15 minutes, or until it thickly coats the back of a spoon. Strain over the pears, cover, and refrigerate for at least an hour until chilled. These pears may be poached 1 to 2 days ahead of time. They become darker the longer they are left in the port.
4. Prepare the cheese topping: Once the pears are cool, mash the cheese until smooth. Whisk in the heavy cream until smooth and thick. Do not overbeat. Transfer the mixture to a pastry bag fitted with a wide star tip and pipe a swirl onto each pear half. Add a pecan half on top, if desired. Serve at once, or refrigerate for up to several hours. If the pears are refrigerated, remove from the refrigerator about an hour ahead of time. Serve on individual plates or in a fruit compote dish.

Did you know? To ripen fruit more quickly, you can put it in a brown paper bag and leave it outside the refrigerator for a couple of days. Remember that fruit needs to breathe, however. So punch some holes in the bag. The new domed plastic ripening bowls, found in many Produce departments, also work well.

Incidentally, a melon baller is also useful for removing the seeds from cucumbers and winter and summer squashes.

PINEAPPLE BOATS WITH PORK, BLACK BEANS, AND MOLE SAUCE

Serves 4 as a main course

- 1 pound boneless pork cutlets
- 1 large ripe pineapple
- 1 tablespoon unsalted butter
- 1 teaspoon vegetable oil
- 1 cup finely chopped onions
- 1 large clove garlic, peeled and crushed
- 8 ounces black beans, cooked just until tender (or 3 cups drained canned beans) and processed or mashed until almost smooth (see note)
- 1 cup beef stock
- 1 teaspoon ground cumin
- 2 tablespoons tomato paste
- 3 tablespoons purchased mole paste
- Salt and freshly ground black pepper to taste
- 1/4 cup chopped cilantro leaves + extra leaves to garnish

Pork and pineapple seem to have a natural affinity. Throw in some black beans and mole paste—the spicy chocolate-based condiment from Mexico found in jars on the same shelf with other south-of-the-border ingredients—and you have a heady fiesta of taste. Make this concoction ahead of time to allow the flavors to mellow. Then spoon it over quartered pineapple shells for an unusual serving idea.

1. Freeze the cutlets for about an hour or just until fairly solid.
2. Split the pineapple into 4 sections, leaving the crown intact, if possible. Carefully remove the pineapple, leaving a 1/2-inch shell. Remove the core, then finely chop enough pineapple to make 1 cup. Cut 12 small triangles to be used as a garnish. Set the pineapple aside, reserving the shells.
3. Once the pork is chilled, trim all the fat, and cut into 1/8-inch thick slices.
4. Melt the butter and oil in a large, heavy skillet over medium-high heat. Stir in the onions and sauté for about 5 minutes, or until softened. Add the pork and cook it for about 3 minutes until just opaque; then add the garlic and cook for 30 seconds. Stir in the beans, stock, cumin, tomato paste, mole paste, and the cup of chopped pineapple. Season with salt and pepper, adjust the heat to medium, and simmer for about 20 minutes. Add the chopped cilantro, and cook for 5 minutes longer.
5. Meanwhile, preheat your oven to 325°F.
6. Put the pineapple shells in a flat pan and heat for 15 minutes. Remove, put a shell on each plate, and spoon on some of the mole-pork mixture. Put 3 small triangles of pineapple standing up in the meat mixture and sprinkle with cilantro. Served with boiled rice, if desired.

NOTE: Black beans, also called "turtle beans," are found with other dried legumes. Most packages are printed with slow and quick cooking instructions. Pick over the beans, put them in a large saucepan, and cover with at least 4 times as much water. Bring the water to a boil, cook for 2 minutes, turn off the heat, and leave the pan tightly covered for 2 hours. After this, the beans may need a little additional cooking time to become just tender. If you prefer them very soft, cook the beans longer. To save time, you can substitute drained canned black beans.

Did you know? Although tougher than the rest of the slice, the core of ripe Hawaiian pineapples is edible. Once removed, it makes a nice "swizzle stick" in a tall drink.

BROILED PINEAPPLE SLICES WITH ZABAGLIONE SAUCE

Serves 6

When pineapples are ripe and juicy, they are wonderful just as they are, cut into either slices or spears. For a little extra pizzazz, I broil the slices briefly and serve them on a decadent pool of cool Zabaglione Sauce. The combination of Marsala, rum, and cream with the tangy sweetness of pineapple is addicting.

Many tropical countries ship their fruit to our markets. For my money, the biggest and best pineapples still come from Hawaii. Rather than trying to pull a leaf easily from the crown to gauge ripeness, look for a firm pineapple whose skin has a minimum amount of green. Put your nose close to the stem end. It should smell fruity and not at all fermented. To distribute the sugar throughout the pineapple, store it upside down until ready to eat. (Otherwise, all the sweetness settles in the bottom.) If I plan on eating it within a couple of days, I don't refrigerate it. For longer periods, up to a week or more, refrigeration is best.

FOR THE SAUCE:

- 4 egg yolks
- 5 tablespoons sugar
- 1/2 cup Marsala
- 1/4 cup light rum
- 1 cup heavy cream

FOR THE PINEAPPLE:

- 6 slices fresh pineapple about 3/4-inch thick, rind and eyes removed
- 3 tablespoons brown sugar
- 1/4 cup chopped pecans

1. Prepare the sauce: In the top of a double boiler and off the heat, beat the egg yolks and sugar with a wooden spoon until pale yellow, about 1 to 2 minutes. Stir in the Marsala and rum.
2. Bring the water in the bottom of the double boiler to a boil. Replace the top, adjust the heat down so that the water is just simmering, and stir the mixture continuously until it thickly coats the back of the spoon, about 5 minutes. Remove the insert from the heat and continue stirring for at least 2 minutes longer to cool the sauce slightly. Stir in the heavy cream, transfer to a bowl, cover, and refrigerate until cold.
3. Broil the pineapple: Turn on the broiler; adjust the rack to about 4 inches from the heat.
4. Put the pineapple slices on a cookie sheet or jelly-roll pan. Sprinkle with brown sugar and broil for about 3 minutes, or just until the sugar is hot and bubbling and the pineapple is warmed through. Remove and let the slices cool slightly.
5. Pour a generous circle of sauce on each plate. Add a slice of pineapple, a sprinkle of chopped pecans, and serve. This dessert may be made ahead of time. Leave the sauce in the refrigerator and the pineapple at room temperature, once it has been broiled. Serve with Molasses Spice Cookies (page 242).

Did you know? Many supermarkets now have pineapple coring machines in their Produce departments. Not only are they amusing to watch, they afford you the opportunity of selecting a better pineapple at the same price as the uncored ones. Make sure the cut pineapple is tightly wrapped. Refrigerate it and use within a couple of days.

Buying ready cut-up fruit, while more costly, saves money because you can see the quality and buy the quantity you want.

PLUM-PEAR KETCHUP

Makes about 2 pints

- 2 pounds plums, split
- 5 ripe Anjou or Bartlett pears, peeled, cored, and coarsely chopped
- 3/4 cup golden raisins
- 1 1/4 cups sugar
- 20 cloves
- 3 sticks cinnamon
- 3/4 teaspoon ground coriander seed
- 1/2 teaspoon salt
- 1/4 teaspoon white pepper
- 1/4 cup raspberry vinegar
- 1/4 cup water

In this intensely flavorful ketchup the combination of fruit, spices, and vinegar are simmered into a wonderful sauce for spreading on toast or plain cookies like Pogachel (page 243) or ladling over ice cream. It's also wonderful with Pheasant Pâté (page 114). What, you thought ketchup was only a bright red tomato sauce? Wrong! The word has a long and colorful past dating back to Marco Polo's adventures in China, where he found the natives using a pickled fish brine called "ket-siap" to liven up the taste of bland food.

Plums are one of summer's nicest gifts. In season, from May through September, market shelves are brimming with several colorful varieties in all sizes and shapes, from the yellow greengage to blue-black Italian prunes, along with bright red and purple fruit. The best plums are firm but not too hard and have smooth skins. When picked too early, plums may ripen, but they never develop the wonderful sweetness that makes them ideal for eating out of hand. If plums are not quite ripe (and many market specimens aren't), leave them out for a day or two, and then refrigerate. Eat them within a couple of days. This ketchup is a good way to use up less-than-perfect plums or pears.

1. In a large, heavy, non-reactive pot, combine the plums, pears, and raisins; cover; and bring to a boil over medium-high heat. Adjust the heat to medium and simmer for about 20 minutes, or until soft.
2. Uncover, mash the fruit with the back of a wooden spoon, stir in the sugar, cloves, cinnamon, coriander, salt, and white pepper, and continue cooking slowly for another 40 to 50 minutes, stirring frequently, until the mixture is quite thick. Remove the cinnamon sticks and reserve.
3. Stir in the vinegar and water. Pass the mixture through a food mill or strain it into a large bowl. Fill sterilized jars and put 1 cinnamon stick in each jar. Cap tightly and store the jars in the refrigerator. The ketchup will keep for at least 4 to 6 months.

Did you know? The term *prune* refers to plums that are dried with the pits still inside. Without a pit, they are "dried plums."

SAUTÉED TURBOT FILLETS WITH SLICED STARFRUIT

Serves 2

These moist fish fillets with a crunchy almond coating, served with starfruit slices, are dramatic to look at and quite pleasing to the taste. The fruit's sweet, citrusy flavor played against the fish and toasted almonds makes this easily prepared dish a winner.

Carambola or "starfruit" are reasonably hearty. I have seen them sitting on shelves for days. Choose one that is unbruised and try it. You needn't even peel it. When cut across the fruit, the slices are a very pretty star. Select firm, shiny-skinned fruit and let it ripen to a yellow-orange color with brown edges for maximum sweetness. Once ripe, starfruit can be stored in a bag in your refrigerator for up to 5 days.

2 turbot fillets, approximately 6 ounces each, blotted dry

1/3 cup ground almonds

2 tablespoons unsalted butter

Salt and freshly ground black pepper to taste

1 medium-large starfruit, approximately 5 ounces, thinly sliced, or sliced mango

2 ounces snow peas or sugar snap peas, strings removed, blanched, for garnish (optional)

1/2 lemon, cut into wedges (optional)

1. Put the fish in a flat dish and press half of the almonds into one side of the fillets.
2. Meanwhile, turn on the broiler and adjust the rack to about 4 inches from the heat.
3. Melt the butter over medium-high heat in a skillet or pan just large enough to hold both fillets. Add the fish with the coated side down. Season with salt and pepper and sprinkle on the remaining nuts. Spoon some of the melted butter over the nuts. Sauté the fish for 2 to 3 minutes until lightly colored.
4. Transfer the pan to the broiler and cook for about 1 to 2 minutes, watching that the nuts do not burn. Remove from the broiler, add the sliced fruit and snow peas, if using, around the outside, and return to the broiler for 30 seconds to 1 minute to warm the fruit. Serve at once with lemon wedges, if desired.

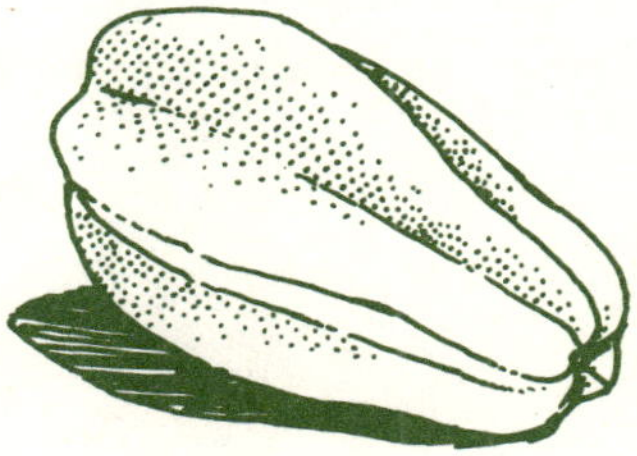

As a variation . . . This beautiful fruit is a delightful addition to curries, stir-fries, and fruit salads. It can be sliced and frozen for later use.

INDIVIDUAL STRAWBERRY CRÈME BRÛLÉE TARTS

Makes 4 individual tarts

FOR THE PASTRY:

4 sheets of phyllo

2 tablespoons unsalted butter, melted

FOR THE CUSTARD AND TOPPING:

3 egg yolks

3 tablespoons sugar

1 1/2 cups heavy cream

1 vanilla bean, split, or 1/2 teaspoon vanilla extract

1 1/2 pints strawberries, washed and hulled

1 teaspoon fresh lemon juice

1 1/2 tablespoons dark brown sugar, strained to remove lumps

This dessert celebrates fresh strawberries. A sprinkle of brown sugar on the vanilla custard topping makes this cream "brûléed" or burned-looking. Each crust is simply a folded square of phyllo lightly brushed with butter and baked. No mixing or rolling is needed. Most of the work can be done ahead of time.

You are likely to find strawberries in the market almost all year, often at reasonable prices. To avoid disappointment at home, check baskets for bruised berries or leakage on the bottom. Strawberries should be firm and bright red. Sort them as soon as you can. Giant Driscoll strawberries, sold with a long stem in some markets, are fine for dipping in chocolate or sour cream and brown sugar. It's a shame to pay extra for them if they are not being used for display. Sadly, bigger isn't always better. Often large strawberries are less sweet and, if green, almost flavorless.

1. Prepare the tarts: Preheat oven to 400°F.
2. Lay 1 sheet of phyllo on a clean work space and lightly brush with butter. Fold it in quarters and trim off the folded edge to make a square (see illustration). Lay the phyllo square on a cookie sheet and lightly brush with butter. Open up the trimmed portion of phyllo (there should now be 2 sheets the same size as the square), lay it on top, and brush with butter. Continue with the remaining sheets of phyllo in the same fashion.
3. Bake in the middle of the preheated oven for 6 to 8 minutes, or until light golden in color. Remove and let cool.

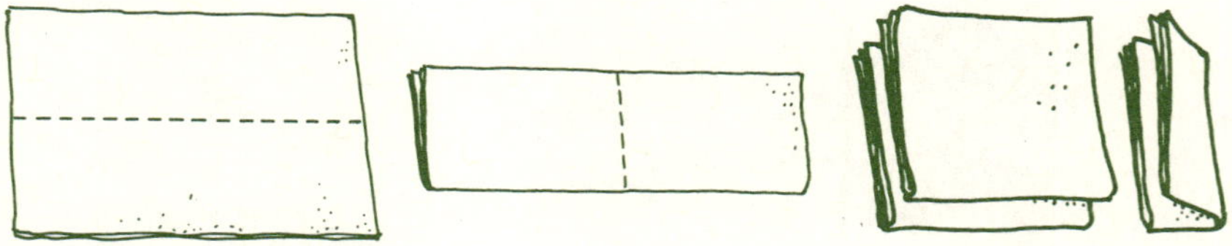

4. For the custard: Off the heat, combine the egg yolks and sugar in the top of a double boiler and stir until pale yellow in color. Add the cream and the vanilla bean. (If using extract, add this after the custard has thickened.)

5. Bring the water in the bottom of the double boiler just to the simmer and set the top over it. Stir the custard mixture frequently with a wooden spoon until it thickens, about 25 to 30 minutes. Try to avoid forming bubbles on the surface. Once the custard thickly coats the back of the spoon, strain it into a small bowl, and chill until cool, about 25 minutes. The custard may be made ahead of time.
6. Turn on the broiler and position the rack close to the heat.
7. Slice the berries into half and arrange on the phyllo squares. Brush lightly with lemon juice and spoon on the custard. Sprinkle about 1 teaspoon of brown sugar over the custard and run the tarts under the broiler until the sugar is just melted, watching carefully that they do not burn, about 30 to 45 seconds. *Or* use a salamander if you have one. Remove and serve at once. As a low-calorie alternative, use 1 cup of Orange-Honey Yogurt Sauce for Fruit (page 206) instead of the crème brûlée. Do not cook.

As a variation . . . Other berries, like raspberries or blackberries, and fruits like peaches, plums, nectarines, or even bananas, will also work with this simple crust. You may also use different extracts to flavor the custard.

GAME BIRDS
Pheasant
Quail
Squab
Cornish Hen
Corn fed chicken

EQUIPPING YOUR KITCHEN FROM THE SUPERMARKET

Beyond food, you may find cooking equipment in your market. Some is pretty basic stuff, like can openers and custard cups, and the supermarket is a good place to buy these items. Other markets recognize that they have a captive audience willing to make more substantial purchases when they see a product they want, and price seems to be less important than the convenience of buying in one place. In some cases, a full Cookware Boutique, complete with heavy-gauge pots, chefs' knives, and professional-grade baking supplies, has been installed. While it is impossible to generalize about the quality and variety of cookware in all markets, two important considerations should enter into your decision-making process.

First, whatever you buy should reflect your degree of interest in cooking. If you cook just to get food on the table, bang your knives and pans around, and wash them in the dishwasher, even the best-quality tools will be ruined in no time. On the other hand, if cooking is something you do for recreation and the results are important, high-quality implements will make your tasks easier and improve the results. With care, equipment will last a very long time. Smart supermarket merchants have put special tools like oyster shuckers or citrus zesters on display near specific foods if they do not have a Kitchen Tools section.

Second, price is not always consistent with quality. Some inexpensive supermarket gadgets, like steamers and rubber pot scrapers, work as well as more costly models sold at boutiques. Some markets mix the quality of items such as spoons made from hard and soft woods and price them the same. As harder woods don't splinter and crack as readily, it is worth looking closely at purchases. Since cookware merchandising is relatively new to markets, the pricing may be out of line with the competition. If the prices are close, the savings in gas and time are worth considering.

The following equipment is usually a good buy at supermarkets:

Measures

- spoons—metal or plastic
- dry measuring cups—metal or plastic
- liquid measuring cups—plastic or glass
- oven, freezer, and instant-read thermometers
- timers

Tools

Make sure each item is in good condition by testing moveable parts, running a finger along edges to see if they are smooth, and checking the points of connection.

- vegetable scrapers—stainless steel with a swivel blade
- metal spreaders with wood or plastic handles
- rubber pot scrapers
- can and bottle openers
- nutmeg graters
- hand graters with changeable drums
- square graters
- zigzag and plain pastry cutters
- pancake turners and spatulas (often Teflon coated)
- pastry brushes—natural bristles

- vegetable and pot brushes
- ice-cream scoops
- strainers—with the basket firmly attached to the rim
- colanders—two-handled with fairly large holes for good drainage
- trivets—to turn almost any pan into a double boiler
- rolling pins—with ball bearings, or a French rolling pin
- nutcrackers and picks
- funnels—plastic or metal
- tweezers (found in Health and Beauty Aids) for removing bones from fish
- 12-inch rulers (from School Supplies) for measuring pastry, etc.
- bulb basters
- whisks—with wires permanently attached to the base

Knives

It is difficult to buy knives in the market, since displaying them is a problem, and there is usually little choice or chance for comparison. Manufacturers of some medium-priced lines have attempted selling their cutlery carded on J-hooks with some success. Inexpensive paring knives are fine for the short term. But for maximum performance, a chef's best friend is a good knife. High-carbon and stainless-steel combinations are the best. They cost money, and few markets are willing to stock these slow-turnover items.

Paper, Wood, and Cloth

These items are generally a good buy. Generic brands of paper goods may be of a thinner gauge and not work as well, especially paper towels. Be sure that towels, mitts, and pot holders are more than just pretty.

- freezer paper and tape
- muffin tin liners
- cheesecloth
- string—tightly twisted without any coating
- bamboo skewers
- toothpicks
- oven mitts—at least above-wrist length and lined or quilted
- pot holders
- towels—should be of a firm weave, linen or cotton are better than blends

Dishes and Bowls

These items are reasonable and readily available.

- Pyrex or porcelain custard cups and soufflé dishes
- stainless-steel or Pyrex mixing bowls in graduated sizes
- glass and metal cake pans, pie plates, tart pans with removable bottoms
- cookie sheets, jelly-roll pans—heavier weight is preferable
- muffin and mini-muffin tins
- metal ring molds

Pots and Pans

These are usually not a good buy in the market unless they are promotionally priced for a demonstration. Teflon skillets are reasonable but wear out quickly. Cast-iron skillets and graniteware roasters may be of interest. The copper pans sometimes sold in markets are usually too lightweight and are still expensive. They are best used for display.

CHAPTER THREE: **POULTRY**

INTRODUCTION 89
The ABCs of Working with Poultry

INTRODUCTION

For a low-fat, inexpensive source of protein, chicken is the number-one choice of supermarket customers, and with good reason. Chicken is incredibly versatile. You can cook it in every conceivable way, from barbecuing to stewing, from whole to minced, and it will be delicious. Ethnic cuisines from around the world combine chicken with local spices and ingredients into an endless array of original dishes. In this chapter you'll find Stir-Fried Chinese Chicken with Cashews (page 95), Individual Mexican Chicken and Cornbread Casseroles (page 94), and Basque Chicken in Red Wine with Olives and Peppers (page 99).

Supermarket cases are filled with chickens, from whole roasters to quartered broilers and fryers and packages of all legs or breasts. In this day when saving time and labor is so important to many of us, cut-up chickens are an appealing convenience, even though they cost slightly more per pound. You'll even find ground chicken and an array of chicken sausages.

Recently, chicken has had to share a little of the limelight with turkey, thanks to a smart market campaign by the turkey people. This once-seasonal bird is now available all year long, not only whole in several sizes including very small, but in cutlets and parts, as well as turkey sausage and ground turkey, too. Like its smaller cousin, turkey is very economical, comparing quite favorably in taste with veal at a fraction of the cost. Look at Sautéed Turkey Cutlets in Lemon Butter (page 105). The ratio of turkey meat to bones is higher than in chicken, particularly with larger birds. Smart merchants have picked up on these facts to bring more options to the customer.

Other poultry choices have expanded, too. Along with fresh Cornish game hens, we find fresh and frozen ducks or even the breast or thigh alone. Markets with a trendy clientele sell goose, quail, and pheasant. Current interest in chickens "like they used to taste" have led to "corn-fed" and "free-range" birds being stocked or available on special order. Prepared items, like breaded chicken nuggets, turkey cutlets, and duck in orange sauce reflect the spiraling interest in poultry.

With the popularity of poultry comes a heightened awareness of the importance of careful selection and storage. Be sure to take a look at "The ABCs of Working with Poultry" in this chapter. For their part, markets sell only USDA-inspected poultry, an indication that the farm was sanitary. There should be a small seal on the package or wing tag. Birds are also graded by the Department of Agriculture. The best grade, "A," indicates that the bird is meaty, with a minimum of skin tears, broken bones, bruises, or other defects.

When purchasing poultry, you may notice some ice crystals on the package. This is because supermarkets store poultry at between 28ºF and 32ºF to retard bacterial growth. To distinguish "fresh chilled" poultry from frozen, push in the flesh. It should not feel solid. Most home refrigerators are substantially warmer than this "chilled" temperature, and it is recommended that poultry be used within two days *even if the "sell by" date is later*. If the package is not broken, supermarket wrapping is satisfactory for home storage for twelve to eighteen hours. Cooked poultry should be used within two days.

Raw chicken should not have an "off" odor. Sometimes the package can have a peculiar smell. If after rinsing the poultry has an odor, either throw it out or return it to the store.

Supermarkets are trying to offer us more choices for varied and healthful eating. This task is surely made easier with fresh poultry.

The ABCs of Working with Poultry

As Americans have become more health conscious, poultry consumption has risen significantly. To meet the demand, supermarkets offer a huge variety of poultry selections. While poultry is nutritious, economical, and versatile, recent news stories emphasize that poultry is also a good source of bacterial food poisoning.

Both *salmonella* and the lesser known *campylobacter* (which, according to some medical sources, is the second-leading cause of food poisoning in the United States today) grow easily in poultry. People infected after eating contaminated foods experience mild to severe cramps, vomiting, fever, and diarrhea, and often attribute these symptoms to "flu." Unless one is very old, very young, or seriously ill, the effects are usually minor and pass quickly. Few people report the experience to the market or a doctor, but they should. If symptoms persist, seek medical assistance.

Rather than experiencing these symptoms or becoming neurotic about the bacteria, become smart and follow these simple tips:

A—Alertness Counts

- **A**lways be an alert shopper when selecting poultry products. Don't just reach without looking at what is wrapped inside. Since most supermarket poultry products are already under plastic wrap, it is imperative to know your market. Does it have a high turnover of product? Can you trust the dating policies (with no switching of dated labels in the back room)?
- **A**lways check the package date to be certain it is current. The plastic wrap should be intact, the tray should be free of excess juices, and the poultry should look moist and fresh with no blemishes.
- **A**sk the department manager if you have questions or concerns about what you see. At the very least, make another selection.
- **A**sk the checker to put your poultry in freezer bags to keep the temperature cooler and to prevent any juices from leaking onto other foods.
- **A**s soon as possible, return home with poultry and put it in the coldest part of your refrigerator. If the ride home has been long or warm, chill poultry in the freezer for about twenty to thirty minutes to lower the temperature rapidly before refrigerating it.
- **A**nd, if not using poultry within twelve to eighteen hours, take it out of the store tray, put it on a clean dish with a lip to prevent spilled juices, and cover loosely with foil to let the air circulate around it.
- **A**fter forty-eight hours from time of purchase, poultry should be rewrapped in tightly sealed freezer paper or resealable plastic bags and frozen. Be sure it is labeled and dated. Defrost in the refrigerator with a plate underneath to prevent juices from contaminating other foods.

B—Be Scrupulously Clean

- **B**efore using any poultry, be sure to wash it under lukewarm water for about a minute while you remove and discard excess fat, unwanted skin, or internal parts. Do not immerse it in water. Drain and pat dry with paper towels.
- **B**owls and dishes used for defrosting or marinating must be washed before being used for cooking or serving poultry.

- **B**lot up any liquid on the counter as soon as possible. After working with poultry, it is *imperative* that all work surfaces, sinks, colanders, knives, and your *hands* be washed with hot sudsy water. Wooden boards easily absorb juices; white opaque plastic ones are safer. Spray these surfaces with an antibacterial cleaner.

C—Cook Thoroughly

- **C**ook all poultry thoroughly to ensure the elimination of any bacteria. Bacteria are killed when the internal temperature reaches 165°F.
- **C**harred flesh on the outside from a barbecue does not mean that the chicken is cooked inside. Pink meat near the bone or in the joints is not only unfashionable, it is dangerous. When poultry is pricked with a fork, the juices should run clear.
- **C**heck poultry by making a deep cut before serving.

D—Don't Give Bacteria a Chance to Grow

- **D**on't stuff poultry ahead of time. Many professionals now bake stuffing in a separate casserole. If birds are to be stuffed, have the ingredients chopped, diced, or sautéed and waiting in the refrigerator. Just before cooking time, mix them together with the dry ingredients and fill the cavity. And don't store cooked poultry with stuffing still inside.
- **D**on't leave raw or cooked poultry out in a warm environment for more than 1 hour.

E—Enjoy

With a little care you can *enjoy* poultry often.

TARRAGON CHICKEN SALAD

Serves 6

Tarragon-flavored chicken salad, flavored with Pommery mustard vinaigrette rather than mayonnaise, is a favorite of mine. Cooking chicken breasts on the bone will keep them juicier.

If you eat a lot of chicken—and who doesn't—look for family packs, especially when they are on sale. You can save up to $1.00 per pound. Divide the large package into serving-size portions and wrap and freeze them for up to 9 months. I find that 2 whole breasts fit nicely into sandwich-size resealable plastic freezer bags.

2 medium whole chicken breasts on the bone, split and skinned
2 cups chicken stock plus enough water to cover the breasts
1/3 cup Pommery or whole-grain mustard (see note)
3 tablespoons red wine vinegar
3 tablespoons walnut oil
3 tablespoons vegetable oil or 6 tablespoons vegetable oil, if not using walnut oil
1 tablespoon dried tarragon, crumbled
1/2 teaspoon salt, or to taste
Freshly ground black pepper
1/2 cup light cream
1 cup coarsely chopped walnut pieces, lightly toasted
1 cup thinly sliced scallions, including most of the green parts
Romaine lettuce leaves, washed and coarse stems removed, to garnish (optional)

1. In a large, deep skillet, cover the chicken with broth and water. Bring the liquid to a simmer, and cook until the chicken is just cooked, about 15 to 20 minutes.
2. Meanwhile, combine the mustard and vinegar in a large bowl. Whisk in the oils in a slow, steady stream to form an emulsion. Stir in the tarragon, salt, pepper, and cream. Add the walnuts and scallions and set aside.
3. Transfer the breasts to a clean counter. Remove the meat from the bones, cut into 1/4-inch cubes, and stir into the sauce. Add the walnut and scallion mixture and toss again.
4. Serve on a platter lined with romaine lettuce leaves, if desired.

NOTE: If your market does not carry Pommery mustard, substitute smooth Dijon mustard.

Did you know? If you sustain a puncture wound while boning poultry, it is vital that you wash it well, treat the injury with a topical ointment, and cover it with a bandage. These cuts easily lead to serious infections.

INDIVIDUAL MEXICAN CHICKEN AND CORNBREAD CASSEROLES

Serves 4

These mini-casseroles are a favorite of children and grown-ups alike. They are festive and easy to make ahead for dinner or a casual party. Prepare the zesty chicken filling ahead and refrigerate it. Ladle the filling into soup bowls (I use the crockery kind usually used for onion soup) and bake them with their cornbread topping. The tomatoes, corn, olives, and spicy jalapeño peppers, seasoned with chili and other Mexican spices, make this chicken dish colorful and tasty. You can also prepare a single, larger casserole.

FOR THE FILLING:

1 pound boneless, skinless chicken meat from any part (see note below if using leftovers)

2 tablespoons olive oil

1 cup finely chopped onions

2 large garlic cloves, peeled and minced

1 tablespoon minced pickled jalapeño peppers or 2 medium jalapeños, seeds and membranes removed, chopped

1 28-ounce can whole, peeled Italian tomatoes, drained and chopped not too fine

1 ½ teaspoons chili powder

1 teaspoon ground cumin

1 teaspoon oregano, crushed

1 cup corn kernels, fresh, frozen, or canned

½ cup thinly sliced pitted black olives

2 teaspoons red wine vinegar

3 tablespoons chopped cilantro or flat-leaf parsley

Salt and freshly ground black pepper to taste

FOR THE TOPPING:

1 cup cornmeal

1 ½ tablespoons sugar

1 ½ teaspoons baking powder

½ teaspoon salt

1 egg

½ cup milk

1. Prepare the filling: Fill a large skillet or casserole with water, add the chicken, bring to a boil, then turn off the heat, cover the pan, and let it sit for 15 to 20 minutes, depending on the thickness of the meat, until the chicken is just opaque. Remove the chicken, blot on paper towels, and cut it into bite-sized pieces.
2. Meanwhile, in a large, heavy skillet, heat the oil until fragrant. Stir in the onions and sauté over medium heat for about 6 minutes, or until limp. Add the garlic and cook for 30 seconds longer. Stir in the jalapeños, tomatoes, chili powder, cumin, oregano, corn, olives, vinegar, cilantro, and salt and pepper. Cook over medium heat for 10 to 15 minutes, stir in the chicken, and taste to adjust the seasonings.
3. Ladle about 1 cup of chicken into 4 oven-safe soup bowls. If not cooking them at this time, cover the bowls and refrigerate. Remove from the refrigerator about 1 hour before baking them.
4. Prepare the topping: Preheat your oven to 425°F.
5. Sift the cornmeal, sugar, baking powder, and salt into a medium-sized bowl. Combine the egg and milk and whisk into the dry ingredients until smooth. Ladle the batter on top of the 4 bowls, smoothing it with a knife or small spatula to cover the chicken. Don't worry if the topping sinks, it will rise during baking. Bake on a cookie sheet in the lower third of the preheated oven for 20 to 30 minutes, or until the tops are puffed and golden brown. The time will vary with the width of the bowl. Remove and serve. These casseroles are also delicious at room temperature.

NOTE: Leftovers are fine for this recipe so long as the chicken is not overcooked and dry. Remove the skin and all fat, and cut it into bite-sized pieces.

Another idea . . . In place of the chicken in this recipe, use leftover turkey or duck meat.

STIR-FRIED CHINESE CHICKEN WITH CASHEWS

Serves 6 to 8

This is my children's all-time favorite chicken dish. The combination of crunchy snow peas, water chestnuts, and cashews, along with mushrooms and chicken, in the gingery hoisin-soy sauce appeals to all of us. Cooks love this dish because it's easy and quick to make in a wok or skillet. Serve with steamed or boiled rice to complete the meal. Change the ingredients to suit your own taste.

Sesame oil, hoisin sauce, rice vinegar, and soy sauce are all in the Asian section of the market.

- 1/4 cup sesame oil
- 1/3 cup rice vinegar
- 1/4 cup sherry
- 2 large cloves garlic, peeled and minced
- 2 pounds boneless skinless chicken breast, cut into 1-inch cubes
- 2 tablespoons peanut or vegetable oil
- 1 1/2 teaspoons cornstarch
- 1/3 cup soy sauce
- 1/3 cup hoisin sauce
- 1 tablespoon sugar
- 2 tablespoons grated fresh gingerroot
- 1/2 pound snow peas, tips and strings removed, blanched for 30 seconds in boiling water
- 1 7-ounce can water chestnuts, thinly sliced
- 1 1/2–2 cups (8 ounces) cashew nuts, lightly toasted
- 1/2 pound white mushrooms, trimmed, wiped, and sliced
- 1 cup thinly sliced scallions, including the green parts

1. Combine the sesame oil, vinegar, sherry, and garlic in a large resealable plastic bag. Add the chicken and marinate for 1 hour.
2. In a wok or large, heavy skillet, heat the peanut oil over high heat until very hot. Transfer the chicken to the wok with a slotted spoon, reserving the marinade. Stir-fry the chicken until it is opaque on all sides, about 3 to 4 minutes.
3. Combine the cornstarch and soy sauce in a small bowl. Add it along with the marinade, hoisin sauce, sugar, and ginger to the wok and reduce the heat to medium-low.
4. Add the snow peas, water chestnuts, cashews, and mushrooms and continue cooking until the vegetables are warmed through, about 5 to 6 minutes. Sprinkle on the scallions, toss to blend, cook 1 minute longer, then serve over cooked rice or Asian noodles, if desired.

Another idea . . . Substitute sea scallops or large shrimp for the chicken. In place of the snow peas, use broccoli florets or mini-ears of corn.

STUFFED CHICKEN BREASTS ITALIANA

Serves 8

8 (4 to 5 ounce) boneless, skinless chicken cutlets

2 tablespoons unsalted butter

1 tablespoon olive oil + oil to sauté chicken

1 medium onion, peeled and chopped

1/4 pound white mushrooms, wiped, trimmed, and thinly sliced

1 cup whole-milk ricotta cheese

1/2 cup freshly grated Parmesan cheese

3 tablespoons finely chopped flat-leaf parsley

1/4 teaspoon freshly grated nutmeg

1/8 teaspoon ground red pepper

Salt and freshly ground black pepper to taste

2 large bunches watercress, large stems removed

Flour seasoned with salt and pepper for dredging

2 eggs

4 tablespoons light or heavy cream

1 cup freshly toasted bread crumbs

2 cups Chunky Homemade Tomato Sauce (page 282), warmed

Finely chopped flat-leaf parsley, for garnish

These rolled chicken breasts, filled with mushrooms, watercress, and ricotta cheese, are substantial enough to satisfy even the heartiest of appetites. They are quickly sautéed to seal in the moisture and flavors, then baked. Once cooked, they can rest in a warm oven for up to an hour while you eat a first course. As a crunchy variation for the coating, mix a little cornmeal with the flour.

Many butchers will flatten the chicken breasts needed for this recipe if you order them in advance.

1. If the butcher has not flattened the breasts, put between 2 sheets of waxed paper and pound to an even thickness of about 1/4 inch, using a meat pounder, the side of a cleaver or chef's knife, or the heel of your hand. Working with the smooth side of the breast down, pound the flesh from the center of the breast outwards, taking care not to break through the meat. The small cutlets may be removed and used for another dish. If used here, be sure to remove the tendon. Cover and set aside.
2. In a medium-sized, heavy skillet, heat the butter and oil over medium-high heat. Stir in the onion and sauté for 5 to 7 minutes until lightly colored. Add the mushrooms and cook for 2 to 3 minutes until they are wilted, stirring occasionally.
3. Combine the mushroom mixture with the ricotta, Parmesan, parsley, nutmeg, red pepper, salt, and pepper in a large bowl. Blanch the watercress for 15 to 20 seconds in boiling water until wilted, drain well, then transfer to the bowl of a food processor and process until almost smooth. Stir it into the cheese-mushroom mixture.
4. Lay the chicken breasts vertically on a clean work space with the narrower end closest to you. Divide the stuffing equally, spooning about 2 tablespoons onto the lower edge of each breast. Roll them up, turning in the sides to form a neat cylinder (see illustration).

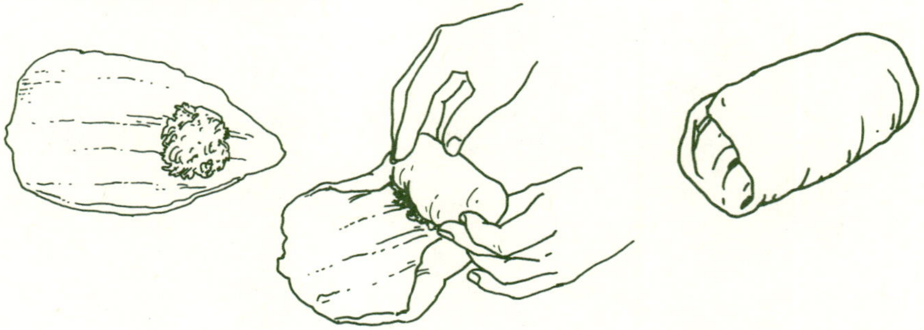

5. Put the flour in a flat dish or pie plate. Beat the eggs and cream in a second dish. Put the bread crumbs in a third dish. Roll each breast first in flour, making sure to pat some on the ends, then dust off any excess. Next, dip it into the egg-cream mixture, and finally, roll in the bread crumbs. Put them on a large flat plate and continue with the remaining breasts. Cover and refrigerate for 1 to 2 hours to seal.
6. Preheat your oven to 350°F.
7. Pour oil into a large, heavy skillet to a depth of ¼ inch and heat until very hot over medium-high heat. The surface will ripple. Add the rolls one at a time to the hot oil, taking care not to crowd them. If necessary, do this in batches. Using wooden spatulas or spoons, turn and brown the rolls evenly on all sides, approximately 5 to 6 minutes.
8. Once they are golden brown, transfer them with a wide spatula to a jelly-roll pan or cookie sheet, and bake for 15 minutes to finish cooking. Test for doneness by partially cutting into one breast to see that the meat is just cooked through. Remove from the oven and serve on a heated platter or individual plates. Ladle a generous spoonful of sauce across each roll and add a little parsley. Pass remaining sauce at the table. Serve with Creamed Spinach (page 311) and a timbale of rice.

NOTE: When preparing chicken breasts ahead of time, reduce the cooking time to about 12 minutes, turn the oven down to low, and leave the breasts for up to 30 minutes.

Did you know? Remember that "a whole chicken breast" refers to both sides of the bird's breast. Chicken breasts are available whole, split (cut in half), and skinless and boneless in the market. If time is short, let the market do the work. Otherwise, save up to $.90 per pound and remove the skin and bones yourself.

To bone a chicken breast, follow the directions on page 106 for boning turkey breast, working the knife against the rib bones. In chickens, the flexible white part of the breastbone is cartilage. You can bend the whole breast in half widthwise, and it should separate from the bony part. Then, grab the top of the cartilage and pull it away from the flesh.

FLOPPY-EARED CHICKEN

Serves 8

- 4 tablespoons unsalted butter
- 2 medium onions, peeled and chopped fairly fine
- 4 whole medium-sized chicken breasts, split, skinned, but not boned
- Flour for dredging
- Salt and freshly ground black pepper
- 8–10 tablespoons Dijon mustard
- ½–⅓ cup heavy cream
- Finely chopped flat-leaf parsley for garnish

A French friend originally prepared this dish for my husband. When he told her that he loved the chicken, she revealed that the chicken had "very floppy ears." Her dish contained rabbit (which is equally delicious). The dish is always well received because the breasts are so moist and flavorful. The generous layer of mustard shields the meat and becomes part of the delicious sauce.

1. Preheat your oven to 325°F.
2. In a large, heavy skillet, melt 2 tablespoons of the butter over medium heat. Add the onions and gently sauté for 6 to 8 minutes until golden brown, stirring occasionally. When the onions are colored, remove with a slotted spoon, leaving as much butter as possible in the pan. Reserve until later.
3. Pat each breast dry with paper towels and dust lightly with flour. Season with salt and pepper, and generously brush with mustard.
4. Melt the remaining 2 tablespoons of butter in the pan, keeping the heat at medium. Add the breasts, flesh-side down, and cook until browned, about 8 to 9 minutes; turn and cook the second side for another 7 to 8 minutes. Transfer them to a heat-proof platter and bake for 15 to 17 minutes.
5. Meanwhile, turn the heat under the skillet to high. Return the sautéed onions to the pan, stir in ½ cup of cream, and bring to a boil, scraping up all the browned cooking bits in the bottom of the skillet. When the cream begins to thicken, reduce the heat to medium and taste for seasonings, adding additional mustard, cream, or salt and pepper, to taste. Return the chicken to the pan; turn once or twice to cover with the sauce. Serve with a generous spoonful of sauce ladled over each breast and a little parsley sprinkled on top.

As a variation . . . If using rabbit for this dish, cut the skinned rabbit into large serving-size pieces and follow the directions for the chicken above. Cooking time will be about 2 minutes less on each side.

BASQUE CHICKEN IN RED WINE WITH OLIVES AND PEPPERS

Serves 6

I first tasted a rustic coq au vin simmered in red wine years ago in the Basque region of southern France. Until then, I thought cooking chicken in white wine was the thing to do. Today we think of using red wine with poultry and even fish where the dish's other ingredients have strong flavors. In this version, colorful peppers and olives give this simple dish a robust taste. It can be made a day or two ahead of time and slowly reheated.

When looking for cut-up chickens in your market, notice that packages labeled "quartered" or "cut-up" fryers are usually the same price. For a stew, the advantage of the cut-up bird is that the almost meatless backbone and tail sections are generally cut away from the thigh and breast. Once the chicken is quartered, this is harder to do. Use these bones and the wing tips for stock.

1/2 pound thick-sliced bacon, cut into 3/4-inch strips

1 3 1/2-pound chicken, wing tips removed, cut into serving-size pieces and patted dry or 3 pounds thighs, excess skin and fat removed

2 large onions, peeled and coarsely chopped

1 large green bell pepper, seeds and membranes removed, coarsely chopped

1 large red bell pepper, seeds and membranes removed, coarsely chopped

4-5 large fresh sage leaves chopped or 1 tablespoon dried sage leaf, crumbled

2 sprigs fresh thyme or 1 teaspoon dry thyme leaves

1 cup oil-cured black olives

Salt and freshly ground black pepper to taste

1 1/4 cups hearty red wine

1/2 cup sour cream (optional)

1. In a large, heavy casserole, cook the bacon over medium-high heat for about 2 to 3 minutes, or until the pieces begin to separate and fat covers the bottom of the pan.
2. Add the chicken, skin side down, and cook for 10 minutes over medium-high heat to lightly brown the skin. If the chicken sticks, use a spatula to loosen it. Turn the pieces, add the onions and peppers, and continue cooking for another 5 to 6 minutes. Drain the fat from the casserole.
3. Add the sage, thyme, olives, salt, and a liberal amount of pepper. Pour in the red wine, adjust the heat to high, and boil for 5 to 6 minutes to reduce it slightly, stirring and scraping up any browned cooking bits. Reduce the heat so the liquid is just simmering and cook for another 15 minutes, stirring occasionally. Stir in the sour cream, if using, and serve.

Did you know? In many chicken recipes, your favorite part may be substituted for the whole bird. If using all thighs or breasts, select pieces of a nearly uniform size for even cooking when timing is vital, as in broiled or roasted dishes. Birds labeled as "fowl" are old and most suitable for soup.

CRUNCHY OVEN-ROASTED CHICKEN

Serves 2 to 4

- 1 corn-fed chicken, if available, about 2 $\frac{1}{2}$ to 3 pounds (see note below)
- 2 tablespoons olive oil
- Salt and freshly ground black pepper
- 4 large fresh sage leaves
- 2 6-inch sprigs fresh rosemary, stems removed
- 2–3 large cloves garlic, peeled
- Salt and freshly ground black pepper
- 3 tablespoons dry white wine
- 3 tablespoons water

In the hills of Tuscany, fresh chickens stuffed with garlic and herbs are roasted to crunchy perfection in wood-burning ovens. After watching an old farmer woman roast her chickens in high heat, I noticed that she left the oven door open for the last 20 minutes. This crisps the skin by allowing the moisture, which might fall back onto the skin, to escape. From that day I have propped my oven door open at the end of the cooking, and my chicken is both succulent and crisp.

Increasingly markets sell free-range and corn-fed chickens. These birds, fed on natural grains and allowed to roam free, taste more like the chickens of years gone by and stay healthier. If a bird eats naturally, we benefit as well. It is worth tasting them. However, the more hand-care the birds get, the costlier they are. Free-range chickens may be $4.00 per pound. Corn-fed birds are usually only about $.50 more a pound than commercially raised chickens, and I buy these when I can.

1. Preheat your oven to 500°F.
2. Wash the chicken under cold water and dry it inside and out. Trim off excess fat and turn the wing tips under the bird. Brush the inside cavity with 1 tablespoon oil and season with salt and pepper. Finely chop the sage, rosemary leaves, and garlic together until they are mixed. Add to the cavity.
3. Brush the remaining tablespoon of olive oil over the skin. Put the chicken, breast side up, on a rack in a shallow roasting pan just large enough to hold it comfortably. Season with salt and pepper. Pour the wine and water around the chicken and put in the middle of the preheated oven.
4. Turn the heat down to 425°F and roast for 50 minutes. If all the liquid in the pan evaporates during this time, add a little more water. Baste the chicken 2 to 3 times and prick the thigh joint with a fork to release any fat.
5. After 45 to 50 minutes, prop the oven door slightly open and continue cooking for another 20 minutes. Remove the pan from the oven and allow the chicken to rest for about 5 to 7 minutes, then cut it into serving pieces. Serve with Zucchini Gratin (page 49).

NOTE: For a larger chicken weighing 3 $\frac{1}{2}$ to 4 pounds, roast the chicken about 20 to 25 minutes longer.

Did you know? If poultry has a "refrigerator smell," squeeze the juice of half a lemon inside the cavity to refresh it.

ROASTED CHICKEN WITH APPLES, CIDER, AND CALVADOS

Serves 4 to 6

The Auge Valley in Normandy is justly famous for its apples and apple products: cider; cider vinegar; and Calvados, or apple brandy. In the sauce for this crunchy roasted chicken, they are all combined with that other celebrated Norman product, cream, for a concert of flavor variations. This is a wonderful main course for an autumn dinner when apples and fresh cider are generally available.

6 tablespoons unsalted butter, at room temperature

1 3-pound chicken, rinsed and dried, wing tips removed

Salt and freshly ground black pepper

3 tablespoons finely chopped fresh chervil or flat-leaf parsley

1/3 cup Calvados or applejack

3/4 cup heavy cream

1 tablespoon vegetable oil

1/2 cup finely chopped shallots

4 large Granny Smith or other tart apples, peeled, cored, and cut into eighths

1/2 cup cider, fresh if possible

1 1/2 tablespoons apple cider vinegar

2 tablespoons unbleached, all-purpose flour

Chopped chervil or flat-leaf parsley for garnish

1. Preheat your oven to 500°F.
2. Spread 1 tablespoon of butter inside the chicken, season with salt and pepper, and add the chopped chervil. Massage 1 tablespoon of butter into the skin, and season with salt and pepper. Put the chicken, breast side up, on a rack in a shallow roasting pan just large enough to hold it comfortably. Put in the middle of the oven, lower the temperature to 425°F, and roast for 50 minutes.
3. Remove the pan from the oven and transfer the chicken to a platter. Tent lightly with aluminum foil. Remove the rack and drain the fat.
4. On top of the stove, pour in the Calvados, stirring up the browned cooking bits. Heat the pan over medium-high heat and carefully ignite to burn off the alcohol. Stir in the cream, return the chicken to the pan, and return to the oven, leaving the oven on but with the door slightly ajar. Cook for 20 minutes more, basting twice.
5. While the chicken is roasting, melt 2 more tablespoons of the butter and the oil in a large, heavy skillet. Add the shallots and cook for 2 to 3 minutes over medium heat, until they are soft and translucent. Add the apples, turn once, cover, and cook for 8 to 10 minutes over medium heat, or until just softened.
6. The chicken is done when the leg moves easily in the socket and the juices run clear when the thigh is pricked. Drain the juices from the cavity into the pan. Transfer the chicken to a heated platter and leave in the turned-off oven while finishing the sauce.
7. On top of the stove, add the cider and vinegar to the roasting pan and bring the liquid to a boil. In a small dish, blend the flour with the remaining 2 tablespoons of butter to make a *beurre manié*. Stir small bits into the sauce until it is thickened. Immediately turn off the heat and taste for seasonings. Stir in the apples. Cut the chicken into serving pieces or serve whole. Spoon the sauce around the chicken on the platter and garnish with a little chopped chervil or parsley.

Did you know? The difference between a frying and broiling chicken is the weight. Under 3 pounds the bird is called a broiler, and it is usually a younger bird. Some markets fudge a bit on this terminology, though, so you are safer buying by the approximate weight you wish. The birds are used interchangeably. With roasting chickens, the bird may be as large as 6 pounds.

DEVILISH CRUNCHY CHICKEN

Serves 2 to 4

- 1 2 1/2 to 3-pound frying chicken, split in half, rinsed and patted dry, excess fat and wing tips and backbone removed
- 1/2 cup fruity olive oil
- 1/4 cup fresh lemon juice
- 1/2+ teaspoon Tabasco sauce
- Salt and freshly ground black pepper to taste
- 1–2 large lemons, cut into wedges

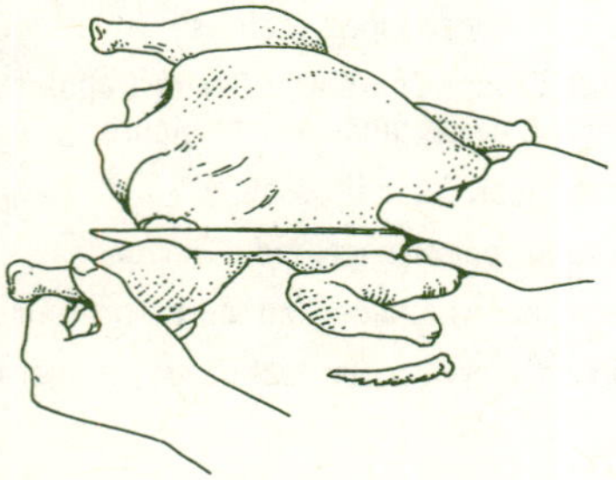

In Italy, this crunchy, piquant chicken is supposedly fare for the devil because of its charred flesh and peppery taste. The chicken is flattened and cooked in a cast-iron (or other heavy) skillet. Once you bite through the darkened exterior, there is succulent, heavenly meat. I also make this with Cornish game hens.

1. With a sharp knife, make an incision between the leg and thigh, partially separating the two sections. Repeat with the breast and wing sections (see illustration). With the skin side up, flatten the chicken with a meat pounder, cracking the bone in several places. Remove broken pieces of bones.
2. In a large, resealable plastic bag, combine the olive oil, lemon juice, and Tabasco sauce and stir to blend. Add the chicken, seal, and refrigerate the chicken for about 2 to 3 hours.
3. Heat a very large, cast-iron skillet over high heat until hot, about 3 minutes. Lift the chicken from the marinade and lay it, skin-side down, in the pan. Reserve the marinade. Put a flat oven-safe plate or large cake pan over the chicken. It should *not* be a tight-fitting lid, or the chicken will steam. Weight it heavily. I use a large saucepan or teakettle filled with water.
4. After about 2 minutes, remove the weight, gently loosen the chicken with a spatula, if it is sticking to the pan, and baste with some of the reserved marinade. Return the plate and weight and cook for 3 to 5 minutes longer, or until the skin is quite crisp and dark colored. Season the top side with salt and pepper. Turn the chicken, baste, season with salt and pepper, and cook the second side uncovered for 5 to 7 minutes.
5. Transfer the chicken to a platter or cut up and serve on individual plates, with the juice of 1 lemon squeezed on it. Pass additional lemon wedges. Serve with a tossed green salad and rice, if desired.

Did you know? While Tabasco sauce may change color from bright orange to rust over a period of time, it does not lose its peppery bite.

MARIA'S CHICKEN AND SAUSAGE IN SAFFRON RICE

Serves 4

During the years I lived in Paris, I remember eating this simple chicken dish, like arroz con pollo, at the home of some friends who had a Portuguese cook named Maria. The wonderful aroma that wafted through the house while it was cooking drew me to the kitchen as soon as I entered the door. When I lifted off the lid, there were the familiar vibrant yellow rice, bright green peas, chunks of garlicky sausage, and chicken to feast on.

Because I love the floral scent of basmati rice, I use it here instead of American long-grain rice, but either will work. I also like turkey kielbasa (Polish sausage) for its spicy flavor and lower fat content.

2 tablespoons unsalted butter

1 tablespoon vegetable oil

1 3- to 3½-pound cut-up chicken, patted dry

3 cups coarsely chopped onions, about 2 large onions

Salt and freshly ground black pepper to taste

¼ teaspoon crushed saffron threads

2½–3 cups chicken stock, heated

1 cup basmati or long-grain white rice

8 ounces turkey kielbasa, cut into ½-inch slices

1 cup frozen petite peas, defrosted

¼ cup coarsely chopped flat-leaf parsley

1. In a large, heavy casserole, heat the butter and oil over medium-high heat until hot but not smoking. Add the chicken, skin-side down, and cook for 3 to 4 minutes until the skin is lightly browned. Turn and cook for another 3 minutes on the second side. Add the onions and sauté for about 7 minutes, stirring occasionally, or until they start to brown. Season with salt and pepper.
2. While the onions are cooking, add the saffron to the chicken stock. Stir the rice into the casserole, cook for about a minute, then pour 2½ cups of the stock over the rice. Add the kielbasa, raise the heat to high, and bring the liquid to a boil. Cover the pan, adjust the heat to medium-low so the liquid is just simmering, and cook for 25 to 30 minutes, until the liquid is absorbed and the rice is tender. After about 20 minutes, check to see if there is enough liquid, adding the remaining stock as needed if the rice is not tender. At this time, stir in the peas and parsley, replace the cover, and finish cooking. The chicken should be cooked through and very tender.

Did you know? In the Deli and the refrigerated packaged Meat departments, there is a whole range of products using turkey in place of other meats. Bologna, pastrami, ham, and hot dogs made from turkey rather than pork or beef are usually dramatically lower in calories. But be sure to read the labels. Most of these products still contain almost as much sodium as their pork or beef counterparts.

SMOKY TURKEY MEATLOAF

Serves 3 to 4

2 tablespoons olive oil
1 1/2 cups finely chopped onions
2 large cloves garlic
1 medium carrot, coarsely chopped
1/2 red bell pepper, seeded and membranes removed, coarsely chopped
1/4 cup chopped cilantro
1 1/4 pounds ground turkey
1 tablespoon Lapsang souchong tea leaves, finely ground
1 egg, lightly beaten
1/2 cup fresh bread crumbs
2 tablespoons + 1 tablespoon sweet Thai chili sauce
1 teaspoon salt or to taste
Freshly ground black pepper to taste

Try this turkey meatloaf perfumed with smoky Lapsang souchong tea and Thai sweet chili sauce. It has a big taste without a lot of calories and it's deliciously juicy. Ground turkey can be used in many preparations where you might use beef or pork. However, as a burger, the meat needs more moisture since it is so lean. You could substitute ground turkey in the Moroccan Lamb in Peppers, as well (page 139). You can easily make this in a food processor, but only pulse as you mix to keep the mixture light.

If you don't like smoky tastes, use any black tea. There are so many teas on the shelf to choose from. The best, by the way, are the loose-leaf varieties because they have fewer "fannings" (tiny broken leaves) and dust. Store tea in a dark spot.

1. Preheat your oven to 350°F.
2. Heat the oil in a large skillet over medium-high heat. Add the onions and sauté until wilted and lightly browned, about 5 to 6 minutes. Set aside.
3. Pulse the garlic, carrot, and red bell pepper in a food processor until minced. Add the cilantro, pulse to blend, then put in the reserved onions, turkey, tea, egg, bread crumbs, 2 tablespoons of the Thai chili sauce, salt, and pepper. Pulse just until blended. Do not over mix. Transfer to a small loaf pan, about 4 by 8 inches, patting lightly until smooth. Spread the remaining tablespoon of Thai chili sauce over the top.
4. Bake for 45 minutes, or until the juices run clear, remove and let stand 5 to 10 minutes, then cut into slices and serve. Or serve at room temperature.

SAUTÉED TURKEY CUTLETS IN LEMON BUTTER

Serves 4

Turkey cutlets, thinly sliced and pounded until flat, are a fine, economical alternative to veal. In fact, since turkey breasts are now sold whole, split, boneless, or cut into slices, it's even easier to try your favorite recipes using turkey. Look at the recipe for Sautéed Veal Cutlets with Mustard, Capers, and Peppers on page 148. An added bonus is that turkey slices stay whole, whereas with veal, if the meat has been cut across muscle groups, you may find the sautéed cutlets breaking into pieces.

This classic version of quickly sautéed cutlets with lemon and butter added to the pan is a breeze for busy evening meals, especially if the turkey is pounded in the morning and refrigerated until needed. When you are cooking, be sure to keep the butter and oil sizzling hot so each cutlet browns as it is added to the pan. Otherwise, you will have soggy, gray meat.

4 tablespoons unsalted butter, at room temperature

2 tablespoons vegetable oil

1–1 1/3 pound turkey breast, sliced and pounded to about 1/4 inch thick (see "Did you know?" below)

Flour for dredging

Salt and freshly ground black pepper to taste

3 tablespoons fresh lemon juice

Finely chopped flat-leaf parsley for garnish

1 small lemon, thinly sliced, for garnish

1. Heat 2 tablespoons of the butter and the oil in a large, heavy skillet over medium-high heat. As it is heating, lightly flour 1 cutlet, shaking off the excess flour. When the fat is very hot, slide in the cutlet. If a second cutlet will fit without crowding, flour it quickly, and add it to the pan. The fat should sizzle with each addition.
2. After about 45 seconds or a minute, the cutlet should be golden brown on the first side. Turn and cook the second side for 30 to 45 seconds. Transfer to a warm platter and season with salt and plenty of pepper.
3. Once all the cutlets are cooked, turn off the heat, add the lemon juice, stirring up all the browned cooking bits, and stir in the remaining 2 tablespoons of butter.
4. Return the cutlets to the pan, turn to coat with the lemon butter, then serve on heated plates. Pour any remaining sauce over the cutlets. Add a couple of thin slices of lemon to each cutlet and a little chopped parsley.

Did you know? Once raw turkey breast is sliced, there appears to be a thin tendon down the center of it. Do not try to remove it, as it disappears during cooking. However, the smaller cutlet(s) that is often connected to the whole or split turkey breast actually has a stringy tendon that you do want to pull out before cooking.

LEAN AND MOIST TURKEY BREAST

Serves 6

2 1/2-pound boned and skinned turkey breast (4 1/2-pound whole turkey breast)

3 tablespoons Dijon mustard

1 1/3 tablespoons paprika

1/4 cup finely chopped flat-leaf parsley

Salt and freshly ground black pepper

1 tablespoon unsalted butter

1 teaspoon vegetable oil

3/4 cup dry vermouth

3/4 cup orange juice

This flavorful boneless turkey roast with Dijon mustard, paprika, and lots of parsley rolled inside, and a sauce made with pan juices and dry vermouth, is an elegant and satisfying meal even for Thanksgiving or Christmas. It's also delicious sliced and served cold. Serve it with Cranberry, Pepper, and Onion Conserve (page 66) and Hearty Bulgur Pilaf (page 293).

Turkey breasts are inexpensive and the calories are minimal, particularly when the skin is removed. Turkey parts are a boon to small families and all-white-meat or dark-meat lovers. Look for smaller whole birds, as well, available almost year around. Fresh turkey meat is best used within 2 days of purchase. Cooked turkey lasts for a week in your refrigerator if tightly wrapped in plastic.

1. If the turkey is not boned and skinned: Carefully slide your fingers between the meat and the skin on one side of the breast close to the ribs. Grab the skin and pull toward the breastbone. Repeat with the second side, pulling toward the center, then up toward the wishbone. The skin should pull off. Use a sharp pointed knife to detach any skin and fat that remain.

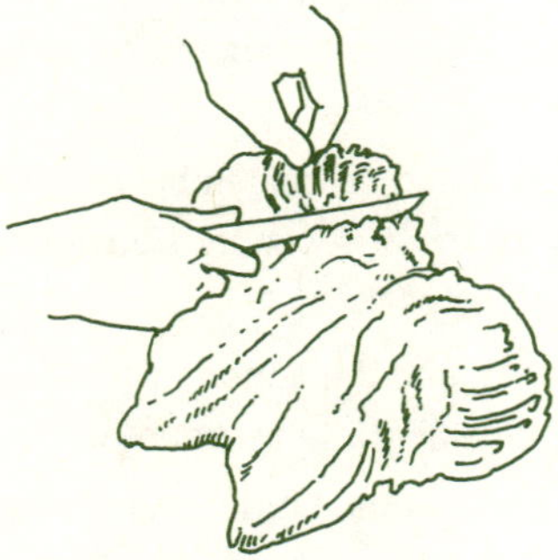

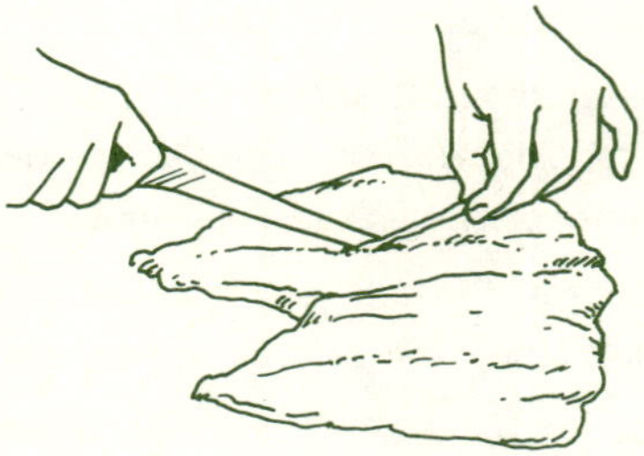

2. With a sharp boning knife, carefully remove the flesh from the bones by scraping the knife against the rib bones and working toward the breastbone. Once at the center bone, carefully work up the breastbone and cartilage, trying to avoid tearing the breast into two parts. (If it does tear, it is not critical, since the roast is tied together.) Repeat with the other side. Remove the tendons from the small cutlets by grabbing the tendon, and scraping the flesh away while pulling the tendon out (see illustrations).

3. Preheat your oven to 350°F.

4. Prepare the roast: Lay the breast, skin-side down, with the tip and wishbone horizontal. Brush the inside and under the small cutlets with mustard. Sprinkle on 1 tablespoon paprika, then the parsley, salt, and pepper. Roll the turkey from bottom to top, forming a cylinder. Tie well with string in several places, including a couple of times lengthwise. The roll will measure about 3 to 4 inches in diameter.

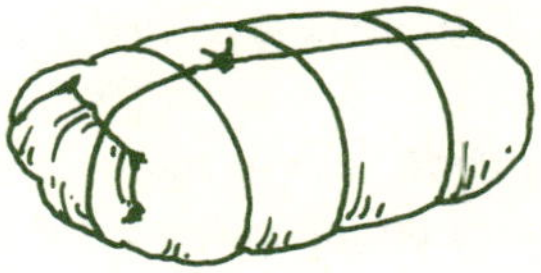

5. In a shallow, heavy roasting pan or skillet, melt the butter and oil over medium-high heat, add the turkey, and brown on all sides, approximately 5 to 8 minutes. Sprinkle the remaining paprika over the turkey, tent with aluminum foil, and roast in the middle of the preheated oven for approximately 25 minutes per pound, basting once or twice, until a meat thermometer registers 145° to 150°F. Remove the foil for the last 20 minutes of cooking. Transfer the turkey to an oven-safe platter and return it to the turned-off oven while finishing the sauce.
6. For the sauce: Deglaze the pan with the vermouth and orange juice, scraping up all the browned cooking bits. Turn the heat to high and boil the liquid until it is reduced and slightly thickened, about 1 to 2 minutes.
7. Remove the strings and let the turkey stand for a couple of minutes before cutting it crosswise into ¾-inch thick slices. Spoon on some sauce before serving.

Did you know? Although many turkeys come with pop-up timers, they are unreliable or broken far too often to be trusted. Instead, remove it and buy an instant-read thermometer, sold in the Meat department or on a J-hook with other cooking tools, for a quick, accurate-temperature turkey. You will be far more secure about the results.

Did you know? Frozen turkeys are usually available in any market. Defrost them slowly on a plate in the refrigerator for minimal moisture and flavor loss. When slowly cooked and basted occasionally, they are fine eating. As for the frozen rolled turkey breast roasts, I much prefer to prepare my own. Mine are less expensive and the texture and taste are better.

TWO-DAYS-AFTER TURKEY HASH

Serves 2 to 3

- 1 medium all-purpose potato, scrubbed and cut into 1/4-inch cubes (about 1 cup)
- 1 1/2 cups cooked turkey, cut into 1/4-inch cubes
- 3/4 cup corn kernels, frozen or canned
- 1 1/2 tablespoons grated onion
- 2 tablespoons finely chopped flat-leaf parsley
- 1 teaspoon Worcestershire sauce
- 1/4 teaspoon dry mustard
- 1/4 teaspoon dried thyme leaves
- Salt and freshly ground black pepper to taste
- 2 tablespoons unsalted butter
- 1–2 tablespoons vegetable oil
- 1/4 cup dry vermouth
- 2–3 poached eggs (optional)

If you think you can't face another turkey sandwich after demolishing a large bird, try this old-fashioned hash for a weekend breakfast or lunch. What a great way to use up those small snippets of meat that are too small to slice. And, it's got just enough seasoning to lift the sautéed turkey, potato, onion, and corn mixture from the mundane to eye-opening satisfaction.

Many people love hash. Because supermarkets sell turkey parts all year, this morning favorite can be made even when there are no leftovers. You could use frozen hashed brown potatoes for a shortcut, avoiding those with preservatives.

1. In a medium-sized pan, cook the potato in boiling salted water for 2 to 3 minutes, until just cooked through; drain and leave in a strainer to dry.
2. In a medium-sized bowl, combine the turkey, corn, grated onion, parsley, Worcestershire sauce, mustard, thyme, salt, and pepper. Add the potatoes and mix well.
3. Heat the butter and 1 tablespoon of vegetable oil in a large nonstick skillet over medium-high heat. Add the hash mixture, flattening it slightly with a spatula. Cook for 15 minutes until it starts to brown on the bottom and become crusty. Turn it with a spatula, adding another tablespoon of oil, if the hash sticks, scrape up the browned bits, and cook for 6 or 8 minutes more.
4. Pour the vermouth over the hash and stir up all the browned bits on the bottom of the pan. Cook only 1 minute longer. Serve on warmed plates, adding a poached egg on top of each serving, if desired.

Did you know? Most markets sell baked turkey breast in their Deli departments. Some also sell packaged "turkey rolls." Since these prepared products require a longer shelf life, many are heavily salted and preserved with chemicals. Be sure to ask whether your market sells sodium-reduced turkey if salt is of concern to your family. Read the label on the packaging to find out about added fillers, too.

RASPBERRY AND DUCK SALAD WITH RASPBERRY VINAIGRETTE

Serves 4

Both the colors and combination of tastes in this dish are dramatic. Vibrant greens shot with ribbons of radicchio form the salad's base. Add julienned strips of duck tossed with mushrooms, cracklings, and fresh raspberries in a raspberry vinaigrette, and this main course salad is a real treat.

With duck breasts now being sold in markets, this is an easy salad to make. In this recipe the breast is skinned before poaching because I loathe eating fatty ducks and prefer to use the skin to make cracklings. Some of the poaching liquid is also used in the vinaigrette.

FOR THE SALAD:

1 whole duck breast

1 cup chicken stock

Salt and pepper

1 small head Bibb lettuce, washed, dried, and torn into bite-sized pieces (about 4 cups loosely packed)

1 small head radicchio, washed, dried, and cut into 1/2-inch strips (about 4 cups loosely packed)

1 large bunch arugula, washed, dried, and coarse stems removed (about 4 cups loosely packed)

4 ounces white mushrooms, wiped, trimmed, and thinly sliced

Cracklings

1 cup raspberries

FOR THE VINAIGRETTE:

1 teaspoon green peppercorns in vinegar or brine, rinsed

1/4 cup raspberry or red wine vinegar

6 tablespoons walnut oil

2 tablespoons poaching liquid (reserved from cooking the duck)

1 tablespoon chopped fresh tarragon or 1 teaspoon dried

Salt and freshly ground black pepper to taste

1. Put the breast in a skillet just large enough to hold it flat, cover with stock, and simmer until the duck is almost cooked through but with a little pink still in the center. Turn off the heat and cool for 15 minutes. Remove and cut into thin strips. Season with salt and pepper. Reserve the poaching liquid.
2. Meanwhile, make the cracklings: Cut the skin and fat into small squares and slowly sauté in a large skillet over medium-high heat. When very crisp and brown, discard the fat, and blot the cracklings on paper towels. Season with salt.
3. In a large bowl, combine the lettuce, radicchio, and arugula. Add the duck, mushrooms, and cracklings.
4. Prepare the vinaigrette: In a small bowl, mash the green peppercorns. Add the raspberry vinegar, then whisk in the walnut oil. Whisk in the poaching liquid, tarragon, salt, and pepper. Pour over the salad and toss. Add the raspberries, turn gently, and serve at once. This salad wilts quickly.

Did you know? Try to use raspberries within 1 day. Raspberries take poorly to moisture, so the covering over the box should have air holes. If you wash the berries, do so at the last possible moment. They start to wilt very quickly. I use a plant mister.

MUSHROOM, FENNEL, AND DUCK STEW

Serves 4

When I want roast duck, I prefer to eat it in fine restaurants where it is cooked so the skin is crispy and the bird is not fatty. At home, I like this wintry stew where the combination of the duck meat blends well with the braised fennel, mushrooms, and pearl onions. It may be prepared ahead and kept on gentle heat for 45 minutes to an hour. Or, cook it up to 2 days ahead of time and keep it in the refrigerator. Slowly reheat before serving.

Almost all ducks in our markets are the Long Island variety, bred with a thick layer of fat to be juicy and tender. Once the fat is rendered, not much meat remains, and an average roasted duck will feed only 2 people, unless it is cut up for a stew such as this one. Use fresh and defrosted birds within a day or two.

- 6 ounces thick-sliced bacon, cut into 3/4-inch strips, or pancetta (see "Have you tried . . .")
- 2 large shallots, peeled and finely chopped
- 1 large clove garlic, peeled and minced
- 3 large bulbs fennel, trimmed and quartered
- 12 ounces white mushrooms, wiped, trimmed, and quartered if large, whole if small
- 1 4- to 5-pound duck
- 2 cups chicken stock
- 12 ounces small boiling onions, peeled, with a small X in each root end, or use frozen pearl onions
- 1 1/2 teaspoons marjoram or 2 sprigs of fresh marjoram
- 1 1/2 teaspoons dried thyme leaves
- Salt and freshly ground black pepper to taste
- 1/2 cup medium-dry Madeira
- 2 teaspoons red wine vinegar
- 2 teaspoons cornstarch

1. Cook the bacon for a few minutes in a large, heavy Dutch oven or casserole over medium heat until the pieces start to separate and the fat covers the bottom of the pot. Stir in the shallots and cook for 5 to 6 minutes until they are translucent, then add the garlic and cook for 30 seconds longer. Stir in the fennel and continue cooking, stirring occasionally, until the fennel starts to brown, about 30 minutes. Add the mushrooms and cook for 2 to 3 minutes longer. Set aside.
2. Meanwhile, wash the duck, trim off any excess fat from around the neck and tail, reserving it for later. Cut off the legs and wings, discarding the wing tips or reserving them for later use with the heart, neck, and gizzard in stock. Chop the duck into serving pieces, removing any extra bones, and pat dry on paper towels.
3. Preheat your oven to 325°F.
4. Put a large piece of duck fat in a large, heavy skillet and render it over medium-high heat until about 2 to 3 tablespoons of fat cover the bottom of the pan. Remove the remaining fat and discard, or retain it for another use. When the fat is very hot, add the duck pieces, skin-side down, and sauté them for 10 to 12 minutes, turning once, until they are light brown; then transfer them to the pan with the fennel. Discard the rendered fat.
5. Adjust the heat to high; stir in the stock, onions, marjoram, thyme, salt, pepper, Madeira, and vinegar; bring the liquid to a boil; cover; and transfer the pot to the middle of the oven for 1 1/2 hours, or until the duck is tender. Stir occasionally.

Have you tried . . . Pancetta is a familiar ingredient in Italian kitchens that is especially useful for sautéing. Like conventional bacon, it is salted and cured, but it's unique because it's not smoked.

6. Remove the casserole from the oven and skim off any fat with a large spoon. Or let the duck cool so the solidified fat can be easily removed. Once the stew is degreased, put the casserole on top of the stove over medium heat. Dissolve the cornstarch in a little water, pour it into the casserole, and mix well. Simmer for 3 or 4 minutes uncovered, then serve over buttered noodles.

INDIAN GAME HENS MARINATED IN YOGURT AND SPICES

Serves 2

1 1- to 1 1/2-pound Cornish game hen
1/2 cup plain low-fat yogurt
1 small onion, peeled and grated
1 small clove garlic, peeled and crushed
2 tablespoons lime juice
1 teaspoon chili powder
1 teaspoon paprika
1/2 teaspoon cinnamon
1/2 teaspoon ground coriander seed
1/2 teaspoon ground cardamom
1/8 teaspoon ground clove
Pinch of ground red pepper
1/2 teaspoon salt, or to taste
1 tablespoon vegetable oil
1/2 tablespoon unsalted butter
1 teaspoon cornstarch dissolved in 1 tablespoon water

After 12 hours of marinating in yogurt and warm Indian spices, this Cornish game hen bakes to incredible tenderness. Sure, it's low in calories and sodium, but the wonderfully intense aroma and taste never let you think about that. Serve it with saffron rice or at room temperature with Orange, Jicama, Watercress, and Olive Salad (page 71).

Many markets only sell game hens in pairs. One bird will freeze beautifully if well wrapped. Or, double this recipe and serve 4. If your market only sells frozen game hens, defrost them slowly in the refrigerator and use them here without a problem.

1. Cut the game hen in half, removing the backbone and tail. Remove the wing tips and pull off the skin. Put in a large resealable plastic bag.
2. In a small bowl, combine all the remaining ingredients except the butter and cornstarch and pour over the game hen. Seal the bag and refrigerate for 12 hours, turning it 1 or 2 times.
3. Preheat your oven to 325°F.
4. Heat the butter in a medium-sized, oven-safe skillet or casserole over medium-high heat. Scrape the yogurt mixture from the game hen, reserving the yogurt. Put the bird, skin-side down, in the hot butter, and sauté for 2 to 3 minutes until lightly browned on the flesh side. Turn the game hen, pour on the yogurt mixture, and transfer to the preheated oven to bake for about 15 to 17 minutes, or until the meat is cooked through.
5. Remove from the oven and transfer the game hen to heated plates. On top of the stove, stir the dissolved cornstarch into the yogurt mixture and bring to a boil over high heat. Cook for 1 to 2 minutes until it is slightly thickened, then spoon it over the game hen. Serve at once or cool to room temperature.

As a variation . . . In place of Cornish game hens, use a skinned frying chicken cut into serving-size pieces and double the quantity of yogurt and spices. It will serve 4. Or, buy just enough chicken thighs to serve 2 and follow the recipe exactly. In either case, cut into a piece of chicken to be certain it is completely cooked.

CARIBBEAN GAME HENS

Serves 4

The sunny flavor of the Caribbean—coconut, banana, ginger, red pepper, and saffron—are blended into the spicy sauce for this tropical dish. Slowly simmered Cornish game hens are a succulent and economical main dish, even for a party. With a very large casserole (or 2), you can double or triple this recipe. Serve with basmati rice or orzo.

Fresh game hens keep for 2 days in the coldest part of your refrigerator. They are often found in the Frozen aisle, as well. When properly wrapped, they will last for up to 9 months in your freezer. The plastic wrap should have no holes or tears. If it does, rewrap the birds before freezing to prevent freezer burn.

- 1 1/2 cups canned coconut milk
- 1/4 teaspoon crumbled saffron threads
- 2 tablespoons vegetable oil
- 2 Cornish game hens, about 1 1/2 pounds each, split with backbone and excess fat removed, blotted dry
- Salt and freshly ground black pepper
- 1 lime
- 1 small orange
- 1 tablespoon vegetable oil, if necessary
- 2 cups finely chopped onions
- 1 1/2 tablespoons minced fresh gingerroot
- 1 very ripe banana, mashed
- 1/2 teaspoon red pepper flakes
- Shredded coconut, toasted, for garnish (optional)

1. Heat the coconut milk until hot. Add the saffron and set aside.
2. In a large, heavy casserole, heat the oil over medium-high heat until very hot. Put in the game hens, skin-side down, adding only enough pieces as fit comfortably without crowding, and cook for 2 1/2 to 3 minutes until the skin is lightly browned. Turn and cook the second side for 2 to 3 minutes. Transfer to a bowl and continue until all the game hens are cooked. Season with salt and pepper.
3. Remove the lime and orange zests and mince; set aside. Squeeze the juice. There should be about 6 tablespoons.
4. If the oil has burned, discard it and add 1 tablespoon of oil to the pot. When hot, stir in the onions and sauté over medium heat for about 5 minutes until wilted, stirring often. Add the juice, turn the heat to high, and boil until the liquid is reduced by half.
5. Turn the heat to medium, whisk in the coconut milk, stirring continuously to blend well. Stir in the ginger, mashed banana, red pepper flakes, and salt and pepper to taste. Return the game hens to the casserole, cover, and simmer for about 25 minutes, turning the pieces over once or twice. The meat should be cooked through. Serve immediately or leave on very low heat for up to 2 hours. Serve garnished with toasted coconut, if desired.

Did you know? If you don't find saffron on the shelf with the other spices, ask at the front desk. Often this golden spice is kept under lock and key because it is packaged in small bottles and is expensive. Figure that the saffron in this recipe will add $1.00 to the cost of the dish. While powdered saffron is wonderful, and it dissolves almost instantly, don't use the powdered substitute or turmeric that some markets sell. Although the dish will turn yellow, the warm flavor of this spice will be missing.

PHEASANT PÂTÉ

Serves 12

1 pheasant, skinned and boned (2–2 1/2 pounds dressed weight), fresh or defrosted

1 pound ground veal

8 ounces pork fat

3 eggs, beaten

6 ounces thick-sliced smoked ham or Canadian bacon, diced

1/3 cup shelled pistachio nuts

1/2 cup finely chopped shallots

10 juniper berries, crushed

1 teaspoon ground thyme

1/4 teaspoon ground nutmeg

1 tablespoon salt, or to taste

Freshly ground black pepper

1/2 cup medium Madeira

1/4 cup brandy

12–16 ounces fatback, sliced about 1/8 inch thick and simmered for 2 minutes, patted dry

2 bay leaves

This elegant, spicy pâté, with a mosaic of smoked ham and pistachio nuts, is one of my favorite hors d'oeuvres for holidays like New Year's Eve. I bake the pâté at least a week in advance and then refrigerate to allow the flavors to mellow. The pale pink pâté looks especially festive when presented on a bed of chicory with small bunches of red grapes. Serve with pumpernickel or dark whole-grain breads, and Dijon mustard or Cranberry, Pepper, and Onion Conserve (page 66).

Along with duck, squab, and other game birds, pheasants have come into the market, as well. While they are often sold frozen, I have purchased fresh birds in a number of markets—especially those that have Service Meat departments. A simple rule of thumb: Find out what day the store received its pheasants. If they are more than a day old, make another choice. Use all poultry within a day or two.

1. Preheat your oven to 350ºF.
2. Divide the pheasant meat in two parts. Reserve half a breast for later. Add the remaining pheasant meat, ground veal, pork fat, and eggs to the bowl of a food processor and pulse until it has a somewhat smooth texture. *Do not overprocess* or the pâté will become too uniform and compacted in texture. Do this in batches if the processor is small.
3. Transfer the mixture to a large bowl and stir in the ham, nuts, shallots, juniper berries, thyme, nutmeg, salt and pepper, Madeira, and brandy. Cook a small amount of the pâté mixture in a skillet to taste for seasoning. The pâté should be highly seasoned.
4. Line a 9-by-5-by-3-inch loaf pan or 6-cup terrine with fatback, extending the slices so they can be folded back over the top of the pâté. Spoon half of the mixture into the mold, patting it down into the corners. Cut the remaining half breast into thin strips and lay it on the meat mixture. Add the remaining pâté mixture and bay leaves, turn the fatback over the meat, cover with a double layer of heavy foil, and punch a hole in the middle for steam to escape.
5. Put the pâté in a larger pan and fill it with boiling water to halfway up the side of the pâté mold. Bake for 1 1/2 to 1 3/4 hours. When done, the juices will run clear and the pâté will have shrunk slightly from the pan.

6. Remove the pans from the oven and lift the pâté from the water. Put about 8 ounces of weight evenly distributed on the pâté. (Another loaf pan with dried beans inside will work well.) Cool for an hour, then refrigerate it with the weight. Remove the weight after several hours. This pâté is best when made at least several days in advance.
7. To serve, remove the pâté from the pan. Wipe off the fat, leaving the fatback lining if desired. Cut into 1/3-inch slices and serve.

Did you know? You may have to order the pork fat for this recipe. When pork comes into the store, it is usually trimmed and the fat is discarded. If there is no fresh pork fat available, use fatback that has been simmered for 2 minutes, then blotted dry and minced.

JACK DANIEL'S ROASTED PHEASANT ON BRAISED CABBAGE

Serves 2 to 3

- 4 tablespoons unsalted butter
- 2 1/2 tablespoons vegetable oil
- 2 large onions, peeled and coarsely chopped
- 1 large green or white cabbage, approximately 2 1/2 pounds, cored, tough ribs removed, and shredded
- Salt and freshly ground black pepper to taste
- 7–8 juniper berries, crushed
- 1 pheasant, cleaned and skinned or plucked (approximately 2 to 2 1/2 pounds dressed weight)
- 2 tablespoons Dijon mustard
- 1 medium onion stuck with 6 cloves
- Flour for dredging
- 2 thick slices fatty bacon
- 1/2 cup Jack Daniel's or bourbon
- 1 cup heavy cream

Once, when I was cooking for a great American lady living near Venice, Italy, I deglazed the pan in which I had roasted a pheasant with her favorite libation, Jack Daniel's. To keep the bird tender and moist, I buried it under caramelized cabbage and onions while it cooked. The results were spectacular. While bourbon packs a good punch, the addition of cream softens and balances the flavor. This is an easy dish to prepare for a special autumn dinner.

Pheasants sold in a supermarket are usually raised in pens or on ranches and they never develop the strong "gamy" flavor of wild birds. Nor are they as tough. In Europe, where strong tastes are more appreciated, they hang whole birds with their feathers for several days to tenderize the meat and develop the flavor of young birds. Americans tend to prefer milder flavors, and many pheasants are sold already skinned and frozen. Freezing tenderizes them by breaking down the meat fiber and protects them from deterioration.

If pheasants are unavailable or not your favorite bird, substitute a small roasting chicken. Or use 2 Cornish game hens and roast for 20 minutes. In both cases, skinning is not necessary, but be sure to brown the birds.

1. In a large, deep casserole, melt 2 tablespoons of the butter and 2 tablespoons of oil over medium-high heat. Add the chopped onions and sauté for 6 to 8 minutes, until lightly colored.
2. Add another tablespoon of butter and the shredded cabbage and cook for 35 to 40 minutes, stirring occasionally, until the cabbage is caramelized and medium brown in color. Use a combination of uncovered and covered cooking. As moisture evaporates and the cabbage browns, cover the pan to prevent burning. When a lot of moisture forms on the pan's lid and drops onto the cabbage, remove it, stir the cabbage to incorporate the liquid, and continue cooking. Repeat as necessary. Season generously with salt and pepper and stir in the juniper berries. Set aside.
3. Preheat your oven to 350°F.
4. Wash the pheasant under cold water and dry well. Season the cavity with salt and pepper, liberally paint with Dijon mustard, and put the whole onion inside. Tie the legs together and turn the wing tips under. Lightly dredge the pheasant in flour.

5. In a heavy skillet, heat the remaining tablespoon of butter and ½ tablespoon of oil and brown the pheasant lightly on one side. Turn and continue cooking until all sides are colored. This will take 6 to 8 minutes.
6. Transfer the pheasant, breast-side up, to the casserole with the cabbage. Lay the bacon on the breast, pack the cabbage around and over the bird, and cover the casserole. Roast for 35 to 45 minutes depending on the size of the bird, basting with the pan juices 1 or 2 times during this time.
7. Remove from the oven, push the cabbage off the pheasant into the pan, and discard the bacon. Return to the oven and cook uncovered for 10 minutes more. Test for doneness by pricking the thigh. If the juices run clear, and the thigh moves easily in its socket, the bird is done. Discard the onion and drain the juices from the pheasant into the casserole. Transfer the pheasant to a heated platter, tent lightly with foil, and leave in the turned-off oven while finishing the sauce.
8. On top of the stove, stir the Jack Daniel's into the pot, turn the heat to high, and boil for 2 to 3 minutes, stirring often to prevent the cabbage from burning. Add the cream, turn the heat down to medium, and continue cooking for 3 to 4 minutes. Either present the bird whole and carve it at the table or cut it into pieces and serve on the cabbage.

Did you know? If a hunter friend gives you a pheasant he has shot, be sure to probe any little dark spots with the tip of a knife. There may be bird shot there, which is tough on teeth and stomachs.

ROASTED SQUABS STUFFED WITH PORCINI AND CHESTNUTS

Serves 8

- 8 1-pound squabs
- Juice of 1 lemon
- Freshly ground black pepper
- 2 ounces dried porcini mushrooms
- 4 tablespoons olive oil
- 1 6-ounce sweet Italian sausage, casing removed
- 1 large onion, peeled and chopped
- 2 medium-sized stalks of celery, trimmed and chopped
- 24 chestnuts, freshly roasted, or 1 15 ½-ounce can unsweetened chestnuts, drained and chopped
- ½ cup currants
- ⅓ cup Marsala
- 3 tablespoons finely chopped flat-leaf parsley
- 1 teaspoon salt or to taste
- ¼ cup toasted bread crumbs
- 2 sprigs fresh rosemary or 2 tablespoons dried rosemary (see note)
- 8 slices bacon
- 1 ½ cups dry vermouth
- 1 tablespoon unsalted butter, at room temperature (optional)
- 1 tablespoon unbleached all-purpose flour (optional)
- 48 seedless red grapes, stems removed, washed

This dish reminds me of autumn in Tuscany when porcini mushrooms and squabs are both in season. Squabs (or pigeons) have a special flavor (some say slightly reminiscent of liver) that complements a well-seasoned stuffing. Here, porcini and chestnuts are combined with sausages, currants, and Marsala. The sauce is made with the pan juices and red grapes. Reminder: Provide extra napkins for this rustic dish; guests may want to pick up the bones with their fingers. Serve with Holiday Cranberry Carrots (page 24) and sautéed rapini.

Some forward-looking supermarket Poultry departments offer game birds in season, including quail, pheasant, and squabs, or they may be special-ordered.

1. Wash the squabs under cold water. Remove and discard any excess fat. Dry well and squeeze the juice of the lemon inside the cavities. Season with a liberal amount of black pepper.
2. Soak the porcini in 1 cup warm water for 25 to 30 minutes, or until soft. Remove all grit and fibrous pieces, then coarsely chop. Reserve. Strain the liquid through several layers of cheesecloth or a fine strainer lined with paper towels into a saucepan. Bring to a boil, cook until reduced to ½ cup, then set aside.
3. In a large, heavy skillet, heat 1 tablespoon of the olive oil over medium-high heat until hot and fragrant. Add the sausage, chopping it into small pieces with a wooden spatula or spoon, and cooking for 4 or 5 minutes or until no longer pink. Stir in the onion and celery, cook until translucent, then add the porcini, chestnuts, currants, Marsala, parsley, and salt and pepper; stir to blend well. Raise the heat to high and boil until the liquid almost completely evaporates, about 2 to 3 minutes. Add the bread crumbs and mix well.
4. Divide the stuffing evenly among the squabs. Tuck the wing tips under and tie the legs together. In a large, heavy casserole, heat the remaining 3 tablespoons of olive oil until fragrant. Cook a few birds at a time, making sure to keep the oil hot. Turn to brown all sides, then remove and set aside.
5. Lay 3 or 4 rosemary leaves on each bird and wrap with bacon slices. Return them, breast side up, to the casserole. Turn the heat to medium, cover the pot, and cook gently for 35 to 40 minutes, basting twice during this time. The birds are done when the thigh moves easily in the socket and juices run clear when the thigh is pricked.

6. Remove the birds to a heated ovenproof platter. Discard the bacon. If the birds are not nicely browned, run them briefly under the broiler. Skim as much fat as possible from the casserole. Deglaze the casserole with the vermouth, scraping up the browned cooking bits; boil until almost completely evaporated. Add the reduced mushroom liquid, and return to a boil. If a thicker sauce is desired, combine the softened butter and flour and stir it into the liquid in small lumps. Immediately turn off the heat. Season with salt and pepper. Stir in the grapes to heat through. Serve the birds on heated plates with a generous spoonful of the sauce.

NOTE: To refresh dried rosemary leaves, put them in a small bowl of hot water for about 2 minutes, then drain and blot dry.

ROASTED SQUABS STUFFED WITH TURNIPS, OLIVES, AND FIGS

Serves 4

The unique stuffing ingredients for these squabs imparts a complex dimension of flavor. Sautéed turnips lend a hint of caramel sweetness that plays off the slightly salty olives and the tangy lemon juice. It's a great dish for cold-weather dining. Serve on a bed of polenta or orzo.

Squabs are young birds that generally weigh between 14 ounces and a pound. They are small in size with plump, meaty legs and are much prized by game fanciers for their sweet eating.

FOR THE STUFFING:

- 4 tablespoons unsalted butter
- 2 tablespoons vegetable oil
- 4 cups grated white turnips, about 6 medium turnips, peeled
- 1 medium onion, peeled and finely chopped
- 8 ounces white mushrooms, wiped, trimmed, and thinly sliced
- 1 ½ cups chopped pitted black olives
- 2 tablespoons finely chopped flat-leaf parsley
- ½ cup coarsely chopped dried Mission figs
- 4 tablespoons fresh lemon juice
- Salt and freshly ground black pepper to taste

FOR THE SQUABS:

- 4 fresh squabs, dressed, livers reserved and cleaned, rinsed under cold water and blotted dry
- 2 tablespoons unsalted butter
- 1 tablespoon vegetable oil
- 4 slices bacon
- ¾ cup medium Madeira
- ½ cup split and pitted black olives
- 1 tablespoon lemon juice

1. Preheat your oven to 400°F.
2. Prepare the stuffing: In a large, heavy skillet, melt the butter and oil over medium-high heat. Add the turnips and cook until softened and lightly browned, about 10 minutes, stirring often. Add the onions, mushrooms, and olives and cook until the mixture is fairly dry and the mushrooms are wilted, about 6 minutes. Add the parsley, figs, lemon juice, salt, and a liberal amount of black pepper; stir; and cook for 30 seconds longer. Set aside.
3. Stuff the birds: Generously season inside with salt and pepper. Fill with the prepared stuffing, tie the legs together, secure the neck skin over the opening with a toothpick or small skewer, and turn the wing tips under. The extra stuffing can be put into individual buttered soufflé dishes or custard cups, covered with foil, and baked with the squabs.
4. Melt 1 tablespoon of the butter and the oil over medium-high heat in a large, low baking pan on top of the stove. Cook the birds, breast-side down, for 2 to 3 minutes to brown the skin. Discard the fat. Turn them breast-side up and put 1 slice of bacon over each bird. Roast them in the oven for 23 to 28 minutes. Prick the thigh; if the juices run clear and the thigh moves easily in the socket, the birds are done.
5. Remove from the oven, discard the bacon, untie the birds, season with salt and pepper, and put on a warm serving platter in the turned-off oven.
6. Strain the pan juices into a medium-sized skillet, skim off as much fat as possible, add the Madeira, and bring to a boil over high heat. Boil until reduced by half. Mash the reserved squab livers into the sauce and cook for 30 seconds longer. They will thicken the sauce. Add the remaining tablespoon of butter and the split olives. Taste to adjust the seasonings, adding more lemon juice, if needed. Spoon the sauce over them. Serve extra stuffing with the squabs.

CHAPTER FOUR: **MEATS:**

BEEF, VEAL, LAMB, PORK, AND GAME

INTRODUCTION

Something wonderful is happening in some supermarket Meat departments: Along with familiar cases piled with cellophane-wrapped pieces of meat, new (or we should say "old-time") Service Meat departments are making a comeback. In consumer-oriented stores, butchers have come out from behind glass walls and stand ready to talk to you with counters full of unwrapped specialty cuts of familiar meats, "value-added" items (partially prepared or stuffed meats and poultry), and unfamiliar game meats. Customers need personalized—not automated—attention to decipher the many variables that can save time and money. When questions are answered and recipes offered, sales are brisker.

Butchering has changed over the years, and so has the meat in your market. The beef and pork industries are breeding leaner animals for our health-conscious society. Animals arrive already cut up. Beef is no longer aged as it once was, making the question "Can I get a good steak anymore?" as valid in a supermarket as in a butcher shop. The answer varies with each market. Some markets sell great steaks.

Buying Meat

Topical concerns relating to meat include whether to buy grass-fed animals raised without hormones, and how our meat stacks up to imported products, such as New Zealand versus American lamb.

In answer to the first, I buy the best-quality, naturally raised beef I can get. I do not, however, invest in premium, superfat beef because I don't think I need the extra fat. Yes, it can make it more tender, but at several dollars more a pound, I'll let my jaw get some exercise.

When buying lamb, imported animals are usually less costly. However, American lambs are typically larger and when making rack of lamb, for example, it is the eye of the chops that is eaten. If all I get is a bite from each, I am paying a hefty premium for that pleasure. Personally, I think American lamb is sweeter, as well.

An aware shopper with basic meat-buying skills is ahead of the game. Food safety is a primary concern of most markets. They make it a rule to use only USDA-inspected meat, which means the animal was healthy and was processed in a sanitary packing house. In general, markets only sell the top two grades of meat: prime and choice, the former having a higher percentage of internal fat. The overwhelming percent of this goes to restaurants.

There are some other important facts you should ascertain on your own for economical and healthful buying.

Consider the Cut

Find out either from the label or the butcher *which primal section* of the animal the piece of meat comes from. Especially in beef and pork, cuts from the working parts—the chuck, shank, brisket, plate, flank, and round—are leaner, tougher, and more sinewy than the more tender rib, loin, and sirloin from the middle or support section of the animal. Since the muscles in this area do little work, they develop more marbling (internal fat) to keep the meat moist and juicy.

Which part of the animal the meat comes from should determine *the most appropriate cooking methods:*

Tougher cuts become tender with slow, *moist cooking:* braising, stewing, or simmering, or by being marinated first.

Tender cuts should be cooked with *dry heat* methods: broiling, frying, or barbecuing. But, since there is no additional moisture added to the meat, overcooking (past medium) is likely to produce dry meat. This is especially important with newer varieties of beef and pork bred to be lower in fat and cholesterol. For maximum flavor and juiciness, cook them to a lesser degree of doneness.

Pork is bred far leaner today to meet the demand for less fat in our diet. Because of this, cooking pork to a high internal temperature will dry the meat out more easily. Years ago, pork was cooked until the internal temperature was 180°F to be sure the trichinosis bacteria were killed. With improved technology, it is now safe to eat pork at 140°F.

Lamb is butchered young, so the locomotive parts do not have a chance to toughen and most parts may be cooked with dry heat.

Veal never develops any internal fat to moisten it, so it is best cooked with moisture (except the thinnest cutlets).

Look at the Meat

Once you settle on a specific cut, look at the piece of meat itself.

Meat needs some *marbling* for tenderness and flavor. The marbling should run evenly through the meat. On the other hand, a thick layer of fat on the outside is not just unhealthful, it is wasteful. Why should you pay for what will be discarded? Meat should be well trimmed, including tails from tougher adjoining muscle groups, which will not cook the same as the whole.

Excess *bones* are another problem, especially with packaged meat. When you cannot see the underside, gently press the meat to feel for concealed or wider bones or gristle underneath.

Color may be an indicator of age and tenderness. The older an animal gets, the darker the meat becomes. Young beef is bright red. Top-quality veal should be whitish pink—not dark rose. However, exposure to air and packaging can affect color, as well.

If the meat is wrapped, be certain that the *package is sealed.* Exposure to air leads to bacteria formation and quality deterioration.

Read the Label

One of the best sources of information about the meat you plan to purchase is the label already glued on the wrapped meat or affixed once the butcher weighs it. It tells you:

✓ the weight

✓ the price per pound

✓ the cost of this package

✓ the kind of meat

✓ the primal part

✓ the specific cut of meat

✓ the date it must be sold by

Most markets also include proper handling techniques, the internal temperature at which to cook it for safety, and storage guidelines on the label.

Other sources of information about meat cookery:

Butchers can tell you about cooking times and temperatures, give you recipe ideas, and may suggest a less expensive or more appropriate cut of meat for a specific recipe.

Printed information cards and pamphlets are now frequently displayed on the meat cases. Pick them up for tips on cooking new recipes, nutritional information, and entertaining ideas.

Cookbooks and magazines are sold in many markets.

Safe Handling

Since meat is extremely perishable, proper handling is vital. Choose meat after staples and other less-fragile items.

Don't leave meat in a warm car for extended periods of time.

Refrigerate meat in the coolest part of the refrigerator as soon after arriving home as possible. If it is very warm, first put it in the freezer for about 15 minutes to cool it down fast.

Different cuts of meat vary in the length of time they remain fresh. As a general rule, the smaller the cut, the more perishable it is, because there is more surface-to-air exposure. Ground meats and organ meats should be used within a day or two.

If the meat will not be used within the time suggested (see tips throughout this chapter), then wrap and freeze it until ready to use. For short periods, it may be frozen in the store packaging if it is sealed.

Defrost meat on a plate in the refrigerator. Be sure to wash any plate used for defrosting or marinating before reusing it to serve cooked meat.

Cook It Right

For cooking meat to perfection, a reliable thermometer is a must. I like the instant-read ones that often are merchandised in the Meat departments. One ruined roast costs more in money and inconvenience than the price of a good thermometer.

One final bit of advice: Remember to remove meat or poultry from the oven when the internal temperature measures five to ten degrees below the desired temperature. Once outside, food will continue to cook those last degrees before serving. This is called the "carry-over cooking time," and it can make the difference between perfection and a near miss.

Hamburger Hints

Ground beef is sold in every supermarket. Because it is reasonably priced, it is used in many dishes from tacos to meat sauce. While "hamburger" is a good choice in most supermarkets, there are some facts you should be aware of for using ground beef to its best advantage.

What's in a Name?

The name "hamburger," or "chopped," or "ground" beef means that this product is made from 100 percent beef. No water, binders, or fillers may be added. It must be at least 70 percent lean meat.

How Lean Is Lean?

Many markets now label their ground beef by the percentage of fat in the mixture, i.e., diet or superlean (8 to 10 percent). The level of fat is not regulated by the USDA. It is determined by the market itself, so the name might be confusing, and the ratio of lean to fat differs from one market to the next. Other markets designate which primal part of the animal the meat comes from, such as the round or chuck, assuming that the customer knows which cut is less fatty. Still another practice markets use is to grind the trimmings and less popular parts of the animal with enough fat to make the determined ratio of fat to lean.

Which Is the Best Choice?

There is more than one "best" choice, depending on how you use ground meat. For strict fat-controlled diets, the leanest meat obviously has the least amount of fat. *But* since fat also gives flavor and moisture to meat, super-lean meat may easily become dry and crumbly, especially if it is overcooked. It is best broiled to no more than medium-rare.

Ground meat with a higher fat content is less expensive. If the meat is drained after it has been cooked, the actual amount of internal fat is very similar, although the quantity of meat is somewhat smaller. A hamburger made this way will be juicier and have more flavor.

Where ground meat is well cooked and well drained, for meat sauce or tacos, even the least-expensive meat is a satisfactory choice.

How to Store Ground Meat

As discussed in the introduction to this chapter, the smaller the cut of meat, the more surface area there is to be contaminated, and the quicker it should be used. All ground meats (beef, veal, pork, turkey, lamb) are highly susceptible to bacteria. Ask when the meat was ground. It should be sold within twenty-four hours. And don't buy an opened package.

Once home, store meat in the coldest part of your refrigerator for up to two days. If the original container is torn or damaged, rewrap the meat in airtight packaging. If you will not use the meat within two days, freeze it and defrost at a later date. It will keep for up to three months.

If ground meat is used for hamburgers, freeze it in patties. It will lose less moisture when defrosted. Otherwise, smaller packages are still better to prevent large ice crystals from forming within the block of meat. Always defrost meat slowly in the refrigerator with a plate underneath.

Because there is a high risk of bacterial infection from ground meat, *do not* eat raw ground meat or steak tartare. For health's sake, it is wiser to select the piece of meat from a Service Meat counter, if available, or buy it from a butcher, have it ground, and use it quickly.

And, don't forget to look at other ground meats. Lamb is wonderful for many ethnic recipes. Pork adds great flavor. Ground veal, turkey, and chicken are lower-calorie alternatives to beef.

MY DYNAMITE, ALL-TIME FAVORITE CHILI

Serves 6 to 8

This heady Southwestern chili is great over rice, but look at the unique way of serving it that follows this recipe. It raises chili to new heights. In my house, we make huge quantities of chili, often with venison, which is also appearing more and more in good markets. The chili is then frozen in serving-size portions, so the kids can defrost it in the microwave. They like it ladled over toasted sourdough bread or baked potatoes.

3 tablespoons vegetable oil
1 large onion, peeled and finely chopped
2 large cloves garlic, peeled and minced
1 jalapeño pepper, seeds and membranes removed, minced (optional)
1 1/4 pounds well-trimmed beef round or venison, cut into 1/2-inch cubes
3/4 pound ground pork
1 28-ounce can crushed Italian tomatoes
3 tablespoons red wine vinegar
2 tablespoons + 2 teaspoons ground hot or mild chili powder, or to taste
2 tablespoons ground cumin
2 tablespoons Worcestershire sauce
1/2 teaspoon ground red pepper, or more, to taste
1 large green bell pepper, seeds and membranes removed, and chopped
2 teaspoons salt, or to taste
Freshly ground black pepper to taste
1 10-once can red kidney beans, drained
3 tablespoons *masa harina* or fine cornmeal, mixed with a little water into a smooth paste (see note)

1. Heat the oil in a very large skillet or Dutch oven over medium heat. Stir in the onion, garlic, jalapeño pepper, and cook, stirring occasionally, until the onion is tender, about 5 minutes.
2. Add the cubed and ground meat, and continue cooking until the meat is no longer pink, about 4 to 5 minutes. Stir in the tomatoes, vinegar, chili powder, cumin, Worcestershire sauce, ground red pepper, bell pepper, salt, and pepper. Bring to a boil, then reduce the heat to medium and cook, uncovered, stirring occasionally, until the meat is tender, about 45 minutes to an hour. The stew should be fairly thick.
3. Stir in the kidney beans and the *masa harina* and heat through. Taste and adjust the seasonings.

NOTE: If your market does not have *masa harina* or cornmeal with the Mexican foods or other flours, the chili may be thickened by cooking it longer.

Did you know? "Chili" refers to dishes made with meat, seasonings, and chilies. A "chile pepper" refers to the varieties of pepper, which range from mild to fiery hot.

INDIVIDUAL CHILI STRUDELS

Serves 8

12 leaves phyllo

6 tablespoons unsalted butter, melted

1 recipe My Dynamite, All-Time Favorite Chili (page 129), chilled

1 cup (4 ounces) coarsely shredded Monterey Jack cheese

Tomato wedges, black olives, sliced green onions, and chopped jalpeño peppers, for garnish

These individual strudels are fun fare for a casual party. Since each roll is a single portion, they are perfect for a buffet table. Prepare them ahead of time (they even freeze) and add the cheese and festive garnishes of tomato wedges, black olives, sliced green onions, and chopped jalapeño peppers (found in the International section) just before serving. Look at page 22 for tips about working with phyllo.

1. Preheat your oven to 400°F. Grease a 15 1/2-by-10 1/2-by-1-inch jelly-roll pan.
2. Lay 1 leaf of phyllo on a towel with the long edge in front of you, and brush lightly with melted butter. Put a second leaf on top, and brush again with butter. Top with a third leaf (do not brush with butter), and cut stack in half crosswise.
3. Spoon about 3/4 cup chili along the near edge of each phyllo stack, leaving about a 1-inch border uncovered on each side.
4. Holding the towel corners nearest you, flip the towel up, causing the phyllo to roll over on itself and cover the filling. (You can do both stacks with one flip.) Turn the edges in over the filling and continue to roll one strudel at a time to the end. Put strudels in the pan, seam side down. Repeat 3 more times with the remaining chili and phyllo. Brush the strudel with melted butter and bake in the middle of the oven for 12 to 14 minutes, or until the strudels are crisp and golden brown.
5. Transfer to an oven-safe serving platter or leave in the pan. Sprinkle on the cheese and bake until it melts, about 3 minutes. Remove and serve strudels garnished with tomatoes, olives, onions, and jalapeños.

BELGIAN BEEF STEW WITH BEER AND SAUERKRAUT

Serves 6

A flavorful, slowly cooked stew is satisfying and economical. Many robust Belgian recipes use beer as the simmering liquid for the distinct malty taste it adds while tenderizing the meat. In this dish, the flavors of the beer, tangy sauerkraut—which mellows during the long cooking—olives, and a touch of brown sugar, blend together into a hearty winter dish. Since stews taste better when made the day before, this one is ideal for a busy household when preparing ahead is necessary.

Beef stew meat is readily available in your market. Choose cubes with a small amount of fat. Beef cut from the round is more expensive and leaner than stew meat from the chuck. Slow cooking tenderizes the meat as the excess fat melts and rises to the surface. The greater amount of fat given off by cheaper cuts results in less meat to serve. Stew meat should be refrigerated and used within 2 days of purchase. Otherwise, freeze it.

- 3 pounds lean stewing beef, cut into approximately $1\frac{1}{2}$-inch cubes
- Flour for dredging
- 3–4 tablespoons vegetable oil
- 2 large onions, peeled and thinly sliced
- 2 garlic cloves, peeled and minced
- Salt and freshly ground black pepper to taste
- $1\frac{1}{2}$ cups (1 12-ounce can) beer
- 2 pounds sauerkraut, rinsed and squeezed dry
- 2 tablespoons dark brown sugar
- 2 teaspoons marjoram
- 1 teaspoon celery seed
- 1 bay leaf
- $\frac{3}{4}$ cup pitted green olives, sliced
- 1 cup cream (optional)
- $\frac{1}{2}$ cup finely chopped flat-leaf parsley, to garnish

1. Preheat your oven to 325°F.
2. Dredge the meat in flour, patting to remove any excess. Heat 3 tablespoons of the oil in a heavy casserole with a cover or Dutch oven over medium heat until hot. Add only enough meat to cover the bottom of the pan without crowding and brown on all sides, scraping and turning the cubes so they don't burn. Remove cubes with a slotted spoon to a bowl, and continue until all meat is browned, adding more oil as needed.
3. If the oil has burned, wipe out the pan and add the remaining oil to the pot. When hot, add the onions and cook for 6 to 7 minutes, stirring frequently, until they are light brown and soft. Stir in the garlic.
4. Add the meat, salt, pepper, beer, sauerkraut, brown sugar, marjoram, celery seed, bay leaf, and olives, and stir to mix well. Cover and cook for $1\frac{1}{2}$ hours, stirring occasionally, or until the meat is tender. Remove the bay leaf, skim off any excess fat, and stir in the cream, if desired. Add the chopped parsley and serve with noodles or boiled potatoes. If preparing this ahead for freezing, do not add the cream until after defrosting.

Did you know? There are two ways of browning stew meat. One is to dredge the meat in flour and then brown it. The second is to dry the meat very well, and brown it in very hot oil. (See Hearty Veal Stew with Ham and Artichokes on page 137.) The light flour coating on the meat thickens the sauce slightly in both cases. Otherwise, the sauce may be boiled down to the right consistency.

OVEN-BARBECUED CHUCK STEAK

Serves 4

- 1 tablespoon vegetable oil
- 2 pounds blade (chuck) steak, patted dry on paper towels
- 1 cup Spicy Tomato Chili Barbecue Sauce (page 283) or purchased barbecue sauce
- 1 large onion, peeled and thinly sliced
- 8 ounces sunchokes, scrubbed and thinly sliced
- Freshly ground black pepper to taste
- 6 ounces white mushrooms, trimmed, wiped, and sliced

This fork-tender steak is easy to prepare and utilizes the reasonably priced blade (chuck) steak. Once the meat is seared, it is smothered with barbecue sauce, onions, sunchokes, and mushrooms and braised in a very slow oven. This is a good method to use with any of the less tender cuts of meat. Serve with cornbread and Mexican Coleslaw (page 21).

When buying meat with the bone in, be sure to let your fingers feel through the packages to find out how much bone there actually is. Turn the package over to look at the underside if you can see it. There can be a large difference from front to back and from one package to the next. Consider, too, how well the meat has been trimmed of fat. Remember that internal fat, or marbling, makes meat tender and adds flavor as it melts during cooking and can be skimmed off once the meat is cooked.

1. Preheat your oven to 250°F.
2. In a heavy ovenproof skillet or casserole, heat the vegetable oil until hot but not smoking. Add the meat and brown it on one side, about 3 minutes, then turn and brown the second side for the same amount of time.
3. Spread the barbecue sauce over the meat, add the onion, sunchokes, and a liberal amount of pepper. Cover with foil or a tight-fitting lid and bake for about 2 1/2 hours. Uncover, add the mushrooms, and allow the sauce to thicken for another 20 minutes, basting the meat occasionally.

NOTE: If using a larger or smaller cut of meat, estimate about 45 minutes cooking time for each 1/2 pound of meat *including* the final 20 minutes when the pan is uncovered.

Did you know? Sunchokes are also called Jerusalem artichokes and topinambour. They are from the sunflower family, hence their name. Scrub them before using. They do not need peeling. They will keep for at least a week in the refrigerator.

MARINATED STEAK TERIYAKI

Serves 5 to 6

This Asian-flavored barbecued beef teriyaki is seared on the outside and rare inside. The marinade tenderizes the meat and imparts flavor. I found that a couple of days in the spicy honey-soy-wine liquid improves the texture and taste of the meat; one day isn't enough. In general, marinating works best with thinner cuts of meat, chicken, and fish where the acidic liquid has a chance to penetrate. (This marinade, by the way, is equally wonderful for chicken breasts or shrimp.) Serve with boiled rice and sautéed snow peas and water chestnuts.

Flank steak is a very lean, economical cut since there is no waste. It keeps in the refrigerator for up to 5 days. Frozen airtight, these steaks last for 6 months providing the temperature remains at 0°F or below.

1/3 cup soy sauce
3 tablespoons red wine vinegar
1/4 cup honey
3/4 cup vegetable oil
2 chopped scallions, including the green parts
2 large cloves garlic, peeled and crushed
1 1/2 tablespoons ground ginger
1 1/2 teaspoons ground coriander seeds
2 teaspoons ground cumin
1 1/2 teaspoons ground cardamom
Freshly ground black pepper
3/4 cup pineapple juice
1/2 cup red wine
1 3/4- to 2-pound flank steak

1. Combine the soy sauce, vinegar, honey, and oil in a resealable plastic bag. Add the scallions, garlic, ginger, coriander, cumin, cardamom, and black pepper. Pour in the pineapple juice and red wine. Add the flank steak, seal, refrigerate for 2 days, turning occasionally.
2. Position the barbecue rack about 4 inches from the fire. Heat the barbecue. When the charcoal briquettes are gray and hot, remove the steak, pat dry with paper towels, and grill for about 5 to 7 minutes on the first side, turn and cook for 5 or 6 minutes. Remove from the grill, let stand for 1 or 2 minutes, then cut into thin diagonal slices across the grain of the meat. For the broiler, preheat the broiler pan for at least 10 minutes. Cook the meat close to the heat for the same length of time, leaving the door slightly ajar.

Did you know? When marinating foods, put them in heavy resealable plastic bags. They'll require less marinade and take up less space in the refrigerator. Turning the food is easy, too.

STEAK 'N' STOUT

Serves 4

- 1 12-ounce bottle stout or dark beer
- 1/4 cup firmly packed dark brown sugar
- 2 tablespoons cider vinegar
- 1 clove garlic, peeled and split
- 1 bay leaf
- 2 1/2–3 pounds sirloin, porterhouse or T-bone steak, bone in steak, about 1 1/4 inches thick
- 3 tablespoons unsalted butter
- 1 tablespoon vegetable oil
- 4 large yellow onions, peeled and thinly sliced
- Salt and freshly ground black pepper to taste

I love grilled steaks that are crunchy on the outside and deep pink inside. As this steak sears on the barbecue, the stout–brown sugar marinade reduces over mounds of onions into a caramelized glaze. Served together, it is a superb summer treat.

There are two reasons for buying meat with the bone in: The cooked meat is juicier and more flavorful, and it is less expensive. When selecting cuts of meat with a bone in, look carefully at the ratio of bone to meat and how well the meat is trimmed. Sometimes a large "tail" is left on a porterhouse or T-bone. That piece is wasteful, since it is less tender than the rest of the steak. Sirloin steaks cost less than steaks cut from the short loin (porterhouse, club, T-bone). Although less tender, they are fine in this barbecued version, especially since the meat is served sliced.

1. Combine the stout, brown sugar, vinegar, garlic, and bay leaf in a large resealable plastic bag. Add the steak, seal, and marinate for at least 1 hour, turning after 1/2 hour. (The meat may marinate several hours or overnight.)
2. Meanwhile, melt the butter and oil in a very large, heavy skillet over medium-high heat. Stir in the onions and cook for 30 minutes, stirring often, until the onions are wilted and lightly colored. Add about 1/2 teaspoon salt, or to taste, and freshly ground black pepper and set aside. (This part of the onion preparation may be done ahead.)
3. Light a charcoal fire and position the rack about 3 inches from the heat. When the briquettes are very hot, remove the steak from the marinade, blot dry, and cook for about 9 to 10 minutes on the first side. Turn and cook the second side for another 4 to 5 minutes for medium-rare.
4. While the steak is grilling, add 1 cup of the marinade to the onions and turn the heat to high. Boil until the liquid evaporates, stirring often, about 6 to 8 minutes.
5. When the steak is done, transfer it to a wooden slicing board, season with salt and pepper, and let it stand for 2 to 3 minutes, then slice across the grain. Serve the onions on top or as a bed under the meat slices.

Did you know? To test the heat of a charcoal barbecue, put your hand palm-side down at cooking level. If you can keep it there for 2 seconds, the temperature is hot; 3 seconds is medium hot; 4 seconds is medium; and 5 seconds is low. Thicker foods require slower cooking temperatures to prevent burning.

Did you know? Winter is a good time to buy and freeze steaks if you have the space, since they are less expensive than in the popular summer barbecue season. Wrap the steaks well, mark the date of purchase, and the amount of meat. They will last for at least 6 months.

SAUTÉED CALVES LIVER LEBANESE STYLE

Serves 2

This is one of the most delicious ways I have ever tasted liver. I learned it from a Lebanese friend from Beirut. Thin strips are marinated in a garlic-mint mixture for about half an hour and then quickly sautéed. Because the cooking time is so quick, all the minced garlic is only warmed through and never gets a chance to become bitter. I serve it over mashed potatoes or cooked orzo to catch every drop of tasty sauce.

Properly prepared, liver is very tender. Of all liver sold, calves liver has the most delicate flavor and is the most expensive. Some markets sell "baby beef liver" at a price between beef and calves liver. Butcher friends of mine tell me this is most often from a full-grown animal, so the higher price is not justified. Lamb livers taste almost identical to calves liver, and the price is usually half, so the savings are great. Select dark-red-colored pieces without any discolored spots.

1 tablespoon minced garlic (3 large cloves)

1 teaspoon salt

1/4 cup olive oil

1 teaspoon dried mint leaves, crumbled

Freshly ground black pepper

8–10 ounces calves liver, cut into 1/2-inch-thick slices

2 tablespoons fresh lemon juice

1. In a medium-sized bowl, mash the garlic and salt together with the back of a spoon. Stir in the olive oil, mint leaves, and plenty of pepper.
2. Cut the liver into 1-by-2-inch pieces and add it to the garlic mixture, stirring to cover, and marinate for 30 minutes.
3. Heat a large, heavy skillet over medium-high heat. Add the liver-and-garlic mixture, stir, and cook just until the liver is cooked through, about 1 1/2 minutes. Remove from the heat, stir in the lemon juice, and serve at once.

VEAL AND SAUSAGE MEATBALLS

Makes 4 to 5 dozen meatballs

- 2/3 pound ground veal
- 3 sweet Italian pork sausages (about 12 ounces), casings removed
- 1 3/4-inch slice stale Italian bread, moistened with milk and squeezed dry
- 2 eggs
- 1/4 cup freshly grated Parmesan cheese
- 3 tablespoons minced flat-leaf parsley
- 1/2 teaspoon salt
- 1/4 teaspoon freshly grated nutmeg
- Freshly ground black pepper
- 1 cup very fine stale or toasted white bread crumbs
- Olive oil for frying
- Lemon slices, flat-leaf parsley sprigs, cherry tomatoes, for garnish
- 1 recipe Caper Mayonnaise (page 277)

Using a mixture of pork and veal makes these meatballs delicious and juicy. Because they are chilled and then rolled in bread crumbs, they have a crunchy golden coating. Serve them on a platter with cherry tomatoes along with cocktails. Dip both meatballs and tomatoes in Caper Mayonnaise (see page 277). Without the coating, they may be cooked and added to tomato sauce for spaghetti or used for sandwiches.

For this recipe, I think that "sweet" sausages are a better combination with the other ingredients. "Hot" sausages contain pepper flakes, fennel seed, and other seasonings. But the choice is yours.

1. In the bowl of a food processor, combine the veal, sausage, Italian bread, eggs, Parmesan cheese, parsley, salt, nutmeg, and pepper and pulse just until well blended, or mix by hand. *Do not overprocess.* Scrape the meat into a bowl, cover, and refrigerate for at least 1 hour.
2. Pour the bread crumbs into a flat dish, shape the meat into 1-inch balls, and roll in the crumbs.
3. Pour the olive oil into a large, heavy skillet to a depth of 1/2 inch and heat over medium-high heat until very hot but not smoking. Add the meatballs slowly to keep the oil hot. Cook only as many as will comfortably fit in the bottom of the pan at one time without crowding until golden brown on all sides, about 5 to 7 minutes. Continue with the remaining meatballs. Remove with a slotted spoon and drain on paper towels. Meatballs may be prepared ahead and kept warm in a jelly-roll pan or pot in a 300°F oven for 30 minutes.
4. Serve the meatballs on a platter with Caper Mayonnaise for dipping. Garnish with lemon slices, parsley, and tomatoes. Once cooked, the meatballs may be refrigerated for several days or frozen.

Did you know? When preparing a dish with raw ground pork—such as meatballs, meat loaf, or any pâté—do not taste it raw for seasonings. Instead, heat a little oil in a skillet and cook a small amount of the meat mixture until it is browned and cooked through. Let it cool slightly and taste. Correct your seasonings accordingly.

Have you tried . . . Some fat-reduced breakfast sausages in the market are juicy and tasty and compare quite favorably with more traditional sausages.

HEARTY VEAL STEW WITH HAM AND ARTICHOKES

Serves 6

In this version of veal stew, ham, mushrooms, and artichoke hearts enhance the delicate taste and appearance of the dish. It's the kind of simple, comforting dish to make ahead and have ready on a cold night. It will keep for 2 days in the refrigerator or 3 months in the freezer. Serve with buttered noodles, parsleyed rice, or couscous.

By far the most reasonable and reliable veal in a market is stew meat cut from the chuck or round where slow, moist cooking usually produces fine results. Buying veal in the supermarket is sometimes risky because what is sold may actually be young beef. Real top-quality veal is "nature" veal—fed only on milk until it comes to market at about 4 months. The meat should be very pale whitish-pink—not red or gray—with a small amount of pure-white fat.

4 tablespoons olive or vegetable oil

3 pounds veal stew meat, cut into 2-inch cubes and patted very dry

1 large onion, peeled and coarsely chopped

1 large clove garlic, peeled and split

1 1/2 cups dry white wine

3/4 cup chicken stock

3 tablespoons finely chopped flat-leaf parsley

1 teaspoon dried thyme

Salt and freshly ground black pepper to taste

3 tablespoons unbleached all-purpose flour

6 ounces boiled ham, cut into 1/4-inch cubes

2 10-ounce packages frozen artichoke hearts, defrosted and patted dry

12 ounces small white mushrooms, wiped and quartered

1/3 cup cream (optional)

2 tablespoons finely chopped flat-leaf parsley, for garnish

1. Preheat your oven to 325°F.
2. Heat 3 tablespoons of the oil in a large, heavy skillet until almost smoking. Add just enough pieces of veal to cover the bottom of the skillet without crowding. Turn and brown on all sides. As the pieces brown, transfer them with a slotted spoon to a large, heavy Dutch oven or casserole.
3. Once the meat is browned, add the last tablespoon of oil to the skillet and when hot sauté the onion over medium heat until golden, 5 to 6 minutes. Add the garlic and cook for 30 seconds longer.
4. Pour the wine over the onions, turn the heat to high, and bring the liquid to a boil, scraping up all the browned bits from the bottom of the pan. Add the stock, parsley, thyme, salt and pepper, and let the liquid simmer for 5 minutes.
5. Turn the heat on under the Dutch oven. Season the veal with salt and a generous amount of black pepper. Sprinkle the flour over the veal, and toss to coat it evenly. Cook over medium heat for 1 to 2 minutes to brown the flour. Stir the wine-stock mixture into the veal, and bring the liquid to a simmer. Add the ham, cover the pot, and transfer to the oven for 1 hour 15 minutes.
6. Add the artichokes and mushrooms, stirring to cover the vegetables, and return the pot to the oven for an additional 30 minutes. The meat should be very tender. Remove the casserole form the oven. Slowly stir in the cream, if desired, and sprinkle on parsley to garnish.

Did you know? While many meats keep well in the refrigerator, store uncooked veal stew meat for a day or two at the longest, because it deteriorates quickly. If the surface starts to feel slightly sticky and you cannot use the meat right away, wipe the meat with vinegar and use within a day.

SAUTÉED VEAL CUTLETS WITH MUSTARD, CAPERS, AND PEPPERS

Serves 4

There is nothing more wonderful than juicy, tender veal cutlets with a scrumptious sauce or even just a little lemon juice squeezed on top. With vibrant red-pepper strips, Dijon mustard, and capers, the finished dish is not only well seasoned, but very colorful.

Alas, buying properly cut veal isn't always easy in a market. You need to use your eyes and ask questions, especially if the meat is already packaged. Besides being the palest pink color, a cutlet should be a solid piece of meat thinly sliced across the grain. If it is sliced lengthwise, you may be buying pieces with connecting membranes that when cooked will separate into different sections.

2 tablespoons unsalted butter

2 tablespoons vegetable oil

1-1 1/2 pounds boneless veal cutlets, sliced thin and pounded, if necessary

Flour for dredging

Salt and freshly ground black pepper to taste

1/2 cup dry vermouth

1 red bell pepper, peeled, seeds and membranes removed, cut into thin strips

2 tablespoons Dijon mustard

1/3 cup heavy or light cream

Salt and freshly ground black pepper to taste

2 tablespoons small capers, drained

1 tablespoon finely chopped flat-leaf parsley, for garnish

1. Heat the butter and oil in a large skillet over medium heat until very hot. Dust both sides of the cutlets in flour, shaking to remove the excess. (Do not stack the cutlets on top of one another, as they will become gummy and won't brown.)
2. Gently slide the cutlets in the hot fat one at a time. The fat should sizzle as each piece is added, so allow a little time in between to keep the fat hot. Sauté only as many pieces as will fit comfortably at one time until lightly browned on one side, then turn and cook the other side, about 1 to 2 minutes more, if the meat is cut very thin. As the cutlets are cooked, transfer them in a single layer to a heated platter in a warm oven. Season with salt and pepper. Repeat with the remaining veal, adding 1 tablespoon of fresh oil, if needed.
3. Discard extra fat. Over medium-high heat, add the vermouth to the skillet, scraping up any browned bits at the bottom of the pan, and stir for about 1 minute. Add the red pepper and cook 30 seconds. Adjust the heat to medium; stir in the mustard; then the cream, salt, and pepper; and cook for 1 to 2 minutes, taking care not to let the sauce boil. Stir in the capers, then return the cutlets to the pan, turn once, and serve on warm plates with the sauce spooned over them. Garnish with a little chopped parsley.

Did you know? The terms cutlets, medallions, scallops, and scallopini are confusing. Actually, they are often used interchangeably. While medallions are usually small (1 1/2-inch) circles of veal cut from the loin, the most expensive part, they may also be called "cutlets," or "scallops," or "scallopini," depending on the nationality of the butcher. Cutlets are usually cut from the different muscle groups in the leg.

For even cooking, the pieces should be about the same thickness. Flatten veal carefully. You don't want to make holes in the meat by brutally pounding it. Instead, gently spread the fibers by striking and pushing the center (or thickest part) outward with a meat pounder or the heel of your hand.

MOROCCAN LAMB IN PEPPERS

Serves 4

Use beautiful colored bell peppers and interchange the tops for these individual serving containers filled with an exotic combination of lamb, almonds, dried fruits, and spices.

We often read the term "spring lamb" in this country; it is used to indicate a young animal. In fact, with modern breeding, we can buy very tender young lamb almost year-round, since the shepherd hardly every walks down the side of the mountain anymore. Another excellent option is frozen New Zealand lamb. The flavor may be slightly stronger than American lamb, but the meat is sweet and the price is often less than that of fresh lamb. Properly stored, large cuts of fresh lamb will keep for 5 to 6 days in the refrigerator. Stew meat should be used within 2 to 3 days. Cook thawed meat within a day.

- 4 large bell peppers (about ½ pound each), red, yellow, or green
- 1 pound ground lamb
- ½ cup drained and chopped canned Italian tomatoes
- ½ cup dark raisins, soaked 20 minutes in warm water and drained
- ⅓ cup coarsely chopped pitted prunes
- ¼ cup slivered blanched almonds
- 2 tablespoons vegetable oil
- ½ pound very well trimmed lamb stew meat, cut into ¾-inch cubes, patted dry
- 1 small onion, peeled and finely chopped
- 2 cloves garlic, peeled and minced
- ¼ cup orange juice
- 2 tablespoons finely chopped flat-leaf parsley
- 1 teaspoon ground ginger
- 1 teaspoon ground cumin
- ¼ teaspoon ground red pepper
- 1 ½ teaspoons salt, or to taste
- Freshly ground black pepper to taste
- 1 egg, beaten

1. Preheat your oven to 325°F.
2. Cut off the stem end of the peppers, about ½ inch from the top, and remove the seeds and white membranes. If the peppers do not stand up straight, slice a very thin layer off the bottom, as well. Save the tops and set aside.
3. In a large bowl combine the ground lamb, tomatoes, raisins, prunes, and almonds. Set aside.
4. In a large, heavy skillet, heat 1 ½ tablespoons of the vegetable oil over medium-high heat until hot. Add the lamb cubes and brown lightly on all sides, about 2 to 3 minutes. With slotted spoon, transfer the cubes to the bowl with the ground lamb mixture.
5. Add the onions to the skillet and sauté over medium heat just until the onions are wilted, about 1 ½ to 2 minutes. Stir in the garlic, cook for 30 seconds, then add the orange juice. Bring the mixture to a boil, stir up all browned cooking bits, and cook until the liquid has almost evaporated. Scrape the onions into the meat mixture, add the parsley, ginger, cumin, red pepper, salt and pepper, and beaten egg, and mix just until blended.
6. Brush the peppers and tops with the remaining ½ tablespoon of oil and put them in an 8- or 9-inch pie plate or round baking dish. Divide the filling among the peppers, replace the tops, and bake until the peppers are tender when pierced with a fork and the meat juices run clear, about 1 hour to 1 hour 10 minutes. Remove, let stand about 5 to 10 minutes, and serve.

Did you know? When working with ground meats for pâtés, meat loaves, and mixtures for stuffing peppers, the texture will be lighter and better if the ingredients are quickly mixed just until blended.

JAVANESE LAMB STEW WITH PEANUT SAUCE

Serves 6 to 8

The combination of peanut butter and molasses in this sauce is surprising. But, try it. I think you will be pleased with both the delicious results and the reasonable cost. Served in a large earthenware bowl, this lamb stew is inviting on winter buffet tables. Serve with steamed white or brown rice, or couscous, and Sautéed Sugar Snaps, Radishes, and Cherry Tomatoes (page 37).

Like most stews, the flavors improve with gentle cooking and reheating—a boon to do-ahead party planning. Another entertaining idea: Double the recipe and freeze half for another night when unexpected guests arrive or you don't feel like cooking. (Be sure to check the Strategy Pages preceding Chapter 9, "Keeping Frozen Food at Its Best.")

3–4 tablespoons vegetable oil

3 pounds well-trimmed lamb stew meat, cut into 1 ½-inch cubes

2 large cloves garlic, peeled and crushed

6 tablespoons soy sauce

1 ½ tablespoons dark molasses

½ cup smooth peanut butter

⅓ cup dark brown sugar

¼ cup fresh lemon juice

¼ teaspoon ground red pepper

Salt and freshly ground black pepper to taste

½–¾ cup water

½ cup chopped peanuts, lightly toasted

3 tablespoons chopped cilantro or chopped flat-leaf parsley, for garnish

1. In a large, heavy casserole, heat 2 tablespoons of the oil over medium-high heat until hot. Add lamb to cover the bottom of the pan without crowding and brown all sides. Remove pieces with a slotted spoon to a bowl. Continue until all the meat is browned, adding additional oil as needed.
2. Add the garlic and, after a few seconds, the soy sauce, molasses, peanut butter, brown sugar, lemon juice, red pepper, salt and pepper. Stir, scraping up any browned cooking bits, and mix well. Stir in ½ cup of the water. Return the meat to the casserole, cover, and simmer until it is very tender, stirring occasionally, about 40 to 45 minutes. If the sauce becomes too thick, add the remaining water. Before serving, stir in the chopped peanuts and sprinkle on the cilantro or parsley.

Did you know? Peanut butter is sold in every supermarket. However, all peanut butters are not the same. Aside from chunky and smooth, some peanut and other nut butters are made the "old-fashioned" way—simply grinding the nuts with or without the addition of salt. Modern peanut butter has salt, sugar, plus saturated and polyunsaturated fats. An opened jar will remain fresh for about 3 months if stored in a cool place. "Natural" peanut butter should be refrigerated.

The good news: Peanut butter has no cholesterol.

BRAISED LAMB SHANKS WITH GLAZED LEMON AND ORANGE SLICES

Serves 4

These slowly cooked lamb shanks are succulent and tender. The meat literally falls off the bone into the slightly sweet tomato sauce flavored with citrus slices, honey, and cinnamon. This dish is ideal for preparing ahead of time as the flavors improve with reheating.

Lamb shanks are readily found in your market. Even through the plastic wrap you can check that the bones have a little red in them; that lets you know that they are fresh and that the animal was not too old. As shanks come from the front legs, the working part of the animal, they have lots of connective tissue, which is tough. With moist cooking (braising), this breaks down and adds a rich flavor to the broth.

2 tablespoons olive oil
4 1- to 1 1/4-pound lamb shanks, patted dry
1 medium onion, peeled and finely chopped
1 large lemon, thinly sliced
1 navel orange, thinly sliced
1 28-ounce can Italian tomatoes, drained and chopped
3/4 cup beef stock
2/3 cup hearty red wine
1/4 cup honey
1 stick cinnamon
Salt and freshly ground black pepper to taste
1 tablespoon finely chopped fresh mint, for garnish

1. Preheat your oven to 325°F.
2. In a large, heavy casserole, heat the oil until almost smoking over medium-high heat. Add the lamb shanks and brown on all sides. This will take about 15 minutes.
3. Stir in the onion, adjust the heat to medium, and cook until the onion is wilted and a pale golden color, about 4 to 5 minutes.
4. Add the lemon and orange, tomatoes, stock, wine, honey, cinnamon, salt, and pepper, and stir to blend. Bring the liquid to a boil, cover the casserole, and transfer to the oven. Cook until very tender, about 1 hour and 45 minutes.
5. Remove the cover, skim off the fat, and return the pot to the oven, partially covered, for another 15 minutes, turning the shanks a couple of times during this time. Serve over mashed potatoes, pasta, or bulgur, with a little mint on top.

Did you know? When buying very bony meats such as lamb shanks or short ribs, figure on about 1 pound per serving, or slightly less if you wish to serve about 4-ounce portions. For bone-in roasts and steaks, up to 1/2 pound per serving is the right amount. When selecting shanks, choose those of a uniform size for even cooking time.

RACK OF LAMB PERSILLADE

Serves 2

- 1 rack of lamb (approximately 1 1/2 pounds), trimmed with the chine bone removed
- 1 tablespoon olive or vegetable oil
- 1/3 cup homemade toasted bread crumbs
- 2 tablespoons finely chopped flat-leaf parsley
- 1 small clove garlic, peeled and finely minced
- 1/4 teaspoon salt
- Freshly ground black pepper
- 1 1/2 tablespoons Dijon mustard
- 2 tablespoons unsalted butter, melted

Rack of lamb is such a festive dish and so easy to make. It is as simple to cook 6 racks as one, if you have the pan and oven space. The meat should come out of the oven slightly undercooked, as the "carryover cooking time" continues the roasting process for another 5 to 10 minutes before carving. Remember, you will need help carving the racks into chops if you are serving individual plates. And, those plates need to be warm. Serve with Those Potatoes! (page 40) and fresh asparagus or Creamed Spinach (page 311).

Racks of lamb are expensive, so look carefully at what you are buying and make a friend of the butcher. Have him help you select racks that have a large eye (center portion), since almost all the fat needs to be cut off. The mustard and flavored bread crumbs in this recipe seal in the juices. The lamb is so juicy and delicious, I serve it without a sauce. If you would like a sauce, Béarnaise Sauce (page 207) is a classic.

1. Preheat your oven to 400°F.
2. Make sure the rack of lamb is well trimmed (Frenched) and that all excess fat has been removed. Brush with oil and put it fat-side down in a heavy, low baking dish in the preheated oven for 15 minutes.
3. Meanwhile, combine the bread crumbs, parsley, garlic, salt, and pepper in a small bowl. Turn the rack over, brush with mustard, then apply the bread crumb mixture with a cupping motion of your hand. Drizzle the melted butter over the crumbs and cook for 10 to 12 minutes for medium-rare meat. Remove from the oven, let it stand 3 to 4 minutes, then slice into chops and serve.

Did you know? The term "Frenched" in meat cookery means that part of the bone is exposed. A whole leg of lamb may also be prepared this way. While some people put paper "panties," sometimes found in the Paper Goods section, on their racks to make them look fancier, I prefer them plain, since the paper often seems to get soggy.

NOISETTES OF LAMB FLORENTINE

Serves 8

This is a grand dish that befits a special occasion. Juicy morsels of lamb on sautéed spinach and toasted croutons are topped with green peppercorn cream sauce. Serve with glazed carrots and Cauliflower and Potato Purée with Parmesan (page 25) or steamed baby vegetables.

It's important to have a butcher prepare the meat ahead of time for you. While boneless rib chops are the most elegant choice for this dish, noisettes may be prepared from the less costly sirloin (see note).

FOR THE CROUTONS:

8 slices firm white bread, cut into 3-inch circles

6 tablespoons unsalted butter, melted

FOR THE SPINACH:

2 pounds fresh spinach, stems removed, washed and lightly shaken

Pinch of salt

3 tablespoons unsalted butter

1 clove garlic, peeled and minced

FOR THE LAMB:

3 tablespoons unsalted butter

1 1/2 tablespoons vegetable oil

8 noisettes of lamb, about 1 1/4 inches thick, patted dry

Salt and freshly ground black pepper to taste

FOR THE SAUCE:

2 tablespoons finely chopped shallots

3/4 cup dry vermouth

1 cup heavy cream

1/4 cup green peppercorns packed in vinegar or brine, rinsed and drained

2 tablespoons finely chopped flat-leaf parsley, for garnish

1. Prepare the croutons: Preheat your oven or toaster oven to 350°F.
2. Brush both sides of the bread with melted butter. Bake in a flat pan in the preheated oven until browned, about 10 to 12 minutes on each side. Keep warm.
3. For the spinach: Cook the spinach and salt in a large pot over medium-high heat until tender, about 5 to 7 minutes. Drain but do not squeeze. Melt 3 tablespoons of butter in a medium-sized saucepan, add the garlic, and shake for several seconds. Add the spinach and sauté, stirring occasionally, for 2 minutes. Season with salt. Remove from the heat and set aside.
4. For the lamb: Melt 3 tablespoons of butter with the oil in a large, heavy skillet over medium-high heat. Add the noisettes and cook, turning once, about 4 to 5 minutes on each side for medium-rare. Season generously with salt and pepper. Transfer to a heated platter and keep warm in a turned-off oven.
5. Prepare the sauce: Discard all but about 1 tablespoon of fat from the skillet used to cook the lamb. Add the shallots and sauté until soft over medium-high heat, about 3 minutes. Pour in the vermouth, turn the heat to high, and bring the liquid to a boil, scraping up any browned bits. Boil until reduced by half. Add the cream and peppercorns, crushing the peppercorns with the back of a spoon, and cook until thickened, about 3 minutes.
6. For the final assembly: Put the croutons on 8 heated dinner plates. Reheat the spinach for 1 minute over high heat, then spoon it on the croutons. Lay the noisettes on the spinach, spoon on generous tablespoons of sauce, sprinkle on parsley, and serve.

NOTE: Have the butcher prepare the noisettes from 2 boned rib chops, well trimmed and tied together, or from a boneless sirloin. Remove all fat and tie each one into a neat circle. Noisettes should weigh about 1/3 pound. Flatten them gently with the palm of your hand before cooking.

JOANNA'S COUNTRY PÂTÉ

Serves 8

1 1/2 pounds lean ground pork
8 ounces ground pork fat
8 ounces ground veal
1/3 cup chopped flat-leaf parsley
1/2 cup minced shallots (about 3 or 4 large)
2 large cloves garlic, peeled and minced
3 eggs, beaten
1 teaspoon dried thyme leaves
1/4 teaspoon ground nutmeg
1/4 cup shelled pistachios
4 ounces smoked ham or Canadian bacon, cut into 1/4-inch dice
10 juniper berries, slightly crushed
1 1/4 tablespoons salt, or to taste
Freshly ground black pepper
1/3 cup Madeira
1/3 cup brandy
16 ounces fatback, sliced 1/8-inch thick, simmered 2 minutes in water, drained, and patted dry or 14 ounces sliced bacon
2 bay leaves
Cornichons (small gherkins)

I have always loved pâtés, especially for picnics with a crusty baguette, Dijon mustard, and a bottle of hearty red wine. This one reminds me of some of the rustic, garlicky versions you find in the French countryside. The trick to keeping a pâté moist and flavorful is not to weight it too heavily when it comes out of the oven. Otherwise, you squeeze out the moisture and seasonings.

1. Preheat your oven to 350°F.
2. Combine the pork, pork fat, veal, parsley, shallots, garlic, eggs, thyme, nutmeg, pistachios, ham, juniper berries, salt, pepper, Madeira, and brandy in a large bowl.
3. Sauté a small amount of the mixture in a skillet until cooked through. When cooled, taste for seasonings and adjust remaining mixture as needed. Pâtés should be highly seasoned.
4. Line a 9-by-5-by-3-inch loaf pan or pâté mold with the fatback or bacon, draping half of the slices over the edge to be used in covering the top of the pâté. If using bacon, line the pan with half the bacon and use the remainder to cover the pâté.
5. Spoon the meat mixture into the mold, add the bay leaves, and fold the fatback over to cover the top. Add additional slices of fatback or bacon, if needed. Cover with a double layer of heavy foil and punch 2 holes to let steam escape.
6. Put the mold in a large pan and fill it with boiling water to a level halfway up the side of the pâté. Bake for 1 hour and 45 minutes. When done, the juices will run clear.
7. Remove the pan from the oven. Cover the pâté with a piece of cardboard or a second pâté mold or loaf pan the same size as the first. Distribute about 1 to 1 1/2 pounds of weight evenly over the pâté. Cool for 2 hours, then refrigerate until cold. Once cold, remove the pâté from the mold, wrap in plastic wrap, and let it rest for 5 to 7 days before serving to develop the flavors.
8. Before serving, let the pâté come to room temperature. Wipe off any congealed juices and remove the pork fat, if desired. When presenting the pâté whole, cut a few slices and put them on bread or crackers. Serve with cornichons, Dijon mustard, crackers, and French bread.

Did you know? The difference between salt pork and fatback is that there are some lean streaks of meat in salt pork and it is brine cured. Fatback has no lean meat, and it is cured in salt. Fatback is actually saltier than salt pork. They are generally sold side by side in Cryovac packages. You can use them pretty much interchangeably, remembering to blanch the pieces to remove some of the salt.

PORK CUTLETS FOR FALL

Serves 8

Pork makes me think of cold-weather dining. Here, boneless chops are served with a sauce blending other wintry flavors: prunes, cranberries, chestnuts, and port.

To save money, buy chops in late summer—when they are usually cheaper—and freeze them. They will keep for up to 4 months. Store fresh pork chops in the coldest part of the refrigerator and use within 2 to 3 days.

2 cups canned or jarred whole unsweetened chestnuts or freshly roasted, if available

1 1/2 cups tawny port

1 1/2 cups pitted prunes, each chopped in six pieces

1 cup cranberries

1 cup orange juice

8 boneless center-cut pork chops, 1 inch thick (about 4 to 5 ounces each), patted dry

Flour for dredging

2 tablespoons unsalted butter

1 tablespoon vegetable oil

Salt and freshly ground black pepper to taste

1/2 cup finely chopped shallots

3/4 cup beef stock

Julienned orange rind, 4 cranberries split in half, and 1 tablespoon finely chopped flat-leaf parsley, for garnish

1. Simmer the chestnuts in the port until just tender, about 10 minutes. Set aside to cool. With a fork, break the chestnuts into coarse pieces, add the prunes, and mix.
2. Meanwhile, in a medium-sized saucepan, simmer the cranberries in the orange juice until softened and split, about 5 to 7 minutes. Add to the chestnut mixture.
3. Lightly dredge the pork in flour, patting to remove any excess. In a heavy skillet large enough to hold all the meat comfortably, melt the butter and oil over medium heat. Add the cutlets, cook for 7 to 8 minutes on the first side, turn, and cook for 6 to 7 minutes more. Remove to a warm platter and generously season with salt and pepper.
4. If all the butter and oil have been absorbed, melt another tablespoon each of butter and oil in the skillet over medium-low heat. Add the shallots and sauté until translucent, about 4 to 5 minutes. Pour in the stock and stir up all the browned cooking bits. Turn the heat to medium-high and boil the liquid until slightly reduced, 6 to 7 minutes. Stir in the chestnut and cranberry mixture.
5. Return the pork and any accumulated meat juices to the pan and reheat for 2 to 3 minutes, turning the cutlets once. Put each cutlet on a warmed plate, spoon on some sauce, and garnish with a few strands of julienned orange rind, a cranberry, and a sprinkle of parsley. Serve immediately.

Did you know? When selecting pork chops, you'll find the center cut (as used above) to be the most costly, because it has the least amount of bone and fat. Chops that come from the rib end have a smaller amount of bone compared with the loin end.

ROASTED PORK TENDERLOIN WITH CHUTNEY

Serves 3 to 4

To speed up your meal preparation, look at the variety of prepared condiments and sauces available. There are hundreds of good tasting and preservative-free products. Don't be afraid to use them out of context. Here, I combine mango chutney and mashed banana with white wine for this succulent roast with a tangy, sweet flavor. It takes minutes to make.

Pork is a good choice in the market as the supply is plentiful and the turnover is usually high. Fresh pork should be pale pink with solid white fat on red bones.

1 teaspoon oil

1 12-ounce pork tenderloin, narrow end tied under, patted dry

Salt and freshly ground black pepper to taste

1/4 cup dry white wine

1/4 cup Major Grey's chutney, fruit finely chopped

1 medium ripe banana, mashed until smooth

1/4 teaspoon dry mustard

1 tablespoon lime juice

1. In a skillet just large enough to hold the meat, heat the oil over high heat until almost smoking. Add the meat and brown it on all sides, about 4 minutes. Season with salt and pepper. Pour in the wine, stir up all browned cooking bits, and boil until it almost evaporates.
2. Meanwhile, combine the chutney, banana, and mustard in a small bowl. After the pan is deglazed, scrape the chutney mixture over the meat, cover the pan tightly with aluminum foil, turn the heat to medium, and cook until the pork is just cooked through, about 20 minutes.
3. Uncover the pan, transfer the meat to a heated platter, stir in the lime juice, and season the sauce with salt and pepper. Slice crosswise and serve with the sauce.

Did you know? Fresh pork roasts will keep for 3 to 4 days in the refrigerator. If the roast is wrapped in plastic, remove it from its airtight covering to prevent bacteria from developing on the meat surface. Put the pork on a plate, cover with foil or paper, and store in the coldest part of the refrigerator. Airtight-wrapped pork roasts will last for up to 6 months in your freezer.

SWEET AND SPICY SPARERIBS

Serves at least 12

Spareribs are one of our all-time favorite family dishes. When I invite friends with kids, I can count on these succulent, mildly spicy slabs to please just about everyone. I serve them with ears of corn, a giant tossed salad, and loaves of garlic bread. It's a winning combination. But, this recipe is easily divided in half, so don't wait for a crowd.

When preparing ribs or other meat dishes with lots of bones, I buy about a pound per person, unless a lot of children are coming. Rather than tiny baby back ribs, I think large, meaty pork or beef ribs absorb the sauce better. Often they are sold partially cut-up to make serving easier once they are cooked. If the ribs are very fatty, I generally boil them first to remove some of the excess fat.

12 pounds pork spareribs

FOR THE SAUCE:

1 cup honey
½ cup firmly packed dark brown sugar
⅓ cup soy sauce
¼ cup dry sherry
¼ cup Worcestershire sauce
¼ cup oyster sauce
2 tablespoons red wine vinegar
2 tablespoons chili powder
1 tablespoon ground ginger
1 cup orange marmalade
1 6-ounce can tomato paste
3 star anise (optional)
1 stick cinnamon

1. Preheat your oven (or both ovens if you have two) to 450°F. Bring a large pot of water to a boil.
2. Divide the ribs between 2 large deep pans, and put in the oven. Pour boiling water over the ribs to cover, cover with heavy foil, and bring the water to a boil. This may take up to 20 minutes. Once the water boils, cook for 15 minutes, remove the pan from the oven, drain and cool the ribs. This may be done in batches and ahead of time. When cool, cut into individual ribs.
3. Make the sauce: While the ribs boil, combine the honey, brown sugar, soy sauce, sherry, Worcestershire and oyster sauces, vinegar, chili powder, and ginger in a medium saucepan and bring to a boil over medium-high heat, stirring frequently. Stir in the marmalade, tomato paste, star anise, and cinnamon; reduce the heat so the sauce is just simmering, and cook for 20 minutes.
4. Turn your oven to 350°F. Return the ribs to the pan, pour on the sauce, turning the ribs to coat evenly, and bake until tender, about 45 minutes, basting occasionally. Remove and serve.

ANN NURSE'S BAKED HAM

Serves at least 24

1 12- to 18-pound smoked ham, bone in
Whole cloves
3 cups pineapple juice
1 pound dark brown sugar
1 16-ounce bottle dark corn syrup

When I served this shiny, darkly glazed ham as a centerpiece for my daughter's 21st birthday, not a bite was left. They ate it at the party, after a late night of dancing, and, for those who returned for breakfast, there were some tiny bites left. My friend Ann Nurse shared this recipe with me. She says it is a holiday tradition in her family; we have shared it with countless guests, as well.

1. Preheat your oven to 325°F.
2. Put the ham in a large, open roasting pan. Score the ham into a 1-inch diamond pattern and stud completely with cloves. Pour on the pineapple juice and bake for 12 minutes per pound.
3. After the first 1½ hours, remove the ham from the oven and carefully pat on the brown sugar, completely covering the top. Pour the corn syrup over the ham, taking care not to disturb the sugar coating. Return the ham to the oven and bake, basting every 15 minutes.
4. Once the ham has baked for the allotted time, remove it and continue basting until the ham is cool to give a beautiful glaze. The remaining syrup may be used to make candied yams, sweet potatoes, or butternut squash.

Have you tried . . . When used as a pan liner, regular-weight foil tears easily during roasting. Instead, line your roasting pan with wide, heavyweight aluminum foil and cleanup will be far easier. A large, disposable aluminum pan will work as well, but put it on a heavy cookie sheet to support the bottom.

VENISON CHESTNUT PÂTÉ

Serves 8 to 12

For years, venison was eaten as a great delicacy in restaurants during game season, or in the home of hunters. Recently, supermarkets have become more adventuresome and have started to sell game. Most venison sold in supermarkets is farm raised under strict growing conditions. Its flavor is quite mild. Nutritionally, venison has outstanding credentials: It's as low in fat and cholesterol as chicken but with a lot more flavor. The flavor of a pâté improves as it ages, so I make mine at least a week ahead of time. Or, I double the recipe and fill 6 mini-loaf pans for holiday gift-giving.

Serve with Cranberry, Pepper, and Onion Conserve (page 66) or Plum-Pear Ketchup (page 80) and dark-bread triangles. Garnish with cornichons.

- 1 1/4 pounds ground venison
- 1 1/4 pounds ground pork (1/2 lean, 1/2 fat)
- 8 ounces venison, cut into strips 1/2 x 1/2 by 1 1/2 inches
- 4 ounces pork fatback, rind removed, blanched, and cut into 1/4-by-1/4-by-1-inch strips
- 8 ounces chestnut meat, fresh-roasted or unsweetened from a can, crumbled
- 1 generous teaspoon ground cloves
- 1 generous teaspoon ground allspice
- 1 1/2 teaspoons freshly grated nutmeg
- 2 large cloves garlic, peeled and minced
- 1/2 cup dried currants
- 1/2 cup Madeira
- 1/4 cup cognac or brandy
- 2 tablespoons raspberry or red wine vinegar
- 2 1/2 teaspoons salt, or to taste
- Freshly ground black pepper to taste
- 3 eggs, slightly beaten
- 16 ounces fatback, sliced 1/8 inch thick, simmered for 2 minutes in water, and patted dry

1. Preheat your oven to 350°F.
2. Combine the ground venison, pork, venison strips, fatback strips, chestnuts, ground cloves, allspice, nutmeg, garlic, currants, Madeira, cognac, vinegar, salt, and pepper in a large bowl and let it stand for 1 or 2 hours.
3. Add the eggs and mix well. Fry a small ball of the mixture until cooked and taste for seasonings, adjusting as necessary. The pâté should be spicy.
4. Line a 9-by-5-by-3-inch loaf pan or 6-cup terrine with fatback slices (see page 144), extending them so they can be folded back over the top of the pâté. Transfer the pâté mixture to the mold, packing it down into the corners. Fold the fatback slices over the top of the pâté. Cover the top of the pan tightly with three layers of heavy-duty aluminum foil and punch 1 or 2 steam holes in the top. Put the loaf pan or mold in another larger pan and fill the larger pan with enough boiling water to come halfway up the outside of the mold. Bake in the lower third of the oven for 1 hour and 35 to 45 minutes or until the juices run clear.
5. Remove the pâté from the oven, lift the foil, and check to see if the pâté has shrunk slightly from the edges. Put the foil back on, put the pâté on a plate, and put a flat board or another loaf pan the same size on top. Weight with 1 to 1 1/2 pounds of cans, jars, or pie weights for 2 hours, then refrigerate overnight. Remove the pâté from the loaf pan, wrap tightly in plastic wrap, and refrigerate for at least 5 to 7 days before eating.
6. Remove the pâté from the refrigerator at least 1 hour before serving. Put it on a platter lined with curly endive or parsley, and cut a few slices. Leave the rest of the pâté uncut, as it will be fresher if cut as needed.

Did you know? The fat of venison has an undesirable taste, so pork or beef fat is used instead to bard or lard the meat. Deer meat is very lean. To tenderize it, venison is often marinated or served very rare. A lot of supermarket venison is frozen, which also breaks down the meat fiber and makes it tender.

GRILLED VENISON MEDALLIONS WITH BLACK BEAN PANCAKES

Serves 6

Inspired by the flavors and simple elegance of Asian cuisines, these marinated venison medallions are served on small black bean pancakes. Yogurt, hoisin sauce, and ginger impart a complexity to the taste of the butter-tender meat, while the crunch of snap peas and the slight nuttiness of the pancakes add texture.

FOR THE VENISON:

3/4 cup plain yogurt

1/4 cup hoisin sauce

2 large cloves garlic, crushed

1 tablespoon minced gingerroot

Freshly ground black pepper to taste

1 3/4 to 2 pounds venison or lamb medallions, about 1 inch thick, cut from leg

FOR THE BLACK BEAN PANCAKES:

1 cup cooked or rinsed and drained canned black beans

1/4 cup water

2 tablespoons dry sherry

2 eggs, beaten

1/4 cup minced scallions, white and light green parts; reserve tops for garnish

1 medium clove garlic, peeled and crushed

2 tablespoons sesame seeds, lightly toasted

2 teaspoons sesame oil

2 tablespoons minced gingerroot

12 drops Tabasco sauce, or to taste

3/4 teaspoon salt, or to taste

3 tablespoons all-purpose flour

Vegetable oil to grease the skillet

1. Marinate the venison: Combine yogurt, hoisin sauce, crushed garlic, ginger, and pepper in a large, resealable plastic bag. Add medallions, turning to coat them on all sides with marinade. Seal and refrigerate for 1 to 2 days, turning twice during this time.
2. Prepare the pancakes: Combine half of the black beans, the water, sherry, and eggs in the bowl of a food processor and process until smooth. Scrape the mixture into a bowl; stir in the remaining beans, scallions, garlic, sesame seeds, oil, ginger, Tabasco sauce, and salt. Sprinkle on the flour, a tablespoon at a time, beating with a fork until blended.
3. Turn your oven to warm. Lightly grease a large, nonstick skillet with oil and heat until hot.
4. Using a measuring tablespoon, pour in 1 tablespoon of batter for each pancake. Cook over medium-high heat until edges begin to brown, about 30 seconds. Turn with a spatula and cook second side for 30 seconds. Transfer cooked pancakes to a warm plate, loosely cover with foil, and keep warm in the oven. Continue until all batter has been used.
5. Cook the venison: Remove the medallions from the marinade and blot dry on paper towels. Heat a large, well-seasoned cast-iron or heavy skillet over high heat until very hot. Lightly coat the surface with oil. Put in only as many medallions in the pan as will fit comfortably without crowding and cook for about 3 minutes on the first side; then turn and cook the second side for 2 1/2 to 3 minutes for medium-rare. Transfer to heated plates. Serve with 3 to 4 pancakes. Slice reserved scallion greens, sprinkle on venison, and serve.

RABBIT IN RED WINE AND BALSAMIC VINEGAR SAUCE

Serves 4

This rabbit, gently simmered in red wine with mushrooms and pearl onions, makes a veritable feast once the rich balsamic vinegar and tangy crème fraîche are added to the sauce. Serve with couscous, polenta, or small roasted Yukon Gold potatoes.

Until recently, if you found rabbit in your market, it was usually frozen. You may find whole rabbits or a boneless saddle, which would be more expensive. Frankly, I think rabbit needs those bones to keep it juicy. The meat of this animal is lean and tender when slowly cooked, and the flavor is quite mild, like chicken.

1 2½- to 3-pound rabbit, dressed, and cut into 8 pieces, blotted dry (see note)

Flour for dredging

4½ tablespoons vegetable oil

1 medium onion, peeled and finely chopped

1 medium carrot, peeled and finely chopped

1 medium rib celery, finely chopped

1 large clove garlic, peeled and minced

1½ cups hearty red wine, such as Zinfandel

1 large bay leaf

⅓ cup finely chopped flat-leaf parsley

1 teaspoon dried thyme leaves

¼ cup balsamic vinegar

Salt and freshly ground black pepper to taste

1 tablespoon unsalted butter

1½ cups pearl onions, peeled and with an "X" cut in the root end

¼ cup beef stock

½ cup currants

8 ounces small white mushrooms, wiped, trimmed, and quartered

6 ounces crème fraîche or sour cream

1. Dredge the rabbit in flour, patting to remove the excess. In a large, heavy casserole or Dutch oven, heat 3 tablespoons of the oil over medium-high heat until very hot but not smoking. Add only as many pieces of rabbit as fit comfortably in the bottom of the pot without crowding. Brown them evenly in batches, about 2 to 3 minutes on each side. Remove the pieces to a bowl with a slotted spoon, season with salt and pepper, and set aside.
2. Add the remaining 1½ tablespoons of oil to the pot and heat over medium heat until hot. Add the onion, carrot, and celery and sauté until they are translucent and soft, about 6 to 7 minutes. Stir in the garlic and cook for 30 seconds longer.
3. Return the rabbit to the casserole and pour in the wine. Turn the heat to high and bring the liquid to a boil, scraping up all the browned cooking bits. Stir in the bay leaf, parsley, thyme, vinegar, salt, and plenty of fresh pepper. Cover and simmer over medium-low heat for 45 minutes.
4. While the rabbit is cooking, melt the butter in a large, heavy skillet over medium-high heat. Add the pearl onions and cook until they start to brown, about 6 to 8 minutes. Add the beef stock and raise the heat, shaking the pan until the liquid has almost completely evaporated and coats the onions.
5. Uncover the pot, add the pearl onions, currants, and mushrooms, and gently boil for 10 to 15 minutes longer to thicken the sauce. Remove the bay leaf, stir in the crème fraîche, and taste to adjust the seasonings.

NOTE: Read the box carefully when buying a frozen rabbit. Select only a "frying rabbit," not a "mature rabbit," which, unless stewed for a long time, will be tough. Frozen rabbits may be cut into more than 8 pieces. Don't worry, this recipe will work with larger or smaller pieces. And a slowly defrosted frozen rabbit (in the refrigerator with a plate underneath) will be fine eating.

Did you know? Traditional balsamic vinegar, originally from Modena, Italy, is distilled in wooden casks and is highly concentrated. Typically only a small amount of the dark liquid is used in a vinaigrette. Since it is now so reasonable in price, I added it in this sauce to balance the flavors of hearty wine and crème fraîche. The acidity seems to "lift" the combined tastes.

KEEPING FRESH FOOD AT ITS BEST

It is a primary tenet of good cooks and great chefs alike, and is repeated many times in this book as elsewhere: The freshest possible ingredients are vital to eating well. Getting food to you in top condition is the supermarket's responsibility. With the help of technology, foods can be delivered rapidly from around the world into your local market. However, I personally look for produce that comes from as close to where I am as possible.

That said, the secret of keeping fresh food at its best is choosing carefully when you buy, then storing it properly once at home, and knowing how long it will last.

The freshest and best-quality food, poorly stored, will soon become mediocre. How food is stored goes hand in hand with where it's kept in the kitchen. When it was purchased and/or prepared is the third part of the equation.

While some whole spices, dried beans, pastas, and canned foods never seem to deteriorate, most foods have a "shelf life" within which you can expect optimum flavor, texture, and color. For a moderate time after that point has passed, the food probably will not be harmful to your body, but you cannot expect the final dish to be first-rate.

Storage Containers

Plastic Containers

There are many practical plastic storage containers available today—some of them for free. Good reusable containers include those used by supermarkets to package their products. The plastic half-pint and quart containers with snap-on lids culled from the Deli or Dairy sections are fine for short-term reuse. Tupperware and Rubbermaid are but two of many manufacturers who make multi-sized and -shaped containers in a heavier, more durable weight. They each make lines of tossable containers, as well.

My biggest reservation about plastic containers is that the plastic tends to absorb the flavors and colors of the ingredients stored. So, a broccoli soup may end up with a haunting taste of peppered shrimp. Wash these containers in your dishwasher or with very hot water, and air them well between uses.

The other objection I have to plastic is that the lids and containers often split, preventing a tight seal. In a refrigerator, this lets circulating air bring other smells to the stored food and causes food to dry out. In a freezer, exposed and improperly wrapped food is often ruined by the formation of ice crystals and by freezer burn. (Check Chapter 9 of this book for detailed freezing tips.) One more concern: Using these containers in microwave ovens may also be unhealthy because, potentially, they might leach PCBs during cooking.

Glass Jars

Before plastics, a lot of food was packaged in screw-top glass jars. If used for preserving, a rubber sealing ring was necessary to the canning process. With a few improvements in lids and canning technology, this remains a viable food storage method. Some of us still preserve fruits and sauces this way. I find that empty glass jars from mustards, baby foods, jams, instant coffee, peanut butter, and the like are perfect for storing small amounts of ground nuts, homemade relishes, and fresh vinegars.

These recycled bottles and jars appeal because glass is impervious to color and odor and is transparent for easy identification. Scrub the lids and jars well and insert a piece of waxed paper between the food and the screw top to form a tight seal. Use new corks, available from hardware stores, for narrow-top bottles.

Heavy Plastic Pouches

Under different storage conditions, the same foods require different treatment. Fish, for example, must be wrapped airtight without moisture for freezing, but should breathe in the refrigerator. Resealable heavy-weight zippered bags, a boon to storage, are ideal for freezing. Push out all the air just before finally sealing the bag. Both solids and liquids, such as soup, can be stored in these pouches, taking up a minimum of storage space.

Plastic wrap, aluminum foil, and freezer paper are other essentials in the kitchen. The specific information on how best to store each item should be available from the supermarket department in which you shop. Make certain to ask. Personnel should to know these key facts; some manufacturers also provide useful storage pamphlets to markets. Look for them.

Storage Tips

Preparation and Labeling for Storage

Whichever type of storage container you choose, cleanliness is vital for food safety and longevity. This includes those largest of containers—your refrigerator and freezer. Always wipe up spills quickly and use an open box of baking soda, as suggested by the manufacturer, to keep the inside of a refrigerator odor-free. (It also sweetens a garbage disposal.)

How many times have you misplaced a choice morsel in the fridge because in haste you put it away without labeling? Make a practice of labeling and dating stored products. For frozen foods, indicating the approximate number of servings is also helpful. A permanent, non-smudge marker prevents these notations from running off due to dampness.

All perishables come with "sell by" or "use by" dates stamped on their packages. Most non-perishables do, as well. These include dairy products, breads, and even cereals.

How to Store Foods

Staples

While it's convenient and attractive to display tins of herbs and spices above the stove or in full view, heat and sun diminish their vitality and flavor. They keep in better shape in a cool, dark spot. Under optimum conditions, dried herbs only last nine months. After this, they should be discarded because they won't add much in the way of flavor to whatever you are cooking. On the other hand, whole spices, like nutmeg, keep for several years.

Smaller packages of herbs and spices marketed in cellophane bags, or those you can scoop yourself, can be more economical because many of us never use a whole bottle of a ground herb or spice before its intensity is lost. If you have fresh herbs, preserve them by spreading them on cookie sheets and air-drying or by putting them in a turned-off oven until dry. I think they retain more flavor than store-bought varieties and can be stored in small jars in the pantry.

Oils and vinegars are also best kept in a cool, dark pantry or cupboard. So are condiments, except those that I open that are marked "refrigerate after opening." The same holds true for jams and jellies. Dried legumes, rice, pasta, and grains should also be kept in a cool spot, away from sunlight. If your house tends to get moths, transfer foods to airtight containers. Even well-wrapped chocolate keeps for nine months under these conditions. I don't freeze chocolate since it develops a "bloom," a dusty appearance on the surface.

I pack all flours—from all-purpose to pastry to whole wheat bread—inside heavy resealable plastic bags in their original boxes or bags and then put them in the freezer to prolong their freshness and prevent little bugs or beasts from attacking them. Some friends of mine put their flours in airtight jars, which also work well.

I reserve those jars for storing nuts—also in my freezer.

Fruit and Vegetables

In Europe, I learned to leave fresh fruit in a bowl on the counter. They taste fruitier at room temperature. Depending on the season, I have an assortment of apples and pears or peaches, plums, and melons ready to eat. There is always a banana or two and often a fresh pineapple. When I buy fresh citrus fruits that I'll use within a few days, I also leave them out. Otherwise, they will keep for a long time in the refrigerator.

But, fruits continue to mature at room temperature, so I try to buy only as much as we will realistically eat within a few days. Because fresh berries are so fragile, unless I will use them within a few hours, I always refrigerate them, discarding any that are bruised before doing so. The same is true with ripe peaches and any other delicate fruit. I cut out any rotten spots, then cut or slice them, and chill them, usually with a little lemon juice squeezed on them to prevent discoloration. All fruit that is cut or is becoming overly ripe should be chilled. For maximum flavor, take it out of the refrigerator at least an hour before serving.

One fruit I try never to refrigerate unless cut is the tomato. (Yes, it is a fruit!) The flavor is dramatically better when left out.

Throughout this book, I indicate the best way to address a particular fruit in recipes where they are used. If it is not indicated in a recipe, check the index for another recipe in which that fruit plays an important role.

With the exception of onions and potatoes, which I keep in a cool, dark place, most vegetables are best refrigerated. Before putting vegetables away, trim any damaged spots or bruised leaves. Store them in the coldest part of your refrigerator, usually at the bottom, near the back. Separate lettuce from pears, cantaloupes, apples, and other fruits that give off ethylene gas that cause rust-colored spots on greens. This is easiest if your refrigerator has two drawers.

Vegetables like green beans, broccoli, and zucchini will keep well for several days, but asparagus and tender lettuces need quicker attention. If vegetables are in jeopardy of deterioration, you can partially cook them. Once blanched, blotted dry, and stored in an airtight container, they can be sautéed a day or two later. Or you can blanche and freeze them in resealable plastic bags. A freezer is also the ideal place to preserve homemade soups, pastas, and fruit purées.

Dairy

The trick to keeping cheese fresh is to recognize that once air is trapped within the package, over time it becomes stale and causes food spoilage. Cheese departments should change the wrapping on cheese each time they cut off a wedge. It's a good habit to get into at home. Most refrigerators have cheese and butter compartments, often on the door or in a drawer, where the temperature is slightly warmer. Although nothing that grows on cheese can hurt you (it's natural penicillin), it can affect the taste and appearance. If so, before using it, cut off a thick slice well below the mold, and discard. Grated Parmesan cheese should be tightly covered and used within a few weeks.

Butter is remarkably porous and readily absorbs flavors from the refrigerator. To keep it sweet, always rewrap it tightly. If you buy pounds of butter to freeze, wrap the cartons before putting them in the freezer.

Poultry, Meat, and Fish

It's worth noting again that care must be taken to prevent poultry, meat or fish from dripping juices that might cause food poisoning onto other foods. Putting them on a plate is good insurance. In the specific chapters on them I have included several tips on how to care for them.

In general, tightly wrapped foods often decay more quickly than those that are allowed to breathe. Once you return from the market, the packing on poultry, meat, or fish should be loosened if you plan on eating it within a few days. For freezing, wrappings should be airtight with all air pushed out. All sausages should be covered but not tightly wrapped. Those made with poultry or fish should be used within a couple of days.

Refrigerator/Freezer Strategies

You can stock your refrigerator and freezer with entire meals from hors d'oeuvres, appetizers, and entrées to ice creams and exotic coffees from around the world. With so many options, a system of organization is useful. These are a few suggestions that work for me.

Group similar kinds of ingredients, such as mustards or preserves, together in both the freezer and refrigerator so you know roughly what and where things are. Retrieval is quicker and easier this way.

Label packages (with a permanent marker) to avoid mysteries. Include a date and the number of portions of stew or chicken thighs, etc., especially when foods are frozen.

Before returning an opened jar or container, check to see that it is clean.

Try to clean up any spills as soon as you discover them.

If a refrigerator is opened and closed numerous times, the temperature inside rises and cold storage is impaired. Put food away quickly, remembering to close the refrigerator between groups of food.

When replacing foods, especially in the freezer, rotate them so that the oldest foods get eaten before the newer ones.

Ice-cube trays are terrific for making small-size portions of stocks, egg whites, and puréed fruits, then transfer to resealable plastic bags.

Periodically, take everything out and evaluate what you have. It's amazing what you can find. The old adage: "When in doubt, throw it out," is a useful maxim. Wash both sections with soapy warm water. Today's freezers are generally frost-free, so the heavy-duty defrosting of years ago is no longer necessary.

With today's markets so well stocked and accessible, loading up on foods is not as necessary as it once was. Yes, freezers are great to hold homemade soups or stews, and the convenience of not having to shop every day is terrific, but too often foods get forgotten and then thrown out.

Just for Nice

And finally a little aside on the subject of storing: Today's supermarkets are loaded with wonderful boxes, baskets, and containers of all sorts. Why not keep some of these in one corner of your pantry with the prettiest empty jars, some snippets of ribbon, a remnant or two of checkered or country-print fabric, and some decorative labels? No gift is so well received as the one you make and give yourself.

CHAPTER FIVE: FISH AND SHELLFISH

INTRODUCTION

Americans have discovered what most other cultures have known for a long time: how rich the harvest from our oceans and lakes can be. In many markets, fish are displayed unwrapped, in full view, on iced counters as they are in the finest fish stores—with all the expertise (cooking tips and recipes) included.

Along with sole, flounder, salmon, and trout, less-familiar fish are now sold in supermarkets. Sadly, some of this is the result of overfishing. Less expensive (but delicious) varieties, like catfish, that used to be thrown overboard are now available. Skate used to be a "trash fish" but is now so popular, the price is sky high. Prepared items, such as stuffed clams and calamari salad, can tempt us with delicious convenience. And there seems to be a ubiquitous sushi section in markets, as well.

Buying Seafood

Smart consumers use their eyes and nose to check quality when buying seafood. I'd suggest taking a little extra time to really study the fish or shellfish you are contemplating. If it is unwrapped, check the *first* clue to freshness: a lack of fishy odor. While we often hear that clear eyes in a whole fish reveal its freshness, this may not be the best indicator. Withdrawing fish quickly from deep waters can result in eyes that bulge, and ice burn can produce clouded eyes. But, there is no hiding the fact that as fish gets older, it smells *fishy*.

Often, you can visually ascertain if the fish has been handled quickly and correctly by the purveyor and market:

✓ With a whole, unwrapped fish, look into the gills or ask the clerk to show you. They should be bright red. As a fish ages, the gills turn brownish.

✓ Even through plastic, you can judge the overall appearance. Is it bright and does the flesh feel firm when lightly pressed? Good. Although some whole fish have a natural light film on their skin, slime develops on fish with poor handling and time.

✓ Bruises, too, are to be avoided. They are a quick port of entry for bacteria.

✓ Fillets should be pearly with the muscle groups holding together. Edges should not be browned or curled.

When choosing fish in the market, it is important to have confidence in the fish buyer's judgment and reliability. Feel free to ask Seafood department personnel about the freshness and origin of the fish. Don't hesitate to ask for a second or third fillet or fish if the first one is an uncomfortable choice for any reason. In packages, look at each item and ask questions, as well; even wrapped fish can be opened and rewrapped by a clerk. The Seafood personnel are there to help you know what you are buying and can usually offer advice and suggestions for handling and preparation.

Ask what are the best buys that day. Is there a more economical cut or size available? I've found that fresh salmon tails work just as well for Warm Salmon Mousse in a Phyllo Crown (page 172) and are usually less costly than fillets. Often, you can find out when the fish is delivered and be there for the best selection. Or ask to have your fish held aside.

For party-quality whole fish, special-order it and discuss your choice with the department manager. And, if a clerk in the Seafood department says that the swordfish isn't great (and you should ask), don't gamble. No matter how great the sauce or the chef, the odds are against the final dish ever being wonderful if the raw fish isn't.

Healthful Eating

Careful handling on the part of the supermarket to ensure freshness is only half of the picture. The responsibility rests with you the minute the fish leaves the store. This means watching where and how the fish is transported home. A long ride in a hot car is like partial cooking. Remember to ask for freezer bags and, where possible, pack the fish surrounded by other chilled items or ice in your bag.

At home, proper storage and preparation ensure good, healthful eating. The sooner the fish or shellfish is cooked, the better.

- ✓ Rinse it under cold water and rewrap in fresh paper, not plastic. This is especially true of live lobsters, which suffocate in airtight bags. Drape them over a bowl of ice and cover to extend their life in the refrigerator.
- ✓ Store fish in the coldest part of the refrigerator and let it breathe.
- ✓ If you won't use your fish within two days, wrap it in airtight covering (plastic wrap or paper) and freeze for up to three months.
- ✓ If freezing a whole fish, gut it first.

✓ Once seafood is defrosted (even if sold as "fresh frozen") do not refreeze; use it within one day.

A revolution in fish eating has occurred. Today's lighter sauces no longer mask delicate flavors. Nor do we overcook fish. Instead, the Canadian Fisheries' standard of nine to ten minutes cooking per inch of thickness has been widely adopted. Whether the fish is whole or in fillets, stuffed or grilled, this rule works wonders to produce moist, delicate, perfectly prepared fish.

We've also heard how healthful fish can be for low-fat/low-cholesterol diets. Even fatty fish like salmon that are high in omega-3 fats are now credited with helping us win the battle against clogged arteries and heart attacks. Yet, next we read that farmed salmon is high in mercury and PCBs.

Tuna is also widely praised for its health benefits, although here, too, there are risks to consider. It and other large predators, like swordfish and shark, have the highest concentrations of mercury. For healthy adults this is not a serious concern. However, pregnant women have been advised that mercury can pose a risk to an unborn fetus.

We must be aware of these concerns, since every day something else that's good becomes potentially "bad." That said, I believe there is lots of good eating available from today's Seafood department. You can make the fanciest Lobster Timbales with Riesling Beurre Blanc (page 173) or swordfish steaks simply barbecued on the grill. With supermarkets upscaling and upgrading, your choices are expanding.

AVOCADO AND SCALLOP SEVICHE

Serves 10 to 12

This colorful hors d'oeuvre is easy and attractive for summer entertaining. It's prepared ahead of time and without a stove; instead, the acidity of the fresh lime juice "cooks" the scallops. The crunch of slightly marinated mushrooms provides an interesting contrast to the soft scallop mixture. Or, serve this seviche on endive leaves.

I think sea scallops are one of the best bets in a supermarket Seafood department. Those huge ones labeled "day boat" are harvested the same day and brought quickly to market. What a feast of sweet, succulent eating! Scallops should look pearly and moist, without any yellowed edges, and with a sweet aroma. They should be "dry," not soaked in chemicals and/or water to keep them plump and white; otherwise they will be watery. Sadly, I find bay scallops often have little taste and are not worth buying.

Make sure to unwrap sealed trays of scallops as soon as you bring them home to avoid an ammonia smell. If the smell is bad, the scallops should be returned to the store. If the smell is only mild, you should squeeze fresh lemon over them and then blot them dry.

1/2 cup fresh lime juice (about 4 limes)
3 tablespoons + 1/4 cup vegetable oil
20–24 green peppercorns, crushed
Salt and freshly ground black pepper to taste
3/4 pound sea scallops, finely chopped
1 large ripe avocado, peeled
2 tablespoons fresh chives or scallions, chopped, plus chives or scallions to garnish
30–40 small white mushrooms
2 tablespoons fresh lemon juice
1 medium clove of garlic, peeled and crushed

1. Combine the lime juice, 3 tablespoons of oil, crushed peppercorns, salt, and pepper together in a glass or ceramic bowl. Stir in the scallops, cover, and refrigerate them for at least 4 hours while they marinate. They should become opaque.
2. Mash the avocado until almost smooth, then add it along with the chives or scallions to the scallops (do not drain them) and mix well. Set aside.
3. About 1/2 hour before serving, remove the stems from the mushrooms and discard. Wipe the caps to remove any dirt. Combine the remaining vegetable oil, lemon juice, garlic, salt, and pepper in a small bowl, and brush the insides of the mushrooms liberally with the mixture.
4. Just before serving, drain the caps and fill with the scallop mixture. Garnish with additional chives, if desired.

NOTE: Any remaining scallop mixture may be spooned onto endive leaves or wide strips of sweet red bell peppers.

Another idea . . . Serve 1 sea scallop per person. Cook a couple slices of bacon in a large skillet; remove from the pan and crumble, reserving the bacon fat. Add a little butter to the pan and sauté the white part of 2 thinly sliced leeks until tender. Add a few drops of cream, season with salt and pepper, and divide among 4 small plates. Reduce 3/4 cup balsamic vinegar to 1/4 cup. Heat a skillet over high heat and sear the scallops for a minute per side. Add the scallops to the leeks, drizzle on the reduced balsamic vinegar, and top with the bacon.

Did you know? Hass avocados, the ones with the dark, almost black skins, have smaller pits and less moisture than the larger, dark green–skinned variety. The flavors are similar, and either variety will work in this recipe. An avocado will ripen faster in a closed paper bag at room temperature. You can keep cut-up avocados for several hours in ice water without their turning brown.

SQUID CAPONATA

Makes 8 ½-cup servings

Caponata is a tasty Sicilian dish traditionally made with eggplant, tuna, anchovies, capers, onions, olives, and garlic in a tomato sauce and served as an hors d'oeuvre or first course. I've added delicately simmered squid for texture and color here.

If you can't find fresh squid, check in the Frozen Foods aisle. Squid is often frozen during the summer months when it is plentiful and less expensive. Even the "fresh" clean squid in the Seafood department may have been previously frozen and defrosted. Be sure to ask. When allowed to come to room temperature slowly, it's a good buy. But, it should be used quickly.

1 2-ounce can anchovies, drained and finely chopped

2 cups Chunky Homemade Tomato Sauce (page 282)

¾ pound cleaned squid, including tentacles

¼ cup red wine vinegar

¼ cup + 1 tablespoon fruity olive oil

2 large cloves garlic, peeled and minced

2–3 tablespoons coarsely chopped flat-leaf parsley

1 3½-ounce jar small capers, drained

¾ cup oil-cured black olives

½ teaspoon salt, or to taste

Pepper to taste

1 large onion, peeled and coarsely chopped

Bibb or romaine lettuce leaves, optional

1. In a medium-sized non-reactive saucepan, combine the anchovies and tomato sauce, and bring to a simmer over medium heat. Partially cover and cook for 10 minutes. Remove from the heat, uncover, and set aside.
2. Rinse the squid under cold water. Remove any of the spotted skin that remains on the outside of the tentacles and any cartilage or hard beak inside. Bring a skillet filled with cold water to a simmer. Add the squid and simmer just until it turns white, about 30 to 45 seconds. Remove the squid, blot dry, and slice into ¾-inch rings. In a medium bowl, combine the squid with the vinegar, ¼ cup olive oil, garlic, parsley, capers, olives, salt, and pepper, and stir to blend. Set aside.
3. In a small skillet, heat the remaining 1 tablespoon of olive oil over medium-high heat until fragrant. Stir in the chopped onion, lower the heat, and cook slowly until lightly colored, about 10 minutes. Stir in the tomato sauce.
4. Combine the tomato sauce with the squid mixture and serve at room temperature or refrigerate in a covered bowl. Serve on small plates with forks as an hors d'oeuvre or as a first course on luncheon-sized plates lined with small Bibb or romaine lettuce leaves.

MINI SHRIMP SPRING ROLLS

Makes approximately 24 to 28

These crunchy 2-bite morsels filled with spicy shrimp make a wonderful cocktail snack. Once you master the technique of making spring rolls, almost anything can be put inside. Serve with Gingery Peanut Dipping Sauce (page 275) and/or hoisin sauce found in Asian sections.

Spring roll wrappers are far thinner than the traditional egg roll wrappers. Check out the Asian section for other spring roll ingredients. One half-ounce of "tree ears" or dried mo-er mushrooms can be substituted for the black mushrooms.

3/4 pound (approximately 40) small shrimp, peeled and deveined

1/2 8-ounce can water chestnuts (approximately 15), drained

1 ounce dried black mushrooms, soaked in warm water until soft, stems removed, drained, blotted dry, and coarsely chopped

1/2 cup thinly sliced scallions, including most of the green parts

2 teaspoons soy sauce

1 tablespoon minced fresh gingerroot

1 tablespoon minced garlic

1 tablespoon dry sherry

2 teaspoons sesame oil

1 teaspoon salt

1 teaspoon sugar

1 teaspoon unseasoned rice vinegar

12 spring roll wrappers or 24 phyllo leaves (see note)

1 egg white

Peanut oil for deep frying

Gingery Peanut Dipping Sauce (page 275)

1. Bring a small skillet half-filled with water to a simmer. Add the shrimp and cook over medium heat until they turn pink. Drain and blot dry.
2. In a food processor, combine the shrimp, water chestnuts, and mushrooms, and pulse about 12 times until the ingredients are the size of small peas. (Or, chop by hand.) Add the scallions, soy sauce, ginger, garlic, sherry, sesame oil, salt, sugar, and vinegar and pulse a few more times to blend.
3. Carefully separate the spring roll wrappers and cut them in half on the diagonal. Put a rounded tablespoon of the filling in the middle of the long edge. Brush the perimeter of the spring roll with egg white. Fold the right corner over the filling, leaving about one-third of the long edge exposed. Fold the left corner over the folded right corner, and then roll into a small cylinder (see illustration). Repeat this procedure until all the filling is used.

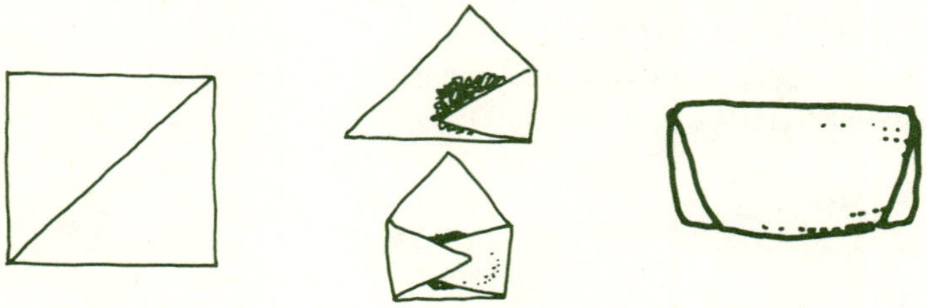

Did you know? Spring roll wrappers are about one-quarter the thickness of egg roll wrappers. They are sold in the Frozen Foods section or defrosted in the Produce or Dairy department. Check that the surface does not have moisture caused by deterioration on it.

Keep unfrozen wrappers chilled and sealed to prevent drying out. Carefully pull wrappers apart; they are actually far more sturdy than they seem at first glance. Tightly wrapped in plastic, wrappers may be frozen for a month.

4. Fill a wok or skillet with peanut oil to a depth of 2 inches. Heat the oil to 350°F or until a cube of bread dropped in turns golden brown quickly. Gently drop in a couple of spring rolls. Add 1 or 2 more, if space permits, and cook just until golden brown on all sides, about 30 to 40 seconds. (If you are using phyllo dough, it will take about 20 seconds.) Remove the rolls with a slotted spoon and drain on paper towels. Continue until all spring rolls are fried, making sure the oil is hot each time. Let the spring rolls cool for at least 10 minutes before serving.

NOTE: To substitute phyllo for spring roll wrappers (which is preferable to traditional thick egg roll wrappers), spread 1 leaf of phyllo with the long edge near you on a work surface, and brush very lightly with peanut oil. Put a second leaf over this. Using a ruler or straightedge, first trim the phyllo into a square, then cut the square in half on the diagonal as with the spring roll wrappers, and continue with the recipe.

Did you know? While sizes vary from market to market, New York's Fulton Fish Market uses the term "jumbo" or "prawn" for a count of up to 15 shrimp per pound. Sixteen to 20 are called "extra large," 21 to 30 are "large," and 31 to 40 are "medium." Prawns, incidentally, are actually shrimp-like crustaceans with two pairs of pincers.

Supermarkets typically carry three or four sizes, with large and medium the most common. However, many Seafood departments have at least eight different sizes that can be specially ordered. Sizes are often interchangeable in a recipe. But, remember, shrimp are made up of lots of water. Between peeling, deveining, and cooking, 3 pounds of uncooked shrimp will weigh about 1½ pounds when ready for eating.

Most shrimp—even in the Seafood department—are previously frozen and then defrosted, unless they have been air-shipped. Check, since refreezing fish is not a good idea. If there are no shrimp in the Seafood department, take a look in the Frozen Foods aisle. The flash-frozen (IQF—individually quick frozen) variety is a good choice as long as the shrimp are slowly defrosted in your refrigerator.

STIR-FRIED SHRIMP WITH TOMATO-CILANTRO VINAIGRETTE

Serves 4 to 6 as an appetizer

For this tasty dish, stir-fried shrimp are showered with chopped tomatoes, cilantro, and balsamic vinegar. Today shrimp are often sold already peeled and deveined, making this a speedy meal.

1½–2 pounds large shrimp, peeled and deveined

2 tablespoons extra-virgin olive oil

1 medium vine-ripened tomato, seeded and finely chopped (about ½ cup)

1–2 tablespoons balsamic vinegar

2 tablespoons chopped cilantro leaves

Salt and freshly ground black pepper to taste

1. Combine the shrimp and oil in a small bowl. Heat a large, heavy skillet over medium-high heat until hot. Add the shrimp and oil and stir-fry until just pink, about 1½ to 2 minutes. Add the tomatoes, 1 tablespoon of balsamic vinegar, and the cilantro, and toss just to warm the tomatoes through. Season with salt and pepper, add more balsamic vinegar, if desired, and serve.

GRILLED STUFFED TROUT

Serves 4

This recipe has an unusual combination of prunes and almonds in the spinach stuffing that is appealing not only for its intensity of flavor but for its low calorie count. I first tasted it at the cooking school of my friend Sabine de Mirbeck, in England. "Sweating" vegetables is a secret for cutting fat in cooking.

The freshest trout is the one you catch yourself. Your next-best choice is to find a market with fresh farm-raised trout swimming in a tank. The seafood clerk can clean them and trim the gills. They will freeze beautifully this way for 3 to 4 months.

4 brook or rainbow trout (approximately 10 to 12 ounces), gutted and boned, rinsed and patted dry

Salt and freshly ground black pepper

FOR THE STUFFING:

1 teaspoon canola or vegetable oil

1 large onion, peeled and finely chopped

1 pound fresh young spinach, washed, patted dry, stemmed, and cut into thin strips

2 ounces small white mushrooms, wiped, trimmed, and thinly sliced

2 ounces pitted prunes, finely chopped

2 ounces sliced almonds, toasted until light brown

Salt and freshly ground black pepper to taste

FOR THE SAUCE:

2/3 cup natural yogurt

2 tablespoons olive oil

Salt and freshly ground black pepper to taste

2 tablespoons freshly snipped chives

Steamed broccoli florets, to garnish (optional)

1. Remove any remaining bones from the trout with tweezers. Generously season the fish with salt and pepper.
2. For the stuffing: Pour the oil into a large skillet and heat over medium-high heat. Add the onion, cover, and let sweat over low heat for 1 minute. Add the spinach and mushrooms, raise the heat to high, and cook for 2 minutes longer. Stir in the prunes and cook 1 minute more. Transfer the stuffing to a flat dish to cool, then combine it with the almonds and season to taste with salt and pepper.
3. Position the broiler rack about 5 to 6 inches from the flame. Turn on the broiler.
4. Stuff the trout with the spinach mixture, packing it well, and put the fish on lightly oiled foil on a cookie sheet or broiler pan. Broil for 4 minutes on each side. Turn off the broiler and leave the fish in the broiler for 4 minutes longer to rest.
5. Prepare the sauce: Put the yogurt in a small bowl and whisk in the olive oil. Liberally season to taste with salt and pepper, then add the chives. Pour the sauce into a gravy boat and pass at the table.
6. Before serving the trout, remove the top skin from each fish. Serve the trout on warmed plates with steamed broccoli florets, if desired.

Did you know? Whole freshwater fish may have a slight, odorless protective film on their bodies. This is not the same as slime from deterioration, which definitely doesn't smell fresh.

SOGLIOLE IN SAOR—SWEET-AND-SOUR SOLE

Serves 6 to 8 as a first course

This unusual dish comes from Venice, Italy, where it is a specialty dating from the Middle Ages. While its background is old, the tastes are a contemporary mixture of tangy and slightly sweet flavors.

There are many varieties of sole available in this country. Any one will work for this do-ahead appetizer. (Look at the "Did you know?" tip at the end of this recipe for a surprising money-saving option.) When selecting recipes, I suggest you read them through. This recipe must be prepared in advance.

- 3/4 cup vegetable oil
- 2 pounds sole or flounder fillets, blotted dry and cut into pieces about 3 by 4 inches
- Flour for dredging
- Salt and freshly ground black pepper
- 3 large onions, peeled and very thinly sliced
- 1 cup apple cider vinegar
- 1 cup dry white wine
- 2/3 cup water
- 1/4 cup golden raisins
- 4 bay leaves
- 1/3 cup pine nuts, lightly toasted
- Sprigs of flat-leaf parsley, to garnish (optional)

1. Add enough oil to a large skillet to cover the bottom; heat over medium-high heat until hot and the surface is rippling. Dredge as many pieces of fish as will easily fit in the skillet, patting to remove excess flour. Cook until golden brown, about 2 to 4 minutes per side, depending on the thickness. With a slotted spatula, transfer the fish to an earthenware or porcelain dish large enough to hold the fish in a single layer. Season with salt and pepper. Continue dredging and cooking the remaining fish, adding oil as needed.
2. Heat the remaining oil and onion slices in the pan, stirring to separate them. Turn the heat to very low and continue cooking, stirring occasionally, until the onions are very soft and lightly colored, about 15 minutes.
3. Pour in the vinegar, raise the heat, and boil until the liquid is almost evaporated, about 5 to 7 minutes. Stir in the wine, adjust the heat to medium-low, and simmer for 20 minutes. Add the water and raisins and simmer 5 minutes longer. Scrape the onions and cooking liquid onto the fish.
4. Add the bay leaves and pine nuts, cover with heavy aluminum foil, and let marinate in a refrigerator or cool place for 12 to 24 hours.
5. Before serving, discard the bay leaves and let the fish return to room temperature. Garnish each plate with a small sprig of parsley, if desired.

Did you know? Lemon sole is much sought after for its fine-textured meat and delicate flavor. It is often one of the most expensive varieties of fillets in the Seafood department. The name lemon sole is actually a marketing term, referring to a large black-back flounder weighing over 3 pounds.

If there is a large whole flounder on the ice in the Seafood department, select this instead of lemon sole. It is the same fish and often dramatically less expensive.

Fluke, halibut, petrale sole, plaice, sand dabs, gray sole, and Pacific turbot are all flatfish belonging to the flounder family. One warning about sole is to be on the lookout for parasitic worms in/under the skin, occasionally found in sole and other bottom feeders. While they're not dangerous, they are unappealing.

INDIVIDUAL CURRIED SCALLOP STRUDELS

Serves 8

This recipe is a great favorite among my friends who entertain, since the strudels can be prepared a day ahead and the portions are easily served to each guest. I love the crunchiness of the phyllo layers. Here I added a small amount of ground nuts and dry mustard between the layers for added flavor. Working with phyllo is quite easy, once you get the hang of it. And, lots of different fillings can be wrapped inside. For a Tex-Mex variation, see Individual Chili Strudels on page 130.

FOR THE FILLING:

3/4 cup clam juice

1 1/2 pounds sea scallops cut in eighths, or bay scallops

2 tablespoons unsalted butter

2 tablespoons flour

1 tablespoon freshly grated gingerroot

4 teaspoons curry powder (hot or mild)

1/2 teaspoon salt, or to taste

Freshly ground black pepper to taste

1/8 teaspoon ground red pepper

2 large cloves garlic, peeled and minced

2 tablespoons fresh lemon juice

1 12 1/2-ounce jar Major Grey's chutney

2/3 cup thinly sliced scallions, including green parts

1 8-ounce can water chestnuts, drained and thinly sliced

FOR THE STRUDEL:

1/2 cup freshly toasted bread crumbs

3 tablespoons finely chopped walnuts

1/2 teaspoon dry mustard

1/2 teaspoon salt

12 phyllo leaves

8 tablespoons (1 stick) unsalted butter, melted

Paprika, to garnish

24 snow peas, 16 cherry tomatoes, sliced scallions for garnish (optional)

1. Make the filling: Pour the clam juice into a medium-sized skillet, add the scallops, and bring to a simmer. Poach the scallops until barely cooked, about 2 minutes. Drain, reserving the broth.
2. Dry the skillet. Melt 2 tablespoons of butter over medium-high heat. Add the flour and cook until pale brown, stirring with a wooden spoon. Whisk in the reserved clam juice, ginger, curry powder, salt, black pepper, red pepper, garlic, and lemon juice. The mixture will be thick. Cook over medium heat for 2 to 3 minutes, then remove the pan from the heat.
3. Before pouring the chutney from the bottle, heat it in a pan of water or (without the top) in a microwave. Strain the chutney, reserving the liquid. Cut the fruit into thin slivers. There will be about 1/2 cup fruit (mango) pieces. Add the chutney, scallions, water chestnuts, and scallops to the curry mixture.
4. Preheat your oven to 400°F and lightly butter a jelly-roll pan.
5. Assemble the strudels: Mix the bread crumbs, walnuts, mustard, and salt in a food processor and pulse a few times to distribute the nuts and mustard evenly, or stir the ingredients together in a bowl.
6. Lay 1 leaf of phyllo with the long edge near you on a towel-lined work surface, covering the remaining phyllo with a dry towel. Brush the phyllo lightly with melted butter and distribute a generous tablespoon of crumb mixture over the entire leaf. Repeat with a second phyllo leaf, buttering and sprinkling with the crumb mixture. Add a third leaf, *do not* butter, and cut the pile of phyllo in half down the middle from top to bottom, using a sharp knife. Brush around the edges of each stack of phyllo with melted butter.

7. Spoon 1/2 cup of the filling along each of the lower edges of the strudel, leaving about 1 inch of phyllo free of filling on either end. Holding each side of the towel in a hand, flip the towel toward the back, causing the phyllo to roll over the filling. Continue to roll until about half of the phyllo is rolled, then turn the side edges in to form neat packets, and finish rolling. Using your hands or a spatula, transfer the strudels carefully onto the buttered jelly-roll pan, placing them seam-side down. Brush with melted butter and sprinkle with paprika. Continue with the remaining phyllo and filling.

8. Bake in the top third of the oven until the strudels are golden brown, about 12 to 14 minutes. Serve at once or leave in a turned-off oven for up to 45 minutes. Place one strudel on each plate with a fan design of 3 lightly steamed snow peas and a couple of cherry tomatoes for garnish. Sprinkle a couple of scallion rings on top, if desired. Pass the remaining chutney and its liquid at the table.

Did you know? Fresh scallops—not previously frozen ones—freeze very well. If properly frozen and defrosted, it is virtually impossible to tell them from fresh. When they are on sale, check the freshness code on the plastic container or ask when they came into the store. If not using them within 2 days of this date, freeze them immediately. When the scallops are packaged in shrink-wrapped trays, be sure to rinse them under cold water, drain, and freeze in airtight containers, leaving a small amount of space at the top for expansion.

WARM SALMON MOUSSE IN A PHYLLO CROWN

Serves 12 for a first course or 8 as a main course

- 2 pounds fresh salmon, skinned and boned
- 4 egg whites
- 1 1/2 cups heavy cream
- 1/4 teaspoon freshly grated nutmeg
- Pinch ground red pepper
- Salt and white pepper to taste
- 1 1/2 tablespoons finely chopped fresh tarragon or 1 1/2 teaspoons dried tarragon
- 1 tablespoon finely chopped flat-leaf parsley
- 10 tablespoons unsalted butter
- 8 phyllo leaves
- watercress sprigs, to garnish (optional)
- 1 recipe Cool and Tangy Watercress Sauce (page 46)

This elegant warm salmon mousse is wrapped in a crown of golden flaky pastry and served with Cool and Tangy Watercress Sauce (see page 46), a pleasing contrast in color and temperature.

IMPORTANT: Have the salmon, egg whites, cream, and all equipment very cold.

1. Divide the salmon almost in half, reserving the smaller amount. Cut the larger amount into 3 to 4 pieces, put it in a food processor and purée until smooth, scraping down the sides as needed. With the motor running, pour the egg whites through the feed tube, blending well; then add the heavy cream. Add the spices and pulse a few times to blend. Remove the blade from the bowl, cover the bowl with plastic wrap, and refrigerate until ready for use.
2. Cut the remaining salmon into small cubes. Melt 2 tablespoons of the butter in a medium-sized skillet over medium-high heat. Add the salmon and sauté for 1 minute, stirring often, then remove from the heat and cool.
3. Preheat your oven to 375ºF and generously butter a bundt pan.
4. Melt the remaining 8 tablespoons of butter. Brush 1 phyllo leaf with butter, covering the remaining leaves with a dry towel until ready to use. Fold the phyllo leaf into quarters lengthwise and drape it inside the pan with the long edge hanging over the outside edge of the pan. The inner edge should come just to the top edge of the center tube. Repeat with the remaining 7 leaves.
5. Fill the pan with half of the salmon mixture. Arrange the salmon cubes evenly over this and scrape the remaining mixture over the salmon, smoothing the mousse with the back of a spoon or a spatula. Cover the mousse with the extended phyllo leaves, gently pushing the leaves together at the center. Brush liberally with butter, and bake in the middle of the oven until the top is crisp and golden colored, about 35 to 40 minutes. Remove pan from the oven, invert onto an ovenproof serving dish, lift off the pan, and return the mousse to the oven for 10 minutes for additional crispness.
6. Remove the mousse from the oven and let it stand for 5 to 7 minutes before slicing. Garnish with some fresh watercress sprigs, if desired. Cut into wedges with a serrated knife, and spoon Cool and Tangy Watercress Sauce around each slice.

Did you know? Before cooking frozen fish, only partially defrost the whole fish or steaks in a refrigerator. They will lose less moisture that way.

LOBSTER TIMBALES WITH RIESLING BEURRE BLANC

Serves 6

If you are a selective shopper, glamorous fare is available from your supermarket. This dish is extravagant, elegant, and delicious—definitely an indulgence for a very special occasion. The pairing of lobster with sweet wine affords a wonderfully rich, complex combination of flavors. The essence of lobster and aromatic vegetables are distilled into the shimmering custard.

2 1 1/2-pound live lobsters

Court Bouillon for Poaching Fish (see page 174) or salted water

5 tablespoons unsalted butter + butter to grease custard cups

2 medium shallots, peeled and minced

1 medium carrot, peeled and minced

1/2 red bell pepper, seeds and membranes removed, and minced (about 1/4 cup)

2 1/2 cups heavy cream + liquid drained from the lobster shells to make 3 1/2 cups liquid

2 whole eggs

3 egg yolks

1/4 cup Late Harvest Riesling or sweet white wine

Pinch of ground red pepper

1/8 teaspoon freshly grated nutmeg

Salt and white pepper to taste

1 recipe Late Harvest Johannesburg Riesling Beurre Blanc (page 209)

18 small scallions, trimmed to 5 to 6 inches, for garnish

1. Fill a pot large enough to hold both lobsters with Court Bouillon or salted water and bring to a boil. Add the lobsters, return the liquid to a boil and cook for 14 minutes. Remove the lobsters and cool slightly. Working with the lobsters over a large bowl to catch the juice, break off the tails and remove the meat. Twist off and crack the claws, removing as much meat as possible. Drain enough of the liquid from within the body of the lobster into the cream to make 3 1/2 cups of liquid. Reserve the meat from 1 large claw to use in the sauce. Cover the lobster meat and set aside.
2. Discard the head. Break the emptied lobster shells into small pieces.
3. In the same pot used to cook the lobsters, melt 3 tablespoons of the butter over medium-high heat. Stir in the shallots, carrot, and red pepper and sauté until softened, about 5 minutes, stirring frequently. Add the cream and lobster shells, including the small legs, and bring the mixture to a simmer. Cook, partially covered, for about 25 minutes.
4. While the cream is simmering, transfer the lobster meat (except for the reserved claw meat) to a food processor and pulse until almost smooth. Scrape into a bowl and set aside.
5. Preheat your oven to 325°F and butter six 3/4-cup custard cups or a 6-cup ring mold. Bring a pot of water to a boil.
6. Line a fine strainer with a double thickness of cheesecloth or heavy-duty paper towels. Strain the simmered cream, vegetables, and lobster shells into a large measuring cup or bowl, pressing with the back of a spoon to extract all the flavor. In a large bowl, whisk the eggs and egg yolks together. Pour the wine into the cream mixture, then add the liquid to the eggs in a slow, steady stream, stirring continuously. (Do not overbeat, or a foam will form on top.) Stir in the ground red pepper, nutmeg, salt, white pepper, and lobster meat.

7. Ladle the lobster mixture into the cups or mold, and set them into a baking dish large enough to hold them. Pour enough boiling water into the large baking dish to come halfway up the side of the cups, and cover the custard with waxed paper. Transfer the pan to the bottom third of the oven and bake for 30 minutes, or until a knife inserted near the middle of the custard comes out clean. Carefully remove the baking dish from the oven and let the cups sit in the water while you prepare the Late Harvest Johannesburg Riesling Beurre Blanc and garnish.
8. Chop the reserved claw meat into fine dice and stir it into the beurre blanc.
9. Before serving, sauté the trimmed scallions in 2 tablespoons of butter until barely wilted, about 2 to 3 minutes, and set aside. Loosen each custard with a sharp knife and invert it onto a heated plate. Spoon the beurre blanc around the timbales. Lay 3 scallions arched around each lobster timbale.

NOTE: To serve the timbales cold, replace the Late Harvest Johannesburg Riesling Beurre Blanc with Cool and Tangy Watercress Sauce (page 46) and garnish with sprigs of watercress.

COURT BOUILLON FOR POACHING FISH

Makes about 1 gallon

Court bouillon is often used to enhance the flavor of a fish as it is poached. It's easy to make, and once the fish has been poached (for example, Chilled Whole Cod Tonnato on page 182) in it, it can be reduced and turned into a fish aspic. It may also then be frozen. If you are not poaching a fish but want fish stock, add the trimmings and bones from 3 or 4 lean white fish to the liquid instead of the whole fish.

- 12 cups (3 quarts) water
- 1 bottle dry white wine
- 3/4 cup white wine vinegar
- 3 large onions, each stuck with 3 whole cloves
- 4 medium carrots, chopped
- 2 medium stalks of celery with leaves, chopped
- 1 bay leaf
- 1 teaspoon dried thyme leaves
- 6 sprigs flat-leaf parsley
- 6 black peppercorns
- 1 tablespoon salt

1. Combine all of the ingredients in a large pot or fish poacher and bring just to a boil; then reduce the heat and simmer for 1 hour before adding the fish to be poached.
2. To turn the bouillon into aspic once the fish (or additional bones and trimmings) has been cooked and removed, strain it into a clean pot through several layers of cheesecloth or a fine mesh strainer lined with two layers of dampened paper towels. Simmer to reduce by about two-thirds, skimming the surface if necessary. Chill until firm.

TANGY CIOPPINO

Serves 6 as a main course

Cioppino is a fish stew that is said to have originated in San Francisco. It is similar to bouillabaisse, from the south of France. As in most stews, ingredients may be substituted for one another. This recipe is meant as a guideline. Use it as a base and improvise from there, selecting what is the best the day you go marketing. I like this version because the addition of vinegar, oil, and garlic at the end really lifts the flavors. Generous bowls of cioppino, served with a crisp green salad, garlicky toasted French bread, and a chilled bottle of crisp white wine, are great for a Sunday supper.

Oysters, mussels, and clams are difficult to buy when shrink-wrapped. In these cases, you must know that the Seafood buyer's sources are reliable. If the shellfish is on ice, touch any open shell to be sure it closes. When steamed, any clam, mussel, or oyster shell that remains shut should be discarded without being eaten.

- 1 pound littleneck clams, scrubbed
- 1 pound mussels, debearded and scrubbed
- 2 cups cold water
- 8 tablespoons fruity extra-virgin olive oil
- 1 large green pepper, seeds and membranes removed, finely chopped
- 1 large onion, peeled and finely chopped
- 2–3 large cloves garlic, peeled and minced
- 1 1/2 cups dry white wine
- 1 6-ounce can tomato paste
- 1 28-ounce can crushed Italian tomatoes
- 2 teaspoons dried basil
- 1 bay leaf
- 1/2 teaspoon red pepper flakes
- 1/4 teaspoon crumbled saffron threads
- 1/2 cup chopped flat-leaf parsley
- Salt and freshly ground black pepper
- 3/4 pound monkfish fillets, cut into 1-inch cubes
- 3/4 pound red snapper fillets, cut into 1 1/2-inch strips
- 3/4 pound medium shrimp, peeled and deveined
- 2 tablespoons red wine vinegar
- 1 tablespoon finely minced garlic

1. Combine the clams and mussels with the water in a large, non-reactive pot. Cover with a tight-fitting lid and cook gently until the shells open, 5 to 6 minutes. Remove the clams and mussels to a bowl and cover. Strain the broth through a double thickness of cheesecloth or a fine-mesh strainer lined with paper towels and reserve. Rinse and dry the pot.
2. Add 3 tablespoons of the olive oil to the pot and heat until fragrant. Stir in the pepper, onion, and garlic, and sauté over medium heat until softened, about 7 minutes.
3. Pour in the wine, bring it to a boil, then stir in the reserved clam-mussel broth, tomato paste, crushed tomatoes, basil, bay leaf, red pepper flakes, saffron, parsley, salt, and plenty of pepper. Reduce the heat and gently boil uncovered until slightly thickened, about 20 minutes.
4. Add the monkfish, simmer for 2 minutes; then add the red snapper and shrimp, and simmer 3 minutes more. Return the clams and mussels to the pot. Combine the vinegar, remaining 5 tablespoons of olive oil, and minced garlic and stir this into the cioppino. Cover and simmer for 10 minutes. Serve at once with thin slices of French bread rubbed with garlic and brushed with olive oil, if desired.

NOTE: Although cioppino is best when served right away, it may be made ahead and gently reheated until hot.

STEAMED MUSSELS WITH CHILE AND LEMONGRASS

Serves 2

- 1 tablespoon unsalted butter
- 1/2 medium red onion, sliced
- 1 stalk lemongrass, trimmed, center portion finely chopped
- 1 clove garlic, finely chopped
- 1/2 Thai chile or 1 small jalapeño pepper, seeded and thinly sliced
- 1 pound mussels, debearded and scrubbed
- 2 cups dry white wine
- 1 cup fish stock, clam broth, or water
- 3 large sprigs flat-leaf parsley
- Juice of 1/2 lemon
- Salt and freshly ground black pepper to taste

There's nothing unexpected about a pot of mussels in white wine and garlic. I simply love them. However, I was surprised and pleased by this pleasantly spicy rendition of mussels in a broth that I tasted in Finland some years ago. The fusion of ingredients from halfway around the world with native Finnish shellfish is outstanding. Serve the mussels directly from the pot with crusty French bread to soak up every last drop of sauce. You could also add a 1/2 cup of canned coconut milk before serving for a slightly richer version.

1. Melt the butter in a deep casserole over medium-high heat. Add the onion and sauté until wilted, then stir in lemongrass, garlic, and chile and cook for 30 seconds.
2. Add the mussels, wine, stock, and parsley. Cover and cook just until the mussels open. Squeeze on the lemon juice, season with salt and pepper, stir, and serve. Discard any mussels that do not open.

ASIAN CRAB-ASPARAGUS SALAD

Serves 4

The colors and flavors of this crab salad are vibrant: green scallions, red-bordered radishes, and golden fried rice sticks.

Live hard- and soft-shelled crabs will seem calm on the ice of your store's Seafood department. As long as they move, they are fine. Watch them scurry about as the temperature goes up. Be sure that the crab, and all seafood on display, is kept cool. If fresh crabs are unavailable or you don't have time to remove the meat from the shell, look for small containers of picked fresh crabmeat in the Seafood department. It is pasteurized to guard against bacteria, like lysteria, but check the dates since freshness makes all the difference in how good it will taste.

Most crabmeat sold in markets comes from Atlantic blue crabs that are lightly steamed to remove the meat from the shells and may then be sold as fresh or frozen. "Lump" crabmeat is from the back legs; the pieces are large and white. It is usually the most expensive. "Backfin" crab is from the body and legs; the pieces are smaller with more shell in it. Some markets also sell "cocktail claws" with the shell still on for easy eating.

Asian rice noodles, also called rice vermicelli, are thin noodles made of rice flour. When added to hot oil they expand,becoming wonderfully crunchy.

½ package Asian rice noodles
Peanut oil for deep frying
1 pound thin asparagus, woody ends and scales removed
1 pound lump or backfin crabmeat, preferably fresh, all cartilage removed
3 tablespoons sesame seeds, toasted 3 to 4 minutes until golden
1 cup thinly sliced scallions, white and light green parts, and additional slices for garnish
½ cup thinly sliced radishes
⅓ cup rice vinegar
2 tablespoons dark sesame oil
2 tablespoons canola or vegetable oil
1 ½ tablespoons lemon juice
½ teaspoon salt, or to taste
Freshly ground black pepper to taste
A few drops hot pepper oil, to taste

1. Break the rice noodles in half. Pour the oil into a wok or deep skillet to a depth of about 2 inches and heat to 375ºF. Add the noodles, turning to cook evenly. This will take seconds if the oil is hot. Watch carefully. When golden brown, remove with tongs or a slotted spoon, and drain on paper towels.
2. Bring a large pot of water to a boil. Add the asparagus and cook until just tender, about 2 to 3 minutes after the water returns to a boil. Remove from the water, plunge into cold water to stop the cooking, and dry on paper towels. Cool, then cut the spears on the diagonal into quarters and set aside.
3. In a bowl, combine the asparagus with the crab, sesame seeds, scallions, radishes, vinegar, and sesame and vegetable oils. Toss, then add remaining ingredients and toss again.
4. Spread the fried rice sticks on 4 plates. Spoon on the crab salad and serve at once. Garnish it with scallion rings, if desired.

Did you know? What is surimi or imitation crabmeat? Right there, next to the crabs, may be a product marketed under the name "sea legs" or something similar. When king crab prices went sky-high, the Japanese started using inexpensive Alaskan pollock plus flavorings and coloring agents to produce this low-cost alternative. While this is an economical substitution in many recipes, my hesitation is due to the additives and extra sugar. Be sure to ask about ingredients.

BAKED SALMON FILLETS IN PARCHMENT

Serves 6

- 4 tablespoons unsalted butter, softened
- 6 5- to 6-ounce fillets of salmon, blotted dry
- Salt and freshly ground black pepper to taste
- 1 small zucchini, trimmed and cut into fine julienne
- 1 small yellow squash, trimmed and cut into fine julienne
- 1 small carrot, peeled and cut into fine julienne
- 12 small sprigs flat-leaf parsley

These salmon fillets are delicious right out of their puffed-up bags, with the julienned vegetables adding a touch of color. Of course, they may be dressed up with a sauce like Confetti Beurre Blanc (page 208), as well. Baking "en papillote" (wrapped in parchment paper) is easy. Simply remember to cut the parchment circles large enough so that the packets do not open up while cooking. The fish may be prepared a couple of hours ahead of time and refrigerated.

Paler-colored Atlantic salmon—like those from Ireland, Scotland, or Nova Scotia—have long been considered the most flavorful by fish fanciers. With dwindling numbers of these prized wild varieties, salmon is now being farmed with great success and is readily available in many markets. Pacific salmon is abundant and is wonderful eating, as well. If you can find wild Copper River salmon from Alaska in season, you are in for a flavorful treat. Of the western species, in season king (Chinook) red is most desirable. Arctic char is a close cousin. This is followed by the coho, sockeye, chum, and finally pink (which is usually canned) varieties.

1. Preheat your oven to 375°F.
2. Cut six 14-inch circles of parchment. Spread a teaspoon of butter on one half of each circle.
3. Rinse the fillets and pat them very dry with paper towels. Put 1 fillet on the buttered half of each parchment circle and season generously with salt and pepper. Put an equal amount of the zucchini, yellow squash, and carrot on each fillet, along with 2 sprigs of parsley. Dot the tops of the salmon with the remaining butter.
4. Fold the parchment paper in half and crimp the edges to seal completely. Transfer the packets to a jelly-roll pan and bake until the paper has puffed, about 13 to 14 minutes. Remove and serve at once on heated plates with orzo or parsleyed small boiled potatoes.

Did you know? Salmon is high in omega-3 oil, thought by many medical professionals to help in lowering cholesterol. If your cholesterol level is a concern, substitute olive oil for butter in this recipe.

QUICK PAELLA WITH MONKFISH

Serves 2 to 3

This saffron-flavored dish with rice, olives, and sausages is reminiscent of the classic Spanish dish paella. While this version uses fewer ingredients, the appeal is great for its ease of preparation, robust aroma, and colorful appearance.

Monkfish was once known as "poor man's lobster." With increased popularity, the price has risen to where it's no longer a poor man's anything, but its firm flesh is perfect here. Since many singles and couples like to "dine well at home," this is a recipe for two hearty appetites to savor together. If you are having a party, see the note at the end of this recipe for the do-ahead party version that serves 8 to 10.

- 3/4 pound monkfish fillets, cut into 1-inch cubes
- 1/4 cup dry white wine
- 3 tablespoons olive oil
- 1 6-ounce hot Italian sausage, cut into 3/4-inch slices
- 1 medium onion, peeled and chopped
- 1 large bulb fennel, trimmed and sliced into wedges
- 1 large clove garlic, peeled and minced
- 1/4 teaspoon crumbled saffron threads
- 1 1/3 cup chicken stock, heated
- 1/2 cup raw rice
- 1 teaspoon dried thyme leaves
- 1/2 cup drained chopped canned Italian tomatoes
- 1/2 cup oil-cured black olives
- 3/4 cup frozen peas, defrosted
- Salt and freshly ground black pepper to taste

1. Combine the monkfish with the wine in a flat glass or porcelain dish or resealable plastic bag just large enough to hold the fish and set aside.
2. In a medium-large skillet, heat 1 tablespoon of olive oil until fragrant. Add the sausage pieces and sauté over medium-high heat for 4 to 5 minutes, turning often to color all sides. Add another tablespoon of oil, stir in the onion and fennel, and sauté for 1 to 2 minutes. Stir in the garlic, cover, and adjust the heat to medium to sweat the vegetables until softened, about 10 to 12 minutes. Stir occasionally.
3. Stir the saffron into the heated stock. Add the last tablespoon of olive oil to the vegetable mixture and stir in the rice. Turn the heat to high, pour in the broth, add the thyme, and stir to blend. Cover the pan and adjust the heat down so that the liquid slowly simmers.
4. After 15 minutes, add the monkfish, wine, and tomatoes and simmer uncovered until almost all the liquid has evaporated, about 5 to 7 minutes. Turn the fish pieces to cook evenly. Stir in the olives, peas, salt, and plenty of pepper and taste for seasonings. Simmer 1 or 2 minutes longer. Serve immediately; it will wait for up to 1/2 hour partially covered over very low heat.

NOTE: For a party-size paella, use a very large, heavy casserole and proceed according to the directions above. Make the following substitutions in measurements:

- Multiply the monkfish, wine, sausage, fennel, garlic, chicken stock, rice, tomatoes, olives, and peas by 4
- Each addition of olive oil should be 3 tablespoons
- Use 2 large onions
- Double the amount of saffron and thyme

STIR-FRIED TUNA WITH GINGERED VEGETABLES

Serves 4

1 ounce dried shiitake or other Asian mushrooms or 3 ounces fresh white mushrooms, wiped, trimmed, and sliced

1/4 cup fresh lime juice (about 2 limes)

1/4 cup soy sauce

1/3 cup dry sherry

2 tablespoons honey

1 1/4–1 1/2 pounds fresh tuna steaks, cut into 1-inch cubes

4 medium carrots, peeled

1 egg white

1 teaspoon cornstarch

4 tablespoons peanut oil

2 large cloves garlic, peeled and split

1 tablespoon finely diced fresh gingerroot

1/2 pound snow peas, washed, strings removed, blanched, and drained

1 cup thinly sliced scallions, including most of the green parts

1 tablespoon sesame oil

Many of us who grew up on canned tuna mixed with mayonnaise and a little chopped celery had no idea how wonderful fresh tuna is. Today it's everywhere. In this recipe, I chose to stir-fry the fish because the cubes of tuna stay very moist and succulent when cooked quickly. They are well balanced by the color and the crunch of the carrots and snow peas in this Asian-inspired dish. Serve with rice or lo mein noodles.

Although fresh tuna steaks have a relatively long shelf life, look to see how the fish is stored. Is it resting directly on ice, or is there a piece of plastic or a metal liner protecting it from losing color and favor? Are the steaks misted periodically to keep the edges from curling and the fish from drying out? Does the surface look pearly? Sometimes a fish's age is less important than how it has been cared for.

1. If using dried mushrooms: In a small bowl, cover mushrooms with warm water, soak until softened, about 20 to 30 minutes, then drain, remove the coarse stems, rinse off any grit, and cut into thick slices.
2. Combine the lime juice, soy sauce, sherry, and honey in a resealable plastic bag and stir to blend. Add the tuna and marinate for 2 hours, turning the cubes after an hour.
3. Meanwhile, make a 1/4-inch-deep cut down the length of 1 carrot. Make a second cut 1/4-inch to the left and slice in at an angle to meet the first cut, removing a V-shaped wedge (see illustration). Repeat these cuts in 4 or 5 more places equidistant around the carrot. Repeat with 3 remaining carrots. (Note: This step is optional. For a simpler method, cut the carrot on the diagonal into long, oval-shaped slices.)
4. Steam the carrots until almost tender, about 3 to 5 minutes. Drain and set aside.
5. Remove the tuna with a slotted spoon and pat dry with paper towels. Reserve the marinade. Whisk the egg white and cornstarch together in a medium bowl, add the tuna, and toss to cover.
6. Heat 1 tablespoon of oil in a wok or skillet until very hot. Working in batches, quickly stir-fry the tuna, tossing to cook all sides, about 1 to 2 minutes. The tuna will become light colored with a slight crispness on the edge. Remove the cooked tuna to a bowl with a slotted spoon. Repeat until all tuna is cooked, adding another tablespoon of oil, as needed.

7. Wipe out the wok and heat 1 tablespoon of oil in it. Add the 2 split cloves of garlic, cook for a few seconds until lightly browned. Add the diced ginger, cook for 30 seconds, then stir in the snow peas, mushrooms, carrots, and marinade and cook over high heat to reduce the liquid by half. Return the tuna plus scallions and sesame oil to the wok. Heat to blend the flavors and serve at once.

NOTE: Shrimp or swordfish work well in this recipe, too.

Did you know? Albacore tuna, called "white-meat tuna," has the lightest meat and is the most valuable canned tuna. It is less oily than other species and has a very mild flavor. Yellowfin tuna is a little darker in color than albacore and, when canned, it is known as "light." It is much in demand for raw tuna dishes such as carpaccio and sushi because of its delicate flavor and light color. Bigeye tuna and skipjack tuna are other mild varieties. Bluefin tuna is oily, darker in color, and has a more pronounced "fishy" flavor. It is recommended that pregnant and nursing women avoid eating a lot of canned tuna, as it contains high levels of mercury that can harm a developing fetus or nursing baby.

CHILLED WHOLE COD TONNATO

Serves 8 to 10

This cod dish is ideal for entertaining because it serves a crowd and tastes better if made the previous day. It's a variation on vitello tonnato, a classic Italian veal dish made with a tuna mayonnaise and served cold.

Whole cod is a reasonably priced fish. Dressed up with layers of cucumber "scales," it makes a dramatic addition to any summer buffet table. And the fish certainly is obtainable. Speak directly to the Seafood manager and let him know what day you need it (a day before the party). The market can possibly even poach it for you.

As a lovely garnish on the platter, lightly steam a pound of julienned carrots and toss with lemon juice, vegetable oil, chopped basil or parsley, salt, and pepper. Arrange the carrots around the fish. Serve with some crusty sourdough bread and a robust white wine, such as a Greco di Tufo. Finish the meal with a fresh fruit tart or Chilled White Wine Soufflé with Apricot Sauce (page 213).

FOR THE TUNA MAYONNAISE (TONNATO SAUCE):

1 6 1/2-ounce can imported tuna packed in olive oil

1/2 2-ounce can anchovy fillets, rinsed and patted dry

1/4 cup small capers

1/4 cup fresh lemon juice

3/4 cup fruity extra-virgin olive oil

1 1/3 cups mayonnaise, preferably homemade with extra-virgin olive oil or a combination of olive and vegetable oils

FOR THE COD:

1 8-pound cod, whole, with head on, cleaned, gilled, and gutted with the center blood vein and air bladder (sound) removed

Court Bouillon (see recipe on page 174) to completely cover the fish in poacher

2 large cucumbers, washed, for garnish

Olive slices, for garnish

1. Make the tuna mayonnaise: In a food processor, combine the tuna, anchovies, capers, and lemon juice, and process until smooth. With the processor on, pour the oil through the feed tube in a slow, steady stream. (If doing this by hand, mash the tuna, anchovies, capers, and lemon juice with a fork. Whisk in the oil in a slow, steady stream.) Fold the tuna mixture into the mayonnaise and blend well. Cover and refrigerate until needed.
2. Poach the cod: Lay the fish on its side and measure its height at the thickest point. Figure on 9 to 10 minutes poaching time per inch of thickness once the poaching liquid returns to a boil. Placing the fish on a poaching rack will make for easier handling; otherwise the fish may be wrapped in a couple of layers of cheesecloth.
3. Fill a fish poacher or shallow pot large enough to hold the fish flat with Court Bouillon. Bring to a boil and lower the fish into the pot. When the liquid returns to a boil, turn down the heat so that it never bubbles or boils. Time as directed above in Step 2.
4. Once the fish is cooked, remove it from the liquid to a platter and let it cool for a few minutes. If cheesecloth has been used, carefully cut it open with scissors. Skin the fish and remove the head if it has fallen apart or you don't want to use it. Slide the cheesecloth from under the cod, using a wide spatula to help. It is not necessary to remove the skin on the underside. Leave the tail intact. Drain and blot any liquid on the platter with paper towels, cover the fish loosely with foil, and refrigerate until cold.

5. Assemble the fish: Spoon off all liquid from the platter. Spread the mayonnaise liberally over and around the fish, covering any cracks in the fish, but leaving the tail uncovered. Reserve the remaining sauce to pass at the table.
6. Run the tines of a fork lengthwise along the outside of both cucumbers. Slice them in a food processor fitted with a very thin slicing blade, or by hand. Cut the slices in half and create scales on the fish, working from the tail toward the head. You can create gills, too.

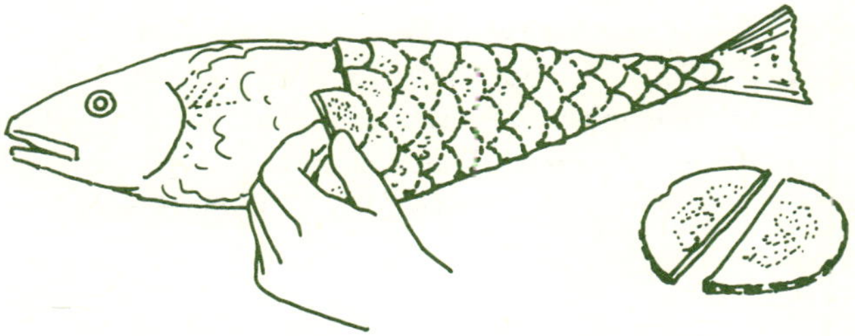

7. If the fish head has been discarded, stop the scale pattern about 2 ½ inches from the front end and re-create a head by changing the direction of the scales and using an olive slice for an eye. Cover the fish loosely and refrigerate for 4 to 6 hours or preferably overnight.

SAUTÉED SWORDFISH WITH MUSTARD-PECAN COATING

Serves 3 to 4

Swordfish is one of my family's favorite summer foods. We often barbecue the steaks well into the fall, as long as the grill will light. (See "Another idea..." below on grilling swordfish.) In this all-weather recipe, the crunchy coating and tarragon cream add an elegant touch, while keeping the fish moist.

This large, firm-fleshed fish is found in warm waters around the world. In supermarkets and fish stores, fresh swordfish steaks are especially popular during the summer and fall months. Swordfish also freezes well. The Japanese ship frozen, individually Cryovac-packed steaks and whole sides, which are cut into steaks on a bandsaw in the market. Under these conditions, I prefer to buy the fish solidly frozen and then cook it when only partially defrosted to retain as much moisture as possible.

- 1 1/2–1 3/4 pounds swordfish steaks, 1 inch thick (1 or 2 large steaks preferred), patted dry
- Flour for dredging
- 1/4 cup Dijon mustard
- 1 1/2 cups finely chopped pecans, not pulverized
- 1 1/2 tablespoons unsalted butter
- 1 1/2 tablespoons vegetable oil
- 1/2 cup heavy cream
- 1 tablespoon freshly chopped tarragon or 1 teaspoon dried
- Tarragon leaves, for garnish

1. Lightly dredge one side of the fish with flour and spread on half the mustard. Press half the pecans into the mustard coating. Turn and repeat the same process on the second side. Put on a plate, tent loosely with aluminum foil, and refrigerate for 30 minutes.
2. Turn your oven on low and heat a platter.
3. Melt the butter and oil in a large, heavy nonstick skillet over medium-high heat. Add the swordfish and sauté for 4 to 5 minutes until golden brown. Adjust the heat down if the pecans begin to burn. With a wide spatula, turn the fish and continue cooking the second side for 4 to 5 minutes. Transfer the fish to the warmed platter in the oven.
4. Add the cream, tarragon, and any nuts that have fallen off the fish to the skillet, turn the heat up to high, scrape up all the browned bits, and boil for 2 to 3 minutes to thicken the sauce. Return the fish and any liquid to the pan. You may wish to cut the fish into 3 or 4 serving-size portions at this point if it has been cooked whole. Turn the heat to low and cook 30 seconds more. Sprinkle a few tarragon leaves on each piece of fish, and serve at once on heated plates.

Another idea . . . To barbecue swordfish steaks, combine 1/4 cup fresh lemon juice, 1 cup olive oil, 2 large cloves of garlic, and 1/2 teaspoon freshly ground black pepper in a flat dish large enough to hold 6 servings of 1-inch swordfish steaks. Turn once to cover both sides, then refrigerate for 2 to 3 hours.

Position the barbecue grill about 6 inches from the charcoal briquettes. When the fire is hot, put on the steaks, baste once, then turn after 4 to 5 minutes with a spatula. Baste again with the remaining marinade and cook for 3 to 4 minutes more. Transfer the fish to a serving platter and serve with 1 or 2 swirls of Red Pepper Butter (page 38) or herbed butter.

BAKED FLOUNDER WITH HAZELNUTS AND SHRIMP

Serves 4

The exquisite balance of flavors in this festive dish comes from the combination of sweet, delicately crunchy fish with hazelnuts and shrimp scattered on top.

Flounder is really a small sole. The fish is available year-round. When buying fish whole, it's best to make your selections from a Service Fish counter, so you can ask about the fish's age and condition. Here is where having a friend behind the counter is important. If wrapped in plastic, flounder may not be as fresh as you'd like. If the head has been removed, look at where the cut was made. Edges yellow and curl with age.

FOR THE SAUCE:

1 cup dry white wine

½ cup fish stock or clam broth

¼ cup dry vermouth

1 tablespoon red wine vinegar

2 tablespoons minced shallots

1 cup heavy cream

¼ cup hazelnut oil

FOR THE FISH

4 1-pound whole flounders, head sliced off at an angle, gutted, gilled, dark skin removed, and white skin scaled only

Salt and freshly ground black pepper

1 tablespoon unsalted butter, at room temperature

10 tablespoons clarified butter

1 cup freshly toasted fine bread crumbs

24 small shrimp, peeled and deveined

3 tablespoons chopped fresh tarragon or 2 teaspoons dried tarragon plus 1 tablespoon chopped flat-leaf parsley

White pepper to taste

Pinch ground red pepper

20 hazelnuts, lightly toasted, and coarsely chopped

1. Prepare the sauce: In a small saucepan, combine ½ cup of the white wine, the fish stock, vermouth, vinegar, and shallots, and bring to a boil over high heat. Cook until the liquid almost completely evaporates. Add the cream and hazelnut oil and boil gently until slightly thickened. Partially cover and set aside.
2. Cook the fish: Meanwhile, preheat your oven to 425ºF and butter a baking dish just large enough to hold the fish comfortably without crowding.
3. Wipe the flounder and season inside with salt and pepper. Brush both sides with clarified butter and lay them in the baking dish, skin-side up. Press the bread crumbs onto the top of each fish and drizzle the remaining butter over the crumbs. Pour the remaining ½ cup of wine around the fish, taking care not to moisten the crumbs. Bake in the middle of the oven for 13 to 14 minutes. Have ready 4 heated plates.
4. Once the fish is cooked and the crumbs are golden brown, remove the dish from the oven and carefully transfer the fish to heated plates. (If the fish is not well colored, run it briefly under a broiler, watching carefully not to burn the crumbs.) Leave the fish in the turned-off oven lightly tented with aluminum foil while finishing the sauce.
5. Stir the shrimp into the thickened sauce and cook until pink, about 1 to 2 minutes. Add 2 tablespoons of the tarragon, salt, and white and red peppers, and taste to adjust the seasonings.
6. Remove the fish from the oven, blot any liquid, add 3 shrimp on either side of each fish, and sprinkle some hazelnuts and some of the remaining tarragon down the middle. Spoon the sauce around the plates and serve at once.

POACHED RED SNAPPER FILLETS WITH SCALLOP MOUSSE IN CABBAGE PACKETS

Serves 2

These red snapper fillets are filled with a chive-flecked scallop mousse, wrapped in delicate green napa cabbage leaves, and poached in the oven. The extra mousse mixture is poached as dumplings, or quenelles, and used to decorate the plates. Served on a light tomato sauce, the fish is beautiful to look at and deliciously satisfying to eat. Steamed carrots and parsleyed new potatoes would be a nice accompaniment.

2 large napa cabbage leaves

FOR THE SCALLOP MOUSSE:

1/2 pound sea scallops, very cold

2 1/2 tablespoons heavy cream, very cold

1 egg white, chilled

2 teaspoons finely chopped fresh chives

Salt and pepper to taste

FOR THE FISH PACKETS:

1 teaspoon unsalted butter

2 6-ounce red snapper fillets, skin removed, as flat as possible

1 cup dry white wine

1 cup fish stock or clam broth

FOR THE LIGHT TOMATO SAUCE:

1 tablespoon unsalted butter

1 large shallot, peeled and minced

1 large ripe tomato, peeled, seeded, and finely chopped or 3/4 cup drained, finely chopped Italian canned tomatoes

2 teaspoons chopped fresh chives

Paprika, for garnish

1. Prepare the mousse: Bring a small skillet partially filled with water to a simmer. Cook the cabbage leaves for about 30 seconds until soft and pliable. Remove, plunge into cold water, then blot dry. With a sharp paring knife, slice away the raised rib on each leaf, taking care not to cut all the way through. Spread the leaves flat on a towel, cover with a damp towel, and set aside.
2. In a food processor, combine the scallops, cream, and egg white, and process until smooth. Scrape down the sides, add the chives, salt, and pepper, and pulse a few times to blend.
3. Preheat your oven to 400°F. Lightly butter a small baking dish.
4. Fill the fish: Put a fillet with the wider end of the fish on the rib-end of the cabbage. Season with salt and pepper. Spoon a rounded tablespoon of the scallop mousse on the wider end of the fish. Begin rolling the fillet up, including the cabbage leaf. About halfway, turn in the edges of the cabbage, and continue rolling to form a neat package, then put in the baking dish. Set aside the remaining mousse for the quenelles.

5. Combine half of both the white wine and stock in a small saucepan, bring to a simmer, then pour over the fish. Or, if the baking dish is able to withstand direct heat, pour the liquid over the fish and bring it to a simmer on top of the stove. Cover with aluminum foil and transfer to the oven for 15 minutes.

6. Prepare the fish dumplings (quenelles): In a small skillet bring the remaining white wine and stock to a simmer. Using a pair of teaspoons, scoop up 1 rounded teaspoon of the scallop mixture. Shape the top into a round form with a second spoon. Then, with the second spoon, scoop under the oval-shaped mound and let it fall gently into the simmering liquid. Continue with the remaining mixture, making about 5 to 6 more fish dumplings.

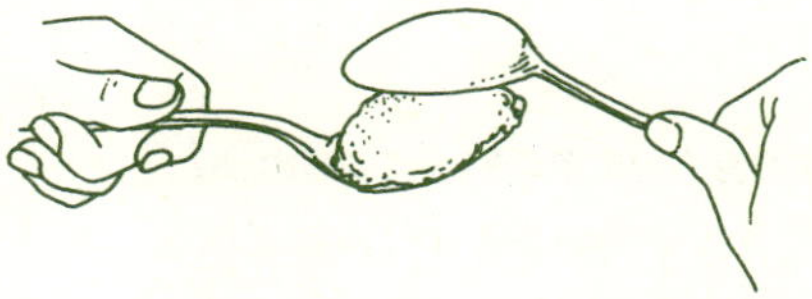

7. Poach for about 2 minutes on the first side, then gently turn, and cook for another 1 1/2 to 2 minutes. Once the dumplings are cooked, turn off the heat, and leave them in the liquid.

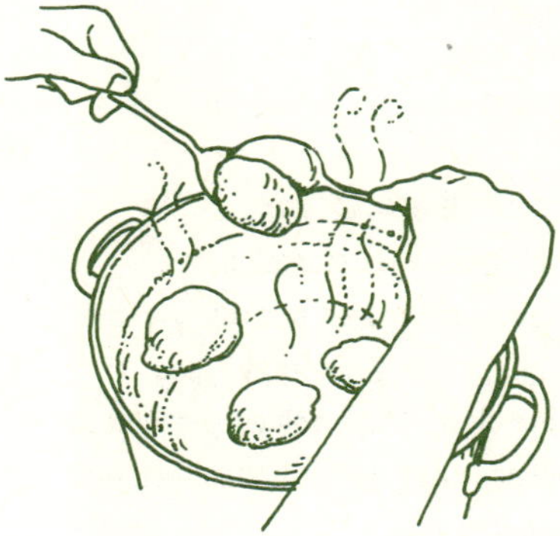

8. Prepare the sauce: In a small non-reactive saucepan, melt the butter over medium-high heat. Add the shallots and sauté for 1 to 2 minutes, stirring occasionally, until softened. Stir in the tomato and continue cooking for another 2 to 3 minutes. Season with salt and pepper.

9. To serve: Remove the fish from the oven, drain the packets on paper towels but do not unwrap them. Divide the sauce between 2 heated plates. Add the red snapper and 3 scallop dumplings alongside the roll. Sprinkle with chives and paprika, and serve at once.

NOTE: This recipe may be doubled to serve 4.

Did you know? When cooking fish fillets, they hold their shape and moisture content better when the skin is left on. They may also be served this way.

MALTESE FISH PIE

Serves 8 to 12

I first tasted this substantial torta tal-lampuki, or deep-dish fish pie, in Malta. Its unusual combination of ingredients reflects how many cultural influences have been blended into that country's cuisine. The robust mixture of fish, onions, olives, capers, and tomatoes, much like a Sicilian caponata, is sealed in a pasta frolla crust. Raisins and mint impart a Middle Eastern flavor. Serve the pie hot or at room temperature.

In Malta, the white, firm-fleshed lampuki, also called dolphin-fish or dorado, is prized for its delicate sweet taste. It is known here as mahi-mahi. If you cannot find it, substitute swordfish, tuna, or shark.

FOR THE PASTA FROLLA:

2 cups unbleached, all-purpose flour

20 tablespoons (2 1/2 sticks) unsalted butter, chilled and cut into pieces

1 teaspoon salt

2 egg yolks

7–9 tablespoons red wine

FOR THE FILLING:

3 tablespoons vegetable oil

1 large onion, peeled and thinly sliced

1 large rib celery, finely chopped

1 large clove garlic, peeled and minced

28-ounce can crushed Italian tomatoes

1/2 cup red wine

2/3 cup dark raisins

20 Calamata olives

2 tablespoons small capers, drained

2 teaspoons each dried basil and marjoram

1 teaspoon dried mint

Salt and freshly ground black pepper to taste

1 medium head cauliflower, boiled until tender, drained, and chopped into small pieces

2 pounds dolphin-fish or other firm-fleshed fish, cut into 1-inch cubes

3 medium red potatoes, boiled until tender, peeled, and sliced

1 egg mixed with 1 tablespoon milk

1. Prepare the crust: Combine the flour, butter, and salt in the bowl of a food processor and process until the mixture resembles small peas. Add the egg yolks, pulse once or twice, then add 7 tablespoons of the wine, and pulse until the pastry begins to pull into a ball, adding more wine by half-tablespoons, as needed. Remove from the processor and divide into two portions, one twice as large as the other. Pat the pastry into discs, dust with flour, cover with plastic wrap, and refrigerate while preparing the filling.
2. Prepare the filling: Heat 2 tablespoons of the oil in a large, heavy skillet over medium-high heat until hot. Add the onions and sauté until translucent, about 5 minutes. Add the remaining tablespoon of oil, stir in the celery, and cook until the onion is golden brown, about 7 minutes longer. Stir in the garlic.
3. Stir in the tomatoes, wine, raisins, olives, capers, basil, marjoram, mint, and salt and pepper. Simmer for at least 10 minutes, stirring occasionally, then add the cauliflower and turn the heat to low.
4. Preheat your oven to 400°F. Have ready an earthenware baking dish measuring about 10 by 14 by 2 1/2 inches. Roll a 3-inch strip of heavy aluminum foil widthwise around a wooden handle.
5. Lightly flour a large work space or pastry cloth. Roll the larger portion of pastry into about a 15-by-9-inch rectangle and 1/8 inch thick. Carefully transfer to the dish. Spoon half the sauce into the dish, distribute the fish and potato slices evenly over this, and add the remaining sauce.

Did you know? Dolphin-fish or mahi-mahi is delicious eating. It is not the mammal that is an endangered species.

6. Roll the remaining pastry into a rectangle large enough to cover the top of the dish and about 1/8 inch thick. Lay it on the dish. Leaving a 1/2-inch border around the edges, trim away excess pastry. Moisten the edges and crimp into a fluted design. Re-roll any trimmed pastry and cut into decorative shapes, such as fish or leaves, and attach to the top with a little water.
7. Cut a 1/2-inch air hole in the top crust. To help prevent the liquid from boiling over onto the crust, gently insert the aluminum vent into the hole. Brush the torta with egg wash and transfer it to the middle of the oven. After 15 minutes, turn the temperature down to 325°F, and cook until the top is a rich dark brown, about 45 minutes more. Remove and let stand for at least 15 minutes with the steam vent in place before serving.

Did you know? In Europe and Asia, fish is often served on the bone; more flavor and moisture are retained that way. If this is not to your liking, carefully split the fish along the center where the rib bones are attached to the backbone. Gently slide a knife along the upper ribs and then the lower ribs, forming 2 half fillets. Put the top fillets to one side. Lift off the skeleton in one piece and discard. Place the two top fillets back over the lower whole fillet, and serve.

LABEL LITERACY: EXTRA! EXTRA! READ ALL ABOUT IT

As an intelligent supermarket shopper, don't ignore the vital information available to you at no additional cost. Being "label literate" can save you money and ensure healthier eating. Increased consumer awareness of the effects of preservatives, fillers, coloring agents, as well as the overall freshness of our foods, has mandated governmental agencies, manufacturers, packers, and supermarkets to provide us with more information about what we are putting into our bodies. This is how it works:

Package Labeling

Dating on Fresh and Packaged Foods

"Sell by" or "pull by" dates indicate at what point the product must be taken off sale. If an item such as meat, bread, or milk is purchased by this date, the manufacturer, packager, or market has built in adequate time for the consumer to use the product safely at home.

"Best if used by" dates are indicated on cans and packaged goods, such as cereals, snacks, and nuts, that are less perishable. This often includes the year. Some refrigerated products use this or an "expiration date," indicating that the manufacturer feels that after this time the product should be discarded.

Another source of protection for the consumer is less obvious. It is the seven-letter-and-number code on some labels. This is used mostly in cases of emergency or recall, and it identifies the exact facility, line, shift, and date at which the product was packaged.

Ingredient Information on Prepared and Packaged Foods

All the ingredients included in a product are listed in order of weight from the greatest to the smallest amount. This includes flavoring and coloring agents, identified as artificial or natural, and preservatives and their use (to prevent caking, to protect flavor, etc.).

Although some foods—such as pasta, ice cream, and peanut butter—used to be made according to a standardized formula listed with the Food and Drug Administration and were not required to identify the basic components, current interest in additives has prompted more and more manufacturers to list all ingredients, including the different types of fat.

Nutritional Information

Manufacturers must list nutritional information including number of portions and portion size; the calories; amount of protein, carbohydrates, fat, and sodium; as well as the percentage of USRDA (U.S. Recommended Daily Allowances) nutrients.

If a label boasts that the product is fortified or enriched with vitamins or minerals, the Food and Drug Administration requires that supporting data be printed on the package. Similarly, if a product is marketed as "low sodium," "low fat," or "low carb"—the latest dietary rage—this must also be substantiated. Be aware that low-fat products are often high in sugar.

Any agricultural product labeled "organic" will soon require a statement confirming that it complies with the U.S. Organic Law. It must be grown and processed in accordance with the law, and this will be monitored by a USDA-approved certifier. As to what constitutes an "all natural" product, so far the USDA and FDA have not come up with a hard definition and the term is bandied around quite loosely.

Weight

While meat, fish, or poultry labels give the exact weight in pounds and tenths of pounds (1.3 pounds equals 1 and 3/10 of a pound, or 1 pound, 4.8 ounces), package or bottle labels indicate net (drained weight without liquid) or volume weight. Some packages also indicate that while the box was full when packed, it will settle during shipping.

Storage and Serving Information

Keeping foods in top condition once they are in your home depends on you. Be sure to check for storage suggestions on the label or packaging that may indicate refrigerating, freezing, or storing on a cool shelf.

Many manufacturers have test kitchens in which recipes and garnishing ideas are developed. This is a good source of primary information if the product is new to you.

Information "hotlines" are sometimes given for consumer problems and information.

Shelf Information

Unit Pricing

Unit pricing is indicated by small signs posted along the edge of each shelf, either above or below the items. Each sign identifies the item by brand, size, and price, and is a useful tool for comparison shopping, telling how much each unit measures:

✓ by weight, such as pounds or ounces for rice or hams

✓ by volume, such as a pint of milk or liquid detergent

✓ by length, such as feet for rolls of paper towels

✓ by quantity, such as number of napkins in each package

The sign also indicates the cost per package and how much this is in standard measurements, i.e., by the pound or gallon. Thus, even if package sizes are different, you can ascertain if one is more expensive than the other. However, even if two different manufacturers' products have the same unit cost, this does not guarantee that the quality will be the same.

Promotional and Sale Items

Some markets place a little flag or banner along the shelf when a certain item is specially priced.

Aisle Indicators

Don't ignore the overhead signs—especially if you are in a hurry. They will aim you in the right direction and allow you to skip unnecessary aisles.

Newer markets are installing electronic locators near the entrance or simplified guides on their carts to speed your marketing.

At the Register: Universal Product Codes

Computerized scanning systems read the UPC (bar) code on bottles, cans, and packages (including meats) with a beam of light. The grid of thin and thick lines on each package indicates the manufacturer and product. As the light passes over this mark, the computer reads the current price for the item in a data bank. All the information is then printed within seconds on your register receipt for future reference. In some cases, the machine also announces each purchase. Uncoded items are weighed at checkout. More and more markets now have self checkout lanes, as well.

It pays to watch as your foods are scanned. Sometimes there are errors, and sometimes the changes in special prices are overlooked. The price posted may differ from the price charged at the register.

Throughout the Market

Smart markets know that informed buyers are better buyers. They want to help you. Work at becoming an informed buyer. Look for consumer information brochures, handouts, hang tags, and warnings about certain products. There is a wealth of information available.

CHAPTER SIX: DAIRY PRODUCTS

INTRODUCTION 197

What's in a Name? • Buying Fresh • Home Care

INTRODUCTION

The familiar statement "I'm going to the market for a quart of milk" reminds us that most people buy dairy products in supermarkets. And with good reason. Since butter, eggs, and milk sell quickly, supplies are normally very fresh. In recent years, dairy shelf space has been expanded to hold a multitude of yogurt products, familiar and lesser-known cheeses, and butter and margarine combinations. Although dairy products have always been popular, recent interest in calcium, lactose-free and fat-reduced varieties, as well as those made with soy products have sparked greater demand for them. Low-carb diets have also initiated a surge in the market for full-fat dairy products.

What's in a Name?

When selecting dairy products, it is important to read labels. Cheese is especially confusing. If it is made from milk with only enzymes and heat added, the Food and Drug Administration allows it to be labeled by its name alone, such as "cheddar" or "Swiss." However, "processed cheese food" is a combination of different cheeses with emulsifiers, water, and coloring agents added. "Cheese spreads" usually include vegetable gums and sweeteners, as well.

Low-fat, low-sodium, and low-cholesterol products should have labeling to back up their claims. If no comparison is given, read the ingredient list. When highly saturated fats, such as palm oil, replace dairy fat, the product is no healthier. Look for added salts, fillers, and chemicals.

There are several low- or no-cholesterol egg substitutes on the market. Here, too, it is important to read their labels because some of them contain monosodium glutamate (MSG) and other chemicals you may want to avoid. The best (least artificial-tasting) product advertises that it is made from 90 percent egg.

Buying Fresh

To guarantee freshness, each dairy product must have a "sell by" date stamped on the package. It may be on a foil wrapper, on the bottom of a cup of yogurt, on the crimped top of a milk carton, or on the label. In most cases, the milk, cheese, or yogurt you buy will be in good condition and the date includes an adequate amount of time for home use.

However, if a distributor or market is careless, and storage temperatures have risen above 39° or 40°F, the cheese may be moldy or the cream almost soured. This often happens during promotions when "specialty items" are left out on display and ignored. Inspect each item as you pick it up. With cellophane-wrapped products and eggs in cartons, your eyes tell you the condition immediately. A strong indication of spoilage is a swollen carton or package. Even if the product is within code, make another choice. Be smart and return any spoiled product. It saves you money and keeps the market vigilant.

Another fact to consider is that markets rotate their stock and push older products toward the front. If you will eat a carton of cottage cheese within a few days, an older date is of little consequence. However, for longer storage, reach toward the back for the freshest date.

Home Care

Dairy products last quite well with a little attention. Refrigerate them quickly after purchase, making sure containers are closed. Cheese needs to be tightly rewrapped after each use. Even with proper wrapping, soft cheeses deteriorate quickly, often within a couple of days. Hard cheeses may last a couple of weeks. Stronger cheeses are best kept in separate plastic containers so the odors don't travel.

With the exception of butter and purchased frozen yogurt desserts, most dairy purchases are better not frozen. Cheese becomes crumbly, and sweet and sour creams separate.

Going to a neighborhood cheese shop is a wonderful experience. You can taste your way through the store, sampling a world of unusual and special dairy products. Supermarkets are trying to match that experience by expanding their inventory of imported and domestic items and bringing that old-fashioned feeling to the market.

While you may still be frustrated looking for a wonderful Reblochon or Taleggio cheese, markets are listening to their customers. Domestic cheeses have dramatically improved in quality and variety. Local and regional specialties are getting well-deserved attention, as well. Beyond offering samples of new products, they are providing printed material, educating their clerks, and trying to make their Dairy departments more diversified.

SPICY AND CRUNCHY LOW-CAL TOFU DIP

Makes 2 cups

With all the emphasis on how healthy soy products are, who says tofu has to be unappealing? This Asian-style dip for cooked artichokes or raw vegetables may surprise you with its rich flavor and texture—yet it is low in calories. Also use it on a green salad with fresh crab or shrimp added for a light summer meal.

Tofu comes in soft and firm styles. I prefer the firmer because it thickens the dressing. If you use part of the package, store the remaining tofu covered in a bowl of fresh water. Change the water every 2 days, and the tofu will last for a week.

1-2 medium cloves garlic, peeled
1 tablespoon minced fresh gingerroot
1/4 cup soy sauce
2 tablespoons sesame oil
1 tablespoon rice vinegar
10 ounces firm tofu
1 6-ounce can water chestnuts, finely chopped
3 tablespoons thinly sliced scallions

1. Put the garlic and ginger in the bowl of a food processor and pulse until the garlic is finely chopped.
2. Add the soy sauce, sesame oil, rice vinegar, and tofu, and process until very smooth, scraping down the sides of the bowl as needed.
3. Add the water chestnuts and scallions, and process until blended. Scrape the sauce into a bowl, cover, and refrigerate 1 hour. It will keep for 2 weeks.

Did you know? Fresh ginger root, cut into small pieces, keeps for weeks in the refrigerator when stored in a jar covered with some sherry. Or simply freeze peeled and sliced fresh ginger in a resealable plastic bag.

HERBED CREAM CHEESE DIP

Makes 1 cup

1/4 cup chopped flat-leaf parsley leaves
2/3 cup loosely packed basil leaves, chopped
1 large clove garlic, peeled and split
8 ounces cream cheese
1/2 teaspoon salt, or to taste
2–4 drops Tabasco sauce
1–2 tablespoons milk (optional)

On the shelves of the Dairy department are containers of cream cheese and herb dips with fancy labels and relatively expensive price tags. Nearby is plain cream cheese. Within minutes, you can make your own dip and vary it to suit your taste. This is a good place to use up little bits of leftover herbs. Because I love basil, I often use it in this dip. But try experimenting with grated onion, grated Parmesan cheese, oregano, roasted red bell peppers, or seasoning blends, like Mrs. Dash. Serve with sturdy raw vegetables, such as carrots, celery, jicama, and red peppers. Or spread on toast, bagels, or sandwiches.

Calorie- and fat-reduced cream cheese, Neufchâtel, and farmer cheese may all be substituted in this recipe.

1. Combine the parsley, basil, and garlic in the bowl of a food processor and pulse until the garlic is finely chopped.
2. Add the cream cheese, salt, and Tabasco and process until smooth. For a creamier consistency, add the milk and blend. Scrape the mixture into a bowl and serve.

Did you know? While the makers of cream cheese advertise that their product has half the calories of butter, remember that this refers to using the same *amount* of cream cheese. Alas, we generally slather on cream cheese while thinly spreading butter.

VERMONT CHEDDAR AND MAPLE CRACKERS

Makes 3 dozen puffs

2 cups shredded sharp cheddar cheese
2 1/2 ounces chopped pecan pieces
1/3 cup mayonnaise
1 tablespoon maple syrup
1/2 teaspoon Worcestershire sauce
36 whole-grain crackers, such as Wheatsworth, Triscuit, etc.

From extra-sharp to mild, cheddar is the most widely consumed cheese in the world. Many of our American varieties are exceptionally good, especially those from Vermont and New York. Today, supermarkets are showcasing regional cheeses, often by displaying a giant whole wheel with small samples alongside to tempt you—a smart move on their part. This is a good opportunity for you to taste a variety you are unfamiliar with.

Speaking of unfamiliar, the combination of cheddar cheese with maple syrup and pecans may strike you as unusual. It is, but it's also a great, easy hors d'oeuvre to throw together when guests arrive. You can make the mixture and keep it for 2 weeks in the refrigerator. It is especially good when served with sherry or port. For an open-faced sandwich, spread the cheese mixture on toast and top with smoked bacon.

1. Mix the cheese, pecans, mayonnaise, maple syrup, and Worcestershire sauce together in a medium bowl. Spread rounded teaspoonfuls of the mixture evenly on crackers.
2. Put the crackers on a flat pan or cookie sheet and broil until the cheese is melted and bubbling. Transfer to an attractive plate and serve at once or keep in a warm oven for up to a half hour.

Did you know? For convenience, some cheeses are sold pre-shredded. This can be a real time-saver if you take a minute to check the package carefully for little beads of moisture or mold. There are code dates stamped on the package to verify freshness. The quality of these products goes from quite good cheddar to pretty awful, artificial-tasting mozzarella for pizzas. Read the labels carefully. Many are not real cheese. You might want to sample one or two that are marked "natural" before serving them to guests.

PUFFY ASPARAGUS AND CHEESE GOUGÈRE

Serves 8

- 8 ounces fresh asparagus pared, woody ends removed
- 1 cup water reserved from cooking the asparagus
- 8 tablespoons (1 stick) unsalted butter, room temperature
- 1/4 teaspoon freshly grated nutmeg
- 1/4 teaspoon dry mustard
- Pinch ground red pepper
- 1/2 teaspoon salt
- Freshly ground black pepper
- 1 cup unbleached all-purpose flour
- 4 eggs
- 3/4 cup (2 1/2 ounces) shredded Gruyère cheese or imported Swiss cheese
- 1 egg yolk mixed with 2 tablespoons of milk
- 1/2 cup (1 1/2 ounces) freshly grated Parmesan cheese

This is an impressive hors d'oeuvre to make in spring when asparagus comes into the market. The pastry (gougère) is a giant cream puff circle, filled with chopped asparagus and Gruyère (or other Swiss cheese) and Parmesan cheese. The top is crunchy with bright green asparagus tips on it. When asparagus isn't in season, substitute finely chopped broccoli and add 1/3 cup chopped parsley in Step 5.

Supermarkets stock many kinds of Swiss cheese, both domestic and imported. While almost any of them will work in this recipe, genuine Gruyère, from Switzerland, has a nutty, sweet, full flavor that most American-made varieties lack. Look for the name stamped on the rind in red. Gruyère is usually sold in square blocks and has almost no holes.

1. Preheat your oven to 400°F. Butter a round oven-safe metal pan (at least 10 inches in diameter) or a cookie sheet and run it under cold water or chill it for a few minutes.
2. Boil the asparagus in 1 1/4 cups salted water until just tender, about 3 minutes. Reserve the liquid. Plunge the asparagus into cold water, drain, and blot dry on paper towels. Cut off the tip plus about 1 inch of 8 asparagus spears and reserve for the final garnish. Cut the remaining asparagus into 1/2-inch slices and set aside.
3. Combine 1 cup of the asparagus cooking water, the butter, nutmeg, mustard, red pepper, salt, and pepper together in a heavy saucepan and slowly bring to a boil. If the liquid does not boil, the dough will not thicken correctly.
4. Remove the pan from the heat and stir in the flour. With a wooden spoon, beat until the dough forms a ball. Return the pan to low heat, stirring and flipping it constantly to dry the dough slightly. This will take from 3 to 5 minutes. A slight film will form on the bottom of the pan.
5. Turn off the heat, add the eggs, 1 at a time, beating to incorporate the first one before adding the next. Stir in the Gruyère cheese and chopped asparagus.

Did you know? It makes good sense to recycle the cooking liquid from vegetables, poultry, etc. In this recipe, you save the asparagus's vitamins and minerals, which otherwise would be thrown out with the water.

6. With a large spoon dipped into warm water to prevent sticking, drop large dollops of the batter onto the baking pan or cookie sheet, forming a circle about 9 inches in diameter. There will be a space in the center. The gougère may be frozen at this point, before the egg wash (see note below). Brush the top of the pastry carefully with the egg-milk mixture, taking care not to let it drip onto the pan. Sprinkle the Parmesan over the top of the ring, reserving about 2 tablespoons.
7. Bake in the middle of the oven for 35 minutes until puffed and golden brown. Lay the 8 asparagus tips on top, sprinkle on the remaining Parmesan, and return to the oven for 5 minutes. Remove the pan from the oven, loosen the gougère, cut it into slices, and serve at once. Once removed from the oven, the pastry deflates quickly. This dish must be served right away.

NOTE: To freeze an unbaked gougère: Put the cookie sheet with the unbaked gougère in the freezer. When hard, slide the gougère off and store in a resealable plastic bag. To cook, put it on a buttered cookie sheet and in the preheated oven while still frozen. Add 10 minutes to the cooking time.

- 1/3 cup + 2 tablespoons fruity extra-virgin olive oil
- 1 5 1/2-ounce log of chèvre (Montrachet), cut into 4 slices
- 2 tablespoons chopped fresh tarragon or 1 teaspoon dried
- 8 thin slices French bread, lightly toasted
- 2 cloves garlic, split
- 1/3 cup fresh-toasted bread crumbs
- Salt
- 2 large red bell peppers, peeled, seeds and membranes removed
- Freshly ground black pepper
- 16 endive leaves

BAKED CHÈVRE ON FRESH RED PEPPER SAUCE AND ENDIVES

Serves 4

This first course celebrates the fact that we now find more high-quality imported and domestic cheeses in our supermarkets. Wonderful regional cheeses are also coming into their own. For years, I devoured goats' milk cheese (chèvre) in France and Italy, loving the tangy cream cheese–like flavor and lamenting that it was only available at specialty cheese stores. Now this first course, composed of a warm pillow of cheese on a bed of red pepper purée surrounded by endive leaves, is easy to assemble from the supermarket.

I have chosen a small Montrachet log for this recipe. You may find it available plain, with herbs, or with a smoky ash coating. Other goat cheeses, such as Bucheron, come in larger logs, and still others in pyramid shapes, each varying slightly in taste and texture.

1. Preheat your oven to 400°F. Lightly oil a cookie sheet.
2. Pour the 1/3 cup of olive oil into a flat dish, and add the sliced chèvre, turning once to coat with the oil. Sprinkle on 1 tablespoon of tarragon and refrigerate for 15 to 20 minutes.
3. Rub the toasted French bread with a clove of garlic and brush with the remaining olive oil. Set aside.
4. Combine the bread crumbs and 1/4 teaspoon salt in a flat dish. Lift the cheese from the oil and coat with the crumbs, turning to cover well. Reserve the oil. Bake on the cookie sheet for 8 minutes, or until golden brown and hot. After about 4 minutes add the sliced bread to heat with the cheese.
5. Meanwhile, purée the red peppers and a half clove of garlic in the bowl of a food processor, scraping down the sides as needed. With the machine running, add the reserved olive oil through the feed tube in a slow, steady stream. Add the remaining tarragon, season to taste with salt and black pepper, and pulse to blend.
6. Ladle the red pepper sauce evenly into the center of 4 luncheon-size plates. Lay 4 endive leaves with the tips pointing out on each plate like a cross. Lift the warmed cheese with a spatula to the center of each plate, add 2 slices of toast, and serve at once.

Did you know? Leftover chèvre is wonderful in vinaigrettes. Follow the recipe for Roquefort Vinaigrette (page 272). Or, simply crumble it and add it to a salad of Boston lettuce, endive, beets, and walnuts, tossed with walnut oil, balsamic vinegar, salt, and pepper.

Did you know? When selecting a piece of plastic-wrapped cheese in the market, make sure that the oils are not separating to ensure that it has been properly refrigerated. Poor storage is the quickest way to ruin the flavor and texture of cheese. Once home, always wrap unused cheese airtight in waxed paper. This wrapping should be changed each time the cheese is opened and exposed to air.

CORNY CHEESY POPOVERS

Makes 12 popovers

Using fine cornmeal instead of flour is a tasty twist on popovers. I add a little cheddar cheese and some corn kernels and serve them with butter and jalapeño pepper jelly for an eye-opening start to the day. These popovers don't rise as high as those made with all-purpose flour. For a south-of-the-border-style brunch, serve these popovers with Huevos Rancheros Casserole Soufflé (page 210) or My Dynamite, All-Time Favorite Chili (page 129).

Look for cornmeal near other flours. Both yellow and white have the same taste. There are different grinds, from fine to coarser stone-ground, that change the final texture of a dish from smooth to gritty.

Unsalted butter to grease a muffin tin
1 1/4 cups whole milk
3 tablespoons unsalted butter, melted
1 cup fine cornmeal
1/2 cup unbleached all-purpose flour
1/2 teaspoon salt
1/4 teaspoon dry mustard
Generous pinch ground red pepper
1/2 cup corn kernels, frozen or fresh
4 eggs
1/2 cup shredded sharp cheddar cheese

1. Preheat your oven to 450°F. Butter a 12-muffin tin or 12 deep porcelain custard cups.
2. Combine the milk, melted butter, cornmeal, flour, salt, mustard, and red pepper, and beat until just smooth. Stir in the corn.
3. Add the eggs 1 at a time, beating until each is incorporated. Using a 1/3-cup measure, fill the muffin tin with the batter, and sprinkle the cheese on top. With your finger or the handle of a spoon, stir each cup of batter once or twice to cover the cheese.
4. Bake in the lower third of the preheated oven for 15 minutes, then lower the temperature to 350°F for 20 minutes more. *Do not open the oven while the popovers are baking.* Once they have "popped," remove the tin from the oven and test one to see if the centers are dried. If not, prick the others with a toothpick and return to the oven for 3 to 4 minutes to let the steam escape. When the popovers are done, immediately loosen with a sharp knife and serve at once.

Another idea . . . If you don't have jalapeño pepper jelly, combine softened butter with a small amount of minced pickled jalapeño pepper.

YOGURT CUCUMBER RAITA

Makes 2 ½ cups

2 large cloves garlic, peeled

Salt

1 ½ cups plain yogurt

1 medium-large cucumber, peeled, seeded, and coarsely chopped

1 large ripe tomato, peeled, seeded, and coarsely chopped

⅓ cup chopped fresh mint leaves

2 tablespoons finely chopped flat-leaf parsley (optional)

Salt and freshly ground black pepper to taste

Did you know? If yogurt develops a little mold on top, scrape off a generous layer of it and discard. The yogurt underneath is usually fine.

In Indian cooking, a "raita" is a cooling sauce often made from yogurt and chopped raw vegetables. It is a nice foil for intensely spicy foods. This chunky version is not only delicious when served with curry, but is also a great sauce for grilled lamb, chicken, or falafel. I also spoon it over mixed greens or cool vegetables.

Because yogurt is a cultured product, it generally has a fairly long shelf life. Be sure to check the code. It is certainly safe for a week or 10 days in your refrigerator. But, yogurt does not freeze well.

1. In a medium bowl, mash the garlic with a little salt to create a paste, then stir in the yogurt and mix well.
2. Add the cucumber, tomato, mint, parsley, salt, and pepper, and blend. Adjust the seasonings, if necessary. Refrigerate until needed.

ORANGE-HONEY YOGURT SAUCE FOR FRUIT

Makes 1 cup

3 tablespoons fresh orange juice

½ teaspoon ground cinnamon

1 cup plain yogurt

2 tablespoons honey

Did you know? When using ground spices like the cinnamon above, it is more effective to mix them first with a small amount of the liquid in the recipe to distribute them evenly.

Here is an almost-instant sauce to serve with fruit. Spoon it over fresh fruit salads or use it for dipping cubes of melon or pineapple, whole grapes, cherries, or even squares of pound cake. The delicately sweet orange-honey flavors complement the slightly tangy yogurt.

When buying yogurt, be sure to read the labels carefully. Although plain yogurt—both low-fat and regular—is low in calories, the benefits are diminished when sweetened cereals, candy toppings, or fruits with lots of extra sugar are stirred in. Drain any extra liquid (whey) from the carton before using the yogurt.

1. Blend the orange juice and cinnamon in a small bowl until smooth. Add the yogurt and honey and mix well. Refrigerate until ready to serve.

BÉARNAISE SAUCE

Makes 1 ½ cups

Béarnaise sauce remains a favorite to serve with roasted meats. It is a classic accompaniment for Rack of Lamb Persillade (page 142) and Châteaubriand steak. The combination of wine, tarragon vinegar, and creamy butter is elegant and rich. Make it for special occasions.

When looking for the freshest butter, buy "sweet" or unsalted butter because salt is a preservative and can mask rancidity. There are also some ultra-creamy, premium regional and imported butters available for those of us who are butter lovers. They have less water and a higher percentage of butterfat. Appreciate them on a fine piece of bread or anywhere their flavor can shine.

To preserve freshness, refrigerate butter in a covered dish, away from foods with a strong aroma. The butter section of your refrigerator is usually several degrees warmer to make butter spreadable. That's fine for a few days. Otherwise, find a cooler shelf (around 39°F), where butter will last up to 2 weeks. It can be frozen for up to 9 months if wrapped in another airtight layer of foil or plastic wrap.

½ cup dry white wine

2 tablespoons tarragon vinegar

2 tablespoons finely chopped shallots

4 black peppercorns

2 tablespoons tarragon leaves + 2 teaspoons finely chopped tarragon leaves or 2 ½ teaspoons dried tarragon

3 egg yolks

12 tablespoons (1 ½ sticks) unsalted butter, melted

½ teaspoon salt, or to taste

Pinch of ground red pepper

1. In a small saucepan, combine the wine, vinegar, shallots, peppercorns, and 2 tablespoons of tarragon leaves (or 2 teaspoons dried)) and bring to a boil over high heat. Cook until the liquid is reduced in half. Strain and cool. Wipe out the saucepan.
2. Combine the egg yolks and wine mixture in the top of a double boiler set over gently simmering water. Whisk until frothy and the yolks have thickened slightly. *Slowly* whisk in the melted butter, beating constantly.
3. Add the salt, red pepper, and remaining tarragon leaves (or ½ teaspoon dried) and taste for seasonings. Serve warm. Keep warm in a double boiler or in a thermos until ready to serve.

CONFETTI BEURRE BLANC

Makes about 2 cups to serve 8 to 10

- 20 tablespoons (2 1/2 sticks) unsalted butter, chilled and cut into pieces
- 2 tablespoons minced carrot
- 2 tablespoons minced onion
- 4 thin green beans, thinly sliced
- 2 tablespoons minced shallots
- 6 tablespoons tarragon vinegar
- 6 tablespoons dry white wine
- 3 plum tomatoes, peeled, seeded, and finely chopped or 1/2 cup finely chopped canned Italian tomatoes, well drained
- Salt and white pepper to taste

Although many people have streamlined their diets, there are still those gala occasions when a beurre blanc, or light-colored butter sauce, is perfect. It is especially appealing for fish dishes and with low-carb diets. In this version, the minced carrot, onion, green beans, and tomatoes are so colorful, they remind me of confetti. It is particularly delicious with Baked Salmon Fillets in Parchment (page 178). Spooned over blanched leeks, steamed asparagus, or chicken breasts, these simple-to-prepare foods become elegant.

The butter in your market is usually U.S. Grade AA (93 Score) or Grade A (92 Score), based on federal standards of evaluation. The best butter (AA) has an appealing flavor with a delicate aroma of fresh sweet cream. It must be smooth with a very even texture. Any salt is distributed equally. Grade A is made from slightly older cream, and the texture may be less even. Grade B (90 Score), is rarely sold in markets. It is made from slightly sour cream and has a more intense, slightly acidic taste.

1. In a medium skillet, melt 1 tablespoon of the butter over medium-high heat. Stir in the carrot, onion, and beans. Cook for 1 1/2 to 2 minutes, or until the vegetables are slightly softened. Set aside.
2. Combine the shallots, vinegar, and white wine in a medium-sized heavy, nonreactive saucepan and bring to a boil. Continue boiling over high heat until the liquid has reduced to about 1 tablespoon. Turn off the heat and whisk in about 2 tablespoons of butter, beating until the butter looks frothy and slightly opaque. Add 2 more tablespoons of butter, and whisk until smooth.
3. Return the heat to low and continue whisking in the remaining butter, 2 tablespoons at a time, making sure to incorporate each lump of butter before adding the next one.
4. Stir in the sautéed vegetables, tomatoes, salt and pepper, and taste for seasonings. This sauce may be prepared up to 30 minutes ahead of time and kept over warm (not boiling) water. Or transfer it to a thermos and the sauce will hold for up to 3 hours.

Did you know? Whipped butter is fine for spreading on toast or seasoning vegetables. However, it contains about 30 to 45 percent air so is not appropriate as a substitute for real butter in baking.

LATE HARVEST JOHANNESBURG RIESLING BEURRE BLANC

Makes about 2 cups

This is a very special sauce to make for a grand meal. The sweet late-harvest wine balanced with tarragon vinegar and shallots is truly exceptional. I serve it with Lobster Timbales (page 173), with some diced lobster meat stirred in. It would be appropriate to serve this sauce with grilled swordfish, roasted game birds, or slices of roasted veal. Drink the remaining wine with an elegant dessert.

Beurre blanc is an emulsified sauce thickened by butter being whisked into a base of reduced vinegar and wine or water. Hollandaise and béarnaise are similar in their preparation, but they are built on beaten egg yolks. There is nothing in this sauce to hide the taste of slightly old butter, so it must be very fresh. Unsalted butter allows you to season the sauce to your own taste.

1/4 cup tarragon vinegar

1/2 cup Late Harvest Johannesburg Riesling

1 tablespoon minced shallots

8 ounces unsalted butter, chilled and cut into pieces

Pinch of ground red pepper

Salt and white pepper to taste

1. Combine the vinegar, wine, and shallots in a small, heavy, non-reactive saucepan and bring to a boil. Continue boiling over high heat until the liquid has reduced to about 1 tablespoon, about 6 or 7 minutes.
2. Turn off the heat and whisk in about 2 tablespoons of butter, beating until the butter looks frothy and slightly opaque. Add 2 more tablespoons of butter and whisk until it is completely incorporated and smooth.
3. Return the saucepan to low heat and continue whisking in the remaining butter in small amounts, making sure to incorporate each piece before adding the next. Add the red pepper and season to taste with salt and pepper. The sauce should coat the back of a spoon. It may be prepared 30 to 45 minutes ahead of time and kept warm over warm (not boiling) water. Check occasionally, whisking to prevent separation.

HUEVOS RANCHEROS CASSEROLE SOUFFLÉ

Serves 6 to 8

- 1½ tablespoons unsalted butter, softened
- 5–6 Italian frying peppers, about 6 inches long
- 12 eggs, separated
- 4 cups loosely packed shredded medium or sharp cheddar cheese
- 2 cups fresh or frozen corn kernels
- 1 cup milk
- 2 chopped jalapeño peppers, seeds and membranes removed, or minced rinsed pickled jalapeños
- 1 teaspoon salt or to taste
- Freshly ground black pepper to taste
- 6 cups Salsa (page 42) or purchased, warmed

When I'm having guests for brunch, these Mexican farmer-style eggs are often one of the dishes I serve. Beaten egg whites add a puff of air, or "soufflé," to keep them light; corn, cheddar cheese, and peppers add zest. They are easy to make and, once baked, they can sit for at least a half an hour. Even at room temperature, they are very tasty.

The baking dish is lined with blanched frying peppers before the egg mixture is poured in. They will help you to cut perfect portions and keep the dish remarkably clean.

1. Preheat your oven to 450°F. Butter a 9-by-13-inch earthenware or glass casserole.
2. Make an incision along the length of each Italian pepper and remove the stem, seeds, and membranes, keeping the pepper in one piece. Partially fill a medium-sized saucepan or skillet with water and bring to a boil. Add the peppers, return the water to a boil, and cook until the peppers are just softened, about 3 minutes. Remove and blot very dry with paper towels. Cool completely, then line the bottom of the casserole with them.
3. In a large bowl, beat the egg yolks until smooth, stir in the cheese, corn, milk, jalapeños, and salt and pepper. In another bowl, whisk the whites into soft peaks, then gently fold them into the yolk mixture until almost blended. Scrape into the prepared pan and bake in the middle of the oven until the eggs are puffy and the top is lightly browned, about 7 minutes. Turn the temperature to 325°F and cook until the eggs are baked through but not dry, 22 to 25 minutes. Test by inserting a knife into the center. It should come out almost clean. Remove and let the eggs sit for a few minutes before cutting into 12 rectangles. Spoon on salsa and serve.

Did you know? Italian frying peppers are very mild. Their tops are quite wide. Jalapeños, on the other hand, are fairly narrow at the stem. You can generally figure that the smaller the top of the pepper, the hotter it is likely to be.

SWISS CHEESE, APPLE, ONION, AND ALMOND FRITTATA

Serves 4 to 5 as a first course

Frittatas are flat Italian omelets made with eggs and almost any other ingredient you may choose. They are a good way to use up leftovers, since the ingredient choices are only limited by your imagination. Once you master the technique, any frittata is a snap.

Making one large frittata is far easier than cooking 4 individual omelets—and a lot more festive. A five-egg frittata will serve 4 to 5 for dinner or may be cut into squares for hors d'oeuvres to serve 12 to 15. All it takes is a mixing bowl, a heavy 10-inch skillet, and a large plate. You can make a frittata in the morning and serve it at room temperature at night.

Apples and cheese are often served together. Here almonds and sautéed onions are added to that combination. Serve with a bottle of chilled white wine for a summer dinner.

5 eggs

1/2 teaspoon water

2 1/2 tablespoons unsalted butter

1 teaspoon vegetable oil

1 medium onion, peeled and chopped

2 medium Granny Smith or other tart green apples, peeled, cored, and chopped fairly fine

1/2 teaspoon nutmeg

1/8 teaspoon white pepper

1/2 teaspoon salt, or to taste

1/3 cup slivered almonds, lightly toasted

1 cup shredded Swiss cheese

1. Beat the eggs and water in a large bowl until blended.
2. In a heavy nonstick 10-inch skillet, melt 1 tablespoon of the butter and the oil over medium-high heat. Add the onion and sauté until light brown, about 6 to 7 minutes. Add the apples and continue cooking until they are limp, about 4 to 5 minutes. Scrape into the egg mixture, add the nutmeg, white pepper, salt, and slivered almonds, and mix well.
3. Melt the remaining 1 1/2 tablespoons of butter in the skillet over medium-high heat and pour in the egg mixture, shaking to distribute the ingredients evenly. After about 1 minute, sprinkle on the cheese. Adjust the heat to medium-low. After 11 to 12 minutes, loosen the edges with a knife or spatula, gradually working under the entire frittata. Shake to be sure it is detached. Flip the frittata by putting a plate about the same size as the skillet upside-down on top of the frittata, inverting the pan so the frittata falls onto the plate, then sliding it, unfinished side down, back into the skillet. Continue cooking for an additional 5 to 6 minutes. Loosen, if necessary, before removing, cutting into wedges, and serving.

SPINACH, MUSHROOM, SCALLION, AND FETA CHEESE FRITTATA

Serves 4 to 5 as a first course

Spinach and feta cheese are favorite ingredients of Greek chefs. They work wonders in frittatas, as well. Serve either hot or at room temperature.

5 eggs

1/2 teaspoon water

3 tablespoons olive oil

4 ounces white mushrooms, trimmed, wiped, and thinly sliced

1/2 cup thinly sliced scallions, green parts included

4 ounces feta cheese, crumbled

1 10-ounce package frozen spinach, defrosted and squeezed very dry

3 tablespoons finely chopped fresh dill leaves or 1 tablespoon dried

3/4 teaspoon nutmeg

1/4 teaspoon salt, or to taste

Pinch of ground red pepper

Freshly ground black pepper to taste

1. Beat the eggs and water in a large bowl until blended.
2. In a nonstick 10-inch skillet, heat 1 1/2 tablespoons oil over medium heat until hot. Add the mushrooms and sauté until just wilted, about 1 to 2 minutes, stirring often. Add the scallions and cook 30 seconds longer. Scrape into the egg mixture. Add the feta, spinach, dill, nutmeg, salt, red pepper, and ground pepper to the egg mixture, and mix well.
3. Add the remaining oil to the skillet and heat over high heat until hot. Pour in the egg mixture and shake the skillet to distribute the ingredients evenly. Adjust the heat to medium-low. After 7 or 8 minutes, begin to loosen the edges with a knife or spatula, gradually working under the entire frittata. Shake to be sure that it's completely free, then flip the frittata (see previous recipe) and continue cooking for 4 to 5 minutes longer. Loosen, if necessary, before removing and serving in wedges.

CHILLED WHITE WINE SOUFFLÉ WITH APRICOT SAUCE

Serves 8

This delicate chilled dessert is light and airy—a perfect finale for a summer meal. My guests are often pleasantly surprised to find out that the soufflé is made from only wine, sugar, and eggs, with a little gelatin and cornstarch for body. It is easy to make and can be decorated glamorously with whipped cream and sugar-frosted grapes, or simply with fresh strawberries. The orange-apricot sauce provides a citrusy accent that complements the flavors of the soufflé.

For healthy people, the potential of salmonella food poisoning from raw eggs is quite small. Those who are pregnant, elderly or very young, and anyone with a compromised immune system should avoid eating raw eggs. Only use grade AA or A eggs that have been properly refrigerated and are clean with unbroken shells. Refrigerate cooked dishes with eggs if not eaten within an hour.

FOR THE SOUFFLÉ:

7 eggs, separated, at room temperature
2/3 cup sugar
2 tablespoons cornstarch
2 cups medium-dry white wine
1 package unflavored gelatin
Pinch cream of tartar

FOR THE SAUCE:

8 ounces apricot preserves
3/4 cup orange juice
Grated zest of 1 lemon
1/4 cup Grand Marnier

FOR THE DECORATION (OPTIONAL):

1 egg white
1/2 cup superfine sugar or processed granulated sugar
16–20 red or green grapes, with stems
4 ounces heavy cream, whipped until stiff and lightly sweetened

1. Prepare the soufflé: In a heavy saucepan, whisk the egg yolks and sugar together until well blended and pale yellow. Stir the cornstarch into the wine, pour into the eggs, and bring the mixture to a boil over medium-high heat for 1 to 2 minutes.
2. Dissolve the gelatin in a little reserved wine or water. When softened, add it to the wine mixture and stir to blend well. Remove the pan from the heat and beat the mixture with a handheld electric mixer or whisk until cool and thick. This process may be speeded up by transferring the mixture into a metal or glass bowl and setting it in another bowl filled with ice while beating.
3. Add the cream of tartar to the egg whites and beat until stiff but not dry. Using a rubber spatula or your hands, gently fold the egg whites into the wine mixture, mixing until just blended, and pour into a 6-cup soufflé mold or glass bowl. Cover and chill for at least 6 hours or overnight.
4. For the sauce: In a small saucepan, heat the preserves with the orange juice and lemon zest until melted, then boil until slightly thickened. Remove from the heat, stir in the Grand Marnier, and cool to lukewarm.
5. Prepare the garnish: In a flat dish, beat the egg white just until frothy. Pour the sugar into another flat dish. Holding each grape by its stem, dip it into the egg, then into the sugar, forming a thin coating. Put on a plate to dry, then remove the stem.
6. Fill a pastry bag fitted with a decorative star tip with the whipped cream and pipe small rosettes onto the soufflé. Serve a generous spoonful of soufflé on each plate, garnished with a couple of frosted grapes and a ribbon of apricot sauce on top.

As a variation . . . Use fresh raspberries and serve with the raspberry coulis from the Fresh Pear Tart with Ginger Cream (page 75).

SOFT PEACH MOUSSE IN CRÊPE FLUTES

Serves 6

This frothy, light dessert not only looks glamorous, it is refreshingly healthy. My friend Carole Walter taught me to make these low-fat crêpes. Make them ahead of time; then, before serving, spoon in the mousse.

FOR THE MOUSSE:

1 1/2 envelopes (1 1/2 tablespoons) unflavored gelatin

1/2 cup orange juice

1 20-ounce package frozen peaches without added sugar, almost completely thawed

1/4 cup sugar

3 tablespoons light rum

16 ounces low-fat vanilla yogurt

1/2 pint fresh raspberries, for garnish

Mint leaves, for garnish

FOR THE CRÊPES:

1/2 cup 1 percent or skimmed milk

1 egg

1/8 teaspoon vanilla

1/2 cup unbleached all-purpose flour

Nonstick vegetable spray, such as Pam

1 egg white, lightly beaten

1. Prepare the mousse: In a small saucepan, sprinkle the gelatin over the orange juice. Once the gelatin is softened, bring the mixture to a boil over medium heat, stirring until the gelatin is melted. Remove from the heat and set aside to cool.
2. Meanwhile, in a food processor or in a blender, purée the frozen peaches and sugar until completely smooth. Add the rum and orange juice-gelatin mixture and blend. Add the yogurt and process until blended. Scrape into a medium bowl, cover, and refrigerate overnight until firm.
3. Prepare the crêpes: Combine the milk, egg, and vanilla in a small bowl. Gradually whisk in the flour, stirring until smooth. It should be the consistency of heavy cream. If not, add a little more milk. Let batter stand for 10 minutes.
4. Spray an 8-inch nonstick skillet with vegetable spray and heat over medium-low heat. Stir the batter. Fill a coffee measure (2 tablespoons) with batter and pour it onto one side of the skillet, removing the pan from the heat with your other hand as you do this. Rotate the pan so the batter will spread evenly.
5. Return the skillet to the heat, and cook the crêpe for about 1 minute, or until the sides begin to brown and leave the sides of the pan. Loosen, if necessary, with a knife, carefully lift up an edge with your fingers, and turn the crêpe. Cook 20 seconds on the second side. Flip the crêpe onto paper towels. Spray the pan for each crêpe. Proceed in the same manner with the remaining batter, separating the crêpes with waxed paper or paper towels. (This recipe will make up to 8 crêpes.)
6. Preheat your oven to 350°F. Spray six 8-ounce Pyrex custard cups with nonstick vegetable coating.
7. Place a crêpe in each cup. They will form scalloped tart shells. Bake in the preheated oven for 15 minutes or until golden brown. Remove the cups and let the crêpes cool for 5 minutes. Remove the shells carefully and invert. Brush the bottoms of the shells with beaten egg white and invert the shells directly onto the oven rack. Bake for 1 to 2 minutes or until very crisp. Watch closely so they do not burn. Remove and let cool.
8. Serve a crêpe shell on each plate. Using a large spoon or ice-cream scoop, divide the mousse among the cups. Add raspberries and mint leaves and serve.

Other serving ideas . . .
Prepare the mousse and transfer it to a decorative 4- or 5-cup soufflé dish or wine glasses. Once chilled, add fresh berries and mint leaves and serve with crisp cookies. Use the crêpe shells to serve a dessert of fresh fruit salad or ice cream.

MANDARIN VELVET CARAMEL CUSTARD

Serves 8

This custard ring, served with mandarin segments and chocolate leaves, wins raves for its velvety-smooth texture and hint of orange. These few supermarket ingredients make an elegant finale to the finest meal.

FOR THE CARAMEL:

½ cup granulated sugar

3 tablespoons water

FOR THE CUSTARD:

1 ½ pints (3 cups) milk

5 eggs

4 egg yolks

¼ teaspoon salt

½ cup sugar

½ teaspoon vanilla extract

1 teaspoon orange extract

24 chocolate leaves (page 257), for garnish (optional)

24 canned mandarin orange segments, drained, for garnish (optional)

1. Line the mold: Combine the sugar and water in a small heavy saucepan and bring to a boil, swirling but not stirring it, until it turns a rich amber brown, about 6 to 8 minutes. Watch carefully that it does not burn. If any sugar crystals start to burn on the side of the pan, wash them down with a wet brush.
2. Using a pot holder to protect your hands, quickly pour the caramel into a 6-cup ring mold and tilt the mold so the caramel covers all sides. As the caramel cools, it will crack. (To easily clean the saucepan after pouring the caramel into the mold, refill it with hot water and bring it to a boil. This will dissolve any remaining caramel.)
3. For the custard: Preheat your oven to 325°F. Scald the milk in a saucepan and set it aside.
4. In a large bowl, blend the eggs, yolks, and salt. Gradually add the sugar, whisking until the eggs are light yellow and frothy, about 2 to 3 minutes. Stir in the milk in a slow, steady stream. Add the vanilla and orange extracts.
5. Pour the mixture through a fine strainer into the caramel-lined ring mold. Put the ring mold into a larger pan *(bain-marie)*, and transfer both pans to the lower third of the preheated oven. Pour enough boiling water into the larger pan to come halfway up the side of the ring mold. Bake until a knife inserted *near* the center of the custard comes out clean, about 40 to 45 minutes. While the custard is baking, the water should never show any bubbles on the surface. Adjust the temperature down, if necessary.
6. Remove the custard from the oven. Cool for 1 hour, then lift the mold from the water, cover, and refrigerate it until cold.
7. To unmold, run a sharp knife around the outside and inside edges of the mold. Agitate the pan to be sure the custard is loose. Holding a serving dish over the mold, invert the pan, shaking slightly to make sure the custard has dropped onto the dish.
8. Add ¼ cup water to the mold. Bring to a boil over high heat to melt any remaining caramel, then strain over the custard. If desired, before serving add chocolate leaves around the outside of the custard and mandarin orange segments between the leaves and custard. Serve each portion with some chocolate leaves, mandarins, and caramel syrup.

Did you know? Foods that bake for a long time continue cooking once they are removed from the oven. Therefore, if a knife inserted near the center of the custard comes out clean, it is done. The small center area that may be soft will firm up as the custard cools.

CHERRIES IN THE SNOW

Serves 12

FOR THE MOUSSE:

3 1/2 cups heavy cream, chilled

10 1/2 ounces (3 bars) white chocolate, broken into pieces

4 egg whites, at room temperature

Pinch cream of tartar

3/4 cup shredded coconut

2 tablespoons white crème de cacao

13 frozen pitted black cherries, defrosted and blotted dry, from a 12-ounce package (reserve the remaining cherries and juice for sauce), for garnish

FOR THE SAUCE:

Cherries reserved from the mousse (above)

2/3 cup white crème de cacao

This white chocolate coconut mousse, with its warm cherry sauce, is a winter favorite of my guests and children, especially my son Ben, who helped create and name it. It proves that while white chocolate may not actually be chocolate (because it has no cocoa solids in it), it sure has appeal to many chocolate- or sweet-lovers.

When possible buy heavy cream labeled "pasteurized" rather than "ultra-pasteurized." Although markets usually stock the latter because the shelf life of an unopened carton is 6 to 8 weeks instead of 1 week, I think pasteurized cream whips better without the risk of the cream turning to butter.

The terms "heavy cream" and "whipping cream" are often used interchangeably. However by general standards of identity, heavy cream must have at least 36 percent milk fat, while whipping cream may have only 30 percent fat. "Light" or "table" cream has between 18 and 30 percent fat, while "half and half" is a combination of cream and milk and has between 10.5 and 18 percent milk fat.

1. Prepare the mousse: Whip 3 cups of the heavy cream in a large chilled bowl until stiff.
2. Melt the chocolate in the top half of a double boiler over barely simmering water. Remove from the heat and stir in about 3/4 cup of the whipped cream to smooth out the chocolate. Set aside to cool.
3. In a large bowl, beat the egg whites with the cream of tartar until stiff but not dry.
4. Using a rubber spatula, fold the chocolate into the whipped cream, then add 1/2 cup of the coconut, the crème de cacao, and finally fold in the egg whites. Scrape the mixture into a 6-cup soufflé dish, cover lightly, and refrigerate until firm, about 3 hours.
5. Whip the remaining 1/2 cup of cream until stiff. (Since the mousse is sweet, no additional sugar is needed for this cream.) Fill a pastry bag fitted with a star tip and pipe a decorative border around the outside edge of the serving dish and a rosette in the center. Place 12 cherries around the outside and 1 in the center. Sprinkle on the remaining 1/4 cup coconut. Cover the mousse lightly with foil or plastic wrap and refrigerate until needed.

6. Prepare the sauce: Combine the reserved cherries and their juice with the crème de cacao in a small saucepan and bring just to a boil. Lower the heat and simmer for 2 to 3 minutes. Cool to lukewarm.
7. Serve a generous spoonful of mousse on each plate and ribbon some of the warmed cherries in the center.

NOTE: This recipe may also be prepared in individual mousse dishes or wine glasses.

Did you know? The rotary egg beater was invented in 1870, providing a real boon to cooks who wished to beat eggs or cream into airy lightness. Before that date, whipping was accomplished by a variety of whisks, much like the ones we use today, or even a wooden rod. Today's cooks have electric stand mixers to make this chore even easier.

DECEPTIVELY DECADENT CHEESECAKE

Serves 8 to 12

FOR THE CRUST:

20 gingersnaps, finely ground

2 tablespoons unsalted butter, melted

FOR THE FILLING:

1 ½ pounds regular or low-fat cottage cheese

½ cup sugar

4 eggs

1 teaspoon vanilla extract

Grated zest of 1 lemon

1 pint fresh strawberries, washed, hulled, and split

Why is this deceptive? Because this rich, creamy-tasting confection is actually made with low-fat cottage cheese rather than ricotta cheese. It bakes in a gingersnap crust and is served with juicy fruit on top. To make this carb-friendly, you could use a sugar substitute, such as Splenda, in the filling and bake crustless in a dish covered with nonstick spray. In that case, use full-fat cottage cheese and top with slivered toasted almonds.

While some cottage cheese is labeled "low fat" (1 or 2 percent), cream-style cottage cheese has only 4 percent fat. (I prefer that tiny extra bit of fat in this dessert.) Cottage cheese is a good source of low-fat protein at a modest cost. Cartons in the market are sealed to prevent shoppers from opening and peeking inside, a reassuring safety precaution. Check the code on the carton. In your refrigerator, cottage cheese will usually last a couple of weeks.

1. Prepare the crust: Preheat your oven to 350°F.
2. Combine the cookie crumbs with the melted butter in a small bowl. Pour into a 9-by-1 ½-inch springform pan, pressing gently with your fingertips or palms to spread the crumbs evenly on the bottom and about a quarter way up the side of the pan. Bake for 8 minutes until slightly crisped. Remove and set on a rack to cool. Leave the oven on.
3. Make the filling: Process the cottage cheese in the bowl of a food processor until completely smooth, about 3 minutes, scraping down the sides as needed. Add the sugar, eggs, vanilla, and lemon zest and process to blend.
4. Put the crust in the pan on a cookie sheet and pour in the cheese mixture. Bake in the middle of the oven until a knife inserted near the center comes out clean, about 45 minutes. Turn off the oven, prop the door slightly open, and let the cake stay in the oven for 15 minutes longer.
5. Remove the cheesecake from the oven and cool on a wire rack for 1 to 2 hours, then tent lightly with aluminum foil and refrigerate until chilled, at least 2 to 3 hours. Run a sharp knife around the edge of the cake and slide off the side of the pan. Decorate the top with the berries, cut into slices, and serve. Fresh or frozen blueberries could be used, as well.

NOTE: One-half cup golden raisins and/or toasted slivered almonds would be a delicious addition to the cake if calories are not so important.

Did you know? While cottage cheese is low in fat and cholesterol, it is relatively high in sodium—457 mg per 4-ounce serving of creamed cottage cheese. The low-fat version has 459 mg per 4-ounce serving. If salt intake is of concern, take note.

RICOTTA-ALMOND TORTE

Serves 8

This torte is a majestic finale for a fancy cool-weather meal. The creamy ricotta filling, scented with crème de cacao and amaretto, is held in a toasted almond crust. Caramelized almonds add visual glamour.

The quality and texture of ricotta cheese varies dramatically with different brands available in supermarkets across the country. Some are quite dry, while others are soupy. If yours is too moist, turn it into several layers of cheesecloth, tie the corners together, and suspend it over the sink or a bowl overnight. Once opened, ricotta cheese only lasts 4 or 5 days in the refrigerator. Do not freeze it.

FOR THE TOASTED ALMOND CRUST:

1 teaspoon unsalted butter

1 3/4 cups ground toasted almonds

1/4 cup + 2/3 cup sugar

4 tablespoons (1/2 stick) unsalted butter, melted and cooled

1/4 cup water

20 whole almonds for garnish

FOR THE RICOTTA FILLING:

2 3/4 cups whole-milk ricotta

1/4 cup + 2 tablespoons sugar

1 tablespoon crème de cacao

1 tablespoon amaretto liqueur

1 teaspoon vanilla

1 cup crème fraîche or lightly whipped cream

3 tablespoons grated chocolate

1. For the crust: Preheat your oven to 375°F. Butter a 9-by-3-inch springform pan. Grease a small baking sheet.
2. Combine the ground almonds, 1/4 cup sugar, and butter in a large bowl, and mix. Press the almond mixture into the bottom and sides of the prepared pan. Bake for 10 minutes in the preheated oven, remove, and cool on a wire rack.
3. Combine 2/3 cup sugar and the water in a small, heavy saucepan and cook over low heat until the sugar is dissolved. Increase the heat to medium-high and cook until the sugar is caramelized and a rich, medium brown. Remove the pan from the heat and quickly dip and swirl the whole almonds in the caramel, placing them on the prepared baking sheet. Set aside for garnish. Quickly pour the remaining syrup over the crust, rotating the springform pan to spread it evenly. Cool the crust for about 30 minutes.
4. For the filling: Combine the ricotta, sugar, crème de cacao, amaretto, and vanilla in a food processor and process until smooth and creamy. *Do not overprocess.* (This mixing may also be done by hand with a wire whisk. Make sure that the cheese is very smooth.) Scrape into a mixing bowl and gently blend in the crème fraîche. Fold in the chocolate. Scrape the cheese mixture into the prepared crust. Cover and freeze for at least 2 hours. (If frozen more than 2 hours, the torte may need to be softened in the refrigerator before serving.)
5. Just before serving, loosen the crust from the pan using a sharp knife. Remove the sides of the pan. Arrange the almonds around the outside, reserving 3 for the center.

Did you know? To make crème fraîche: For each 1/2 pint of pasteurized (not ultra-pasteurized) cream, add 1 tablespoon of buttermilk to the cream in a screw-top jar, shake gently, and leave in a moderately warm spot (about 70°F), such as your kitchen counter, for 24 to 36 hours. Ultra-pasteurized cream is heated to a high temperature, so the enzymatic action may have been destroyed and the cream will not thicken.

CHOCOLATE CHIP ANGEL FOOD CAKE

Serves 12

Angel food cakes made from scratch bear little resemblance to the packaged variety containing powdered egg whites and other ingredients that may have been sitting on the shelf for a long time. Homemade versions are far moister and usually not as cloyingly sweet. This angel food cake, with tiny chocolate bits suspended throughout, may be decorated with a mixture of confectioners' sugar and cocoa sifted over the cake and served with fresh sliced berries or peaches. For a splurge, split and frost it with the heavenly mocha whipped cream frosting at the end of the recipe.

FOR THE CAKE:

12 egg whites, room temperature
1 ½ teaspoons cream of tartar
½ teaspoon salt
1 ½ cups granulated sugar
1 ½ teaspoons vanilla extract
½ teaspoon almond extract
1 cup sifted cake flour
1 cup mini chocolate chips

FOR THE FROSTING:

2 tablespoons instant coffee
1 tablespoon hot water
¼ cup unsweetened cocoa
1 ½ cups sifted confectioners' sugar
2 cups (1 pint) heavy cream, chilled

1. Prepare the cake: Preheat your oven to 350°F.
2. In a large bowl, combine the egg whites, cream of tartar, and salt and beat with a handheld electric mixer until foamy. Add ¾ cup of the granulated sugar, a tablespoon at a time, beating continuously until soft peaks form. Stir in the vanilla and almond extracts.
3. Combine the flour and remaining ¾ cup of sugar and sift about ½ cup of the mixture over the egg whites. Using a rubber scraper, gently fold until the flour is no longer visible. Continue gently folding in the sugar-flour mixture by half-cupfuls. Fold in the chips, then scrape the batter into an ungreased 10-inch tube pan, and gently cut through the batter with a knife in several places to remove air pockets. Bake in the lower third of the oven until the top springs back when lightly pressed with your finger, about 40 to 45 minutes.
4. Remove the cake and invert it while still in the pan on a bottle neck or inverted funnel to cool completely, about 1 ½ hours. Once the cake is cool, loosen with a sharp knife or spatula, and transfer to a serving plate.
5. To prepare the frosting: While the cake cools, stir the coffee and hot water together. Set aside to cool. Sift the cocoa and confectioners' sugar together and set aside.
6. In a large chilled bowl, beat the cream with a wire whisk until it starts to thicken. Add the coffee and sift in the cocoa-sugar mixture, beating continuously just until the cream is the consistency of frosting. Take care not to overbeat.
7. With a long serrated knife, cut the cake in half horizontally, placing the top to one side. With a metal spatula, spread about one-third of the frosting over the middle of the cake. Replace the top and press down gently. Spread the remaining frosting over the top and sides of the cake. Refrigerate until needed. To serve, use a special angel food cake cutter or a serrated knife to carefully cut the slices without exerting pressure on the cake.

Did you know? While some supermarkets pride themselves on selling eggs delivered right from the farm, angel food cake and meringue recipes work better with eggs that are at least 3 or 4 days old. For the tallest cake, use eggs that are freshly separated (not defrosted egg whites) in this recipe. Save the yolks for Béarnaise Sauce (page 207), or Mandarin Velvet Caramel Custard (page 215).

A pinch of cream of tartar in egg whites has the same effect as beating them in a copper bowl. They both stabilize the egg whites once beaten. As a general rule, use ⅛ teaspoon of cream of tartar for each egg white, except with meringues, when the ⅛ teaspoon is enough for every 2 egg whites.

CELESTIAL CARAMEL SAUCE

Makes 3 ½ cups

If you asked what this outrageously decadent sauce was best on, I'd probably say my fingers since I am completely addicted to it. However, with our interest in premium ice cream at an all-time high, this would make a perfect topping. Or spoon some on Chocolate Chip Angel Food Cake (page 220), any cookie, or poached pears.

10 tablespoons unsalted butter
3 cups firmly packed light brown sugar
1 cup light corn syrup
1 teaspoon salt
1 cup heavy cream
2 tablespoons dark rum

1. In a medium saucepan, combine the butter, brown sugar, corn syrup, and salt and slowing bring to a boil over medium-high heat. Boil until the sugar has melted, about 8 minutes, then boil 2 minutes longer, stirring often with a wooden spoon.
2. Stir in the cream, bring the mixture back to a boil, and continue to let it slowly boil for 2 minutes more. Stir in the rum and let it cool and thicken. Pour into a covered glass jar and refrigerate. If very cold, remove from the refrigerator at least 1 hour before serving.

FLOUR
BRAN
CORNMEAL
OATS
CHOCOLATE
COCONUT
NUTS
RAISINS

STOCKING A BAKER'S PANTRY

Stocking a baker's pantry in this age of expanded supermarkets is far easier than ever before. In fact, because most of us find storage space at such a premium, I would not buy large quantities of any items regularly stocked in a market. Unless you do a lot of baking, let their shelves hold those cumbersome bags and boxes of specialty flours, nuts, and chocolates until you need them.

But a totally empty pantry isn't advisable, either. If you get the urge to bake late at night, as I do, especially when the weather is dreary, then provisions should be handy. To save time, I group them together in the pantry. My bare-bones list of baking essentials includes:

- ✓ unbleached all-purpose and whole wheat flour
- ✓ granulated, dark brown, and confectioners' sugar
- ✓ baking soda and baking powder
- ✓ vanilla and almond extract
- ✓ ground cinnamon and ginger and whole nutmeg
- ✓ whole and slivered almonds and walnut pieces
- ✓ jar of jelly or preserves (raspberry, apricot, currant)
- ✓ raisins
- ✓ 3-ounce bar of premium-quality bittersweet chocolate
- ✓ packets of dry yeast
- ✓ envelopes of unflavored gelatin
- ✓ flavorless vegetable oil

I also have the following non-food items:

- ✓ waxed paper, plastic wrap, aluminum foil, paper towels, and parchment paper
- ✓ muffin liners
- ✓ sandwich- and gallon-size resealable plastic bags
- ✓ toothpicks and string
- ✓ dried beans for pie weights

Shopping for Staples

Freshness Counts

When it comes to commercial baked goods, typically we shun two-day-old bread. Attention to freshness is just as vital with homemade confections, although we have a longer grace period with baking staples before they begin to spoil.

- Check for freshness code dates on packaged nuts, cereals, or dried fruits.
- Look to see that all boxes, cellophane bags, and jars are sealed in the store and show no sign of deterioration.
- At home, cool to cold storage is usually best. Butter, delicate flours, and nuts belong in the refrigerator for short-term storage, in the freezer if stored longer than a week. Keep spices, sugars, and extracts in a cool, dark place.
- Buy small amounts of fragile seeds and dried fruits if using them for a special recipe.
- Keep all packages tightly closed. Plastic bags over bags of flour and/or sugar deter pests and keep brown sugar moist.
- Label refrigerator- and freezer-stored foods for future reference—e.g., "1 cup ground walnuts with sugar, 4/17/04."

Quality and Price

Be as quality- and price-conscious a shopper here as you are throughout the store.

Packaging costs money. Consider the quality of products sold in fancy boxes or clear bags. There is a price code marker on the edge of each shelf giving the net price per pound. If the store has a Bulk Food section, and it is well tended and has a good turnover, this is a good place to save money, providing the quality is high. In larger quantity, whole shelled walnut halves may be priced the same as broken pieces and you can realize a nice savings. Store these products in airtight bags or clean jars at home.

Sometimes bigger is better, but only if you will use the product within a reasonable period of time. Since it is less costly to pack in larger containers, almost twice the amount of orange marmalade costs about one-third more. But if the jar is left to take up your shelf space for months and eventually goes bad, the savings are lost.

Look at generic products. Buy a can of the market's brand of mandarins and one from a well-known supplier. Compare the two for size, color, uniformity, broken pieces, etc., and decide if the difference makes the savings economical or wasteful. Sometimes large manufacturers ship a product of the same quality in both generic and fancy-labeled packaging.

Creativity and Convenience

Be adventuresome. Take the time to explore new possibilities to add to your baked goods. Do some creative tasting. But be sure to read labels to avoid preservatives and hidden sweeteners.

- The Flour and Grain sections of the market have expanded because recreational bakers find great satisfaction in baking homemade loaves.
- Nuts and seeds add texture and flavor.
- Convenience packaging, like chopped dried fruits or shredded coconut, makes baking easier.

Also, think about the presentation and packaging for your baked goods if you enjoy them as gifts. Supermarkets are a good source for inexpensive and recycled containers.

- Doilies, gift ribbons, and festive baskets are all sold in the market.
- Tins and jars from mustards, jams, or crackers are excellent containers for your own storage.
- Use inexpensive disposable aluminum trays, which come in the right sizes to bake in, to give brownies and tarts as gifts. Look at the professionally baked products in the Bakery for inspiration. Ask questions.

Finally, let your market work with you to meet your needs. Call ahead and give your market the time to order larger quantities of items you may need. Don't risk finding depleted shelves. Most of the time, however, supermarkets have everything you need when you want it—even late at night and on weekends.

CHAPTER SEVEN: **STAPLES:**

FLOUR, SUGAR, NUTS, AND CHOCOLATE

INTRODUCTION

In this day of prebaked, prepackaged convenience foods and upscale supermarket bakeries, one might argue that baking is less popular than it used to be and that time limitations have wiped out this homey art. Why, then, have grocery aisles expanded with more varieties of flour, nuts, and luxury-quality chocolate than ever before? Pick up almost any food magazine, and the answer is there—if not on the cover, then throughout the pages and in beautiful photographs.

Baking is one of the most creative and therapeutic endeavors in the entire cooking repertoire. It connects us from one generation to the next, and it is an experience to share with young and old. The same simple ingredients—flour, sugar, butter, nuts—available in every market, produce special confections unique to each country. And it is a sensual, satisfying experience, the perfect retreat from a pressure-filled day. Even though just a few aisles over from the Staples section there are cookies with names such as "Like Home" and "Grandma's Best," they cannot begin to compare with the fresh-from-the-oven, homemade ones with their diet-wrecking aromas and tastes.

There are some extraordinary supermarket Bakery departments today that offer scrumptious brick-oven baked breads (either baked on the premises or the dough is baked off), fresh fruit tarts, and cookies. There are also some excellent-quality bread mixes available. (Other markets, unfortunately, still sell the same mass-produced, average-tasting fare that they have for the past twenty years.) But nowhere can you buy the satisfaction of baking from scratch without doing it yourself. Dazzlingly glamorous creations, the kind no market and few bakeries could ever offer without a giant price tag, are yours to be had from this section.

With a little time and practice, fresh, professional-quality baked goods can be yours. I'm not suggesting that you attempt to make everything from scratch. Most of us don't have that kind of time. But, a pile of frozen tart shells will enable you to quickly make a heavenly Blackberry Tart (page 61) when you find the fruit in the market. Your own refrigerated cookie dough and even frozen waffles will taste better than store-bought ones.

Invest a little time in wandering slowly up and down these aisles and find out how your market is reflecting the growing fascination with baking. When I see new products, my mind races forward to envision contemporary combinations: a whole yam (including the healthful skin) puréed and combined with rye flour into Day-After-Thanksgiving Sweet

Rye and Yam Muffins (page 235) or Irish Oatmeal Hermits laced with coconut and dried fruits (page 241).

Look for hazelnuts, marzipan, and candied fruits on the shelves in the fall for holiday sweets. Cornmeal and wheat flours; sourdough bread starters; improved, preservative-free packaged mixes; even miniature fluted-foil and colored-paper cups in which to serve candies and tiny hors d'oeuvres are some of the many options we have. But some items seem impossible to find in a market. Cake flour is frequently missing, supplanted by mixes. Slower-selling items rob the market of vital space.

If you don't find what you are looking for, ask the manager. Some ingredients are in more than one section. Chocolate, for example, is often found in the Baking section and in a separate Candy department. Or, write to the market's Consumer Affairs department. Smart stores are listening to their valued customers.

Although it's not as obvious with Baking Staples as with produce or fish, ingredient freshness is still very important. Delicate flours, nuts, and chocolates do not last forever. Take a look at the Strategy Pages just preceding this chapter entitled "Stocking a Baker's Pantry" for some suggestions for more successful supermarket baking.

One final note: I prefer to use *unbleached* all-purpose flour. When I measure it, I use the spoon and sweep method: spooning the flour into the measuring cup and then leveling it with a spatula or knife. Where eggs are used in my recipes, they are standard (USDA) large, unless otherwise indicated.

BASIC PÂTE BRISÉE PASTRY

Makes one 11-inch tart or two 8-inch tarts

This all-purpose pastry made in a food processor is ideal for savory as well as sweet dishes. It is extremely easy to make and may be prepared up to 5 days in advance and refrigerated until ready for baking. The texture is light and flaky.

When working with pastry, a large aluminum sugar shaker filled with flour makes it easy to sprinkle small amounts of flour on the dough or bread. You can find them with the non-food items.

1 2/3 cups (7 1/2 ounces) unbleached all-purpose flour

2 tablespoons sugar

1/4 teaspoon salt

9 tablespoons (1 stick plus 1 tablespoon) chilled unsalted butter, cut into small pieces

3 tablespoons solid vegetable shortening or lard, chilled

4–5 tablespoons cold water

1. Combine the flour, sugar, and salt in the bowl of a food processor. Add the butter and shortening and pulse until the mixture resembles small peas. Add a scant 4 tablespoons of water and process just until the dough begins to pull into a ball. If the dough seems very dry, add additional water by the teaspoon, as needed. But don't overprocess.
2. Remove the dough from the processor. Dust with flour and flatten into a disc about 3/4 inch thick. Wrap in plastic wrap and let it rest in the refrigerator for at least 2 hours.
3. Preheat your oven to 400°F.
4. Remove the dough from the refrigerator, unwrap, and put on a lightly floured board or pastry cloth. Massage gently with your fingertips until it begins to soften and be workable, turning it over a couple of times. Dust lightly with flour. Using a lightly floured rolling pin, roll it into a circle about 14 inches in diameter and 1/8 inch thick.
5. If using a pastry cloth, flip the dough into a tart pan. If not, roll the dough back onto the pin or fold it into quarters, position it over the pan, and carefully ease the dough into the tart pan, working to flatten the bottom, then gently pushing the dough well into the corners and against the sides with your thumb and fingertips. Trim off excess dough by rolling the rolling pin over the top of the pan or by using a knife. Cut excess dough into decorative shapes and bake on a cookie sheet along with the tart. Or, refrigerate and use later for little tartlets.
6. Smooth a square of aluminum foil, shiny-side down, on the crust and against the edges, prick well with a fork (through the foil), and fill the pan with dried beans or pie weights (see note). Bake in the middle of your oven until the crust is pale-beige-colored, set, and starts to pull away from the edge of the pan, about 12 to 15 minutes.

Did you know? Lard and vegetable shortening added to pastry make them flaky; butter gives wonderful flavor. Therefore, many recipes use a combination of the two fats for the best results. Pieces of fat the size of small peas make a lighter crust. When these little bits melt and brown the flour during baking, the empty spaces that the fat leaves are like a fine honeycomb—making the crust less compact and more tender.

7. Carefully remove the foil and beans. Discard the foil and reserve the beans or weights for future use. Prick the bottom again with a fork and lower the heat to 350°F. Return it to the oven and cook for another 10 to 15 minutes, or until pale gold-colored. Check from time to time, pricking any air bubbles, if necessary. Remove and set on a rack to cool.

NOTE: Pie weights are small aluminum pieces used to keep pastry flat while baking. They are sold in packages along with other baking supplies in markets that stock cooking equipment. Personally, I think dried beans, such as Great Northern or kidney, are less expensive and a better choice. The weights, being metal, get far hotter than the beans. Beans can be reused (but not eaten) many, many times before being discarded.

WALNUT PASTRY CRUST

Makes one 11-inch crust

- 2 cups unbleached all-purpose flour
- 12 tablespoons (1 1/2 sticks) unsalted butter, chilled, cut into small pieces
- 1 egg
- 1 tablespoon milk
- 1 teaspoon vanilla extract
- 2 tablespoons sugar
- 1/4 teaspoon salt
- 1/4 cup finely chopped walnuts

This buttery-rich nut crust is one of my favorite pastries for making fancy desserts in a hurry. Add a dense layer of chocolate and plenty of raspberries, strawberries, or plums to this cookie-like sweet crust, and a luscious confection is yours (see page 257 for Raspberry Chocolate Tart).

If you chop nuts in a food processor, take them directly from the freezer (where it is best to store them) and pulse them rather than letting the machine run continuously. Otherwise, you might get a nut butter. If a pastry recipe calls for sugar, add a tablespoon to the nuts as they are chopping to prevent them from clumping together. Fresh walnuts in shells are usually available during the fall. However, bagged shelled nuts are found all year.

1. Combine the flour, butter, egg, milk, and vanilla in the bowl of a food processor and pulse process until the butter is the size of small peas.
2. Add the sugar, salt, and walnuts and process until the dough starts to pull together. *Do not overprocess.* Remove from the bowl, pat into a ball, flatten into a disc about 3/4 inch thick, and dust with flour. Cover with plastic wrap and refrigerate for at least 2 hours or overnight.
3. Preheat your oven to 375°F.
4. Remove the dough from the refrigerator. Gently massage it until it is workable, turning it over a couple of times, and start to flatten it with your fingertips. Dust with a little flour. Lightly flour a rolling pin and board, and roll the dough into a

circle about 14 inches in diameter and 1/8 inch thick. If the dough sticks, add a small amount of flour and loosen with a dough scraper or long, thin-bladed knife. (I prefer to work on a pastry cloth because I can turn the cloth quarter-turns and roll the dough more evenly. It also makes it easy to flip the dough over into the tart pan.)

5. Carefully roll the dough over the pin (or fold into quarters), and position it over the pan. Unroll, and ease the dough into the pan, flattening the bottom and then gently pushing the dough well into the corners and against the sides with your thumb or fingertips. Trim off any excess dough by rolling the pin over the pan or trimming it with a knife. Excess dough may be cut into decorative shapes (like leaves or apples) and baked alongside the tart. Once baked, glaze them and put them on finished tarts for decoration.

6. Lay a piece of aluminum foil large enough to cover the tart shell, shiny-side down, on the dough. Prick the dough well with a fork (through the foil), and fill with pie weights or dried beans. Bake in the middle of the oven until the crust begins to pull away from the pan, about 15 minutes. Carefully remove the aluminum foil and beans or weights, saving the beans for another use. Remove the sides from pan (optional), prick the pastry if it swells up, and return to the oven for 6 to 8 minutes, or until golden. Remove from the oven and cool on a rack.

Did you know? You can freeze pastry crusts in the tart pan both uncooked and cooked. Make sure that the pastry is double wrapped. I use plastic wrap or waxed paper for the first layer, and a resealable plastic bag for the second. Squeeze all the air out. The uncooked and cooked tarts may be frozen first, removed from the tart pan, and then carefully stacked for easier storage. Uncooked pastry should be slowly defrosted before baking, but should still be chilled. Return it to the tart pan for baking. The cooked shells should be reheated without defrosting at 350°F for 5 to 7 minutes to crisp them. Crusts will keep for at least 6 months if they are properly wrapped and your freezer is kept constantly at 0°F. As a rule, unbaked pastry has a slightly longer shelf life.

WHOLE-WHEAT CREAM PUFF SHELLS (PÂTE À CHOUX)

Makes about 30 puffs, 2 1/2 inches in diameter

Who said cream puffs can only be used to serve sweets? These savory shells are perfect for a cocktail party or elaborate tea, when finger foods and individual servings are especially appreciated. I find the more substantial whole-wheat flavor appealing when the puffs are filled with Tarragon Chicken Salad (page 93). Or, make mini versions to hold single Veal and Sausage Meatballs (page 136).

Make your market work for you: Fill puffs with a prepared salad like turkey or tuna from the Take-Out department. Drizzle a little shredded cheese on top, heat for a minute or two, and let your guests be impressed with your talents.

3/4 cup low-fat milk

6 tablespoons unsalted butter, cut into cubes

1/2 teaspoon salt

1/8 teaspoon white pepper

1/2 cup unbleached all-purpose flour

1/4 cup whole wheat flour

3-4 extra-large eggs at room temperature + 1 extra-large egg combined with 2 tablespoons milk, for egg wash

1. Preheat your oven to 400°F.
2. Combine the milk, butter, salt, and pepper in a heavy, medium-sized saucepan and bring it to a full boil. Remove from the heat and add both flours all at once, stirring with a wooden spoon until smooth.
3. Return the pot to medium heat and continue stirring and flipping the pastry to dry it out, about 5 to 7 minutes. A slight coating will form on the bottom of the pan, and the dough will be smooth and slightly shiny. Make sure it does not burn.
4. Remove the pan from the heat and add the eggs, one at a time, completely incorporating each egg before adding the next. A good test to determine if a fourth egg is needed is to pinch off a small amount of the dough between your thumb and index finger. Separate your fingers slowly. If the dough breaks into two parts, it is too dry and another egg is needed. It should form a U-shaped strand between the two fingers.
5. Butter 2 cookie sheets and then briefly run them under cold water, shaking to leave just a few drops on each pan, *or* line the pan with parchment paper. Fill a pastry bag fitted with a plain number 4 tip and squeeze the dough into small mounds about 1 1/2 inches in diameter and height, about 2 inches apart (see illustration). Brush carefully with egg wash, taking care not to let it drip onto the cookie sheet or the puffs will not rise properly.
6. Immediately transfer the pan to the upper third of your preheated oven and bake until puffed and a rich amber color, about 25 minutes. Remove from the oven and with a spatula transfer the puffs to a rack to cool.
7. Once the puffs cool, carefully cut in half horizontally, and remove any uncooked dough from the center with a spoon. Cooled cream puffs may be frozen in resealable plastic bags for 2 to 3 weeks.

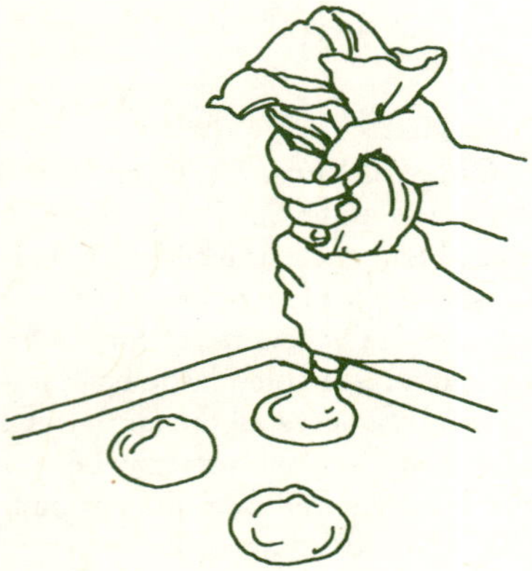

As a variation . . . For sweet cream puffs, use only all-purpose flour and add 1 teaspoon of sugar and 1/8 teaspoon nutmeg to the boiling milk, butter, salt, and pepper in Step 2. Fill with vanilla ice cream, fresh fruit, and top with The Ultimate Raspberry Chocolate Sauce (page 316).

HEAVENLY BLUES

Makes 50 to 60 dollar-size pancakes

The talented cook and author Marion Cunningham first served me these melt-in-your-mouth little morsels at Bridge Creek, her breakfast restaurant in Berkeley, California. They are sinfully delicious when drizzled with warm maple syrup. To gild the lily, I borrowed Rose Levy Beranbaum's (founder of The Cordon Rose Cooking School) idea of adding solidly frozen fresh blueberries directly to the pancakes when on the griddle. They stay plump and juicy that way. This works well for other frozen berries and pieces of fruit like peaches and cherries as long as they will have adequate time to cook through.

4 eggs

1/2 teaspoon salt

1/2 teaspoon baking soda

4 tablespoons cake flour or 3 1/2 tablespoons unbleached all-purpose flour (see note)

2 cups sour cream

3 tablespoons sugar

Vegetable shortening for greasing the griddle or skillet

2 cups blueberries, solidly frozen

1. Mix the eggs, salt, baking soda, cake flour, sour cream, and sugar together in a large bowl and beat with a wooden spoon until smooth. This can also be done in a food processor or blender.
2. Heat the griddle or skillet until very hot. Add just enough shortening to cover with a thin film. Drop small spoonfuls of the batter measuring about 2 1/2 inches in diameter when spread out onto the hot griddle. When a few bubbles appear on top of the pancakes, drop a few berries onto each pancake, quickly turn, and cook the second side briefly. Serve with maple syrup or confectioners' sugar. The batter keeps for up to 1 week when covered and refrigerated.

NOTE: In this recipe, substituting all-purpose for cake flour wouldn't make much difference with the results. When larger amounts of all-purpose flour are substituted for cake flour, reduce each cup of all-purpose flour by 2 tablespoons. While the results will be satisfactory, they will not be identical. Cake flour is milled from softer, spring-summer wheat and is about 9 percent protein. All-purpose flour is a combination of harder, winter flour and summer flour and is 12 to 13 percent protein. Do not use cake flour in a recipe calling for all-purpose; it won't work.

Did you know? Freezing blueberries when they are plentiful is easy. Pick over the berries, discarding any that are unsuitable. Rinse and blot as dry as possible. Spread the berries on a jelly-roll pan and put them directly in the freezer for about 1 hour or until frozen solid. Then, quickly transfer them by cupfuls to resealable plastic bags, gently squeezing out all the air, and freeze. They will keep for 4 to 6 months. Small freezer containers just large enough to hold each batch of berries will also work. Leave a small amount of headroom and make sure that the containers are very dry.

WILD RICE, PECAN, BUTTERMILK WAFFLES

Makes 12 waffles, serves 4 to 6

2 cups unbleached all-purpose flour

2 teaspoons baking powder

2 tablespoons sugar

½ teaspoon salt

2 cups buttermilk

2 eggs, separated

6 tablespoons (¾ stick) unsalted butter, melted and cooled slightly

¾ cup chopped pecans

½ cup cooked wild rice, cooled

These crunchy waffles are loaded with texture, taste, and old-fashioned goodness. Wild rice used to be a scarce autumn product but it has recently risen in popularity and availability. You can make these waffles ahead of time and leave them in a warm oven for at least 45 minutes. Or, let them cool on a rack and freeze them in resealable plastic bags. They reheat better than the store-bought varieties! Serve them with Very Berry Compote (page 313) on top. All those crunchy indentations will catch the tangy juice.

Breakfast has made a big comeback in recent years, especially on weekends. There is something very satisfying about pancakes, hot cereals, and waffles. We know that they are a good source of sustained energy. Markets reflect this trend with every variety of breakfast bar and frozen breakfast food imaginable. Alas, many of them are sugar, salt, and chemical rich, as well as nutrient poor, so read the labels before buying.

1. Heat an electric waffle iron (see note).
2. Sift together the flour, baking powder, sugar, and salt into a large bowl.
3. In a small bowl, combine the buttermilk and egg yolks. Stir in the melted butter, then the dry ingredients, and mix just until the batter is well blended. Stir in the pecans and wild rice.
4. Beat the egg whites into soft peaks, then gently fold into the batter.
5. Ladle about ⅓ of the batter onto the heated waffle iron, covering about ⅔ of the surface. Close and cook for 7 to 8 minutes. The red indicator light will usually go off by this time and the waffle will have stopped steaming. Test for doneness by carefully lifting the top. If it opens easily and the waffle falls off without sticking, it is done. If there is resistance, let the waffle cook for another minute. Remove and serve at once, or leave in a warm oven for up to 45 minutes.

NOTE: Waffle irons should be properly seasoned. Newer electric models come with directions in the box. Many also have a nonstick coating. Once an iron is seasoned, you should only wipe the pan clean; do not wash it. You should not need to grease it further, since the batter has plenty of butter in it.

DAY-AFTER-THANKSGIVING SWEET RYE AND YAM MUFFINS

Makes 12

These muffins are a moist and delicious by-product of our Thanksgiving table when there is often an extra yam left over. One year I puréed one—nutrient-rich skin and all—in the processor and combined it with rye flour and sour cream. Served with a combination of cream cheese and strawberry preserves, these muffins are a festive morning-after treat.

It's best to refrigerate or freeze specialty flours like rye and whole wheat in airtight bags to keep them fresher tasting and free of pests. Given a choice, I'd buy the smallest bag possible if I weren't planning to use it quickly.

- Unsalted butter for greasing the muffin tin or 12 muffin liners
- 1 3/4 cups rye flour, preferably stone-ground
- 2 1/2 teaspoons baking powder
- 1/2 teaspoon baking soda
- 1/2 teaspoon salt
- 1 cup mashed baked yam, fibrous tip and burned spots removed, but skin left on (approximately 1 large yam)
- 2 eggs
- 1/4 cup dark molasses
- 1/4 cup orange juice
- 4 tablespoons (1/2 stick) unsalted butter, melted and cooled slightly
- 2 tablespoons caraway seeds
- 1 cup sour cream
- 3/4 cup currants or chopped prunes (optional)

1. Preheat your oven to 375ºF. Grease or line a 12-muffin tin.
2. Put the rye flour in a medium bowl and sift in the baking powder, baking soda, and salt.
3. In a large bowl, stir the yam, eggs, molasses, orange juice, butter, caraway seeds, and sour cream until well blended. Toss the currants or prunes with the dry ingredients, then stir in the wet ingredients with a wooden spoon until just combined. The batter will be quite stiff.
4. Fill the muffin tins evenly with the batter. Bake in the middle of your preheated oven for 25 to 30 minutes, or until a toothpick or knife comes out clean when inserted in the middle of a muffin.
5. Remove, loosen with a small knife, if necessary, and gently turn muffins on their sides to cool.

Did you know? Although sour cream contains 18 percent milk fat, it has only 25 calories per tablespoon, making it lower in calories than butter and most salad dressings. A lower-calorie option is sour half-and-half, with 10.5 percent milk fat. Both will keep in your refrigerator for at least a week after purchase. Sour cream should be smooth and thick with a slightly tangy taste and only minimal separation, if any. Do not freeze sour cream.

ALMOST-IRISH SODA BREAD

Makes one 8-inch round loaf

Irish soda bread has long been one of my favorite quick breads. Its sweetness and slightly crumbly texture make it perfect for a snack in the afternoon or for a family dessert instead of rich cake or cookies. I lightly butter warmed slices and spread on apricot preserves. The addition of wheat germ and toasted sesame seeds gives it a more substantial, nuttier flavor, and the buttermilk adds a nice tang. Although it's not authentic, it certainly tastes good.

- 4 1/2 cups unbleached all-purpose flour
- 1 teaspoon baking soda
- 1 teaspoon baking powder
- 2 teaspoons salt
- 1/3 cup sugar
- 1 cup toasted wheat germ (see note)
- 1/3 cup sesame seeds, lightly toasted
- 6 tablespoons (3/4 stick) unsalted butter, at room temperature
- 1 cup golden raisins
- 2 cups buttermilk

1. Preheat your oven to 350°F. Butter and flour a round 8-inch cake pan.
2. Sift 4 cups of the flour with the baking soda, baking powder, salt, and sugar into a large bowl. Stir in the wheat germ and sesame seeds.
3. Using a pastry cutter, two knives, or your fingertips, cut the butter into the dry ingredients until the mixture resembles fine cornmeal. Add the raisins.
4. Pour in the buttermilk and mix with a wooden spoon or your hands just until all the ingredients are moistened. The dough will be sticky. Turn onto a floured board and knead for about 1 to 2 minutes, adding small amounts of the remaining 1/2 cup of flour, until it is smooth and no longer sticky.
5. Form the dough into an 8-inch ball and put it in the prepared cake pan, flattening it slightly. With a sharp knife, cut an X across the top extending beyond the edges. Bake for 75 to 80 minutes in the lower third of your oven until the bread has shrunk from the edges of the pan and makes a hollow sound when tapped on the bottom.
6. Remove from the oven, turn out of the pan, and cool on a rack for at least 1 hour. Once completely cooled, the bread may be sliced with a serrated knife and toasted, if desired. Serve with softened butter and apricot preserves, or softened cream cheese and orange marmalade.

NOTE: Wheat germ is the outer layer of the wheat that is removed during the milling process. When toasted, it becomes nutty and slightly sweet in flavor. While it was once found only in health food stores, it is readily available in jars and boxes with most other cereal products in the market. With all the discussion of fiber's benefits, this deliciously crunchy addition to breads, cookies, and other baked goods is even good for us.

Another idea . . . What do you do with leftover buttermilk? A couple of tablespoons makes a tangy addition to creamed vegetable soups; stir it in after the soup is heated. Use buttermilk in place of whole milk in waffles (see page 234), pancakes, or biscuits. There is also a good powdered buttermilk available in many markets. It keeps a long time on the shelf and combines with other liquids in baking to add the buttermilk flavor.

DILLED POTATO BREAD

Makes 1 large loaf

When I make this beautiful golden-brown braided loaf, I remember the wide-eyed amazement of my children as they first watched it rise in the oven. Try this lightly toasted, spread with chive-flecked cream cheese with thinly sliced smoked salmon on top, and cut into small canapés.

1 cup milk

1 teaspoon + 1/2 cup sugar

1 package active dry yeast

12 tablespoons (1 1/2 sticks) unsalted butter, at room temperature

1 tablespoon salt

2 eggs, beaten, at room temperature + 1 egg beaten with a few drops of water

3/4 cup freshly mashed potatoes

3 tablespoons chopped fresh dill leaves or 1 tablespoon dried

5 1/2–6 cups unbleached all-purpose flour

Vegetable shortening to grease a cookie sheet

1. In a small saucepan, heat the milk until it measures 110° to 115°F on an instant-read thermometer or until a few drops feel warm when dropped on your wrist. Stir in the 1 teaspoon of sugar, sprinkle the yeast over the milk, stir, and let stand 8 to 10 minutes in a warm, draft-free place (a turned-off oven works well) until the mixture has swollen and has small bubbles on the surface.
2. Meanwhile, cream the butter until light in color. Add the remaining 1/2 cup of sugar, the salt, and 2 eggs, and beat until smooth. Add the yeast-milk mixture and stir until blended. Add the potatoes and dill and mix well.
3. Begin adding the flour, a cup at a time, stirring with a wooden spoon. Continue adding flour until a soft dough is formed, working it in with your hands when it becomes difficult to stir. Turn the dough onto a lightly floured board and begin to knead. Continue adding flour until you have a stiff dough. Knead for another 10 to 12 minutes until the dough is smooth and elastic.
4. Roll dough into a ball and set into a lightly oiled bowl, turn once, and cover with a slightly dampened towel. Let it rise in a warm, draft-free place until doubled in size, 2 to 3 hours. Punch down and divide it into three equal parts.
5. On a lightly floured board, roll each part into a rope about 1 1/4 inches in diameter and about 14 to 16 inches in length. Lay the three ropes side by side and braid, pulling slightly as you braid the strands (see illustration). Pinch the ends together, tucking them under, and put the loaf on a lightly greased cookie sheet. Cover with a damp towel and let it rise in a warm, draft-free place until doubled in size, about 1 1/2 to 2 hours.
6. Preheat your oven to 350°F.
7. Brush the bread with the remaining beaten egg and water and bake for 30 to 35 minutes until well browned on top and hollow-sounding when tapped on the underside. Cool thoroughly on a rack before cutting.
8. When cool, the bread may be wrapped in aluminum foil or plastic, placed inside another plastic or resealable plastic bag with the air squeezed out, and frozen for up to a month. Reheat before serving.

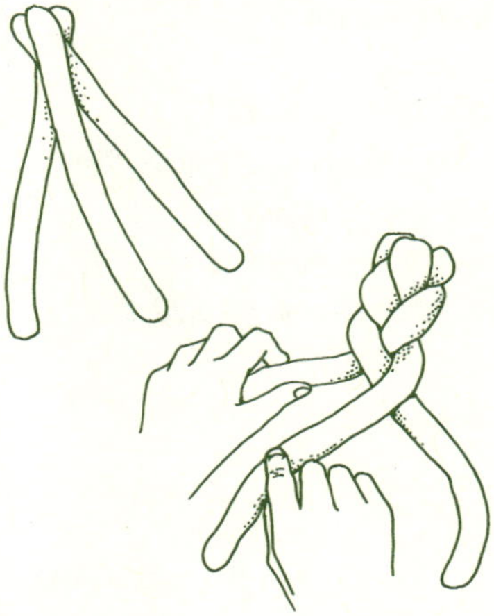

Did you know? Fresh bread doesn't have preservatives and dries out faster than commercially baked loaves. To refresh bread, sprinkle with a few drops of water, put in a preheated 350°F oven inside a closed brown paper bag or aluminum foil, and heat for 15 to 20 minutes. Open the bag or foil and continue cooking for another 5 minutes to crisp the crust.

CRANBERRY HOLIDAY BRAID

Makes 1 large loaf

This buttery rich yeast bread, braided with a cranberry-orange filling, looks especially festive if decorated with pine boughs (well rinsed and dried) around it and extra cranberries sprinkled on the greenery. It's wonderful for breakfast and good enough to pass for dessert, as well.

When choosing preserves, jams, and jellies, look for labels where the fruit is listed first. That tells you that there is more fruit than sugar or any other ingredient. Sealed jars of preserves will keep in a cool pantry for at least a year. Once opened, they should be refrigerated.

FOR THE DOUGH:

3/4 cup milk

1 teaspoon + 6 tablespoons sugar

1 package active dry yeast

4–4 1/2 cups unbleached all-purpose flour

12 tablespoons (1 1/2 sticks) unsalted butter, at room temperature

2 eggs, at room temperature

FOR THE FILLING:

1 cup sweet orange marmalade

1 1/2 cups fresh or frozen cranberries, coarsely chopped

1 stick cinnamon

FOR THE GLAZE:

3/4 cup confectioners' sugar, sifted

2 tablespoons orange juice

1 teaspoon vegetable oil

7–8 cranberries, for decoration

1. Make the dough: In a small saucepan, heat the milk until it measures 105° to 115°F on an instant-read thermometer or until a few drops feel slightly warm when dropped on your wrist. Stir in the 1 teaspoon of sugar, sprinkle the yeast over the milk, stir, and let stand 8 to 10 minutes in a warm, draft-free place until the mixture has swollen and has small bubbles on the surface. Stir in 1 cup of the flour, cover with a towel, and let it rise in a warm, draft-free place (a turned-off oven works well) until doubled in size, about 1 to 2 hours.
2. In a large bowl, cream the butter and sugar until light and fluffy. Punch down the risen sponge and stir it into the butter-sugar mixture with a wooden spoon. Add the eggs one at a time. Stir in about 2 1/2 cups of the flour and blend well. Once the dough starts to pull away from the sides of the bowl and is too stiff to mix with a spoon, begin to knead by hand. Turn it out onto a lightly floured board and begin adding the remaining flour by 1/2 cupfuls until the dough is smooth and no longer sticky. Knead the dough for 10 minutes, or until very smooth and elastic.
3. Form it into a ball and put in a lightly oiled bowl, turn once, cover it with a towel, and set in a warm place to rise until almost doubled in size, 45 minutes to 1 1/2 hours.
4. Make the filling: Combine the marmalade, cranberries, and cinnamon stick in a medium saucepan, cover, bring to a boil over medium heat, and cook for 5 minutes, stirring occasionally. Uncover and continue boiling gently for 5 minutes more, stirring frequently. Remove the cinnamon and let the mixture cool.
5. Punch down the dough. On a lightly floured board, roll it into a rectangle approximately 10 x 14 inches and 1/4 inch thick.

6. Spread the filling in a thin layer lengthwise down the center third, leaving a small border at the top and bottom. Cut the outer thirds into 7 diagonal strips approximately 1 ½ inches wide, so that they are attached at the filling side. Lace the strips alternately over one another and tuck the ends under (see illustration). Lightly grease a cookie sheet and transfer the braided bread to it. Cover with a slightly dampened towel and let it rise in a warm place until doubled in size, about 30 minutes to 1 hour.

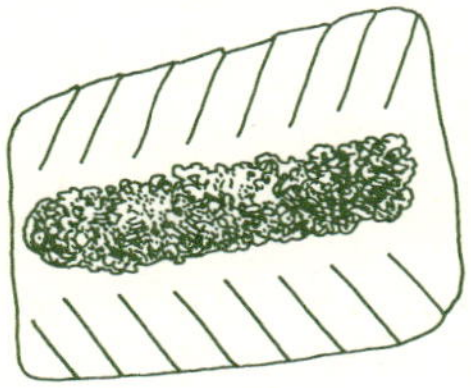

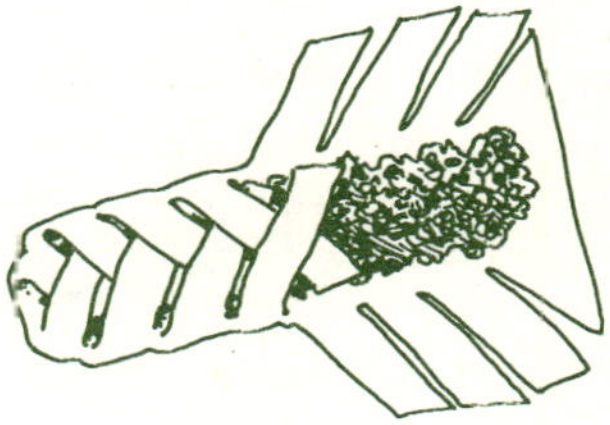

7. Preheat your oven to 350°F.
8. Bake in the middle of the oven for about 35 minutes until it is a rich golden color on top and when lightly pressed with your finger, the indentation springs back up. Put on a rack to cool.
9. Prepare the glaze: While the bread is cooling, stir the confectioners' sugar and orange juice in a small bowl until smooth. Stir in the oil. Brush the glaze generously over the cooled loaf and add the extra 7 or 8 cranberries down the middle where the bread is braided. Cool completely before slicing. It may be sliced and reheated, if desired.

Did you know? Cranberries freeze beautifully. Wrap them in an airtight bag, squeeze out excess air, and they will keep for almost a year. When adding them to a recipe, do not defrost; they will be much juicier that way.

Recently, the cranberry industry changed their standard bag size. Whereas we used to buy a 16-ounce bag (which contained 4 cups), we now get only three-quarters of that. Make sure to check amounts given in older recipes.

LEMON SHORTBREAD COOKIES

Makes 18 pieces

I love shortbread cookies for their firm, wonderful-to-dunk-in-tea texture. This slightly festive version, with a lemon glaze and rectangular shape, makes a tempting addition to a plate of cookies served with custard, ice cream, or sherbet. The combination of crunch with soft is most satisfying.

Fresh lemons are always available in the market and infinitely superior to bottled lemon juice. Fresh-frozen lemon juice, near the condensed orange juice and lemonade in the freezer, is a reasonable substitute in a pinch. But, don't use dried lemon rind in a jar. The flavor and texture are very different from fresh.

FOR THE DOUGH:

12 tablespoons (1 1/2 sticks) unsalted butter, at room temperature

2/3 cup confectioners' sugar, sifted

1/2 tablespoon grated lemon zest

1 tablespoon fresh lemon juice

1 3/4 cups unbleached all-purpose flour

1/2 teaspoon salt

FOR THE GLAZE:

1/3 cup confectioners' sugar, sifted

1 tablespoon + 1 teaspoon fresh lemon juice

1. For the shortbread: Cream the butter with a wooden spoon until fluffy and light in color, about 2 to 3 minutes. Add the confectioners' sugar and blend well. Stir in the lemon zest and lemon juice. These first steps can be done by hand or with an electric mixer.
2. Sift the flour and salt into the butter mixture and blend with your hands or a wooden spoon into a smooth dough.
3. Preheat your oven to 325°F.
4. Press the dough into an 8-by-8-inch cake pan and smooth it with your hands or the back of a wooden spoon to make as even as possible. Score the dough halfway through into 6 equal horizontal strips, then into thirds vertically. A short ruler and sharp paring knife will help. Prick each rectangular piece 3 or 4 times with a fork (see illustration).
5. Bake in the lower third of the oven until the cookies are set when touched and light brown around the edges, 45 to 50 minutes. Remove from the oven and cool on a wire rack. Cut through the rectangles where the dough was scored and run a sharp knife around the outside.
6. For the glaze: Mix the confectioners' sugar with the lemon juice. Brush on the warm shortbread. Allow the cookies to cool completely before covering. Shortbread cookies may be stored in the baking pan for at least a week.

NOTE: Supermarkets sell disposable aluminum baking pans in just the right size to make these shortbread cookies and then give them as a gift.

Did you know? When working with pastry brushes, always smell them before using to guarantee they were put away clean. Rancid tastes are easily transmitted to baked goods this way and can ruin your best efforts. Wash brushes in warm, soapy water, then rinse well. If this does not do the trick, soak them in some hot water with a little bleach added. Rinse very well.

IRISH OATMEAL HERMITS

Makes 2 dozen 3 1/2-inch cookies

These cookies could be called "true grit" for the crunchy toasted oatmeal, chewy coconut, and dried fruits they contain. They are the result of foraging in the Staples aisles with my children. We decided to experiment with ingredients we don't usually have on hand. The Irish oatmeal, found in cans, lends a healthy nuttiness to these hermits, and the mixed fruit bits are a fast and helpful addition that are much easier than chopping everything by hand. After consuming quite a few, we pronounced them a success.

Shortening for greasing cookie sheets or parchment paper

1 cup Irish oatmeal, not the quick-cooking variety

12 tablespoons (1 1/2 sticks) unsalted butter, at room temperature

1/2 cup firmly packed light brown sugar

2 eggs

1 teaspoon orange extract

3/4 cup shredded coconut, sweetened or unsweetened

1 cup unbleached all-purpose flour

1 teaspoon salt

1 teaspoon baking powder

1 teaspoon baking soda

1 1/2 teaspoons cinnamon

1 1/2 teaspoons ground coriander seed

1 1/2 cups chopped mixed dry fruits

1. Preheat your oven to 325°F. Lightly grease a cookie sheet or line it with parchment paper.
2. Spread the oatmeal in a thin layer in a flat pan and toast in the preheated oven until lightly browned, about 15 minutes. Set aside to cool.
3. In a medium bowl, cream the butter with a wooden spoon or handheld electric mixer until light and fluffy. Beat in the brown sugar, then the eggs, orange extract, and coconut. Sift in the flour, salt, baking powder, baking soda, cinnamon, and coriander into the bowl, and mix well. Add the oatmeal and fruit and stir to blend.
4. Drop the mixture by rounded tablespoonfuls onto the cookie sheet, leaving about 3 inches between each cookie. Bake in the middle of your oven until lightly colored around the outside and puffed in the middle, about 12 to 14 minutes. Do not overbake. Remove from the oven and cool on the cookie sheet for 5 minutes before transferring them to a wire rack. Store in airtight tins. They will last at least 1 week.

Did you know? To keep brown sugar soft: Once the bag has been opened, either transfer the sugar to an airtight container or carefully fold the plastic inner bag down and clamp closed. I have purchased small colored wire clothes pins which are excellent for this purpose. If sugar does become hard, place a piece of soft bread or an apple slice in the bag, close it tight, and leave it for a few days. The moisture from the bread or apple will soften the sugar.

MOLASSES SPICE COOKIES

Makes about 4 to 5 dozen

- 12 tablespoons (1 1/2 sticks) unsalted butter
- 1 1/2 cups sugar + 1/2 cup sugar, for coating balls of dough
- 1/4 cup dark molasses
- 1 egg
- 2 cups unbleached all-purpose flour
- 2 teaspoons baking soda
- 1 teaspoon ground cinnamon
- 1 teaspoon ground ginger
- 1 teaspoon ground clove
- 3/4 teaspoon salt
- Shortening for greasing cookie sheets

Supermarket shelves are crammed full of old and new cookie varieties. Yet nothing quite matches the aroma and flavor of the fresh-from-the-oven variety. These buttery, spicy cookies are our family favorite. These days, it's my daughter Nicole who is the champion at making them for our friends and family.

When first out of the oven, these cookies are soft and chewy. After cooling on a rack, they become crisper. You can choose the texture you prefer—crisp or soft. By adding a piece of soft bread to the storage tin, you can soften crunchy cookies. They are wonderful served with Nutmeg-Scented Cantaloupe Sherbet (page 64) or custards.

1. In a medium saucepan, melt the butter over low heat, let it cool to room temperature, then stir the sugar, molasses, and egg.
2. Sift the flour, baking soda, cinnamon, ginger, clove, and salt into the butter mixture, mix well, cover and refrigerate until dough is firm, about 45 minutes.
3. Preheat your oven to 375°F. Lightly grease 2 cookie sheets.
4. Form the dough into 1-inch balls, rolling each in granulated sugar before putting it on the cookie sheet. Leave about 2 inches between each cookie. Bake in the middle of the oven for 8 to 10 minutes, or until the cookies are golden brown and the tops are cracked. They will still be soft. Remove the pan and transfer the cookies with a wide spatula to wire racks to cool. Store in an airtight tin. (Add a piece of soft bread if you prefer softer cookies.)

Have you tried . . . To measure molasses easily, lightly film a measuring cup with a little flavorless vegetable oil. When you pour out the desired amount of molasses, it will all slip into whatever you are baking instead of sticking to the cup. No spatulas and no scraping needed.

POGACHEL

Makes about 32 cookies

These simple hard biscuits are not too sweet and are perfect for dunking in cocoa, tea, or sherry. Sometimes I serve them with rich fruit compotes or strawberries soaked in Grand Marnier, and I savor each soaked crumb. I learned to make them just as my Hungarian great-grandmother made hers, by hand. When I was teaching my daughter to make them, we tried a batch in the food processor. My great-grandmother must have been smiling as we discovered that the handmade batch had a much finer, more delicate texture than the machine-mixed version.

8 tablespoons (1 stick) unsalted butter, at room temperature

3/4 cup sugar

1 egg

2 tablespoons sour cream

2 cups unbleached all-purpose flour

2 teaspoons baking powder

1/2 teaspoon salt

1. Preheat your oven to 350°F. Lightly flour 2 cookie sheets.
2. In a medium bowl, cream the butter and sugar until fluffy and light in color. Beat in the egg and the sour cream.
3. Sift the flour, baking powder, and salt into the bowl, then knead the mixture by hand into a smooth dough.
4. Lightly flour a wooden board or counter. Carefully roll out the soft dough to an even thickness of slightly more than 1/4 inch. Using a round cookie cutter or a glass about 2 1/4 inches in diameter dipped in flour, cut out the cookies. Carefully transfer them to a cookie sheet with a spatula dipped in flour. Gather up the scraps, re-roll them, and repeat.
5. Prick the center of each cookie in 2 places with a fork. Bake in the middle of the preheated oven until lightly browned around the edges, 18 to 20 minutes. Remove and transfer cookies to wire racks to cool.

Did you know? Where you bake your cookies in the oven makes a difference. If too close to the heat source, they can burn on the bottom before the top is cooked. Good heat circulation produces even baking. Cookie sheets should be at least 2 inches narrower than the width of the oven. If 2 sheets are used, try to stagger them so that they are not right on top of one another. It helps to rotate their position in the oven, as well.

CHOCOLATE PECAN ICEBOX COOKIES

Makes about 4 dozen

- 8 tablespoons (1 stick) unsalted butter, at room temperature
- 1 cup firmly packed dark brown sugar
- 1 egg
- 2 tablespoons bourbon or freshly squeezed orange juice
- 1 tablespoon grated orange zest
- 2 1/2 cups unbleached all-purpose flour
- 1/2 teaspoon baking soda
- 1 teaspoon salt
- 1/2 cup chopped pecans
- 1/2 cup mini chocolate chips

Those rolls of prepared cookie dough calling to you from the Dairy case have nothing over these easy-to-prepare cookies. Besides having no preservatives, these pecan slices have plenty of crunch and flavor, thanks to the chocolate, orange zest, and a nip of bourbon.

Make the dough up to a week in advance, wrap in plastic wrap, and slice and bake as desired. Or, make 2 batches and freeze one. It will be there waiting for you 4 months later. Remember to defrost dough slowly in the refrigerator until it can be easily sliced. When you slice, cookies should be uniform in size and thickness to bake evenly.

1. In a medium bowl, cream the butter and sugar until light and fluffy. Beat in the egg, bourbon, and orange zest. Sift the flour, baking soda, and salt into the butter mixture and blend well. Stir in the pecans and chocolate chips.
2. Shape the dough into a roll about 2 inches in diameter, wrap tightly in plastic wrap or waxed paper, and refrigerate overnight or for up to 1 week.
3. Preheat your oven to 350°F.
4. Using a sharp thin-bladed knife, cut the dough into 1/4-inch slices and put them on *ungreased* cookie sheets. Bake in the middle of the oven until lightly browned and set, about 15 minutes. Remove from the oven and transfer the cookies to wire racks to cool. Store in a jar with a loose-fitting lid to maintain the crispness. They will keep for up to 1 week or they may be frozen (see "Did you know?," page 245).

Did you know? Aside from use as a leavener and as an air freshener for your refrigerator, baking soda will also extinguish small kitchen fires.

CHOCOLATE-DIPPED BUTTER WALNUT CRESCENTS

Makes 18

The delicate texture and toasted-nut flavor of these crescents has made them a family favorite for generations. Inspired by a passion for chocolate and finding high-quality imported and domestic bars available in supermarkets, I began dipping the cookies in chocolate. I found that coating each cookie halfway made them particularly attractive. Alternatively, after the cookies have cooled, dust them with confectioners' sugar rather than dipping them in chocolate.

Choose the variety of chocolate you like—from extra-bitter to milk chocolate. But read the labels and buy only real chocolate. If you wrap it in a double layer of paper or foil, chocolate will keep well in a cool pantry for at least 9 months. The gray "bloom" that develops on chocolate that gets too warm will not affect the taste and will disappear if the chocolate is melted for baking.

8 tablespoons (1 stick) unsalted butter, at room temperature

1/2 cup confectioners' sugar, sifted

1 teaspoon vanilla extract

1/4 cup firmly packed, finely ground walnuts

1 cup unbleached all-purpose flour

1/2 teaspoon salt

3 ounces bittersweet chocolate

1. Preheat your oven to 350°F.
2. In a medium-sized bowl, cream the butter until light and fluffy. Stir in the confectioners' sugar. Add the vanilla and walnuts and mix well. Sift in the flour and salt and stir until smooth.
3. Lightly flour a cookie sheet. Scoop up enough dough to form a 1-inch ball. Roll each ball between your palms into a 3-inch cylinder, form into a crescent, and put on the cookie sheet leaving about 2 inches between cookies.
4. Bake in the middle of your oven until the edges of the crescents are golden brown, about 13 to 15 minutes. Remove and transfer the cookies to a wire rack to cool.
5. Melt the chocolate in a small saucepan over low heat or in the top of a double boiler. Let it cool slightly and dip one end of each cooled crescent in the chocolate. Put on waxed paper to harden.

Did you know? Cookies freeze beautifully, for 3 to 4 months. Wrap each variety of cookie separately in airtight tins or freezer wrap. If the recipe calls for a final dusting of confectioners' sugar, do this once they have been defrosted—approximately 10 to 15 minutes. For added crispness, unglazed cookies may be reheated for 2 to 3 minutes in a 325°F oven.

PRINCE ALBERT'S CAKES

Makes 32 squares, 2 1/2 by 3 inches

These old fashioned fruit-filled squares with their flaky cookie crust and sweet glaze are royal indeed. England's Queen Victoria liked to bake them for her husband, Prince Albert, and their 9 children when in their private apartments at Windsor Castle. They appeal to all ages and are the perfect sweet for late-afternoon tea or a large holiday open house.

Rona Deme, the charming British proprietor of Country Host, a take-out shop originally in New York City, helped me modify her bakery-size recipe into this smaller version.

FOR THE FILLING:

2 cups raisins (golden and dark mixed or either one alone)

1 cup currants

1/2 cup candied diced lemon peel, finely chopped

2 tablespoons unsalted butter

1/4 cup unbleached all-purpose flour

1/4 cup water

1/4 cup sweet sherry

FOR THE PASTRY:

2 pounds (6 1/2 to 7 cups) unsifted all-purpose flour

2 cups sugar

2 teaspoons salt

1 cup (1/2 pound) solid vegetable shortening or lard

1/2 pound (2 sticks) unsalted butter

2/3–3/4 cup milk

FOR THE GLAZE:

3/4 cup confectioners' sugar

3 tablespoons hot water

1/2 teaspoon vanilla extract

1/2 teaspoon flavorless vegetable oil, such as canola

1. Make the filling: Combine the raisins, currants, lemon peel, and butter in a medium size saucepan and add just enough water to cover. Bring to a boil, then turn the heat down, and simmer for 10 minutes. While the fruit is cooking, mix together the flour and 1/4 cup water and gradually stir it into the fruit mixture.
2. After the fruit thickens, stir in the sherry. Remove the pan from the heat and spread the fruit on a dish to cool completely while preparing the pastry.
3. Prepare the pastry: Combine the flour, sugar, and salt in a large bowl and cut in the shortening and butter until it is the size of small peas. Gradually add the milk, mixing until you have a smooth, soft dough. Vary the amount of milk as necessary.
4. Preheat your oven to 350°F.
5. Roll out half the pastry to fit an 18-by-12-by-1-inch pan. It will be easier to roll the pastry on an apron or non-terrycloth dish towel dusted with flour. Flour the rolling pin to keep it from sticking to the dough. Once the desired size is reached, roll the dough and cloth around the rolling pin. Unroll the dough and cloth so that the cloth is on top and the dough is in the pan. Remove the towel, patch as necessary, and using your thumb or a knife, cut the pastry even with the top of the pan. (See note.)
6. Spread the fruit mixture evenly over the pastry.
7. Roll out the remaining pastry and lay it over the fruit. Press the edges together to seal and prick the top in several places. Bake in the middle of the oven for 45 minutes or until the pastry is golden brown. Remove and let cool.
8. Make the glaze: In a small bowl, mix the sugar and water together until smooth. Stir in the vanilla and oil. If the glaze stiffens, add a few drops of hot water and stir to smooth it out. When the pastry is cool, brush the top crust with the glaze. When it dries, cut the pastry into 32 squares. When storing these squares, cover loosely with foil; otherwise, they get soggy.

Did you know? When storing boxes of dried fruits, make sure they are tightly closed. I slip a resealable plastic sandwich-size bag over mine. If they do dry out, soak them for a few moments in warm water or a little sherry, port, or brandy until softened, then drain before using.

NOTE: Don't get discouraged if the dough breaks when you transfer it to the pan. This large amount can be unwieldy and slightly sticky. Patching and smoothing it does not adversely affect the final taste or appearance. If this happens with the bottom layer, simply flatten the dough with your fingertips. For the top, gather the dough back into a ball, dust lightly with flour, and re-roll. For small cracks, add a piece of the dough and smooth it with your fingertips.

Excess dough scraps can be wrapped and refrigerated for 1 week. I make it into tartlet shells and fill with Lemon Curd (page 59), or make it into sugar cookies.

"KILLER" TRIPLE-CHIP BROWNIES

Makes 32 brownies

If you like decadence, these brownies are it. They have a thin, cake-like topping and the richest fudgy interiors imaginable. They were dubbed "killers" because the moment my kids knew they were around, all their aggressive instincts came out and they attacked any suspected hiding place. Along the way they learned that unfortunately, when taken from the oven, the brownies have to chill for several hours before cutting; otherwise, the result is a gooey mess. I used to send these to my kids when they were away at camp during the summer. When a directive came that parents were not to send food to campers, some counselors asked that I bring these brownies to the staff on visiting day.

- Shortening to grease the foil
- 16 tablespoons (2 sticks) unsalted butter, softened
- 2 cups sugar
- 8 ounces semi- or bittersweet chocolate, melted and slightly cooled
- 2 teaspoons vanilla
- 4 eggs
- 1 cup unbleached all-purpose flour
- 1 teaspoon salt
- 1 cup chopped walnuts
- 1 cup *each* dark chocolate, milk chocolate, and butterscotch bits

1. Preheat your oven to 350°F. Line an 8 3/4-by-13 1/2-inch glass or metal pan with a large piece of foil, smoothing it into the corners. Butter the foil.
2. In a large bowl, cream the butter and sugar until light in color. Using a handheld electric mixer, beat in the melted chocolate, the vanilla, and the eggs, one at a time, until well blended.
3. In another bowl, combine the flour and salt. Add the walnuts and all the bits, tossing to coat with flour. Add to the chocolate, stirring until all the ingredients are just blended. *Don't overmix.* Scrape the batter into the pan, holding the foil so it doesn't move, and bake in the middle of the oven until a toothpick inserted in the center comes out almost clean, about 50 minutes.
4. Remove the pan, let it stand for an hour, then cover, and refrigerate for several hours or overnight until firm. Turn the cooled brownies onto a clean work space, lift off the foil, and cut into 32 squares. Refrigerate or freeze in an airtight tin.

CURRIED CORN NUT AND SUNFLOWER SEED NIBBLE

Makes 1 ½ cups

This "nibble" is addicting. In fall, I make big bowls of it for open houses and cocktail parties. It is economical, festive, and ideal to make and package in jars for hostess presents. Use the variety of curry powder that suits your palate.

1 cup corn nuts

½ cup sunflower seeds

2 teaspoons sugar

2 teaspoons vegetable oil

1 teaspoon curry powder, mild or hot

½ cup dark raisins

Did you know? Most sunflower seeds and corn nuts—those large, roasted puffed kernels of corn—that we buy in supermarkets are already salted unless marked "salt free" or "raw." Therefore, there is no additional salt in this recipe. Salted seeds and nuts like these don't freeze well.

1. Preheat your oven to 350°F.
2. Combine the corn nuts, sunflower seeds, sugar, and oil in a small, oven-safe bowl and toss to blend.
3. Bake in the oven for 10 minutes.
4. Remove, toss with the curry powder, stir in the raisins, and cool. Store in airtight containers.

COCOA PECANS

Makes 1 pound

This kind of glazed nut treat is often sold in expensive food boutiques, although it is really very easy to make. You can use the general principle of dipping nuts into egg whites and add any combination of sweet or savory coating you desire—coconut and cocoa; or Parmesan cheese, ground red pepper, and nutmeg. Even lavender and rosemary lend a nice flavor. The shiny nuts are very tempting. Packed in clean, empty mustard jars or colorful tins, they make nice gifts.

1 tablespoon vegetable oil to grease cookie sheets

1 egg white

1 pound pecan halves

⅓ cup sugar

3 tablespoons unsweetened cocoa powder

½ teaspoon salt

½ teaspoon cinnamon

¼ teaspoon ground cloves

Did you know? Cookie sheets are usually buttered when baking time is short, as with cookies, where the butter will add flavor and not burn. For longer baking with exposed pans, a flavorless vegetable oil is recommended.

1. Preheat your oven to 350°F. Lightly oil 2 cookie sheets.
2. Put the egg white in a deep bowl, beat until frothy, then add the pecans and toss to cover evenly.
3. Combine the sugar, cocoa, salt, cinnamon, and cloves in another bowl. Transfer the pecans to this bowl and toss to cover.
4. Divide the nuts evenly between the cookie sheets, keeping them in 1 layer. Bake for 15 minutes. Remove and let cool. Store in airtight containers.

DATE AND NUT MERINGUE KISSES

Makes about 100 pieces

These delicious candy nibbles from my Great-Aunt Ann are an easy and unusual confection to serve either with other desserts, with cheese, or with a cup of tea in the afternoon. They are slightly crunchy on the outside—thanks to the toasted coconut—and chewy and nutty inside. Supermarkets sell pitted and chopped dates—a time-saving convenience for those of us in a hurry. But many markets only stock them from the fall through the holidays.

Unsalted butter to grease a cookie sheet or parchment paper

1 pound pitted soft dates, coarsely chopped

1/2 pound walnuts, coarsely chopped

1/2 teaspoon grated orange zest

3 egg whites

Pinch of salt

2/3 cup superfine sugar

2 cups moist shredded coconut

1. Preheat your oven to 250°F. Butter a cookie sheet or line it with parchment paper.
2. Combine the dates, walnuts, and zest in a bowl, mix well, and form into small balls about 3/4 inch in diameter.
3. In a large bowl, whisk the egg whites and salt until the whites are just foamy. Slowly add the sugar, a teaspoon at a time, and continue beating for 30 seconds longer until you have a stiff but not dry meringue.
4. Toss half the date/nut balls in the meringue, coating them with your fingers; then roll them in coconut and place on the cookie sheet. Repeat with the remaining balls. Bake for 30 minutes, or until light brown in color and nearly dry to the touch. Remove from the oven and cool. Store in a dry area.

NOTE: For best results, choose a dry day to prepare these. If they become tacky during storage, dry them for a few minutes in a 200°F oven.

Did you know? When you can't find superfine sugar, you can process granulated sugar by pulsing in a blender to the finer consistency necessary. But go easy—you don't want powdered sugar. The finer the sugar crystal, the more sweetening power to each cup of sugar.

MANDARIN CRANBERRY SORBET

Serves 8 to 12

- 2/3 cup sugar
- 2/3 cup water
- 1 12-ounce package cranberries, fresh or frozen
- 4 11-ounce cans whole mandarin segments in light syrup, drained
- 1 1/2 tablespoons grated orange zest
- 2 tablespoons Cognac (optional)

This refreshing, richly berry-colored sorbet is especially beautiful when garnished with mandarins and cranberries. It is a lovely palate refresher served between courses of a substantial meal or as a lighter dessert with cookies.

Canned fruits in light syrup or their own juices are perfect for making homemade sorbets. Sorbets and other fruit confections, in which the ingredients are puréed, offer an opportunity to buy less expensive brands of fruit; the less-than-perfect size does not affect the final presentation as long as the quality is not inferior.

1. Combine the sugar and water in a small saucepan. Over medium heat, bring the liquid to just below the boiling point. Set the syrup aside to cool.
2. For the garnish, set aside 6 cranberries and 12 nice mandarin segments (or a couple extra for mistakes). Add the remaining cranberries, mandarins, sugar syrup, zest, and Cognac to the bowl of a food processor and purée until smooth. Pour into a shallow glass or metal dish and freeze until solid, about 6 to 10 hours.
3. Return the frozen mixture to the bowl of the food processor and process, starting with an on-off motion, until the mixture is smooth. Return it to the shallow dish and refreeze for another hour or until firm.
4. Remove the sorbet from the freezer and let it stand at room temperature for about 10 minutes. Serve in small scoops. If desired, garnish with mandarin segments, split in half lengthwise, with a split cranberry added.

SPICY PUMPKIN MOUSSE

Serves 6

Pumpkins are native to the New World. They were brought back to Europe by Christopher Columbus, where they were used in vegetable dishes (see Pumpkin and Porcini, page 39) and pasta. This lightly spiced mousse recipe is ideal for Thanksgiving—you can easily double the quantities of the ingredients—or anytime you want a flavorful do-ahead dessert. You can also serve the mousse in ready-to-fill chocolate cups now sold in many markets.

Supermarket shoppers are used to buying cans of puréed pumpkin, not realizing that they may cut up a pumpkin, and bake and purée one, as well (see how below). Or, in many recipes winter squash substitutes just fine. If canned pumpkin is a staple in your house, buy an extra can or two between October and December. At other times, it may not be stocked.

1 3/4 cups fresh or canned pumpkin purée
1 teaspoon cinnamon
1/2 teaspoon freshly grated nutmeg
1/2 teaspoon ground ginger
1/2 teaspoon salt
1/8 teaspoon white pepper
Grated zest of 1 orange
3 tablespoons Grand Marnier or triple sec
1 package unflavored gelatin
2 tablespoons fresh orange juice
4 egg yolks
1/3 cup sugar
1 1/4 cups heavy cream
1 teaspoon vanilla
6 ginger snaps, crumbled for garnish

1. In a large bowl, stir the pumpkin, cinnamon, nutmeg, ginger, salt, pepper, orange zest, and Grand Marnier until well blended.
2. Dissolve the gelatin in the orange juice in a small bowl.
3. Combine the egg yolks and sugar in a small bowl and beat until thick and lemon colored.
4. Scald 1/4 cup of the cream and the vanilla in a small saucepan. Add the softened gelatin to it and stir until entirely dissolved, then pour this into the egg yolks, beating continuously. Scrape the cream-egg mixture into the pumpkin and stir until smooth.
5. Whip the remaining 1 cup of cream until stiff; reserve about 1/3 cup for the garnish. Fold the cream into the pumpkin mixture then scrape it into a 2-quart mold or 6 individual ramekins. Cover and chill for several hours or overnight.
6. To serve, pipe the reserved whipped cream in rosettes on top of the mousse for decoration and sprinkle on the ginger snap crumbs.

Did you know? To make pumpkin purée, lightly oil a jelly-roll pan or cookie sheet, and preheat the oven to 325°F. Wash the pumpkin and scrape out the seeds; cut the pumpkin into large chunks and place them shell-side up in the oven. Bake for an hour or until the flesh is easily scraped from the skin. Purée in a food processor or pass through a food mill. Once cooled, the purée may be frozen for up to 3 months.

CARAMEL CURLS WITH APRICOT CREAM

Makes 16

These lacy, crunchy caramel rolls are so delicious I often eat them just as they cool. Or I fill them with custard or cream whipped with a little instant coffee and mini chocolate chips. In this party version, the gingery apricot cream provides a stunning contrast in flavor and texture to the curls. Since crispness is important, avoid making them on humid days. Also, fill them just before serving for the same reason.

Dried apricots are often found in boxes, bags, and sometimes loose in the Health Food bins of markets. While bags and boxes are often about the same price, bulk dried fruits can be less costly and fresher. Store dried fruits in a cool pantry or refrigerator until needed.

Shortening to grease 2 cookie sheets

FOR THE CARAMEL CURLS:

1/4 cup light corn syrup
4 tablespoons (1/2 stick) unsalted butter
1/3 cup firmly packed light brown sugar
1/4 teaspoon ground ginger
1/2 tablespoon brandy
1/2 cup unbleached all-purpose flour

FOR THE APRICOT CREAM:

5 ounces dried apricots
1 tablespoon finely grated fresh gingerroot
3/4 cup light cream
2 tablespoons superfine sugar (or regular sugar processed in a food processor, see "Did you know?," page 249)
1 tablespoon brandy
1 pint heavy cream

1. Make the caramel curls: Preheat your oven to 350°F. Generously grease 2 cookie sheets.
2. In a medium size saucepan, combine the corn syrup, butter, brown sugar, ginger, and brandy and bring it to a boil. Remove the pan from the heat, slowly stir in the flour, and mix well.
3. Drop the batter by generous rounded teaspoonfuls onto the prepared cookie sheets. They should measure about 2 1/2 inches once they flatten before baking. Bake only 4 at a time, since they spread to about 5 inches in diameter. Bake in the middle of the oven for 8 to 9 minutes, or until dark golden in color.
4. Remove the pan from the oven and cool the cookies on the cookie sheet for about 1 to 2 minutes, then lift them off, one at a time, with a cake spatula or your fingers. Wrap each cookie around a clean broom handle or a metal cannoli form, and hold for a few seconds until firm, then carefully slide off and cool on a cake rack before filling. If cookies become too brittle to bend, put them back in the oven for 15 to 30 seconds.
5. Prepare the apricot cream: Combine the apricots and ginger in the bowl of a food processor. Start by pulsing, then process until quite smooth. Add the light cream, sugar, and brandy and process until very smooth.
6. Using a chilled bowl and beaters, beat the heavy cream until very stiff. Fold in the apricot mixture.
7. Fill a pastry bag fitted with a wide decorative tip (6B) and pipe the cream into both ends of the caramel curls. Serve as soon as possible.

NOTE: These curls become soggy if refrigerated. Once they are made, store them in a dry place. The apricot cream may be made ahead of time and refrigerated.

Did you know? These cookies may be served plain or slightly bent over a rolling pin. Two flat cookies may be sandwiched with a few drops of melted chocolate.

CARAMELIZED BRAZIL NUT STRUDEL

Serves 10 to 12

This sinful giant nut roll with its flaky crust has a wonderfully intense, spicy combination of flavors—apricots, apples, rum, cinnamon, lemon, and more—that are beautifully balanced by softly whipped unsweetened cream. What a heavenly combination!

½ cup golden raisins
½ cup chopped apricots
⅓ cup dark rum
6 tablespoons unsalted butter
1 large Granny Smith or other tart apple, peeled, cored, and finely chopped
¾ cup firmly packed dark brown sugar
2 tablespoons lemon juice
Grated zest of 1 lemon
1 ½ teaspoons cinnamon
½ teaspoon ground cloves
½ teaspoon salt
1 pound shelled Brazil nuts, coarsely chopped
8 phyllo leaves
6 tablespoons toasted bread crumbs
Confectioners' sugar for dusting
3 whole shelled Brazil nuts, for garnish
1 cup heavy cream, lightly whipped

1. Combine the raisins and apricots with the rum and set aside.
2. Melt 2 tablespoons of the butter in a large, heavy skillet over medium heat. Stir in the apple and cook for about 5 minutes until softened, stirring occasionally. Add the brown sugar, lemon juice, lemon zest, raisin-apricot mixture (including the rum), cinnamon, cloves, and salt, and mix well. Turn up the heat and boil gently until the mixture is thickened and slightly reduced, about 5 to 6 minutes. Stir in the Brazil nuts. Set aside.
3. Preheat your oven to 400°F. Lightly butter a cookie sheet or jelly-roll pan at least 14 inches in length.
4. On a clean work surface, spread a large towel horizontally. Melt the remaining 4 tablespoons of butter. Lay one leaf of phyllo with one long edge close to you on the towel and brush about a 1-inch strip of the upper edge lightly with butter. Place the lower edge of a second leaf of phyllo along the buttered upper edge of the first sheet, overlapping about ¾ inch. Brush both sheets lightly with butter and sprinkle about 2 tablespoons of bread crumbs evenly over this. Lay the third sheet of phyllo over the first and repeat the above procedure. Do the same with the fifth and sixth leaves of phyllo. Lay the seventh and eighth leaves on top of the phyllo layers, but do *not* brush with butter.
5. Spoon the nut mixture to the lower edge of the phyllo, forming it into an even cylinder, and leaving a 1 ½-inch border on each side. Holding the towel by the lower edge, flip it, causing the phyllo to roll over on itself. Turn in the sides and continue to roll. When the strudel is about two-thirds rolled, brush across the top and sides with butter; then finish rolling.

6. Carefully transfer the strudel to a cookie sheet, seam-side down, by lining up the edge of the towel with the cookie sheet and rolling the strudel onto it. Brush the top and ends with butter and bake in the middle of the oven for 15 minutes, or until crisp and golden colored.
7. Remove from the oven and let it stand at least 10 minutes before serving. Dust with confectioners' sugar. Garnish with the 3 remaining Brazil nuts, and cut with a serrated knife into 1-inch slices. Serve with unsweetened whipped cream.

NOTE: Once the strudel is prepared, it may be covered with buttered aluminum foil and refrigerated for up to a couple of days. Put it directly into a preheated oven and add a couple extra minutes to brown. If the foil sticks to the pastry, do not try to remove it. It will come off easily after a few minutes in the oven. This strudel can stay in a turned-off oven for several hours after baking.

Did you know? When buying frozen phyllo, open the cardboard box and look inside. The roll of phyllo should be tightly sealed in plastic. If it isn't, or the sheets look dry and broken, check another box. Slowly defrost it according to the package directions. Quickly defrosted phyllo develops moisture and the sheets then stick together.

If fresh phyllo is available, that is preferable. Phyllo keeps for months in a refrigerator without spoiling when tightly wrapped, but refreezing causes it to become brittle. When working with phyllo, keep the unused portion covered with a towel. Air is the enemy of phyllo because it dries out quickly. However, don't panic if you have to patch; it will not show in most preparations.

TUSCAN PINEAPPLE UPSIDE-DOWN CAKE

Serves 8

Mita Antolini is a farmer who lives in the hills of Tuscany in the tiny hamlet of Cortona. One afternoon she made this special treat for me in her old wood-burning stove. To my surprise, it turned out to be the best pineapple upside-down cake I'd ever tasted. The texture of the cake was unique—kind of firm but light at the same time. I tried to re-create the effect of Italian durum wheat flour by adding a little whole-wheat flour to this batter.

- 3/4 cup sugar + 7 tablespoons sugar, strained to remove lumps
- 3 eggs, separated
- Grated zest of 1 lemon
- 1 20-ounce can sliced pineapple packed in its own juice, drained, juice reserved
- 2 tablespoons brandy
- 1 teaspoon vanilla extract
- 1 1/4 cups bleached all-purpose flour
- 1/2 cup whole-wheat flour
- 1 1/2 teaspoons baking soda
- 8 tablespoons (1 stick) unsalted butter, melted
- 1 cup chopped walnuts and almonds

1. Preheat your oven to 375°F.
2. In a large bowl, stir 3/4 cup of the sugar, the egg yolks, lemon zest, 1/4 cup reserved pineapple juice, brandy, and vanilla until well blended. Sift in the white and whole-wheat flours and the baking soda, and mix until smooth. Stir in the melted butter.
3. Put the 7 tablespoons of sugar in a heavy, oven-safe 10-inch skillet (see note). Heat over medium-high heat until the sugar melts and lightly caramelizes. Immediately remove the pan from the heat and rotate it to cool it slightly. (Sugar will continue to cook once off the heat, so be careful not to overbrown it while cooking. Any remaining sugar crystals will melt while you are rotating the pan.)
4. Lay enough pineapple slices to cover the bottom of the skillet, about 7 or 8. Sprinkle the chopped nuts over the pineapple. Beat the egg whites into soft peaks and fold them into the batter. Pour the batter over the pineapple and spread with a spatula.
5. Bake in the top third of the oven until the cake is lightly browned on top and the center springs back when gently pressed, about 20 to 25 minutes. Remove from the oven, run a knife around the inside edge of the skillet, and invert onto a plate. Cool on a cake rack and serve.

NOTE: A seasoned cast-iron or other heavy skillet would be ideal to bake this cake. If your skillet is not oven-safe, caramelize the sugar first in a skillet, then pour it into a 10-inch cake pan.

Did you know? If you over-beat egg whites and they become dry and lusterless, add an extra unbeaten white and stir gently just to distribute it evenly. The texture should then be correct. If the volume of your cake, mousse, etc., will be affected by the extra white, remove approximately the amount of a beaten egg white (1/4 cup) before continuing.

MEXICAN CHOCOLATE CAKE

Serves 8 to 12

This cake is a celebration of south-of-the-border flavors: dark rich chocolate, almonds, espresso, black pepper, and cinnamon. There is very little flour so it is dense, like a torte. A little goes a long way, even for chocoholics. The cinnamon-laced whipped cream spooned on top provides a nice complement to the flavors. Olé!

FOR THE CAKE:

8 ounces bittersweet chocolate

12 tablespoons (1 1/2 sticks) unsalted butter, at room temperature

1/4 teaspoon salt

1 teaspoon finely ground black pepper

1 tablespoon powdered instant espresso (not granular)

2 teaspoons cinnamon

1 teaspoon vanilla extract

3/4 cup firmly packed dark brown sugar

3 eggs

3/4 cup unbleached all-purpose flour

1 cup finely ground toasted almonds

FOR THE GLAZE:

6 ounces bittersweet chocolate

1 egg

1 egg yolk

3 tablespoons unsalted butter, at room temperature

1 teaspoon light corn syrup

FOR THE FINAL DECORATION:

12 whole blanched almonds

1/2 cup heavy cream

1/4 teaspoon cinnamon

1/4 teaspoon sugar

1. Preheat your oven to 375°F. Butter a 9-by-1 1/2-inch straight-sided cake pan with a removable bottom, or springform pan.
2. Prepare the cake: Melt the chocolate in the top of a double boiler or over very low heat. Set aside to cool.
3. Cream the butter until light and fluffy. Add the salt, pepper, espresso, cinnamon, vanilla, and brown sugar, and beat until well blended. Add the eggs, one at a time, beating after each addition.
4. Stir in the chocolate, then add the flour, mixing only until it is blended. Fold in the ground almonds. Scrape the batter into the cake pan. Bake in the bottom third of the oven until a toothpick inserted in the center comes out with a little moist batter on it and the cake is set, about 25 to 30 minutes.
5. Remove from the oven, slide off the sides of the pan and cool cake on a wire rack for at least 30 minutes. With a sharp, thin-bladed knife, separate the bottom of the pan from the cake. Once cooled, brush the cake gently with a pastry brush to remove any crumbs.
6. Prepare the glaze: Melt the chocolate in the top of a double boiler or over very low heat. Stir in the egg and egg yolk, mixing well. Stir in the butter and corn syrup, remove the top of the pan from heat, and let the glaze thicken for 5 to 10 minutes, then pour it over the cooled cake. Smooth over the top of the cake, allowing some of the glaze to run down the sides. Smooth the sides with a metal spatula, then swirl the top into a design. Place the whole blanched almonds evenly around the outside of the top.
7. Transfer to a serving dish and let the glaze harden for a couple of hours. Serve with softly whipped cream flavored with cinnamon and sugar.

Did you know? Some dramatic presentations are actually the simplest. In this Mexican Chocolate Cake, blanched almonds are a stark contrast against the shiny dark glaze.

RASPBERRY CHOCOLATE TART

Serves 8

This is the wonderful tart I described with the Walnut Pastry Crust. It's so special that my daughter Nicole thinks of it as her birthday "cake." The marriage of buttery walnut pastry with rich chocolate crowned with firm, juicy raspberries is magical. Add some chocolate leaves and caramelized walnuts, and this dessert will win applause. (Note that I combine bittersweet and milk chocolate because the added sweetness of milk chocolate seems to be a better combination with the berries. If you prefer, use all dark chocolate.)

FOR THE TART:

1 recipe Walnut Pastry Crust (page 230), baked and cooled

3 ounces imported bittersweet chocolate

3 ounces imported milk chocolate

2 1/2 tablespoons unsalted butter

1 1/2 pints raspberries or 1 1/2 quarts uniform-size strawberries, split

FOR THE GLAZE:

4 ounces red currant jelly

2 tablespoons sugar

FOR THE CHOCOLATE LEAVES

2–3 ounces imported bittersweet chocolate

16–24 waxy, nonpoisonous leaves, such as camellia, orange, etc.

FOR THE CARAMEL WALNUTS:

1/2 cup vegetable oil

8 walnut halves

1/2 cup sugar

1/4 cup water

Softly whipped sweetened heavy cream (optional)

1. Assemble the tart: Melt the chocolate in the top of a double boiler. Remove the insert from the heat and stir in the butter. Spread the chocolate over the inside of the baked and cooled tart shell. Add the raspberries on the chocolate before it is set.
2. Prepare the glaze: Combine the currant jelly and sugar in a small saucepan and bring it to a boil over high heat for about 3 minutes, or until the sugar dissolves and the glaze coats a spoon. Brush the outside and top edge of the tart shell. Glaze the raspberries, if desired. Refrigerate extra glaze for another time.
3. Make the chocolate leaves: Melt the chocolate in the top of a double boiler. Wash and dry the leaves. Brush the underside with chocolate and refrigerate on a flat dish until firm. Carefully peel off the leaf, holding the stem end (see illustration). Return the chocolate leaves to the refrigerator or freezer until needed.

4. For the caramel walnuts: Heat the oil in a small saucepan until hot. Drop the walnuts into the oil for 30 to 45 seconds, or until lightly colored. Remove with a slotted spoon, and drain on paper towels.
5. In a small saucepan, bring the sugar and water to a boil. Once the sugar is dissolved, add the walnuts and turn the heat down to maintain a slow boil. Cook for 10 to 12 minutes, until the nuts are shiny and coated, then remove with a slotted spoon to a lightly buttered piece of waxed paper to cool.

6. For the decoration: Either lay 8 walnut halves evenly spaced around the outside edge of tart with 2 leaves on either side of each walnut *or* put 8 leaves evenly around the outside edge of the tart with the stem edge pointing toward the center. Put 8 more leaves slightly overlapping the first leaves, working toward the center. Add the last 8 leaves in the same way, again overlapping slightly. You should have eight even sections of the tart. Add 4 walnuts equally spaced around the outside, and put the remaining 4 walnuts in the middle on the rows of leaves that do not already have a walnut (see illustrations). If desired, serve with softly whipped heavy cream.

QUEEN VICTORIA'S CHRISTMAS TRIFLE

Serves 10 to 12

This fanciful, old-fashioned dessert can be made almost entirely with staples from the pantry and in a very short time. In Victorian England, trifles were often served in elaborate pedestal dishes as the flamboyant finale to a holiday meal. They are just as appropriate today in simple or elegant glass bowls, especially since this version may be made ahead of time for a dozen Yuletide or other revelers.

- 2 cups Crème Brûlée custard sauce (see page 82)
- 1 small sponge cake or 1 package ladyfingers
- 1/2 cup sweet sherry
- 1/4 cup brandy
- Grated zest of 1 lemon
- 2 ounces slivered almonds, toasted until light brown
- 1 cup raspberry or strawberry preserves
- 2 small bananas, sliced
- 1 1/2 cups fresh or canned bite-size pieces of pineapple in its own juice
- 12 1 1/4-inch macaroons or amaretti cookies, crumbled
- 1 pint heavy cream, whipped until stiff, sweetened with sugar

1. Pour the custard into a deep compote or trifle dish. Slice the sponge cake into 3-by-1-by-1-inch pieces, arrange over the custard and against the sides of the dish, and moisten with sherry and brandy. Sprinkle on the lemon zest and almonds, spoon on the preserves, and add the bananas, pineapple, and crushed macaroons.
2. Using a pastry bag fitted with a star tip, pipe heavy cream in a decorative design over the top.
3. To serve, spoon the trifle from the bottom of the dish to combine all ingredients.

NOTE: Victorian trifles were often decorated with angelica or candied flowers and fruit. It's difficult to find these today. Chocolate bits, maraschino cherries, and more nuts would all make attractive garnishes.

Did you know? Ladyfingers and sponge cakes may be located with Packaged Baked Goods, in the Produce department near berries, or even with Frozen Foods. Use them with any fresh or frozen fruit, custards, or ice cream for a quick dessert idea. If your market has an Italian festival, you may also find savoiardi, a Piemontese biscuit that resembles ladyfingers but is thicker. It's used in tiramisù.

THE ULTIMATE DECADENT ORANGE-CHOCOLATE DACQUOISE

Serves 8 to 12

This is, perhaps, the most beautiful and delicious dacquoise I've ever tasted—and I've tasted many, since I am passionate about this meringue-and-buttercream dessert. It is well worth the effort and proves again what extraordinary foods are available from your supermarkets, since the ingredients are all right there. The chocolate-dipped orange segments will be the first visual seduction. But, taste the orange-chocolate buttercream: The balance of flavors between the bitter, sweet, and sour is out of this world and is heightened by an imperceptible amount of salt (1/2 teaspoon). Swiss buttercream, made with egg whites, is lighter than those made with whole eggs, so the flavors are even more intense. Finally, there is the crunchiness of the meringue layers. What a way to go!

Butter and flour for cookie sheets

FOR THE MERINGUE LAYERS:

6 extra-large egg whites (1 scant cup), at room temperature

Pinch cream of tartar

1/2 cup sugar

1 1/3 cups (6 ounces) ground almonds

FOR THE CHOCOLATE-DIPPED ORANGES:

1 navel orange

3 ounces imported bittersweet chocolate

1 teaspoon vegetable oil

FOR THE BUTTERCREAM:

6 extra-large egg whites (1 scant cup), at room temperature

1 1/2 cups superfine sugar

1 pound unsalted butter, cut into pieces, at room temperature

6 ounces imported bittersweet chocolate, plus chocolate left over from dipping the orange pieces

1 tablespoon orange extract

Grated zest of 1 orange, reserved from above

2 tablespoons Grand Marnier

1/2 teaspoon salt

1. Make the meringue layers: Preheat your oven to 250°F. Generously butter and flour 2 cookie sheets. Shake excess flour from the sheets. Trace 3, 8-inch circles on them.
2. In a large bowl, beat the egg whites and cream of tartar with a wire whisk into soft peaks. Gradually add 1/4 cup sugar and beat until stiff. Add the remaining 1/4 cup sugar to the ground almonds. Reserve 1/3 cup of the sugar-nut mixture for later. Fold the remaining sugar-nut mixture into the egg whites.
3. Fill a pastry bag fitted with a plain (number 3) tip with the egg white mixture and pipe circles onto the cookie sheets, working from the outside to the center. Smooth any missed spaces with a metal spatula. Pipe or spoon any extra egg white mixture in dollops around the circles.
4. Bake in the middle of the oven until firm to the touch and lightly colored, about 55 to 75 minutes. Rotate cookie sheets for even cooking. After 55 minutes, press lightly with a fingertip. If they are not firm, return to the oven and check again in 5-minute increments. Meringues can take 80 minutes to cook.
5. Run a long, thin-bladed knife or spatula carefully under the meringues to loosen. Carefully transfer them to wire cake racks to harden. Meringues may be made the night before and left out uncovered in a cool, dry spot.
6. For the orange segments: Remove the zest, mince it, fold it in waxed paper or cover in a custard cup, and reserve for later use. Peel the orange and remove as much pith as possible. Carefully separate into segments without breaking the membranes.
7. Melt the chocolate in the top of a double boiler and stir in the vegetable oil. Cool slightly, then dip each segment halfway into the chocolate. Let extra chocolate

drip off each segment and back into the pan, then place the segments on waxed paper to harden. (The design will be more attractive if all segments are dipped and placed in the same direction.) Use 8 of the nicest segments for the garnish. Once the chocolate hardens, lightly cover the segments with plastic wrap and refrigerate until needed.

8. Prepare the buttercream: Put the egg whites in a large metal mixing bowl and set it *over* (not touching) a pot of boiling water. Using a wire whisk, gradually add the sugar and beat until the mixture is slightly thickened and measures 105°F on an instant-read or candy thermometer.

9. Immediately remove the bowl from the water and begin beating with an electric mixer. Continue beating while slowly adding the butter. Beat until the mixture is room temperature and thickened, about the consistency of stiff filling, about 10 to 15 minutes. The buttercream will look ugly and you'll think that it won't come together. Keep beating; it will!

10. Meanwhile, melt the chocolate in the same double boiler used for the garnish, including any leftover dipping chocolate. Add the orange extract, zest, Grand Marnier, and salt and stir to blend. (The chocolate may seize up slightly, but it will smooth out again when the buttercream is added.) Stir in ½ cup of the buttercream and beat until the chocolate is smooth. Scrape the chocolate mixture into the bowl of buttercream and mix well. Cover and refrigerate for 10 to 20 minutes.

11. Assemble the dacquoise: Reserve the nicest meringue for the top. On a cake plate or 8-inch cardboard circle and turntable, if you have one, put a dab of buttercream in the center to anchor the dacquoise and put the first meringue over it. Spread on a generous quarter of the buttercream with a long metal spatula, making it a little thicker toward the outside. Add the second meringue, press *slightly*, *and* spread another quarter of the buttercream. Add the final meringue layer and spread a generous fourth of the buttercream to cover the top and sides.

12. Crumble the extra dollops of meringue into a bowl and combine with the reserved sugar-nut mixture. Using a cupping motion with your palm, pat this around the sides of the dacquoise. Arrange the chocolate-dipped orange segments in the center of the top. Fill a pastry bag fitted with a star tip and pipe the remaining buttercream into rosettes around the top outside edge. Refrigerate, uncovered, until an hour before serving.

NOTE: Meringues are like sponges; they absorb moisture like mad. So choose to make this dessert on a cool, low-humidity day. Otherwise, there is no crunch. If the meringues start to sag, refresh them briefly in a warm oven and let them cool on a rack.

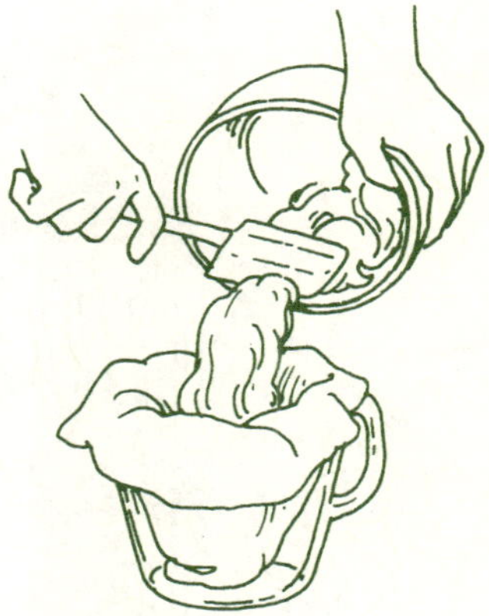

Did you know? Filling a pastry bag is easier if you twist the bottom of the bag and stuff some of the fabric down into the tip, sealing off the opening. Rest the pastry bag in a tall Pyrex measuring cup and open the top of the bag over it while filling the bag, so both hands remain free. When the bag is about two-thirds full, hold the top closed, position the pastry bag, and untwist the bottom.

A WELL-STOCKED CUPBOARD

The Staples aisles—canned vegetables, dried beans and rice, oils, vinegars, and prepared sauces—have expanded into entire ethnic sections. Years ago, for example, our choice was maybe two different brands: a can of medium tomatoes or tomato paste. Today we can choose from whole peeled or puréed tomatoes, those that are crushed or diced, Italian, Spanish or Mexican flavored, and several other varieties of the same product.

With products packed in cans, jars, aseptic boxes, and even tubes, how do you select from the proliferation of new products? How much should you buy? What is the best way to organize your cupboard? It requires thought and careful selection to utilize your space most effectively. Again, as in "Stocking a Baker's Pantry," less is usually best; let the market's shelves work for you.

Except in convenience stores, most large supermarkets have their aisles labeled overhead or at eye level, for example Aisle 4—canned vegetables and rices. Some stores have installed electronic aisle finders at the entrance where you can punch your needs into a terminal. These indicators are useful for quickly locating products. If you shop at the same store most of the time, chances are you don't even look at the signs. But you may actually be cheating yourself by skipping certain aisles. Sometime, when you are not in a hurry, slowly walk up and down the Staples section. Stop and examine the varied products there.

SHOP CAREFULLY FOR SHELF LIFE AND QUALITY

Packaging

There are many kinds of packaging available today. The same product is frequently in more than one of these. Tuna, for example, comes in cans and pouches. Be sure to compare prices after determining that the quality is equal.

Cans

The contents will last for months and even longer when kept cool. Once the can is opened, transfer the food to a clean glass or plastic container and refrigerate. A little dent is usually not harmful, but bulging or rounded bottoms indicate bacterial activity, which can be fatal if consumed by people or animals.

Jars

These should be vacuum-sealed. If the seal is broken, make another choice. Storage times vary with the ingredients, but try to keep them in a cool, dark place. Once opened, some prepared sauces like mustard and ketchup are shelf-stable for months. Others, like delicate oils, should be refrigerated. Whole spices, such as nutmegs and peppercorns, last indefinitely.

Tubes

Tubes are a good choice for mustard, tomato paste, or other ingredients where a small amount is used and the rest is stored. Be sure the bottom end is well crimped and there are no small cracks or punctures. Once the tube is opened, you can refrigerate it for a month or two.

Cardboard Boxes

Boxes need to be sealed when purchased and show no signs of any pests. Check that the bottom is tightly glued. Boxes need not be resealed, but they should be closed. If there is a plastic or paper liner inside, as with cereals and crackers, roll this down. The contents will last well in a cool, dry place.

Aseptic Boxes

Be sure these are not dented or broken. They keep tomato sauces, milk, and juices fresh for a month or longer in a cool place. Check the stamped freshness code for the expiration date or "best if used by" information. If the box can be sealed tightly once it has been opened, put it in the refrigerator for up to a week. Otherwise, transfer the contents to a clean glass or plastic container first.

Plastic and Cellophane Bags

Bags should be sealed at the time of purchase. Because they are clear, it is easy to determine the quality of what is inside. Once they are opened, twist and seal them with a tie. Dried beans and rice keep well in a cool, dry cupboard. For spices in bags, seal or tie the bag to protect the spice from the air and store in a cool, dark place. An airtight jar would work well also. Most people keep herbs and spices way too long.

Fabric Bags

These are fine for imported rice and grains as long as they do not get wet or develop holes or tears. Be sure to close them before storage. However, for long-term, pest-free storage, transfer them to a clean jar or resealable plastic bag.

Labels

Beyond the wide variety of shapes and sizes available for canned and bottled products, there are many attractive and inviting labels to capture your attention and your food dollars. Before making a selection, be sure to read what is written on the package.

Origins

Tomatoes, for example, are shipped from Italy, Spain, and the United States. More specifically, the tomatoes from the San Marzano region of Italy are preferred by many cooks, and some clever manufacturers print "San Marzano–type" on their labels. There is a difference.

Form

Look to see if the tomatoes are peeled and whole, crushed, puréed with basil, or made into a sauce. Some recipes ask that the tomatoes be drained first and then crushed. Crushed tomatoes affect the consistency of the dish.

Additives

"Hidden" sugars, especially in cereals and packaged mixes, are a real liability to health. Words that end in "ose" are all forms of sugar. They are often combined with honeys and corn sweeteners. Ingredients are listed in the order of greatest use in a food, i.e., the first ingredient listed is in the greatest quantity and the last the smallest.

Many canned and packed products contain salt. No- or low-salt products are now often found alongside their salted version rather than in a Health Food section.

BHT, BHA, and EDTA are all chemical preservatives that should be avoided.

Dietetic/Health Foods

Be sure to compare prices among products. Sometimes the same product merchandised as "dietetic" because it has no salt or is juice-packed will be substantially less expensive if sold with the regular canned goods rather than in the Diet Foods section. Fruit cocktail and tuna, for example, are often sold in both sections. Some dietetic products are a real boon, and others are filled with chemicals and taste like it. Until recently I eschewed all no-calorie sugar substitutes until I tasted Splenda, a new product made from sugar but combined with a lot of cellulose. It is being used in a lot of low-carb recipes. But Olestra, marketed as a fat substitute, has given several people I know acute gastrointestinal upsets. If you don't want to cook with butter, try olive oil. Margarine has a lot of hydrogenated fats and trans-fatty acids and is probably more unhealthy than butter.

INVENTORY CONTROL

How Much to Buy

Although many unopened cans and bottles last a long time, why clutter up your cupboard with extras that will be used only occasionally? Buy what you need, and let the supermarket warehouse what you can pick up easily. Unless you use a lot of a certain product quickly (or have a cellar), buying a case on sale will rob your precious storage space.

Buy smaller rather than larger sizes, unless you will use the remainders up quickly. A large can of garbanzo beans costs only 30 percent more than a smaller one. But, if the remainders go bad in the refrigerator, there is no savings. Delicate oils quickly turn rancid, and mustards and vinegars lose their bite.

Develop an inventory-control habit. Once a staple that you use often is opened and removed from your shelf, be certain to add it to your week's shopping list.

Whenever trying a product for the first time, buy only enough for one meal, no matter how tempting it looks. Better to buy more later than be stuck with something you won't use.

What to Keep on Hand

This is a personal choice and depends on your own style of cooking. Most supermarkets are well stocked with these provisions, and I try not to stockpile items that are easily purchased. I generally have the following items in case I need to improvise:

- two boxes of pasta—a longer one, such as spaghetti, and an extruded variety, such as elbows or penne
- long-grain and Arborio rices; couscous or bulgur
- at least two varieties of dried beans or legumes, such as split green peas or lentils, Great Northern white beans, garbanzo beans, or black beans
- oils: polyunsaturated vegetable oil, virgin and extra-virgin olive oil, and a nut (hazelnut/walnut) oil
- vinegars: red wine, balsamic, herb (tarragon), and rice vinegar
- wines: medium sherry, red wine, and dry white wine or dry vermouth
- condiments like Dijon mustard, ketchup, mayonnaise, Worcestershire, Tabasco, soy sauce, horseradish, and capers
- beef, chicken, vegetable, and clam broth
- whole and crushed Italian tomatoes, tomato paste, and sun-dried tomatoes
- cans of tuna in olive oil
- a jar of oil-cured olives
- seasonings and dried spices: kosher or sea salt, pouring salt, black peppercorns, basil, bay leaves, chili powder, cumin, curry powder, ginger, dry mustard, whole nutmeg, oregano, ground red pepper, rosemary, sage, and thyme.

Storage

To ensure that your purchases are accessible and easily found in your cupboard, a personal system is invaluable. I use the following method:

- Group foods the way the market does: all soups and stocks together, tomato products, rices and dried beans, spices, etc.
- Wipe products clean after each use before putting them away.
- Label open packages with the name and date.
- A turntable or lazy Susan is useful for herbs and spices, condiments, and oils and vinegars.
- I separate my oils and vinegars. It's especially useful when reaching for something to dress salads with.

CHAPTER EIGHT: **STAPLES:**

OILS, VINEGARS, BEANS, TOMATOES, PASTAS, RICES, AND GRAINS

INTRODUCTION

Don't be a modern-day Mother Hubbard! An empty cupboard is an invitation to culinary disaster, while a few well-chosen staples will always provide a backup when drop-in guests, a long day at the office, or bad weather send you foraging for "just about anything" to eat. Many basic necessities of our food life, such as soups, pastas, and vinaigrettes, start with the ingredients kept in our cupboards. Sometimes those cans work wonders.

Canned tomatoes are the perfect staple to keep on hand. In fact, except for the few months of the year when the fresh varieties are truly outstanding, I prefer the San Marzano-region Italian tomatoes or those from Muir Glen in California for all my sauces, soups, and stews. Combine tomatoes with onions, garlic, tomato paste, and herbs, and a Chunky Homemade Tomato Sauce (page 282) is ready in a short period of time. Grab another staple—pasta—and you are well on your way to satisfying large appetites. Since the sauce freezes beautifully, it may be used as the basis for other sauces, such as in Squid Caponata (page 165) where it becomes marinara style.

As you peruse the aisle with sauces, vinegars, and condiments, notice how contemporary cooking has influenced our choices in the supermarket. Rich green and gold extra-virgin olive oils and delicate nut oils, once found only in specialty food boutiques, fill the shelves. Raspberry, balsamic, and rice vinegars are likewise easy to find. Wasabi and mole paste, too, are also available to add their special touch to dishes.

As Americans have fallen in love with ethnic cuisines, they want to buy authentic provisions in the same place they find most of their food—the supermarket. Originally these new foods were merchandised in Gourmet Foods sections (where they were difficult to locate). They are now sensibly placed alongside similar products.

Our awareness of ethnic cuisines has increased our consumption of legumes, rice, and grains, as well as a host of salsas and condiments. In many cultures, meat is used sparingly, like a condiment or flavoring for a pasta sauce that is mixed with the higher-carbohydrate pasta. Today we also find alternative pastas that are lower in carbohydrates or those that are wheat free.

Look for couscous, both plain and flavored, in small and larger sizes—it's terrific in Couscous Salad with Radishes and Pine Nuts (page 290). Use bulgur (cracked wheat) to make Hearty Bulgur Pilaf (page 293) with sausages, chestnuts, raisins, and pine nuts. Chicken, Pecan, Avocado, and Wild Pecan Rice Salad (page 291) is tossed with a chickpea, sesame, and soy vinaigrette that is full of flavor and texture. There are so many exciting staples to experiment with; all are worth investigating.

Mrs. Dash and many other salt-free seasonings found near herbs and spices add flavor but eliminate sodium or calories. Mix them with curry powder and mayonnaise as a coating for broiled fish. Salsa, mustards, and chutneys may be combined into your own flavorful original creations.

Supermarkets are trying to meet the demand for a wider selection of convenience foods to make your job easier. Look at the proliferation of prepared canned, bottled, and packaged foods available. When you are considering buying any item to feed yourself, your family, or friends, really read the label on that product. If the bottled Alfredo sauce has starch, sugar, and preservatives, it won't taste like your own and the chemicals won't nourish your body.

I am not against convenience. When I don't have the time to make stock or mayonnaise, I buy them. I have doctored up a bottled spaghetti sauce. We all make compromises at certain times. Just select carefully. There are countless excellent choices available in these aisles.

MUSTARD VINAIGRETTE

Makes 1 cup

This is our "house dressing." It can be changed to suit a salad ingredient or to reflect your preference in vinegars and oils. We use it for the Green Bean and New Potato Salad from Vernon (see page 29), and on tossed greens. Red wine or sherry vinegars can replace the lemon juice. Delicious walnut or hazelnut oils are elegant additions to salads with cheese or bitter greens. The herbs, too, may be changed.

Along with the new "designer label" jars of vinegars and oils, mustards have spread out on the shelves, too. Since I use a lot of Dijon mustard in my cooking, I buy it in ample quantities, reading labels carefully to find a product made in France (where there is governmental control of ingredients) without any flours or sugars. Often, a large, simple jar contains a perfectly respectable mustard for about half the cost of the smaller, fancier bottle. Although mustard won't spoil, per se, it loses its bite. If you use it slowly, buy smaller jars. Refrigerate mustard after opening.

2 tablespoons Dijon mustard

1–2 cloves garlic, minced very fine or crushed

4 tablespoons lemon juice

3/4 cup olive or vegetable oil, or a combination of both

2 tablespoons chopped flat-leaf parsley, or fresh dill

Salt and freshly ground black pepper to taste

1. Stir the Dijon mustard, garlic, and lemon juice in a small bowl to blend well. Slowly whisk in the oil in a steady stream to form an emulsion. Stir in the parsley, salt, and pepper, and taste to adjust the seasonings.

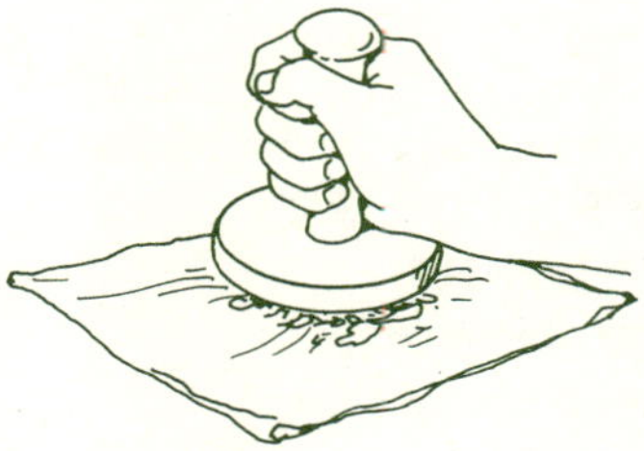

Did you know? An easy way to crush garlic is to fold the peeled and split clove(s) in a piece of waxed paper and pound it into a pulp with a meat pounder or flat-bottomed glass. Scrape the garlic into the bowl and throw away the paper.

ROQUEFORT VINAIGRETTE

Makes about 3/4 cup

1/2 tablespoon Dijon mustard
2 tablespoons red wine vinegar
1/2 cup olive oil
1 tablespoon chopped fresh dill
2 ounces Roquefort cheese, crumbled
Salt and freshly ground black pepper to taste

This is another easy salad dressing that goes especially well with stronger-flavored greens like chicory and arugula. I like it combined with Boston lettuce, endive, arugula or watercress, thinly sliced scallions, walnut pieces, and thinly sliced oranges.

1. In a small bowl, combine the mustard and vinegar. Slowly whisk in the oil in a steady stream to form an emulsion. Add the dill and crumbled cheese. Stir in salt and black pepper and taste to adjust the seasonings.

Did you know? The word *vinegar* comes from the French *vin aigre* or soured wine. Most vinegars have between 5 and 7 percent acidity. They will last for a very long time if sealed. However, once opened, vinegars react with air and lose their bite after about six months. To reduce the acidity of vinegars in a vinaigrette, add a tablespoon of water, milk, or even stock.

PURÉED CHICKPEA VINAIGRETTE

Makes 2 cups

1 1/2 cups cooked or canned chickpeas (garbanzos), drained
1 large clove garlic
1/3 cup rice vinegar
2 tablespoons soy sauce
1/4 cup sesame oil
1/4 cup vegetable oil

This is a wonderfully thick and spicy sauce to spoon on everything from the Chicken, Pecan, Avocado, and Wild Pecan Rice Salad (page 291) to steamed asparagus or sautéed veal cutlets. The combination of Asian flavors—rice vinegar, soy sauce, and sesame oil—with the puréed chickpeas is very satisfying.

For purists, freshly cooked chickpeas (garbanzos) can't be beat. But for people in a hurry, the drained canned variety works wonderfully well here. Both dried and canned legumes stored in a cool pantry will keep at least a year.

1. Combine the chickpeas, garlic, vinegar, and soy sauce in the bowl of a food processor and purée, scraping down the work bowl as needed. With the motor running, pour the sesame and vegetable oils through the feed tube in a slow, steady stream. The vinaigrette will be creamy and thick. Scrape into a screw-top glass jar and refrigerate until needed.

Did you know? Oils keep best in cool, dark cupboards. More fragile oils, such as walnut, hazelnut, and sesame, go rancid very easily. Store them in the refrigerator and only buy small quantities. Always smell or taste an oil before using it. What a shame to ruin a dish by adding bad oil.

SPICY OLD BAY TOMATO DRESSING

Makes 1 cup

This tangy dressing is reminiscent of the creamy Louis sauces often used with crab or shrimp salads. Sometimes the spice section of the market is stocked with tins or jars that have combined ingredients to produce a unique-tasting product. Old Bay seasoning is one, most often used in seafood preparations. Try this dressing with a combination of shrimp, blanched snow peas, cubed jicama, and diced red pepper. Use it for the Papaya, Avocado, and Chicken Salad (page 73) as well. With any prepared package or bottle, be sure to read the list of ingredients and add salt at the end if needed.

1 tablespoon capers, drained
1 large clove garlic, peeled and split
3 tablespoons tomato paste
1 egg, at room temperature (see note if not using a food processor)
1 tablespoon tarragon vinegar
1½ teaspoons Old Bay seasoning
½ teaspoon dried tarragon, crumbled
¼ teaspoon dry mustard
½ cup vegetable oil
8–10 drops Tabasco sauce
Freshly ground black pepper to taste
3 tablespoons finely chopped shallots

1. Combine the capers, garlic, tomato paste, egg, and vinegar in the bowl of a food processor or electric blender and process until smooth. Add the Old Bay seasoning, tarragon, and mustard and pulse to blend. With the machine running, pour the oil through the feed tube in a slow, steady stream to form an emulsion. Add Tabasco sauce and pepper to taste. Add the shallots and pulse just to blend. Transfer to a glass screw-top jar and refrigerate for at least 3 hours.

NOTE: If making this salad dressing by hand, use only the yolk of the egg. Mince the capers, garlic, and shallots as finely as possible and whisk the ingredients together in a bowl. Add the oil slowly, as with the processor version.

Did you know? Capers are sold in small jars near the olives and pickled onions. There is a big difference in price between those marked "fancy" (which are usually very small) and others, which can be at least twice the size. In a recipe where the capers will be puréed or chopped, as in this dressing, buy the less-expensive variety. In a salad or other dish where the capers remain whole, I prefer the smaller size. The taste is the same. By the way, the capers we buy are the pickled unopened flower buds of the caperbush. They are not nasturtium seeds, as some people believe.

SWEET AND TANGY ASIAN VINAIGRETTE

Makes 2 cups

1/3 cup hoisin sauce
1/2 cup rice vinegar
2 tablespoons finely chopped gingerroot
2 tablespoons soy sauce
2 1/2 tablespoons honey
12-24 drops hot pepper oil
1/2 cup sesame oil
1/3 cup vegetable oil

In our house, we are always looking for new dressings for salads. I first used this gingery sweet and spicy vinaigrette on Asian Broccoli Salad (page 19). But, it is also good on simple mixed greens, pasta salad, or a composed salad with turkey, orange slices, almonds, and scallions.

I use a combination of oils because sesame oil alone is too assertive and the pepper oil adds a good bite. The hoisin sauce (from the Asian section) thickens the dressing and adds a nice sweetness.

Keep clean, empty olive oil and sauce bottles to store your own preservative-free dressings—in the refrigerator, of course. Soy sauce, because it is fermented, need not be refrigerated. If kept closed, it will last a long time. Any crystals may be removed and the remaining soy is fine.

1. Blend the hoisin sauce, vinegar, ginger, soy sauce, and honey together in a small bowl. Whisk in the hot pepper, sesame, and salad oils in a slow, steady stream. Cover and refrigerate.

NOTE: This recipe is better made ahead to allow the flavors to develop. It keeps well tightly covered in the refrigerator for a couple of weeks.

Did you know? Soy sauce is another product that may be confusing. First, there are several kinds: Chinese and Japanese are the most popular. Japanese is the more commonly available in supermarkets, and most brands are of a good quality. It is lighter and less salty tasting than Chinese soy. "Lite" soy means that the salt is reduced. With Chinese soy, it is essential to read the label, looking for a product that is really made from soybeans, not just coloring and flavorings (as one of the leading brands is). Chinese soys range from thin/light (more delicate in flavor and saltiness) to dark/heavy. Double-dark and flavored soys are infrequently sold in supermarkets. Tamari is good-quality soy sauce without preservatives.

MUSTARD CUSTARD

Makes 1 ½ cups

This piquant dipping sauce for raw vegetables or Jarlsberg fingers is one of Barbara Soyster's gifts for making and giving. It is also wonderful spread on sandwiches. I use it as a base for my Gingery Peanut Dipping Sauce (see following recipe) to serve with Mini Shrimp Spring Rolls (page 166).

English-style dry mustard is made from yellow mustard seeds that are ground into a fine powder. It is intensely spicy. A tin will keep its bite for at least 6 to 9 months if stored in a cool spot away from sunlight.

½ cup (2 1½-ounce tins) loosely packed English-style dry mustard

½ cup white wine vinegar

¼ cup dry vermouth

¾ cup sugar

2 eggs, well beaten

1. In a small bowl, mix together the mustard, vinegar, and vermouth. Cover and let stand overnight.
2. The next day, add the sugar and beaten eggs and mix well.
3. Transfer the mixture to the top of a double boiler and cook over boiling water, stirring constantly with a spoon or whisk, until thickened, about 3 to 5 minutes. Remove the insert from the heat and continue stirring until the mixture stops steaming. This sauce is best if refrigerated overnight before serving at room temperature. It keeps for months in the refrigerator. For a hotter sauce, increase the dry mustard to ¾ cup.

GINGERY PEANUT DIPPING SAUCE

Makes ¾ cup

This is a piquant condiment that can be served with Mini Shrimp Spring Rolls (see page 166) or crudités. I also spread it on melted Jarlsberg or Muenster cheese sandwiches.

¼ cup Mustard Custard (see previous recipe)

2 tablespoons dry sherry

5 drops (or more) hot pepper oil

1 tablespoon minced fresh gingerroot

2 teaspoons rice vinegar

1 teaspoon soy sauce

¼ cup chunky peanut butter

1. Combine all the ingredients in a small saucepan and heat gently over low heat, stirring constantly until the mixture thickens, about 2 to 3 minutes. Cool to lukewarm and serve with Mini Shrimp Spring Rolls (page 166). Or serve with roasted pork or sliced cold meats.

BASIC WHOLE-EGG MAYONNAISE AND VARIATIONS

Makes about 1 1/4 cups

- 1 egg, at room temperature
- Pinch of salt
- 1 tablespoon lemon juice or white vinegar
- 1 teaspoon Dijon mustard or 1/2 teaspoon dry mustard
- 2/3 cup vegetable oil
- 1/3 cup olive oil

Homemade mayonnaise is a great pleasure. The taste may be delicate (if it is made with a flavorless oil) or gutsy (when a fruity olive oil is used). In any case, it is superior to most commercial varieties and will last more than a week in the refrigerator if stored in a screw-top glass jar.

Making mayonnaise is easy, especially in a food processor or blender. It is one of those versatile staples of cooking that changes color and flavor easily to suit the surroundings. Take a look at some of the variations listed at the end of this recipe, then try your own combinations. Also, note that if making this sauce by hand, you should use only the egg yolk and have all ingredients at room temperature.

1. Combine the egg, salt, lemon juice, mustard, and 1/4 cup oil in a food processor and process for 3 to 4 seconds to mix well. With the motor running, pour the remaining oil through the feed tube, pouring in a slow, thin stream. The mixture should thicken immediately. Taste to adjust the seasonings, then transfer to a clean glass screw-top jar and refrigerate. If the mayonnaise is too thick, thin it with a little warm water.

AS A VARIATION . . .

Russian Dressing, for salads and spreading on sandwiches: To a cup of mayonnaise, add 3 to 4 tablespoons of ketchup or chili sauce, 1 tablespoon minced onion, and 2 teaspoons minced fresh parsley.

Thousand Island Dressing, for salads and spreading on sandwiches: To 1 cup of mayonnaise, add 2 tablespoons of ketchup, 2 tablespoons minced celery, 2 tablespoons minced green pepper, 1 finely diced hard-cooked egg, and 1 tablespoon minced sweet pickle.

Red Pepper Mayonnaise, for grilled scallops and chicken breasts: To 1 1/2 cups mayonnaise made with lemon juice and vegetable oil, add 2 large red bell peppers that have been roasted, peeled, seeded, patted dry, and puréed (*or* 2 jarred peppers packed in water and also puréed), 3 to 4 drops Tabasco sauce, and 1 1/2 to 2 tablespoons extra lemon juice to taste.

Green Mayonnaise, for cold poached fish: To 1 cup of mayonnaise made with mostly olive oil, fold in 1 1/2 tablespoons minced fresh parsley, 2 teaspoons fresh snipped chives, 2 teaspoons minced fresh tarragon (*or* 1/2 teaspoon dried and crumbled), and 1 to 1 1/2 teaspoons extra lemon juice or white vinegar to taste.

Did you know? Commercially prepared mayonnaise tastes fresher with a little wine vinegar or lemon juice added. Herbs are another welcome addition. If using dried herbs, crumble them to release the oil, then let the mayonnaise stand a while before using. Once a jar of mayonnaise is opened, it will keep in the refrigerator for at least 2 to 3 months.

Curried Mayonnaise, for broiled fish steaks and dipping raw vegetables: To 1/2 cup mayonnaise, add 2 teaspoons Mrs. Dash or other citrus-herb blend without salt, 1 teaspoon curry powder (hot or mild), and 1/4 teaspoon dry mustard. Spread on fish and sprinkle with toasted bread crumbs. Broil at least 6 inches from the heat for 5 minutes (if steaks are 1 inch thick), carefully turn, spread mayonnaise and crumbs on second side, and cook another 5 minutes.

Caper Mayonnaise, for Veal and Sausage Meatballs (see page 136): To 1 1/2 cups of mayonnaise made with olive oil, add 2 tablespoons of crushed capers, 1 to 2 tablespoons anchovy paste, and freshly ground black pepper.

TAPENADE

Makes 3 cups

One often finds this kind of olive dip in the south of France, where it is usually served with a large, tempting basket of raw vegetables. Although the horseradish is not part of the classic version, I like the tang it imparts. Beware, tapenade is addicting on a lazy summer afternoon. The warm colors and wonderful fragrances of Provence seem to come back to me with each bite. Often tapenade sold in supermarkets tastes like it has a lot of extraneous additives. Make your own; it's so easy.

You can find oil-cured olives in 6 1/2-ounce jars in the Staples section or in the Deli department. Look either next to canned olives or where other Italian and Greek specialties are located.

- 1 6 1/2-ounce jar black oil-cured olives, pitted +8 whole olives, for garnish
- 1 2-ounce can anchovies, drained, rinsed in warm water, and patted dry
- 1 tablespoon Dijon mustard
- 3 eggs, at room temperature
- 3 tablespoons lemon juice
- 1 1/2 tablespoons prepared white horseradish
- 1 1/2 cups olive oil

1. Combine the pitted olives, anchovies, mustard, eggs, lemon juice, and horseradish in the bowl of a food processor and process until smooth. With the machine running, pour a few drops of the oil through the feed tube. The first few drops should begin to emulsify before the remaining oil is added. Pour in the remaining oil in a very slow, steady stream. The mixture will resemble a mayonnaise. For a thicker consistency, refrigerate for 2 to 3 hours before serving.
2. Scrape into a serving bowl, garnish with the whole olives, and serve with a basket of fresh vegetables, such as fennel, endive leaves, carrots, and red peppers, and/or thin slices of French bread brushed with olive oil, dusted with crumbled dried basil, and toasted until lightly colored. Tapenade will last for a couple of weeks when refrigerated.

Did you know? When adding prepared horseradish to a dish, be sure to cut back on salt. During processing, vinegar and salt are usually added. Once a jar of either red or white horseradish is opened, it will lose its bite within 4 to 6 weeks.

As a delicious sauce for smoked salmon, drain and chop 1 1/2 tablespoons of capers and mix with 1 tablespoon of prepared horseradish. Fold them into 1 cup of lightly whipped cream.

HEARTY EIGHT-BEAN SOUP

Serves a crowd

My friend Barbara Soyster volunteered this recipe as a unique gift-giving idea: Purchase a variety of eight dried beans and barley, usually packaged in 1-pound bags. Set out 9 bowls, pots, or kitchen containers and empty each bag into one bowl. Reach in and take a generous handful (about 1/2 cup) of each and put it into a plastic food storage bag with a twister. Continue making packages of mixed beans until all beans are used. Tie the Hearty Eight-Bean Soup recipe to the top closure with a ribbon, and you have a gift from the hearth! By all means, substitute other favorites, such as black beans, cannellini beans, green split peas, etc. Serve this soup with a tossed salad and hearty bread.

(All beans are dried)
1/2 cup Great Northern beans
1/2 cup pinto beans
1/2 cup Michigan pea (navy) beans
1/2 cup lima beans
1/2 cup black-eyed peas
1/2 cup red kidney beans
1/2 cup chickpeas
1/2 cup lentils
1/2 cup barley
3 quarts water
1 ham hock (optional)
1–2 celery stalks, preferably with leaves attached
1 large carrot
Several sprigs of flat-leaf parsley
2 medium onions, peeled and coarsely chopped
2–3 bay leaves
1 large garlic clove, minced
1 teaspoon dried thyme leaves
1 28-ounce can crushed Italian tomatoes
1 tablespoon fresh lemon juice
1 tablespoon balsamic vinegar
1 teaspoon chili powder
Coarse or kosher salt and freshly ground black pepper to taste

1. The night before, sort through the beans and remove any unwanted material. Rinse well. Put the beans in a large bowl, add enough water to cover by 3 inches, and soak overnight or for 8 hours.
2. In the morning, drain the beans well. Put them in a large stockpot or soup pot. Add 3 quarts of water and the ham hock, if using, and bring to a boil. Reduce the heat and slowly simmer for 2 hours, occasionally skimming off any surface foam.
3. Tie the celery, carrot, and parsley together with kitchen string and add to the soup pot. Stir in the onions, bay leaves, garlic, thyme, tomatoes, lemon juice, vinegar, chili powder, salt, and pepper, and simmer for at least another half hour, adding more water if necessary.
4. At the end of the cooking time, remove the vegetable bundle, ham hock, and bay leaves. (Pieces of ham may be returned to the soup, if desired.)

Did you know? Most soups and stews may be served immediately after cooking or refrigerated or frozen for future use. However, they improve in taste if refrigerated for a day or two before serving so flavors have a chance to blend. It's economical to make big batches of stews and soups and freeze them in serving-size portions.

PUMPKIN BLACK BEAN SOUP

Serves 8

Many people love a hearty black bean soup, including me. Served with thick slices of bread, it is the perfect winter's lunch or supper. In this version, the puréed pumpkin adds a slight sweetness that nicely balances the tangy sherry vinegar and produces a rich, satisfying combination of flavors. I serve the soup with toasted pumpkin seeds in place of croutons. It is festive enough for any great meal. A tiny glass of sherry is a perfect partner to serve with the soup.

When buying dried beans, be sure to compare prices in different sections of the store: the dried legumes versus the ethnic foods. Sometimes there is a pretty big difference in price between brands, though the quality is about the same. If substituting canned beans, drain and rinse them well. You will need about 4 1-pound cans. Since the quality of canned beans varies widely—with some brands the beans are almost mashed because they are overcooked and overprocessed—you will have to do a little experimenting.

1 pound black beans, washed and picked over for foreign objects

3/4 cup canned Italian tomatoes, drained

1 cup canned pumpkin or puréed fresh

6 ounces boiled ham, diced in 1/8-inch cubes or meat from a leftover ham bone

2 1/2–3 cups beef stock

3 tablespoons unsalted butter

1 1/2 cups finely chopped onions

3 large cloves garlic, peeled and minced

1 tablespoon ground cumin

Salt and freshly ground black pepper to taste

3–4 tablespoons sherry or red wine vinegar

1/2–1 cup medium sherry

1 cup hulled pumpkin seeds, to garnish

1 tablespoon canola or vegetable oil

1/2 cup sour cream, to garnish (optional)

1. Put the beans in a heavy saucepan and pour in boiling water to cover by at least 2 inches. Bring the liquid to a boil, then turn down the heat and simmer, partially covered, for about 2 to 3 hours, or until the beans are tender. Add more water if the beans become dry.
2. Stir in the tomatoes and transfer the mixture in batches to a food processor. Pulse until the beans have started to smooth out but are still somewhat chunky. Return the beans and tomatoes to the saucepan and stir in the pumpkin, ham, and 2 1/2 cups of the stock.
3. Melt the butter in a heavy skillet over medium heat. Stir in the onions and sauté for 8 to 10 minutes, or until lightly colored. Add the garlic and cook 30 seconds more. Stir in the cumin, salt, and pepper, add to the bean mixture, and stir in the vinegar.
4. Bring to the boil, reduce the heat, and simmer for 15 to 20 minutes longer. Stir in the sherry and taste to adjust the seasonings. If the soup is too thick, add additional stock or sherry.
5. Toss the pumpkin seeds with the oil and toast for 7 to 9 minutes in a toaster oven or on a cookie sheet in a preheated 400°F oven or until well colored. Remove and sprinkle lightly with salt, if desired.
6. Ladle the pumpkin soup into bowls, sprinkle on a few pumpkin seeds, add a dollop of sour cream, if desired, and serve.

Did you know? "Cooking sherry," because of the addition of salt, can be sold in supermarkets that otherwise do not permit the sale of alcoholic beverages. I don't recommend it. Less expensive California or imported sherries are fine for this recipe, however.

SPLIT PEA SOUP WITH KIELBASA

Serves 8

A steaming bowl of split pea soup is a great favorite in our house—especially during the fall and winter months. The ham and kielbasa (Polish sausage, found in the Meat department) make this thick soup more substantial—and perfect for a casual Sunday supper. It's an easy supermarket soup to make because the ingredients are readily available and the preparation is uncomplicated. Try doubling the recipe and freezing it in 2- or 4-cup containers. Serve with peasant bread cut into hearty slices.

1 pound dried split green peas
6 cups water
4 cups chicken stock
1/3 cup salt pork, diced in 1/4-inch cubes
1/2 cup chopped carrots
1/2 cup chopped celery
1/2 cup chopped onion
1 small bay leaf
2 ham hocks (see note)
1 1/2 teaspoons ground cardamom
Salt and freshly ground black pepper to taste
1 1/2 cups diced kielbasa

1. Rinse the split peas in a colander or strainer under cold water and discard any sediment.
2. Put them in a large, heavy saucepan or stockpot with the water and chicken stock. Cover and boil over high heat for 2 minutes. Turn off the heat, leave the lid on, and let the peas soak for at least an hour, or until very tender.
3. In a heavy skillet, sauté the salt pork over medium heat for 5 minutes, stirring occasionally, until it is opaque but not brown. Add the carrots, celery, and onion and cook until tender, 6 to 8 minutes.
4. Add the vegetables and bay leaf, ham hocks, cardamom, salt, and pepper to the pot with the peas and return to a boil. Adjust the heat to low and simmer until the meat begins to fall off the bones, 1 1/2 to 2 hours.
5. Remove the ham hocks and bay leaf from the soup and pull the meat off the bones. Discard the bones and bay leaf. Chop the ham into fine pieces and reserve until the soup is finished.
6. Transfer the soup to the bowl of a food processor and pulse until it is slightly chunky. Return it to the pot, add the ham and kielbasa, and simmer for at least 10 minutes to warm the meat. Taste to adjust the seasonings.

NOTE: If you cannot find ham hocks, a leftover ham bone with some meat on it, or even a smoked turkey leg may be substituted.

Stock or Broth? The terms are usually used interchangeably. If time does not permit making your own, you can enrich a canned broth by simmering it for about 10 to 15 minutes with some diced or sliced aromatic vegetables—an onion, a couple of carrots, and a stalk of celery—along with some parsley sprigs and a bay leaf. This is most acceptable when using it with hearty vegetables, meats, cream, and other strong-flavored ingredients.

SAUTÉED WHITE BEANS WITH PORK AND SAGE

Serves 8 to 10

There are only a few ingredients in this dish and it's wonderfully simple to make. But, don't let the ease of preparation fool you. This northern Italian classic is the perfect accompaniment for roast leg of lamb—especially in spring. I like the flavor of lamb drippings as they combine with the beans. Be sure to pass a fruity high-quality extra-virgin olive oil at the table when you serve them. White beans are very porous and absorb lots of liquids. Additional salt and pepper are also a good idea.

If time is short, the beans may be cooked, drained, and refrigerated in a covered bowl for up to 4 days ahead of time. Drizzle them with a little olive oil to prevent drying out. In a pinch, some brands of canned beans, well rinsed, will work, although the texture won't be as pleasing. You will need two 19-ounce cans, drained.

1 1-pound bag white kidney beans (cannellini-type)

1½ cups ¼-inch cubes diced salt pork

½ cup fruity extra-virgin olive oil

2 teaspoons finely chopped fresh sage or rosemary leaves

Kosher or coarse salt and freshly ground black pepper to taste

1. Cook the beans according to package directions, drain, cover, and leave on a very low heat. (Or drain and rinse canned beans.)
2. While the beans are cooking, put the salt pork in a small pan, cover with boiling water, and gently simmer for 10 minutes. Drain and blot dry.
3. In a medium-size saucepan, heat the olive oil until hot and fragrant and almost smoking. Stir in the salt pork, lower the heat, and sauté until cooked through but not browned or crisp, about 10 to 13 minutes. Add the drained white beans and sage, stirring to coat evenly. Season with salt and a generous amount of black pepper. If you are using canned beans, cook until the beans are heated through.

NOTE: Leftovers of these beans are marvelous with a splash of red wine vinegar. Serve at room temperature as a salad.

Another idea . . . In Tuscany, beans are so popular that it is often said that their specialties are beans, beans, and more beans. To make a quick white bean soup, reserve some of the cooking liquid from these beans. Prepare the beans as directed above. Then purée them in batches, leaving them slightly chunky. Return the purée to the pot and add enough of the liquid to dilute the mixture to the consistency of a thick soup. Add 2 sweet Italian sausages, skinned, and cut into ¾-inch slices. Simmer until the sausages are cooked through, about 10 minutes. Serve with thick slices of bread rubbed with garlic and brushed with olive oil.

CHUNKY HOMEMADE TOMATO SAUCE

Makes 2 quarts

This tomato sauce is not only quick and easy to make with cupboard staples, it is also delicious and freezes beautifully. If you choose flavorful canned tomatoes, it is guaranteed to bring raves. Besides saucing pasta, I use it over Stuffed Chicken Breasts Italiana (page 96), and as a base for Squid Caponata (page 165). Good-quality canned Italian tomatoes are generally superior to fresh tomatoes for sauces and stews except in the summer when regional, vine-ripened ones are available. As a variation, near the end of the simmering, add 2 cups sliced mushrooms sautéed quickly in a little olive oil. Or, to make a Bolognese sauce, brown 1 pound ground lean hamburger in the skillet before the onions are added. Add 2 thin strips of orange zest, about 1 by 3 inches each, during the simmering and stir in ½ cup heavy cream just before serving.

3 tablespoons olive oil

1 large onion, peeled and chopped

1–2 large cloves garlic, peeled and minced or crushed

1 28-ounce can crushed Italian tomatoes, undrained (some imported cans come larger; the extra ounces will not make any difference in this recipe)

1 tablespoon dried basil or oregano or 3 tablespoons chopped fresh basil

1 teaspoon dark brown sugar

1 6-ounce can tomato paste

Salt and freshly ground black pepper, to taste

1. In a large, heavy non-reactive saucepan, heat the oil over medium-high heat until hot and fragrant. Stir in the onion and sauté until soft but not brown, about 5 to 6 minutes. Stir in the garlic and cook for about 30 seconds longer. Add the tomatoes, basil, sugar, tomato paste, salt, and pepper. Simmer, partially covered, over medium-low heat for at least 40 minutes, stirring occasionally with a wooden spoon, before serving.

NOTE: This sauce may be prepared and eaten immediately or stored in a tightly covered container in the refrigerator for up to 5 days. It freezes well in airtight containers. Make sure to leave some headroom for expansion.

Have you tried? Today there are improved jarred spaghetti sauces. Some are quite good and don't contain a lot of sugar, salt, and starches. Be sure to read the label, don't just admire the design. To dress up bottled sauces, add freshly chopped basil, oregano, or parsley. Fresh garlic, sautéed chopped onions and peppers, or a dash of olive oil and red wine vinegar will all liven up these prepared products. Refrigerate any leftovers in a tightly closed container.

There are also some fresh-pasta manufacturers who supply sauces like Bolognese, Alfredo, and Puttanesca in plastic 1-pint containers. These sauces are found in the refrigerated sections of the market near packages of fresh pasta. Some are terrific and real time-savers. Again, the quality of the ingredients and freshness are the keys. Buy and taste before using them for party fare.

SPICY TOMATO CHILI BARBECUE SAUCE

Makes 1 cup

This tangy, spicy barbecue sauce is easy to prepare and not loaded with preservatives, either. It is wonderful brushed on grilled shrimp or a pork roast during the last few minutes of cooking. But our favorite uses are for roasted chicken or Oven-Barbecued Chuck Steak (page 132). I always make extra chicken or brisket to serve at room temperature the next day. After the first time, perhaps you will double or quadruple the recipe since it keeps for a couple of months when refrigerated in a screw-top jar.

1/2 cup tomato ketchup
1/3 cup orange juice
1/4 cup Worcestershire sauce
3 tablespoons dark brown sugar
2 tablespoons chili powder
1 large clove garlic, peeled and crushed
1 large lemon, ends removed and thinly sliced
1 stick cinnamon

1. Combine all the ingredients in a small saucepan and bring to a boil over medium-high heat. Reduce the heat to medium-low, partially cover, and simmer for 25 minutes, stirring occasionally, then strain, if desired, before eating.

TUNA NIÇOISE VINAIGRETTE

Makes 2 ½ cups

A Niçoise salad is usually made with tuna, small black olives, green beans, tomatoes, and boiled potatoes. Using the tuna in the vinaigrette and tossing it on a salad with fresh tuna (see following recipe) is a variation on this theme. "Niçoise" evokes the French Riviera and Nice, the town famous for its little olives.

Tuna packed in olive oil and shipped from Italy, Spain, or Portugal is usually sold with other canned fish. It has a substantially richer flavor than the water-packed variety. Even tuna in vegetable oil is, for me, superior in taste. If you plan on breaking up the tuna into flakes for a salad, less-expensive grades are a better buy than "solid pack" tuna. The meat is the same quality. If you are concerned about mercury levels, chunk light is lower than solid white canned tuna.

- 1 6 ½-ounce can imported tuna in olive oil, undrained
- 5 tablespoons red wine vinegar
- 1 tablespoon Dijon mustard
- 1 large clove garlic, peeled and minced or crushed
- 2 tablespoons finely chopped flat-leaf parsley
- 2–4 tablespoons lemon juice
- 1 cup extra-virgin olive oil or ½ olive oil and ½ vegetable oil
- Salt and freshly ground black pepper, to taste

1. In a small bowl, mash the tuna with a fork; stir in the vinegar, mustard, garlic, parsley, and 2 tablespoons of lemon juice. Slowly whisk in the oil in a steady stream. Add salt and plenty of pepper and taste to check if it needs additional lemon juice and seasonings. Set aside while preparing Double Tuna Niçoise Salad (which follows).

Did you know? "Extra-virgin olive oil" refers to the acidity of the oil. As long as the level is less than 1 percent, an olive oil may be called "extra-virgin." It may be the result of the first cold pressing or the first and second pressings. It usually tastes very fruity and varies in color from rich green to pale green-gold. Use it for foods where the flavor can be appreciated.

DOUBLE TUNA NIÇOISE SALAD

Serves 4

This double hit of tuna—canned and fresh—is exciting for tuna lovers.

8 romaine lettuce leaves, coarse stems removed, washed, dried, and torn into pieces

1/2 pound small red or Yukon gold potatoes, scrubbed, boiled until tender, then quartered

1/2 pound young green beans, tips removed, steamed until just tender

2 eggs, hard-cooked, peeled, chilled, and quartered

3/4 cup tiny Niçoise olives, if available, or oil-cured black olives

1 medium red onion (or 1/2 large), peeled and thinly sliced

2 ripe tomatoes, cut into eighths

4 4-ounce premium tuna steaks, about 1 inch thick

1 tablespoon olive oil

1 recipe Tuna Niçoise Vinaigrette (page 284)

Salt and freshly ground black pepper to taste

1. Divide the lettuce among four plates. Add the potatoes, green beans, quartered eggs, olives, onions, and tomatoes.
2. Brush the tuna with oil. Heat a cast-iron skillet over high heat until hot. Sear the tuna for 1 1/2 to 2 minutes per side, for rare or medium-rare fish. Remove, cut each across the grain into 4 to 5 thin slices, and arrange on the salads. Ladle some Tuna Niçoise Vinaigrette over the salad and pass the remainders at the table.

Did you know? To keep the yolks in the center of hard-cooked eggs, turn the eggs over about halfway through the cooking time. It makes deviled eggs, etc., more attractive.

A PASTA PRIMER

There is nothing quite as versatile or satisfying as a plate of pasta. Recipes for pasta are found throughout this book. Gnocchi with Peas and Tomato Sauce (page 30), Fettuccine with Asparagus and Lemon Cream (page 17), and Convenient Vegetarian Lasagna (page 312) show some of the many possibilities. A recipe for making homemade pasta in a food processor is given, too.

Although once served as a separate first course, pasta has become just as popular as a salad and, of course, many people make a meal of it. The noodles can be flat, round, wide, or narrow; shaped into twists, shells, or tubes; cut into squares and filled; or left in long sheets to layer.

There should be some balance between pasta size, shape, and sauce. A light sauce calls for a lighter strand of pasta, while a heartier, more rustic sauce seems appropriate with a heavier shell or tubular shape. But mix and match to your own preference. Pasta assumes an infinite number of personalities.

Types of Pasta

There are three general types:

- dried pasta (either imported or domestic)
- fresh pasta (prepared commercially and sold in markets by weight or prepackaged)
- homemade pasta—the freshest of all

Amount Needed

One pound of dry pasta will feed six to eight as a first course or three to four people as a main course.

To Cook

1. In a large pot, bring five to six quarts of water to a rapid boil for each pound of pasta. If you have more than two pounds of uncooked pasta, use more than one pot for easier draining. Adding salt to the water is optional. I prefer this, unless the sauce and other ingredients are very salty, e.g., feta cheese or anchovies.
2. Add all the pasta at once, stirring to separate the strands.
3. Cover the pot to return the water quickly to the boil, then uncover, and start timing. If enough water is used so the pasta can swirl around, if the water boils rapidly enough, and if the pasta is separated by early stirring, it will not stick together. Do not

add oil to the cooking water; if you do, your carefully prepared sauce will slip off the cooked pasta. And do not rinse cooked pasta unless you want it chilled for a salad. (Note: For pasta salads, drain, rinse, and drain again. Mix the pasta with part of the dressing/sauce. Add more sauce just before serving. Pasta salads are best served at room temperature.)

Cooking Time

Timing is of the utmost importance. In general, the fresher the pasta, the shorter the cooking time. Aim for *al dente* pasta—tender but firm to the bite—and no more. While close clock-watching is inherent to your success, tasting for doneness just as the cooking time is approached is imperative. Drain immediately in a colander.

- homemade pasta cooks in thirty to fifty seconds
- fresh (commercial) pasta cooks in a minute or so (according to package directions)
- dried pasta generally cooks from six to twelve minutes (according to thickness and cut of pasta and box directions)

To Sauce

Use a moderate amount of sauce, approximately 1 ½ to 2 cups per pound. You will need a larger amount for thicker sauces. Toss well. If you like, top with about ½ to 1 cup additional sauce. It is unattractive to have pasta swimming in a pool of sauce because you have been overgenerous. Yet remember, pasta is porous and absorbs sauce quickly; some sauce should be reserved and kept warm in the event you need more.

And just a reminder from pasta experts: Refrain from ladling sauce over a mound of cooked pasta. Instead, combine it with pasta by tossing several times to coat the strands or shapes thoroughly. Serve hot on warm plates.

SPAGHETTI ALLA PUTTANESCA

Serves 4 as a first course, 2 to 3 as a main course

- 3 tablespoons fruity olive oil
- 1 large onion, peeled and chopped
- 1 green bell pepper, seeds and membranes removed, chopped
- 2 large cloves garlic, peeled and minced
- 1 28-ounce can crushed Italian tomatoes
- 1 2-ounce can anchovies, drained and chopped
- 16 green olives, coarsely chopped
- 1 tablespoon capers
- 1/4 cup chopped fresh basil leaves or 2 teaspoons dried
- 1/4 teaspoon dried red pepper flakes
- Freshly ground black pepper to taste
- 12 ounces dried spaghetti
- Freshly grated Parmesan cheese

In Italian, a puttana is a "lady of the night." While this sauce tastes as if it has been slowly simmered for a good part of the night, it actually takes only half an hour to make—ideal for the working wives or husbands who rush home, prepare this aromatic favorite, and let their spouses think they have been tending the hearth. You can also make the sauce in advance, like the night before, and reheat it when needed.

Crushed Italian tomatoes make preparing sauces easier and quicker when a smoother texture is appropriate. For larger chunks, or when less liquid is important, buy whole peeled tomatoes.

1. In a large, heavy skillet, heat the oil over medium-high heat until hot and fragrant. Add the onion and green pepper, and sauté for 5 to 7 minutes until soft. Add the garlic and cook 30 seconds longer. Add the tomatoes and anchovies and simmer for 10 minutes.
2. Stir in the olives, capers, basil, red pepper flakes, and black pepper and simmer for an additional 20 minutes.
3. Meanwhile, prepare the pasta according to package directions. Drain the pasta, pour on the sauce, toss, and serve with sprinkled Parmesan cheese.

QUICK HOMEMADE FETTUCCINE

Makes 1 pound of pasta

Making pasta in a food processor is quick and easy. So easy, in fact, that my children do it themselves. The long kneading and incorporating of flour are avoided, while the fun part (for us) of rolling the dough through a hand-crank pasta maker is retained. The results are a good-quality fresh pasta, which I serve often because it is so simple.

I first learned this method from an Italian friend, Lorenza de' Medici, whose family had been making pasta by hand for centuries before she added this twentieth-century touch.

3 large eggs, at room temperature

2 1/4 cups unbleached all-purpose flour

1. Break the eggs into a glass measuring cup with a pouring spout, making sure all the white is removed from the shells.
2. Put the flour in a food processor and process for about 10 seconds. With the motor running, pour the eggs into the bowl through the feed tube, allowing the measuring cup to rest on the feed tube for several seconds to make sure all the egg is added. Continue processing for about 45 to 50 seconds, at which time the dough should be the consistency of coarse cornmeal. Stop the machine and scrape down the sides of the bowl. Process for 15 to 20 seconds longer. The dough should just start to come into a ball and 2 pieces should stick to one another if pinched together. If the dough feels sticky, add a teaspoon more flour and process a few seconds. If very dry, add up to a teaspoon of water and process.
3. Remove the dough, divide in half, and flatten into 2 small rectangles of a size to fit through your hand-crank pasta maker. Cover 1 rectangle with a clean, slightly dampened towel while working with the other. With the rollers set on the widest setting, feed the dough through. Fold it into thirds, flatten with your fingertips, and pass it through the machine twice more, or until the dough is smooth and the edges are even.
4. Adjusting the machine to ever-narrower settings, continue to pass the dough through until it is as thin as needed, usually the thinnest or next to thinnest setting. Take care not to pull or stretch the pasta. The easiest way to hold the strip is to drape it between your left thumb and forefinger, while cranking with the right hand.
5. Cut the pasta strip in half horizontally. Change the rollers to the fettuccine cutter, and pass the pasta through. Spread the fresh pasta on clean, dry towels and lightly dust with flour, tossing to separate the strands, or hang it over a pasta drying rack or kitchen chair. Repeat with the second rectangle.

6. Fresh pasta gradually dries when left out. This affects the cooking time but not the taste, tenderness, or quality. Within an hour after it has been prepared, it will take only a minimum of cooking time—as little as 30 seconds. This increases to 5 to 7 minutes after a few hours. Always taste pasta to determine when it reaches the *al dente* stage.

NOTE: When preparing fettuccine for a dish in which the pasta will cook further in a sauce, such as Alfredo, drain the pasta when slightly firm, so that it does not become too soft with the added cooking time.

COUSCOUS SALAD WITH RADISHES AND PINE NUTS

Serves 12 as a side dish

1 1/2 cups chicken or vegetable stock
3 cups water
1 teaspoon salt
3 cups dry, medium-grain quick-cook couscous
1 1/2 cups orange juice
Grated zest of 2 oranges
1 cup chopped cilantro or basil leaves
1/4–1/3 cup vegetable oil
3 cups thinly sliced radishes
3/4 cup pine nuts, toasted
1/4 cup apple cider vinegar, if needed
Salt and freshly ground black pepper to taste

This tempting orange-scented grain salad complements any roast chicken or grilled meats. Most of the work can be done ahead, but add the pine nuts and radishes just before serving so they are crisp and the radishes retain their bright red border. The recipe is easily divided in half for smaller groups.

1. In a medium saucepan, bring the stock, water, and salt to a boil. Slowly add the couscous, stirring until all the liquid is absorbed, 2 to 3 minutes. Remove from the heat and let the pan stand until the couscous is tender, about 2 minutes. Turn into a large bowl to cool, 10 to 15 minutes, rubbing it gently with your fingers or tossing with large spoons.

2. When cool, add 1 cup of the orange juice, the orange zest, and coriander, and toss to blend. Before serving, add the oil, radishes, pine nuts, and remaining orange juice. Taste, add vinegar, if desired, season with salt and pepper, and serve.

CHICKEN, PECAN, AVOCADO, AND WILD PECAN RICE SALAD

Serves 6 to 8

Thanks to the unique Wild Pecan Rice, avocado, and the Middle Eastern–inspired Puréed Chickpea Vinaigrette (page 272), this chicken salad is a sophisticated variation on the mayonnaise classic. Serve it for a summer lunch or dinner. As an easy picnic idea, bring along pita breads and let guests make pocket sandwiches.

Wild Pecan Rice is a variety of brown rice from Louisiana marketed under the brand Konriko. It contains neither nuts nor wild rice, but the texture is firm and slightly chewy, and the flavor is somewhat reminiscent of pecans. Look in the Staples aisles near the ever-popular long-grain white rice to find this and other newer rice varieties. Opened boxes of rice should be closed and stored in a cool place; that way, they will keep fresh for at least 6 months.

- 1 1/2 pounds boneless skinless chicken breasts or leftover chicken cut into cubes
- 3 cups chicken stock
- 1 7-ounce package Wild Pecan Rice
- 3 ounces (1 cup) pecan halves, lightly toasted and coarsely chopped
- 1 1/2 cups thinly sliced scallions, including most of the green parts
- 12 cherry tomatoes, cut in half
- 1–2 large, ripe avocados
- 1 recipe Puréed Chickpea Vinaigrette (page 272)
- Salt and freshly ground black pepper to taste
- Boston lettuce leaves, to garnish (optional)

1. In a large skillet, cover the chicken breasts with stock and bring the liquid just to a boil. Turn the heat to low and poach the breasts until just cooked, about 15 minutes. Remove, cool, and cut into 3/4-inch cubes.
2. Cook the Wild Pecan Rice according to the package directions, making sure all the water evaporates, then set aside to cool.
3. In a large bowl, combine the rice, chicken cubes, pecans, and scallions. Add the cherry tomatoes. Peel the avocado, cut into 3/4-inch cubes, and add to the salad. Pour on the vinaigrette and toss to blend. Add salt and freshly ground black pepper to taste. Serve on Boston lettuce leaves, if desired.

Did you know? Cut-up avocados will not blacken, change texture, or lose their taste for up to 4 hours if kept in a bowl of ice water. After that time, they start to soften. Blot dry on paper towels before using.

CURRIED RICE SALAD

Serves 4

This cool, refreshing rice salad is a perfect lunch for a hot summer day. It's like a combination of my favorite condiments from a large curry dinner: Yogurt Cucumber Raita (sauce; see page 206), mango chutney, chopped nuts, currants, and rice, all blended together.

Aromatic, long-grain basmati rice is called the "queen of fragrance" in India for the milky, floral aroma it gives off during cooking. It is also grown in the United States. You can also use brown rice as a delicious and healthful alternative. White or brown basmati rice is commonly available in natural foods stores, natural foods sections, and many supermarkets.

1 teaspoon salt
1 cup basmati or brown rice
1 cup plain low-fat yogurt
2 tablespoons curry powder, hot or mild
1/2 cup currants
1/2 cup sunflower seeds
1 cup peeled and thinly sliced cucumbers, quartered with seeds removed
1 cup thinly sliced scallions, including most of the green parts
1/2 cup dry roasted peanuts
1/4 cup finely chopped Major Grey's chutney
1/2 Granny Smith or other tart apple, peeled, cored, and diced
Salt and freshly ground black pepper to taste
Boston lettuce leaves, for garnish (optional)

1. Following the package directions, bring the quantity of water indicated to a boil in a heavy saucepan. Add the salt and rice and simmer, covered, until all the water is absorbed. Drain and transfer it to a large bowl to cool.
2. Stir in the remaining ingredients: yogurt, curry, currants, sunflower seeds, cucumber, scallions, peanuts, chutney, apple, salt, and pepper, and taste for seasonings. Serve on Boston lettuce leaves, if desired.

NOTE: For a more substantial salad, add 1 cup cooked shrimp or turkey cubes.

Did you know? Commercial curry powder is a mixture of many spices—often as many as 16. Each brand varies in heat intensity and actual spices. As a rule, a jar labeled "Madras" is the hottest. Like other ground spices, curries should be stored away from light. And, if the jar or tin looks as if it has been sitting on the grocer's shelf for several months, even though it has exotic packaging, chances are that it has lost some of its punch.

Curry paste is now widely available. Because the spices are lightly cooked in a little oil, it tastes and keeps better (in the fridge) than curry powder. Simply stir in the quantity that suits your palate to flavor a stew or sauce. Or, combine a tablespoon or two with 1 cup mayonnaise and/or sour cream as a tasty dipping sauce for blanched vegetables.

HEARTY BULGUR PILAF

Serves 8

Bulgur, or precooked cracked wheat, has long been a staple throughout the Middle East. In this dish, the grain is combined with the raisins, pine nuts, and chestnuts and baked into a golden ring. It's a fine side dish for an autumn meal.

Bulgur lasts a long time in a dry cupboard and is quick to prepare. Look for sizes from coarse to fine in many markets. Finer grinds seem to work better for stuffings, while a coarser grind is more appropriate when used in a pilaf. But use the size that appeals to you or mix them. The nutty taste of bulgur adds flavor and good nutrition to pilafs, soups, and salads. Sometimes bulgur comes packaged with a premixed spice packet. If your market does not sell bulgur alone or you are inclined to experiment, use the grain and save the spices for another use (like mixing them with low-fat yogurt for a baked-potato topping).

- 2 teaspoons vegetable oil (optional)
- 1 6-ounce Italian sweet sausage, casing removed (optional)
- 2 tablespoons unsalted butter + butter to grease a 5-cup ring mold
- 3/4 cup chopped onion
- 1 cup bulgur (fine or coarse grind)
- 8 chestnuts, roasted, peeled, and chopped or canned in water, drained, and chopped
- 1/3 cup golden raisins
- 1/4 cup pine nuts, toasted
- 1 3/4 cups chicken stock, heated

1. In a small skillet, heat 1 teaspoon of oil until hot but not smoking. Add the sausage meat, breaking it into small pieces with a spatula, and cook until browned. Set aside. (Omit this step if not using sausage.)
2. In a large, heavy skillet, melt the 2 tablespoons of butter and remaining teaspoon of oil over medium-high heat. Stir in the chopped onion and sauté until translucent and soft, about 5 or 6 minutes. Add the bulgur, chestnuts, raisins, pine nuts, and heated chicken stock. Bring the liquid to a boil, reduce the heat to medium-low, cover, and cook for about 15 minutes, fluffing the bulgur every 5 minutes, until the liquid has evaporated.
3. Preheat your oven to 325°F. Butter a 5-cup ring mold. If you are not using sausage meat, a 4-cup mold will be sufficient.
4. Spoon the pilaf into the ring mold, smoothing it to make it even, cover with foil, and bake in the oven until lightly browned around the edges, about 15 minutes. Remove from oven and run a sharp knife around the outside and inside edges. Put a serving plate over the mold, invert, shake gently to be sure the ring is loosened, and let stand for 1 to 2 minutes before taking off the mold. If desired, fill the center with a green vegetable, such as minted green peas sautéed with finely chopped scallions or steamed broccoli florets.

Did you know? If you want to serve this pilaf or other rice dishes individually on a plate, pack the pilaf or rice into a 1/2-cup measure or ramekin, cover with a wide spatula or cake server, and invert onto the dish, slipping the spatula out once the cup is positioned.

RISOTTO ALLA PARMIGIANA

Serves 6 to 8

- 3 cups beef, chicken, or vegetable stock, preferably homemade
- 3 cups water
- ½ teaspoon saffron threads, crumbled
- 6 tablespoons unsalted butter
- 2 tablespoons vegetable oil
- 1 small onion, peeled and finely chopped
- 2 cups raw arborio rice
- ⅔ cup freshly grated imported Parmesan cheese
- Salt and freshly ground black pepper to taste

Risotto has been cooked in Milan, Italy, since the late sixteenth century and prepared as below, "alla Milanese." It's traditionally served as a separate pasta course. But contemporary cooks serve it with simple grilled meats, fish, and poultry, as well. Once mastered, this dish may be prepared with everything from chicken livers and fresh vegetables to squid.

Short-grained, oval-shaped arborio rice, which slowly absorbs the right amount of liquid to remain creamy and firm at the same time, is found in boxes or in white fabric bags. Either will do, but I have found that the bags seem to have fewer broken grains of rice.

1. Bring the stock and water to a simmer in a medium saucepan and keep hot. Stir in the saffron.
2. In a large, heavy skillet or saucepan, melt 4 tablespoons of butter and the oil over medium-high heat. Add the onion and slowly sauté until translucent and tender, but not browned, about 5 to 6 minutes. Add the rice and stir for 2 to 3 minutes to coat it evenly with butter.
3. Add approximately ½ cup of the simmering stock to the pan, stirring frequently to prevent sticking. Continue adding stock, a half cup at a time, stirring until it has been absorbed before adding the next amount. It should take about 25 to 30 minutes until the rice will be *al dente* (slightly firm to the bite). Turn off the heat.
4. Stir in the Parmesan cheese, the remaining 2 tablespoons of butter, salt, and pepper, and taste to adjust the seasonings. The risotto will be somewhat lumpy. Serve immediately and pass a peppermill at the table.

Did you know? The "Parmigiana" in this recipe title refers to the wonderful hard Grana-type cheese made from partially skimmed cow's milk and produced in the Parma region of Italy. The best quality is called Parmigiano-Reggiano; the name is stamped all over the rind. It has a rich nutty flavor. Although most often used for grating, Parmigiano is wonderful in small pieces with a glass of wine or for dessert. It will be fresher if you buy a chunk in the Deli department and grate it at home as you need it. Store the remainder wrapped in a slightly damp paper towel inside a resealable plastic bag. It will keep fresher and longer that way.

SOUTHWESTERN CLAM PUFFS

Makes about 36 small puffs

Do you have a mini-muffin tin? If so, use it to make these amusing little Southwestern-flavored clam cups. You can keep almost all of the ingredients in your cupboard and toss them together for this hors d'oeuvre in no time. Serve the baked puffs in tiny fluted cups and decorate the tray with colorful flowers and greenery.

If you don't have a muffin tin, leave the bread rounds flat, or check near the cracker section of the grocery store for a tin or package of mini pastry shells. As these prepared products vary widely in quality and taste, it's best to test before serving them to guests.

3 tablespoons unsalted butter, melted

12–18 thin slices fresh white or wheat sandwich bread

3 tablespoons vegetable or olive oil

1 medium onion, minced

2 small cloves garlic, peeled and minced

1/4 cup minced flat-leaf parsley

2 teaspoons dried oregano

Pinch dried thyme leaves, crumbled

Pinch dried basil leaves, crumbled

1 cup dried bread crumbs (approximately)

2 6 1/2-ounce cans minced clams, not drained

1 6-ounce can corn kernels, well drained

1 pickled jalapeño pepper, seeds removed and minced

Salt and freshly ground pepper to taste

1/2 cup finely shredded Monterey Jack or Muenster cheese

Diced roasted red pepper, to garnish

1. Preheat your oven to 350°F. Brush the muffin tin with butter.
2. Using a 2 1/2-inch glass or cookie cutter, cut out 36 circles from the bread, and press each gently into the tin so the bread conforms to the base of each muffin cup. Reserve the trimmings for fresh bread crumbs, if desired, or discard. Toast until lightly browned, 5 to 8 minutes. Remove the tin and set aside. Leave the oven on.
3. In a medium-sized skillet, heat the oil over medium heat. Add the onion and sauté until translucent, about 5 minutes, stirring occasionally. Stir in the garlic, parsley, oregano, thyme, and basil and cook for 1 to 2 minutes longer.
4. Add half the bread crumbs, the clams and their juice, corn, jalapeño pepper, salt, and pepper and mix well. Add enough additional bread crumbs so the mixture just holds together and cook for 1 minute. Taste to adjust the seasonings.
5. Divide the mixture evenly among the toast cups, pressing to mound slightly. Sprinkle with cheese. (Clam puffs may be prepared ahead and refrigerated for 1 day.)
6. Transfer the shells to a jelly-roll pan lined with aluminum foil, for easy cleanup, and bake until bubbly and golden, 12 to 15 minutes. Top each puff with a tiny piece of red pepper and serve at once.

Did you know? Canned minced clams have a much softer texture than fresh or frozen clams. They are fine in this sort of mixture, but best not used in stews or soups. Finely chopped fresh or frozen clams with a little broth will certainly work in this recipe.

KEEPING FROZEN FOOD AT ITS BEST

Storing fresh and already frozen foods correctly will provide you with top-quality foods in excellent condition. Consider the following:

FREEZER BASICS

Foods to be frozen need to be as fresh as possible. Freezing will not destroy bacteria or make old food taste better. If you will not use food within the appropriate time, don't take a chance. It is far safer to freeze it and then defrost it at a later date.

Your freezer should be set at 0°F or below to maintain the optimum quality of foods. A hanging freezer thermometer will help verify this. Another test is a container of ice cream. If it becomes soft, turn down the thermostat.

When adding foods to your freezer, put in only the amount that will freeze completely within 24 hours. For upright freezers, packages should be laid out with maximum surface area exposed so they freeze as quickly as possible, without touching other frozen foods already in the freezer, which can cause freezer burn. For chests, against the walls is best. In refrigerator-freezer combinations where the door is opened frequently, the back is cooler. After foods are solid, they can be put in another section. Label each item with a waterproof marker, writing on the bag or on masking tape what the item is, portion size, and the date/year.

Cleanliness and order are important. An orderly plan for storing different foods in different sections of your freezer will help you locate what you have on hand and what needs to be restocked. Rotate packages of food so older ones are used first.

Containers and Wraps

Foods must be wrapped airtight to retain their flavor, texture, and appearance. Freezer-burned foods that have been exposed to air may be safe to eat, but the quality will be inferior. There are several options for good protection.

- Sealed heavy-gauge resealable plastic bags with the air squeezed out are excellent for fruits and vegetables first frozen on trays (page 233), puréed herbs and stocks frozen in ice-cube trays, cooled servings of stews, and as extra protection around already-wrapped food. They take up a minimum of space.

- Rigid plastic containers in many sizes with tight-fitting snap-on lids are useful for stews, purées, and tray-frozen fruits and vegetables. Leave about one inch of headroom for expansion of the water in foods. Some of these containers can go directly into a microwave. However, tossable thinner containers often crack in a freezer.
- Aluminum trays with foil-cardboard lids or covered with freezer paper are good for heat-and-eat items that can go from the freezer to the oven. They also protect baked goods.
- Freezer-wrap paper sealed with tape is useful for fresh meat, poultry, and fish. The shiny plastic-coated side should be next to the food for protection. Be sure to fold it as closely around the food as possible and seal tightly.
- Aluminum foil is not recommended, as it cracks and tears easily where it is folded. If using foil, put the item inside a plastic bag, as well.
- Most plastic wraps are also too thin to protect food adequately.

What to Freeze

When deciding what will freeze well, consider the following general guidelines. Other suggestions are found with specific foods in the recipes.

Dairy

With the exception of butter and separated eggs, which will keep for nine to twelve months, it is best not to freeze dairy products. You can freeze hard cheese, but it will become crumbly. Soft cheeses change texture and cream separates. Buttermilk, though it is still useful for cooking for up to three months, is not good to drink after it has been frozen.

Meats

These will freeze very well when wrapped properly. Meats should be taken out of their original wrapping (often thin plastic, soggy liners, or too much air) and put in resealable plastic freezer bags. Larger cuts of meat, such as roasts and steaks, will last far longer than smaller pieces. Beef roasts last up to nine months, pork for six months. Chops, steaks, and midsize cuts will last for four to six months. Ground beef lasts up to three months, and ground pork and sausage only two months. With processed and cured meats, such as ham and corned beef, the texture and taste change so they are best not frozen. Game meats will last for eight to twelve months depending on the cut.

Poultry

Poultry freezes very well. It should be frozen within a day of purchase. Then it will last at least six months.

Fish

The fattier the species, such as bluefish or mackerel, the shorter the time it will keep, up to three months. Less fatty fish, such as sole, will last up to six months. Purchased breaded frozen fish products will keep only three months or until an expiration date on the package. Many fishermen suggest freezing fish in blocks of ice, especially whole, cleaned trout.

Vegetables

These are best when cleaned—meaning the ends are trimmed—and, when needed, they are cut into serving-size portions and blanched to retain their color, texture, taste, and vitamins. The blanching time will vary with the size and density of each vegetable. Blanch by submerging them in boiling water for a short period of time, steaming them over boiling water in a covered pot, or microwaving them according to the manufacturer's instructions. Potatoes, beets, and lettuces do not freeze well. Other vegetables will last for up to nine months in the freezer.

Fruit

The best fruit to freeze are berries (page 233), melons, and stone fruits that will be puréed so their appearance is less important. They are useful in sherbets (page 64), ice cream, coulis, or compotes. If you have a bumper crop of peaches or apricots that risk deterioration, blanch them, then slice and store them in resealable, heavy plastic bags. Cooked apples may also be frozen. Even bananas can be frozen if they will be puréed once they are defrosted.

Bakery

Most purchased baked products will keep at least two to three months. Unbaked and partially baked products have an expiration date stamped on the package. Fruitcakes and homemade cookies will keep from ten months to a year.

Defrosting

When defrosting foods, do so slowly to maintain as much internal moisture as possible. The best place is in the refrigerator on a plate to prevent any juices from leaking onto other foods. On a counter at room temperature is not safe. This is particularly true for meats, poultry, and fish because dangerous bacteria can grow in fewer than two hours, or even a single hour on hot days.

Times will vary depending on the size and density of what you are defrosting. Figure a day for every 5 pounds of a turkey's weight. A solid 3-pound roast can take more than eight hours. Even chopped meat can take six hours in the refrigerator.

CHAPTER NINE: **FROZEN FOODS**

INTRODUCTION

For years, I was a "periphery shopper," buying primarily fresh foods—produce, meat, dairy—that lined market walls. Occasionally I navigated up and down the Staples and Frozen Foods aisles for orange juice concentrate, peas, frozen berries out of season, or ice cream. But, as a serious cook, I was convinced that everything made from scratch was best, including puff pastry.

That viewpoint changed abruptly when I was working on a project emphasizing convenience foods and I looked more closely at the Frozen Food aisles. I discovered a whole world of preservative-free, top-quality ingredients and prepared products that did not compromise the quality of my dishes. They simply made the cooking process easier and quicker.

Enterprising companies have done a remarkable job of improving frozen foods. They supply high-quality entrées, desserts, and hors d'oeuvres that can be heated in both traditional and microwave ovens. Well-known chefs have jumped on the bandwagon, too, recognizing how important saving time is in our lives. Some of these heat-and-eat products are very good but they tend to be pricey. Mundane frozen slice-and-bake cookies now share space with upscale, mouth-watering varieties. There are quiches made with wholesome ingredients and a vast array of foods marked "all natural." In considering these items, the trick is to read the labels—some are misleading—and taste the product before using it for guests.

With all frozen foods, it is important that the market monitor the condition of the freezer cases. A constant temperature below 0°F is essential to preserve the quality of foods. Packages should be sealed airtight and in good condition.

Some of my favorite frozen foods that I find convenient include:

Puff Pastry

Select the all-butter variety, if possible. It produces wonderful results in a minimum of time when you follow the directions. Frozen puff pastry is a boon to entertaining, from Crisp Cheese Palmiers (page 306) to Mediterranean Tomato Tart (page 307).

Vegetables

In soups and purées, flash-frozen vegetables are a real time-saver. Corn and Shrimp Chowder (page 309) can be made in minutes. I'm really enthusiastic about baby peas, which are almost always superior to the fresh ones in the Produce aisle; and spinach is another good buy, especially for saving time. On the other hand, I shy away from vegetables prepared in sauces. They often have preservatives and end up being soggy or salty.

Fruits

Individually quick-frozen berries, melons, and summer fruits are a good buy especially in winter when they are more reasonable than out-of-season varieties sold fresh. The Ultimate Raspberry Chocolate Sauce (page 316) is a good test of this. Fruits packed in sugar syrup are usually overly sweet and the texture is inferior.

Ice Creams and Sorbets

Markets are reflecting the national craze for designer ice creams as well as providing options for those who are lactose intolerant or watching carbohydrates. There are many wonderful flavors and brands available to use straight from the carton or as part of other desserts.

Fast Foods

From veggie burgers, Indian entrées, Mexican burritos, to pizzas, every day, new, more creative and healthier frozen products appear in the Frozen Foods aisles. Some will be wonderful. Unfortunately, there is no way to tell except by tasting. I still avoid prepared foods that have preservatives and flavor enhancers. But in our fast-paced world, isn't it nice to know that this industry is on our side, trying to help us eat better with quicker preparation?

MUSHROOM SWIRLS

Makes about 40

Palmiers, also called "elephant ears," are cookies made of sheets of puff pastry where two opposing sides are rolled toward the center, forming two connecting ovals, then thinly sliced and baked. They resemble palm leaves. Palmier is the French word for palm tree.

Traditionally, they are made with sugar that caramelizes during baking. Recently savory varieties are being served as tasty hors d'oeuvres or garnishes for soups and salads. In the following recipe, the pastry is spread with mushroom filling and rolled in one direction.

2 tablespoons of olive oil

2/3 cup finely chopped onions

1/2 pound white mushrooms, wiped, trimmed, and finely chopped

1/3 cup grated imported Parmesan cheese

1 teaspoon dried chervil leaves, crumbled

Salt and freshly ground black pepper to taste

1/2 pound puff pastry, defrosted according to package directions

1. Heat 1 tablespoon of olive oil in a large skillet over medium-high heat until hot but not smoking. Add the onions and sauté until just limp, 3 to 4 minutes. Add the remaining oil, stir in the mushrooms, adjust the heat to high, and sauté the mushrooms until moisture has almost completely evaporated, 3 to 4 minutes, stirring often. Remove the pan from the heat and stir in the cheese, chervil, and salt and pepper. Set the fillings aside while rolling out the pastry.
2. Lightly flour a work space and rolling pin. Roll out the pastry into a rectangle that measures about 6 x 18 inches. Brush excess flour off the pastry and spread the mushroom mixture over it, leaving a 1-inch border at the uppermost edge. Starting with the bottom long edge, roll up the rectangle jelly-roll fashion, gently pressing the top edge to seal the pastry. Carefully wrap tightly in plastic wrap. Flatten slightly by pushing gently on the sides so the spirals will be oval shaped. Refrigerate until the pastry is firm, at least 2 hours. This may be done up to 4 days ahead of time.
3. Preheat your oven to 375° F and line a cookie sheet with baking parchment. Remove roll from refrigerator. Using a sharp knife, cut crosswise into 3/8-inch slices and lay on the parchment, leaving 1 1/2 inches of space between them. Bake in the middle of the oven until tops are lightly browned and centers are cooked through, 8 to 9 minutes. Turn each swirl with a spatula and bake until the second side is lightly browned and centers are cooked through, 8 to 9 minutes. Remove pan, slide swirls onto a rack to cool, and continue until all swirls are baked.

CRISP CHEESE PALMIERS

Makes 3 dozen

½ pound puff pastry, defrosted according to manufacturer's directions

6 tablespoons grated Parmigiano-Reggiano

Pinch ground red pepper

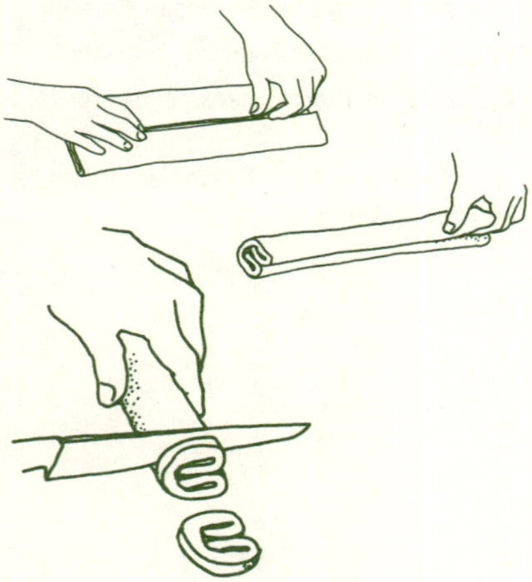

With frozen puff pastry tucked away for unexpected guests, these delicately crunchy morsels with a touch of Parmesan can appear magically from the oven.

For the flavors to be their best, use the best-quality Parmesan cheese available. When buying puff pastry, there are two types to consider. One is relatively reasonable but is made with vegetable shortening. The other is at least twice the price and worth every penny, since it is made from pure butter. It rises to great heights and is truly a gift for making fabulous confections in a matter of minutes. The real work has been done for you.

1. Lightly dust a work surface and rolling pin with flour. Carefully flatten the pastry and cut in half lengthwise. Rewrap the second half and use it for another dish like Mediterranean Tomato Tart (page 307). Roll the pastry into a 5 ½-by-15-inch rectangle and make a light indentation lengthwise to indicate the middle.
2. Combine the cheese and red pepper; spread about 4 tablespoons of the mixture over the pastry. With your fingertips, gently push the cheese into the pastry.
3. Bring both long edges to the middle and push down gently. Sprinkle 2 more tablespoons of the cheese over the pastry, gently press it in, and then bring the 2 sides to the center. Cover the pastry with plastic wrap or foil, and refrigerate for about ½ hour, or until firm. (See illustration.)
4. Preheat your oven to 375ºF. Line 2 cookie sheets with parchment paper or aluminum foil with the dull side up.
5. Cut the roll into ⅜-inch slices and put it flat on the pan with about 2 inches of space around it. If the pastry becomes soft and sticky, return to refrigerator until firm. (If you only have 1 cookie sheet, store the uncut half in the refrigerator while the other bakes.) Bake in the middle of the oven until golden brown, about 15 minutes. With a spatula or knife, carefully turn the palmiers, and bake for 5 minutes longer.
6. Remove from the oven, loosen the palmiers, and cool slightly, then serve on a doily-lined tray. They can be served at room temperature, as well.

Another idea . . . To make traditional sweet palmiers or elephant ears, spread a work space with about ¼ cup sugar. Roll out ½ pound of pastry on the sugar to the same size as above, flattening any folds. Flip the pastry over and press into the sugar. Score the center. Fold the pastry as above, sprinkling on 2 tablespoons of sugar after the first fold. Wrap and chill for ½ hour. Cut the roll into ⅜-inch slices. Press both cut sides of each palmier into sugar before putting on a lined cookie sheet. Bake in the upper third of a 375°F oven for 15 minutes until golden. Loosen carefully with a spatula, turn, and bake for 4 to 5 minutes, or until the second side is golden brown. Remove to a rack to cool.

MEDITERRANEAN TOMATO TART

Serves 8 as first course, 16 as an hors d'oeuvre

This flat tart with a sauce of tomatoes and anchovies is reminiscent of the flaky open-faced snack called "pissaladières" one finds in the south of France.

The advantage here is that frozen pastry and handy staples make this impressive hors d'oeuvre or first course a breeze to make even ahead of time. The sauce can be spread over the pastry, then lightly covered, and left in the refrigerator for at least 2 days.

1/2 pound frozen prepared puff pastry, defrosted according to manufacturer's directions

1 tablespoon + 1 teaspoon olive oil

1/2 cup finely chopped onion

1/4 cup finely chopped green bell pepper

1 large clove garlic, peeled and crushed

3 tablespoons tomato paste

1/2 cup canned tomato sauce

1 teaspoon dried basil

1/2 teaspoon dried oregano

1 tablespoon small capers

1/2 tablespoon anchovy paste or mashed anchovies (about half of a 2-ounce can), drained and rinsed

1 teaspoon sugar

Salt and freshly ground black pepper to taste

1. On a lightly floured board, roll the puff pastry out with a floured rolling pin into a 5-by-14-inch rectangle. Transfer to a cookie sheet lined with baking parchment, roll up the edges slightly to form a little border, and refrigerate while preparing the tomato sauce.
2. In a large, heavy skillet, heat the tablespoon of olive oil over medium-high heat until fragrant, about 1 minute. Add the onion and sauté it until translucent, about 5 to 6 minutes. Stir in the green pepper and cook for 2 minutes more. Add the garlic and cook for 30 seconds.
3. Stir in the tomato paste, tomato sauce, basil, oregano, capers, anchovy paste, sugar, salt, and pepper; bring the mixture to a boil; reduce the heat and simmer for about 15 minutes. Remove from the heat and cool for about 15 minutes.
4. Preheat your oven to 400°F.
5. Spread the tomato sauce evenly over the pastry and bake in the middle of the preheated oven for about 7 or 8 minutes, until the pastry has begun to puff. Turn the heat down to 350°F and bake until the crust is golden brown, about 12 to 15 minutes. Remove from the oven, brush the remaining 1 teaspoon of olive oil over the filling, and let it sit for a few minutes before cutting into 8 or 16 servings.

As a variation . . . There are many toppings that could be used on this tart. Tuna, olives, sliced onions, and even tiny meatballs are but a few.

A SOUTHERN SALAD

Serves 6

- 2 medium yams (about 1 pound), peeled and cut into 1-inch cubes (approximately 4 cups of cubes)
- 1 10-ounce package frozen black-eyed peas, cooked according to the package directions until just tender and drained
- 8 ounces ham, cut into ½-inch cubes (approximately 2 cups)
- 1 cup chopped celery
- ½ cup chopped red onion
- ½ cup coarsely chopped flat-leaf parsley
- ⅔ cup mayonnaise
- 2–3 tablespoons spicy mustard (American, German, or French)
- Salt and freshly ground black pepper to taste

This is a salad I make for friends from the South and it always elicits a chuckle for the familiar fare—ham, black-eyed peas, and yams—combined in this unconventional manner. It's a great buffet dish using leftover ham. Frozen black-eyed peas are a snap because they are easily defrosted and cooked. Although frozen yams are available, cooked fresh yams or sweet potatoes have a better texture.

1. In a medium saucepan, boil the yams until just tender, about 5 minutes. Drain and put in a large bowl. Add the peas, ham, celery, red onion, and parsley. Combine the mayonnaise and mustard in a small bowl, pour on the salad, and toss gently. Season with salt and pepper, toss again, and serve.

CORN AND SHRIMP CHOWDER

Serves 4 to 6

Almost everyone loves a good cup of chowder. This colorful version of corn chowder—made with corn, bell peppers, and shrimp—is a snap to make with a food processor. It is a Pruess family favorite.

Frozen kernels are esteemed among corn aficionados. For eating, the "shoepeg" variety of canned corn is also quite tasty. For this soup, it is so simple to open a large package of frozen corn. I like yellow corn here, but there are white kernels and even packages labeled "tiny sweet yellow kernels" to choose from, as well. Since most of the kernels are puréed in this chowder, the least expensive package is the best buy here.

- 2 tablespoons unsalted butter
- 1 medium onion, peeled and finely chopped
- 1/2 each green and red bell peppers, seeds and membranes removed, finely chopped
- 3 cups corn kernels, defrosted frozen or fresh
- 2 cups chicken, vegetable, or fish stock
- 1 cup light cream or half-and-half
- 3/4 pound medium shrimp, peeled, deveined, and cut into 3/4-inch slices
- 1 teaspoon salt, or to taste
- Freshly ground black pepper to taste
- 1/4 cup freshly chopped cilantro leaves + extra leaves for garnish

1. In a large, deep skillet or saucepan, melt the butter over medium-high heat. Stir in the onion, sauté for 3 to 4 minutes, add the bell peppers, and cook for 3 to 4 minutes more.
2. Purée 2 cups of the corn in the bowl of a food processor, then scrape into the pan with the onions. Stir in the chicken stock and cream, and simmer for 2 to 3 minutes. Stir in the remaining 1 cup corn, the shrimp, salt and pepper, and cilantro and gently simmer until the shrimp are just cooked through. *Do not overcook the shrimp.* Taste for seasonings, then ladle the soup into bowls. Garnish with a few cilantro leaves in each bowl.

NOTE: You can use frozen chopped bell peppers in this soup in place of fresh ones. Be sure to seal the bag tightly once it has been opened for maximum shelf life.

FRENCH PEA SOUP

Serves 6

6 tablespoons (3/4 stick) unsalted butter

1/4 cup finely chopped shallots

1 small Boston or Bibb lettuce, washed, cored, shaken of excess water, and cut into thin strips

1 1/2 pounds frozen tiny peas, defrosted and drained

2 teaspoons salt, or to taste

2 teaspoons sugar

3 cups chicken stock

2 cups water

3 ounces boiled ham, cut into fine julienne (optional)

1 cup croutons, if desired (optional)

Did you know? Frozen tiny peas need no further cooking if they are to be used in salads. Once they are defrosted, they may be used directly or briefly rinsed under warm water for a slightly softer texture.

This is one great pea soup! It is simple to make and has no cream. The peas are cooked in the French manner—with butter and lettuce leaves providing the moisture—and then puréed. Little bits of ham added at the end provide a nice balance to the sweet taste of the peas. It is equally as appealing served hot or at room temperature when the weather is warmer.

Of all vegetables available frozen, peas are my favorite. In fact, except for a couple of weeks in the late spring or early summer, when tender peas may fleetingly grace the grocers' shelves, I buy frozen ones exclusively. It's worth paying more for the ones marked "tiny." They are more tender and sweeter. Larger-size plastic bags of tiny peas are a good value since you can return the extras to your freezer.

1. In a large saucepan melt the butter over medium heat. Add the shallots and cook until translucent, about 3 to 4 minutes. Add the lettuce and the peas–reserving about 1/2 cup for the final garnish–salt and sugar. Cover the pan and cook gently for 10 minutes.
2. Transfer the mixture to the bowl of a food processor and purée, or pass them through a food mill. This will have to be done in batches. Reserve any liquid not used to purée the peas in the pan. Pass the puréed peas through a strainer to remove the skins.
3. Return to the pan, add the stock and water, and cook over medium heat for 5 to 7 minutes. Add the ham, if desired, and reserved peas. Taste for seasonings and serve with croutons, if desired.

EASY GLAZED PEARL ONIONS

Serves 4 to 6

These delicious pearl onions are glazed with beef stock and a little sugar, with a splash of vinegar added at the end to perk up the flavor. My son Justin always asks for them at Thanksgiving.

- 1 16-ounce package frozen pearl onions
- 2 tablespoons unsalted butter
- 3 tablespoons sugar
- 1 1/2 cups beef stock
- 3–4 tablespoons red wine vinegar
- Salt and freshly ground pepper to taste

1. Rinse the onions in a strainer, just to separate them and remove extra ice. Blot on paper towels.
2. In a large, heavy skillet, heat the butter over high heat. Add the onions and sugar and cook for 5 minutes, shaking often, until the onions are lightly colored. Pour in the beef stock, turn the heat to medium-high, and cook until the liquid is almost completely evaporated, about 20 to 25 minutes. Stir in the vinegar, cook for 30 seconds, season with salt and pepper, and serve.

CREAMED SPINACH

Serves 8

I am always amazed at how much people love well-seasoned creamed spinach. It is wonderful served plain or as a filling for hollowed-out tomatoes or potato baskets. Frozen spinach is an excellent alternative to the fresh vegetable.

- 2 10-ounce packages frozen leaf or chopped spinach or 2 1/2 pounds fresh spinach, washed and stems removed
- Salt
- 4 tablespoons unsalted butter
- 1 large onion, peeled and finely chopped
- 2 tablespoons unbleached all-purpose flour
- 1 cup milk
- 1/2 teaspoon paprika
- 1/8 teaspoon ground red pepper
- Generous pinch freshly ground nutmeg
- Freshly ground black pepper to taste

1. In a medium saucepan, cook the spinach according to the package directions, drain well, and set it aside. *Or* shake most of the water from the fresh spinach, combine with 1/2 teaspoon salt in a large, deep saucepan, cover, and cook it until tender, about 5 to 7 minutes. Drain well in a strainer.
2. Melt 2 tablespoons of butter in the saucepan over medium-high heat. Add the onion and sauté for 6 to 8 minutes, or until lightly colored. Combine the spinach with the onion.
3. Melt the remaining 2 tablespoons of butter in a small saucepan. Add the flour and cook over medium-low heat for a few minutes to cook but not brown the flour, stirring with a wooden spoon. Add the milk all at once and whisk until the mixture is smooth and thick. Add the paprika, red pepper, and nutmeg; scrape into the spinach-onion mixture; season with salt and pepper to taste; and serve.

CONVENIENT VEGETARIAN LASAGNA

Serves 8 to 12

- 2 pounds whole-milk or low-fat ricotta
- 4 eggs
- 1 cup grated Parmesan cheese
- 1/3 cup chopped flat-leaf parsley or 2 tablespoons dried
- 2 tablespoons chopped fresh basil or 2 teaspoons dried
- Freshly ground black pepper to taste
- 1/2 cup olive oil
- 1 1/2 cups chopped onions or 1 12-ounce package frozen chopped onions, defrosted and blotted dry (see note)
- 1 cup sliced carrots, blanched or frozen carrots, defrosted and blotted dry
- 1 cup diced bell peppers or 10-ounce package frozen cut red and green peppers, defrosted and blotted dry
- 1 1/2 cup blanched broccoli florets or 1 16-ounce package frozen chopped broccoli, defrosted and blotted dry
- 3 cups Chunky Homemade Tomato Sauce (page 282) or prepared spaghetti sauce
- 1-1 1/2 pounds Quick Homemade Fettuccine (page 289) or store-bought fresh pasta left in broad strips, and cut into lengths to fit a lasagna pan or dried lasagna noodles, cooked according to package directions and drained
- 2 cups shredded mozzarella cheese

Did you know? Since frozen chopped onions are difficult to brown because of the moisture, they are best used in stews and soups where they can add a sweet, subtle, uncaramelized flavor. For them to color in sautéeing, they must be blotted very dry on paper towels. At this point, it is usually faster to chop a fresh onion.

This colorful, aromatic lasagna will feed you and a goodly tribe of your friends remarkably well. It's a testament to the value of vegetables that can be waiting in your freezer and folded into the basil-flavored ricotta filling.

Boxes and bags of frozen vegetables adorned with an endless variety of sauces and in exotic combinations have multiplied over recent years. The pictures look so tempting, especially when otherwise the same old boring vegetables stare you in the face. Unfortunately, many of the packaged seasonings contain a generous dollop of chemicals and the vegetables end up being a sorry imitation of the promised product. Stick to individual flash-frozen vegetables.

1. In a large bowl mix the ricotta with the eggs, Parmesan, parsley, basil, and pepper.
2. In a large saucepan, heat the olive oil until fragrant over high heat. Stir in the onions and sauté them for 5 to 6 minutes, or until translucent but not brown. Add the carrots and cook for 2 minutes; then stir in the bell peppers and broccoli. Turn the heat to medium and cook the vegetables until tender, another 5 to 6 minutes. Scrape them into the ricotta cheese and mix well.
3. Preheat your oven to 350°F.
4. In an 11-by-14-inch lasagna pan, spread 1 cup of tomato sauce evenly over the bottom. Lay 2 lengths of fresh pasta, or enough of the cooked dried pasta, lengthwise to cover the bottom of the dish. Spread on 4 cups of filling evenly over the pasta. Sprinkle on 1 cup mozzarella.
5. Add 2 more lengths of pasta, ladle on another cup of sauce, and then scrape the remaining filling into the lasagna dish and spread evenly. Cover with 2 to 3 more lengths of pasta, using a part of the third length only if necessary to cover the filling. Ladle the last cup of sauce over the pasta and sprinkle on the remaining mozzarella.
6. Cover with aluminum foil and bake for 50 minutes, or until hot and bubbling. Remove, let the lasagna stand for at least 10 minutes, carefully uncover, and cut into 8 to 12 servings.

NOTE: An easy way to drain whole packages of frozen vegetables is to let them defrost, then puncture 3 or 4 holes in one end and gently squeeze the water out.

VERY BERRY COMPOTE

Makes about 5 cups

Spoon this combination of berries, orange juice, and spices on your favorite breakfast fare. It's superb on Wild Rice, Pecan, Buttermilk Waffles (page 234) or Heavenly Blues (page 233). Or try it over ice cream and chocolate brownies.

The beauty of this sauce is that frozen fruits can go directly from the freezer to the saucepan. Remember to buy individually quick-frozen fruits rather than those in sugar syrups. The quality of the fruit is generally higher and you can use only the portion needed at one time and return the remainder to the freezer. Seal the bag tightly and replace it as quickly as possible.

1 12-ounce package frozen raspberries
1 12-ounce package frozen blueberries
1 20-ounce package frozen strawberries
½ cup dark or light raisins
1 10-ounce jar raspberry jelly or jam
1 stick cinnamon
12 whole cloves
Grated zest of 1 orange
½ cup orange juice
2 tablespoons finely chopped candied ginger

1. Combine the berries, raisins, jelly, cinnamon, cloves, orange zest, orange juice, and ginger in a large non-reactive saucepan and bring to a boil over medium-high heat. Once the jelly melts, lower the heat and gently boil for about 1 hour, stirring occasionally, until the mixture is slightly thickened. Remove and let stand for about 20 minutes. As it cools, it will become thicker. Serve warm or cool. It will last several weeks in your refrigerator. Remove the cinnamon stick before serving.

Another idea . . . Save decorative jam and jelly jars to use for gifts. Fill the empty jar from the raspberry jelly with this compote, cover the lid with a wide circle of printed fabric, and tie it with a pretty bow.

EASY ORANGE SHERBET

Makes 1 pint

3/4 cup water
3/4 cup sugar
1/2 cup undiluted orange juice concentrate
2 egg whites

This is a very quick and easy way to make orange sherbet, especially if you keep frozen orange juice on hand in the freezer. Use it with Oranges in Orange Sauce with Orange Sherbet (page 72), or as a filling for hollowed-out oranges.

Frozen orange juice comes in several varieties in the market: low-acid, home-style with more pulp, and regular. Frozen cartons of citrus juices last up to 6 months in your freezer. Other fruit juices last for 10 to 12 months. Refrigerate once the juice has been reconstituted and use within 5 to 6 days.

1. Combine the water and sugar in a small saucepan and bring just to a boil over high heat. Remove from the heat, pour the syrup into a jar, and cool. *Or*, let it cool in the saucepan.
2. Combine the syrup and orange juice, pour into a flat metal brownie pan, cover, and freeze until solid, 3 to 4 hours.
3. Cut the frozen juice into squares. Combine with the egg whites in the bowl of a food processor and process until the mixture is frothy and pale orange in color. Cover again and return it to the freezer for 2 hours. Serve in scoops.

As a variation . . . Other varieties of juice that will work in this recipe include pineapple-orange, grapefruit, and even grape.

HONEYDEW-CANTALOUPE SEMI-FREDDO

Serves 6

3/4 cup sugar
3/4 cup water
2 20-ounce bags frozen melon balls
2 tablespoons lemon juice
2 egg whites, separated
2 tablespoons lime juice

This is a dessert to literally "whip up" for friends. With a couple of bags of frozen melon balls, this Italian soft-style frozen dessert can be made in minutes in a food processor. Once the fruit is puréed, it will keep for a couple of hours in the freezer before hardening. Serve 1 scoop of each flavor with some crisp cookies for a light dessert.

Like its name says, this dessert is only "semi-cold." The texture is softer than frozen sherbet or ice cream.

1. Combine the sugar and water in a small saucepan and bring it just to a boil to dissolve the sugar crystals, then let it cool.
2. Separate the melon balls into cantaloupe and honeydew. You should have about 3 1/2 to 4 cups of each. Combine the cantaloupe balls in a food processor with 1/2 cup of the sugar syrup and process until the melon is almost smooth, about 10 seconds. Add the lemon juice and 1 egg white and process until light in color and smooth, about 10 seconds. Scrape the semi-freddo into a metal or plastic container, cover, and freeze for up to 2 hours before serving. (If your freezer is not very cold, this dessert may stay soft longer.)
3. Repeat the process with the honeydew balls, using the lime juice and remaining egg white. Serve small balls of each.

NOTE: This simple dessert can be made with many fruits by cutting the fruit into bite-sized pieces and freezing them first on a cookie sheet. Or use any frozen fruit without sugar. These semi-freddi are wonderful eaten right away. When they become too solid, process again.

Did you know? If you have several frozen egg whites that have been defrosted, measure out 2 tablespoons for the equivalent of 1 large egg white. One egg yolk measures 1 tablespoon.

THE ULTIMATE RASPBERRY CHOCOLATE SAUCE

Makes 2 1/2 cups

- 1 12-ounce package individually quick-frozen raspberries, defrosted
- 3/4 cup Dutch process cocoa
- 3/4 cup heavy cream
- 4 tablespoons unsalted butter, softened
- 1 1/2 cups sugar
- 1/3 cup light corn syrup

When it comes to chocolate sauces, I like mine dark and rich. This sinfully decadent sauce blends cocoa, sugar, cream, and butter with puréed fruit for a thick topping to slather on ice cream, pound cake, or brownies. (Some of my friends say to forget the ice cream and serve a bowl of this sauce with a spoon!)

Frozen raspberries are marvelous when puréed for this sauce or in sherbet and ice cream. But you cannot expect them to look as beautiful as fresh fruit. If you want to preserve as much of their shape as possible when using them for decoration, keep them separate and frozen until ready to serve. Without a lot of handling, there will be a number of presentable berries in the package.

1. Purée the raspberries in a food processor, then pass them through a fine strainer. Or pass them through a food mill. Set aside.
2. In a medium-sized heavy saucepan, whisk together the cocoa and heavy cream. Add the butter, sugar, corn syrup, and raspberries and stir until well blended. Slowly bring to a boil over medium heat, stirring often. Once it boils, continue boiling slowly for 8 minutes *without* stirring. Remove from the heat and pour the sauce into a heatproof container. Cool for 15 minutes if serving hot, or cover and refrigerate until needed. It will last for at least 1 month. The sauce may be slowly reheated.

Did you know? "Dutch process" cocoa refers to cocoa that is processed with a slight amount of alkali. It darkens the cocoa and changes the taste slightly as compared with natural cocoa. Cocoa is made of chocolate from which most of the cocoa butter has been removed. It is then cooled and pulverized into a powder.

PRALINE CANDY ICE-CREAM CUPS

Serves 8

These festive dessert cups take advantage of the premium-quality ice creams sold in every supermarket. And who doesn't love ice cream? Here, scoops of the flavor of your choice are served in crunchy candy cups made from ground Amaretti—Italian almond macaroons—and caramelized almonds. Top with The Ultimate Raspberry Chocolate Sauce (page 316) or purchased hot fudge topping. I have used vanilla, coffee, and strawberry ice creams. But there are so many wonderful flavors now, the choice is up to you.

Buying "gourmet" or "premium" ice creams is expensive. Typically they are higher in butterfat content with rich ingredients added in. Think Ben and Jerry's to start, and go up from there. If the ice cream is served naked—relying solely on its flavor and texture—then serve the best quality. However, when it will be sauced or used as part of another confection, a good-quality, less-costly product will never be noticed. Ice creams are best when used within 2 to 4 months.

- Shortening to grease aluminum foil
- 1/2 cup sugar
- 2 tablespoons water
- 3/4 cup slivered almonds, toasted until rich brown
- 10 pair Amaretti cookies, crumbled
- 3 tablespoons unsalted butter, melted
- 1 quart premium-quality ice cream

1. Lightly grease a piece of aluminum foil.
2. In a small, heavy saucepan, combine the sugar and water and bring to a boil over high heat. Let the mixture bubble slowly, continuously swirling the syrup but not stirring it, for about 6 minutes, or until it is a rich amber color. If some sugar crystals begin to burn, rinse down the side of the pan with a brush dipped in water. Immediately remove the pan from the heat, stir in the almonds, and scrape the mixture onto the aluminum foil, separating the pieces with a couple of forks. Set aside to cool.
3. When the almonds are cool, add them with the cookie crumbs to the bowl of a food processor and process into very fine crumbs, add the butter, and pulse to mix evenly.
4. Line an 8-muffin tin with foil or colored liners. Spoon about 3 tablespoons of the crumb mixture into each cup, and press the crumbs against the bottom and sides. Freeze the cups until hard, about 1/2 hour. They may be made several days in advance and left ready to fill or already filled and lightly covered with foil. Reserve any extra crumbs.
5. Scoop a large ball of ice cream into each cup, and sprinkle on some of the remaining crumbs. If the ice cream has softened, return the cups to the freezer until firm. Serve with or without sauce. The muffin liners may be pulled off, leaving an attractive ridged pattern.

NOTE: Look for foil and colored muffin liners in the Kitchen Tools section.

As a variation . . . As a variation, before adding the ice-cream scoops, spoon 1 tablespoon of The Ultimate Raspberry Chocolate Sauce (page 316) in the bottom of each cup and let it harden for about 40 minutes in the freezer before adding ice cream. Another fun idea is to buy the mini muffin tin and liners, line them with a generous tablespoon of crumbs, and use mini scoops of several flavors of ice cream. Each guest may have a couple of different cups.

Did you know? Take a look to see if the product you are buying is really pure dairy cream with natural sugar, honey, and other ingredients. Products with air whipped into them will deflate quickly with a little stirring.

TAKING TAKE-OUT ONE STEP FURTHER

These Strategy Pages are meant to offer suggestions on how your supermarket can make entertaining easier and how you can make "supermarket take-out food" look and taste like your own. These are some general guidelines to consider for successful menu planning.

PREPARATION

- For me, the most important factor is that a majority of the work be done ahead of time so I can spend time with my guests.
- Special-order meats, produce, and other special ingredients need to be ordered at least a week in advance. Be sure to recheck the order a few days before you need it. Markets have a way of forgetting or getting orders mixed up.
- All table settings, platter selection, beverage, and appropriate garnishes (where possible) should be decided upon ahead of time.
- Some dishes may be partially prepared in advance and finished at the last minute. Others can be made, frozen, and then reheated.
- Be realistic. Select only a few dishes that require a lot of last-minute preparation. Be sure to consider the number of burners, broilers, and ovens you have as well as refrigeration space. Also think about how many hands are required for stirring, chopping, etc.
- Where possible, clean up as you go during preparation and during the meal to avoid a last-minute pile-up. Sometimes a conscientious high-school student will be grateful for a little extra money for washing dishes.

FOOD SELECTION

- Consider seasonality. Lighter foods, chilled or at room temperature, work well in the summer. They can be prepared early, before the day becomes hot.

A more substantial meal takes away the chill in winter. Foods that are appropriate to the season will usually be fresher and a better buy, as well.

- Make use of color. You have a giant paintbox of colors to choose from in the market. Think about the balance of hues and shades as you select dishes. You may want to select a color scheme appropriate to the setting or the time of year. Remember that we see our food before we taste it.
- Textures and shapes should be mixed. All-puréed or all-crunchy foods are less satisfying than a combination of smooth, soft, firm, and rough. If your plate has thin rectangular slices of meat on it, sliced carrots and a purée of spinach afford contrasting optical and taste sensations.
- Use creamy or rich foods sparingly. You can serve a greater variety of courses when moderation is used.
- Let the menu be appropriate to the guest list. If the group is not familiar with game meat or unusual delicacies, choose foods that will make everyone comfortable and happy. Menus where children will be present, unless the kids are quite sophisticated, should include choices they are sure to eat.
- Don't forget to think about garnishes. They need not be complicated. Even poached chicken breasts look more glamorous with a sprig of watercress and a cherry tomato next to them. Again, look in the next chapter for some new serving ideas.
- Finally, have some familiar recipes in your repertoire that you can make with no hesitation. Each new dish requires concentration. When you are trying several at once, select some that can be made ahead of time.

ENTERTAINING FROM THE SUPERMARKET

Until recently, the idea of entertaining from the supermarket might have seemed like a strange one. Although it was a fine place for everyday shopping, those elegant prepared foods and the accessories for special occasions were missing. When you wanted someone else to take care of an entire event, you called a caterer. For many people, this is still the case. However, look around your market. You might be surprised at what you will find.

The biggest area of expansion in the entire supermarket business is in the realm of Take-Out, Prepared Foods, and Catering. This reflects the current need for convenience as a result of our changing lifestyles. In many homes, either both partners work, there is a single parent, or other interests draw one away from the home and kitchen. The time crunch has curtailed our running from one food boutique to the next. Yet, the desire to entertain remains constant.

Recognizing these trends, supermarkets have started to add trained personnel to meet customers' needs. Chances are a chef or even a sophisticated consulting company is directing these changes. In Deli cases, mundane, commercially made salads share space with more contemporary combinations of ingredients prepared on the premises. Nearby, fresh soups, vegetables, entrées, and desserts may be displayed. Throughout the store, in the Meat, Poultry, Fish, and Produce departments, there are fresh foods ready to eat or to be cooked at home.

While the prices of these convenience foods may seem more expensive, they can save lots of time and effort for everyday or special meals and are worth trying. You will find that some are wonderful; others are best forgotten. Across the country, the quality ranges from superior to mediocre. If you take a little time to familiarize yourself with the services available, your results will be more predictable.

Entertaining can be a combination of store-bought and homemade foods. "Doctoring up" and "dressing up" already prepared foods can make them taste and appear more homemade. Toss a pasta salad with a simple vinaigrette or a handful of fresh vegetables to perk up the taste and appearance. Or pack a chicken or rice salad in a ring mold and unmold it on a large platter with curly endive leaves for a border. Add cucumber "scales" to a piece of poached fish. Or, serve tartar sauce in a hollowed-out red bell pepper. Supermarkets are full of garnishes, centerpieces, and serving containers that are imaginative and inexpensive.

To meet an even broader range of needs, some supermarkets rent or sell almost any service or piece of equipment for catering your party from musicians or bartenders to chafing dishes and glassware. Depending on state laws, this may also include wine and spirits. Explore these services, because supermarkets are working to make entertaining easier and more enjoyable for all of us, including the host/chef.

Before You Buy

Before deciding to buy ready-made items or have the market cater your entire party, a little detective work of your own will give you a better idea of the final results.

1. Look critically at the foods display in the Prepared Foods department. Do they look fresh? As salads sit, acidic vinegar or lemon juice leaches out the color of vegetables. Cream- or mayonnaise-based salads develop an unattractive skin if not turned or stored correctly. The edges of sliced meats will brown and curl as they dry out. Ask when foods were prepared. Does the store make its own? Are there preservatives? Does it move quickly (a good indication of quality)? And, how long and under what conditions have they been stored?
2. How is each preparation displayed? Bowls and platters should be neat and clean. If there is not a separate serving utensil for each preparation, then utensils should be washed after each use. Food should not be left out of refrigeration for a long time, as it deteriorates quickly. What does the market do with the food that is left over each day?
3. Watch the clerk who serves. Has he or she been snacking and then handling your food? Gloves and a hat or some protection against falling hair should be worn.
4. Always ask to taste at least a few (if not all) of the items you are considering buying to get an idea if they are well seasoned and made without preservatives. Unfortunately, many great-looking salads are made with bottled or packaged dressings and have a chemical taste. Find out what is in them.
5. Discuss quantities with the clerk. He or she should be able to tell you how much you will need for light or heavy eaters. Be sure to indicate if you are serving it alone or with other items.

6. Freshly packaged prepared foods sold in the Deli and Prepared Foods departments should have the date of preparation stamped on the serving container along with reheating and storage directions. Trays should be sealed and neatly organized. Most foods are best used within a day or two unless otherwise indicated.
7. When possible, order larger quantities in advance to save time and to ensure that the particular selection is in good supply.
8. Pick up perishable prepared foods toward the end of your shopping, especially if you will be in the market for a long time. Refrigerate them as soon after purchase as possible.

Simple Ideas for Enhancing Purchased Food

With the vastly expanded Prepared Foods and Deli departments, everything from salads to entrées to desserts are available to make elegant or casual dining less work and more convenient. As good as some of these items taste, for store-bought food to look and taste homemade, simple garnishes, seasonings, or additional ingredients may be helpful.

These suggestions are meant as a guide only. There is a never-ending number of ways to dress up food. Once you look over these ideas using familiar Deli and Prepared Food fare, I'm sure you will have several of your own.

1. Pasta is incredibly porous and in salads it often absorbs most of the flavor and vinaigrette before you are ready to eat it. Ask what variety of oil, vinegar, and herb was used and then add a little more of them just before serving. Or, add Mustard Vinaigrette (page 271).
2. Vegetable salads dressed with an acid-based sauce lose their color and texture when prepared in advance. You might add a few blanched broccoli or cauliflower florets or some frozen tiny peas for more color, taste, and texture. Often they can be found already cut-up in the Produce department. Toasted nuts are another crunchy addition.
3. Potato salad will taste brighter with some fresh parsley, a little sour cream, and/or freshly chopped dill. You can also add a shredded hard-cooked egg and chopped small pickles. Serve the salad in hollowed-out bell peppers. This works for macaroni salad, too.
4. Marinated cucumber-and-onion salad will taste special if you drain it, add some plain yogurt, chopped fresh dill and/or mint, and serve it in hollowed tomatoes as a side dish. Add leftover chicken or shrimp and serve with pita bread.

5. Purchased coleslaw tastes livelier if caraway seeds, finely shredded carrots, and/or a chopped green apple are stirred in. Serve it with Jarlsberg cheese and brown bread.

6. Refresh mayonnaise-based chicken and turkey salads with a few drops of lemon juice and some finely chopped celery or onion. Cut off one end of a pita bread and open the pocket. Add some shredded lettuce, alfalfa sprouts, sunflower seeds, and sliced tomato along with a scoop of one of these salads for a satisfying lunch or light supper.

7. Or, make curried chicken salad by adding curry powder or paste, lemon juice, sliced radishes, sliced almonds, and raisins. Serve in a small melon half cut with a zigzag pattern.

8. Enliven prepared tuna salad with a little red wine vinegar, diced celery, and minced chervil. Scoop it into a split avocado. Garnish with a lemon twist.

9. Toast flour tortillas with thinly sliced Muenster or Jack cheese on top in a 400°F oven until the cheese is hot and bubbling. Add a dollop of sour cream, thinly sliced pickled jalapeños (from a jar), and some salsa or a little mole sauce. Top with a second tortilla and bake for a few minutes. Cut into wedges and serve.

10. For nachos, cover purchased taco chips with shredded cheddar cheese, add sliced jalapeños, and bake until hot.

11. Make individual pita-bread pizzas. For two seven-inch pitas: Combine 1 cup ricotta cheese, 1 egg, 1 ½ tablespoons chopped basil or 1 ½ teaspoons dried, ½ cup Parmesan cheese, 1 teaspoon olive oil. Spread over the pitas and top with a thin layer of spaghetti sauce and thin slices of pepperoni; or thinly sliced zucchini, yellow squash, and red pepper lightly brushed with oil, etc. Bake for fifteen minutes in a preheated 425°F oven.

12. Prepared soups often benefit from fresh herbs, a splash of vinegar, a little cream, and/or freshly ground black pepper.

13. Split a purchased croissant in half, add thinly sliced ham and Swiss cheese, and grill until bubbling and hot. A touch of Dijon mustard will help, too. Or, fill the croissant with tuna or chicken salad.

14. Make a "Muffaletta"—a New Orleans–style hero sandwich. Buy a large round Italian or French bread. Slice off the top and hollow out the center. Start by spreading the inside with about ¾ cup of any salad (olive, onion, etc.) in a vinaigrette. Add ½ pound of ham, ½ pound thinly sliced salami, ⅓ pound thinly sliced provolone, lettuce, and tomato

slices. Replace the top of the bread, wrap tightly in plastic wrap, and refrigerate for a couple of hours. Then unwrap and cut into wedges.

15. Decorate poached fillets or a whole salmon with cucumber slices (see page 183) or thinly sliced lemons and dill.

16. Heat a purchased whole roasted fillet of beef or roasted chicken and present it on a platter with Holiday Cranberry Carrots (page 24), Creamed Spinach (page 311), or Cauliflower and Potato Purée (page 25) piped around the edge, sprinkled with Parmesan cheese, and briefly broiled for a little color. Serve with a sprig of watercress and a couple of cherry tomatoes, too.

17. Fresh mint, Grand Marnier, lemon juice, and shredded coconut all enhance fruit salads. Add prepared fruit salad to hollowed-out grapefruit halves or melons, including the fresh fruit with the purchased fruit. Or serve a large spoonful over a mound of purchased rice pudding.

18. Purchased custard cups baked in disposable individual aluminum cups can be unmolded and served with The Ultimate Raspberry Chocolate Sauce (page 316) or purchased fudge sauce. Add some chocolate shavings on top of a dollop of whipped cream.

19. Decorate dessert mousses with whipped cream piped around the edge in a decorative design or carefully spoon them into purchased (or made) dessert cups—chocolate or pastry—and top with fresh fruit or whipped cream.

20. Serve purchased baked apples with a scoop of French vanilla ice cream and crumbled candied nuts on top.

Decorative Serving Containers to Make

1. Buy a large round French bread, cut off the top about a quarter of the way down, and hollow it out (save the bread for bread crumbs or croutons). Toast it briefly, line the bottom with foil, and use it to serve Veal and Sausage Meatballs (page 136) or even My Dynamite, All-Time Favorite Chili (page 129). Line the platter with some rich-looking leaves, like beet greens.

2. Choose a large purple or green cabbage. If it does not sit steady, cut off a narrow slice from the root end. Cut off the top about a quarter of the way down, and hollow out a space in the cabbage large enough to accommodate a pint or half-pint plastic container from the market. Use it for a spinach dip or other sauces. Fill extra plastic containers and

refrigerate until needed; then replace the empty with the filled one.

3. When lemons, limes, or oranges are hollowed out, they become festive cups to hold sorbets (see Lime Sorbet, page 70), relishes, and dipping sauces. Cut them in half with a zigzag pattern and leave a narrow strip to become a handle, if it won't be in the way.
4. Cucumbers may be scored around the outside, hollowed out into little cups about 2 ½ inches in height, and filled with fish mousse, mashed potatoes, or condiments.
5. Split zucchini in half lengthwise. Hollow it out, leaving a half-inch border, then chop and sauté the removed zucchini and blend with rice, chopped parsley, seasonings, and grated Swiss cheese. Refill the shells, bake, and serve as a side dish.
6. Pumpkins make handsome tureens in which to serve Pumpkin Black Bean Soup (page 279) or My Dynamite, All-Time Favorite Chili (page 129). Hollowed-out melons also make bowls for Margarita's Fruit Salad (page 68).

7. Use tablequeen squash as individual soup or stew bowls.

8. Large red, yellow, green, or purple peppers make a beautiful medley of containers for dipping sauces or condiments. Use two or three colors at once; see Moroccan Lamb in Peppers (page 139). Cut off a tiny slice from the bottom if the peppers do not stand steady.

9. Stuffed potato skins have been used for everything from taco fixings to chicken salad.

10. Hollowed-out avocado shells can be filled with guacamole.

11. And tomatoes will hold tossed or Marinated Three Onion Salad (page 35) or Creamed Spinach (page 311).

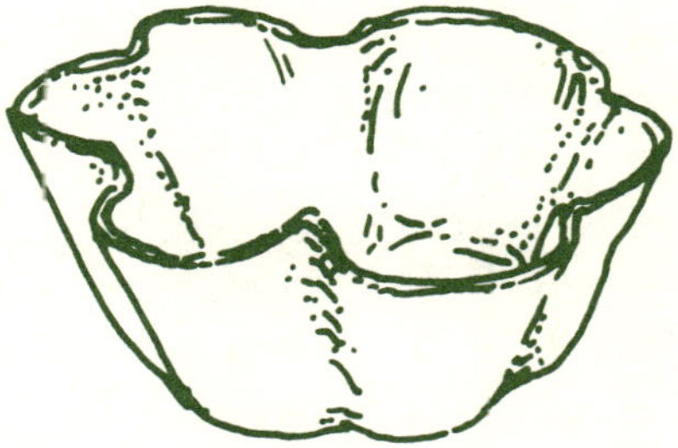

GLOSSARY

AL DENTE (to the tooth) Usually refers to pasta or vegetables that are cooked until just tender yet retaining some "bite."

BAIN-MARIE A method of cooking foods over or in another vessel that contains water.

BARD To cover lean meat, poultry, or fish with a thin layer of fat to keep it moist during cooking.

BASTE To moisten the surface of foods with a liquid or fat while cooking.

BEURRE MANIÉ Usually equal parts of softened unsalted butter and flour kneaded together and used as a last-minute thickener of sauces, soups, and stews.

BLANCH To partially cook foods in boiling water to set the color, remove an outside skin (such as with tomatoes), or to soften the texture of vegetables. In many cases, vegetables are immediately plunged into cold water to stop the cooking and retain the color.

BOIL To cook food in rapidly bubbling liquid.

BRAISE A moist-heat method of cooking foods in a covered pan, usually used with larger, tougher cuts of meat.

BROIL To cook foods under a direct heat source. (Grilling is the same but the heat source is below the food.)

BROTH/STOCK The liquid derived from slowly simmering bones, herbs, and aromatic root vegetables in large quantities of water. The foundation for many dishes.

CHOP To cut into coarse, irregular pieces.

CLARIFY To remove impurities in stocks or milk solids in butter. Clarified butter can be heated to a much higher temperature without burning.

DEGLAZE To stir a liquid into a hot pan that has been used for sautéing or roasting foods, thereby incorporating and dissolving the browned cooking solids that remain in the pan. A good source for pan sauces and juices.

DICE To cut foods into small, uniform cubes.

EMULSION The binding of two normally insoluble ingredients into a suspension. Oil with vinegar or butter and egg yolks in Hollandaise sauce, are examples.

GRATINÉ To run food under a broiler to add additional color.

JULIENNE To cut foods into thin, matchstick-like strips.

LARD To insert small strips of fat into lean meats to make them more tender and flavorful.

MINCE To chop finely.

MIREPOIX A classic combination of aromatic vegetables: carrots, celery, and onions or leeks, frequently used as the foundation for stocks and stews.

MISE EN PLACE All ingredients for a specific recipe gathered together. (Getting your "mess in place"!)

POACH To submerge foods in a gently simmering liquid.

PURÉE To turn a solid food into a semi-liquid state.

REDUCE To boil a liquid to reduce the volume and concentrate flavors.

REFRESH To plunge hot food into cold water to arrest the cooking and set the color or to reconstitute, as with dried herbs.

ROAST A dry-heat method of cooking, usually in an uncovered, shallow pan.

ROUX Equal parts by weight of flour and fat cooked together to create a thickening agent. It may be cooked to various stages from white to lightly colored to dark brown, depending on its final use.

SAUTÉ To cook foods quickly in a small amount of fat over high heat.

SIMMER The stage just below boil when bubbles begin to break the surface.

STEAM To cook foods over rapidly boiling water in a covered pan.

SWEAT To soften vegetables in a minimum amount of fat in a covered pan over low heat.

ZEST (v.) To remove the colored outside layer of citrus fruit; (n.) the colorful outside layer of citrus fruit.

INDEX

D

E

F

T

U

V

W

Y

Z